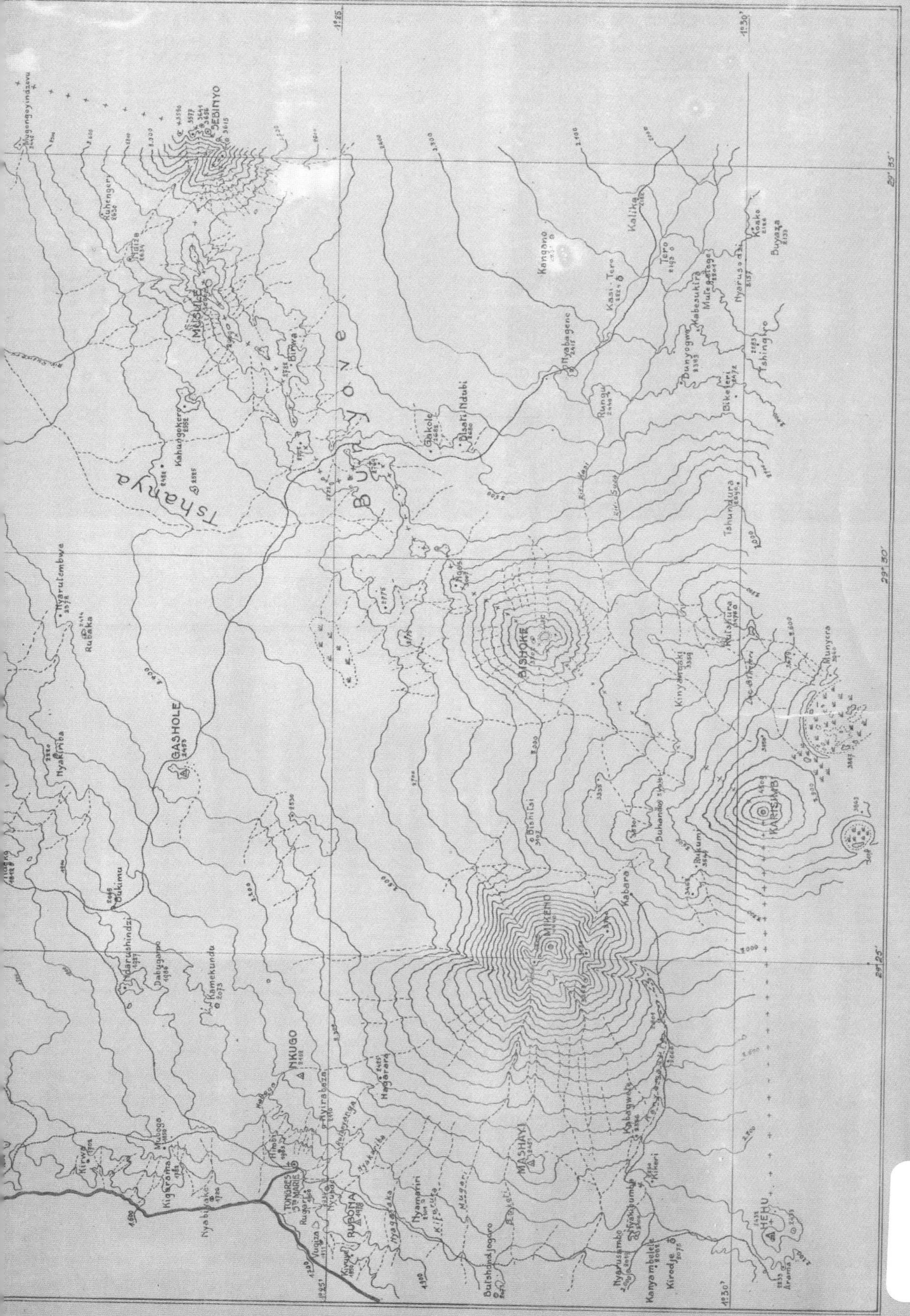

After 100 years of existence, with its ups and downs, Virunga National Park is still alive and kicking.

Emmanuel de Merode
Director of Virunga National Park

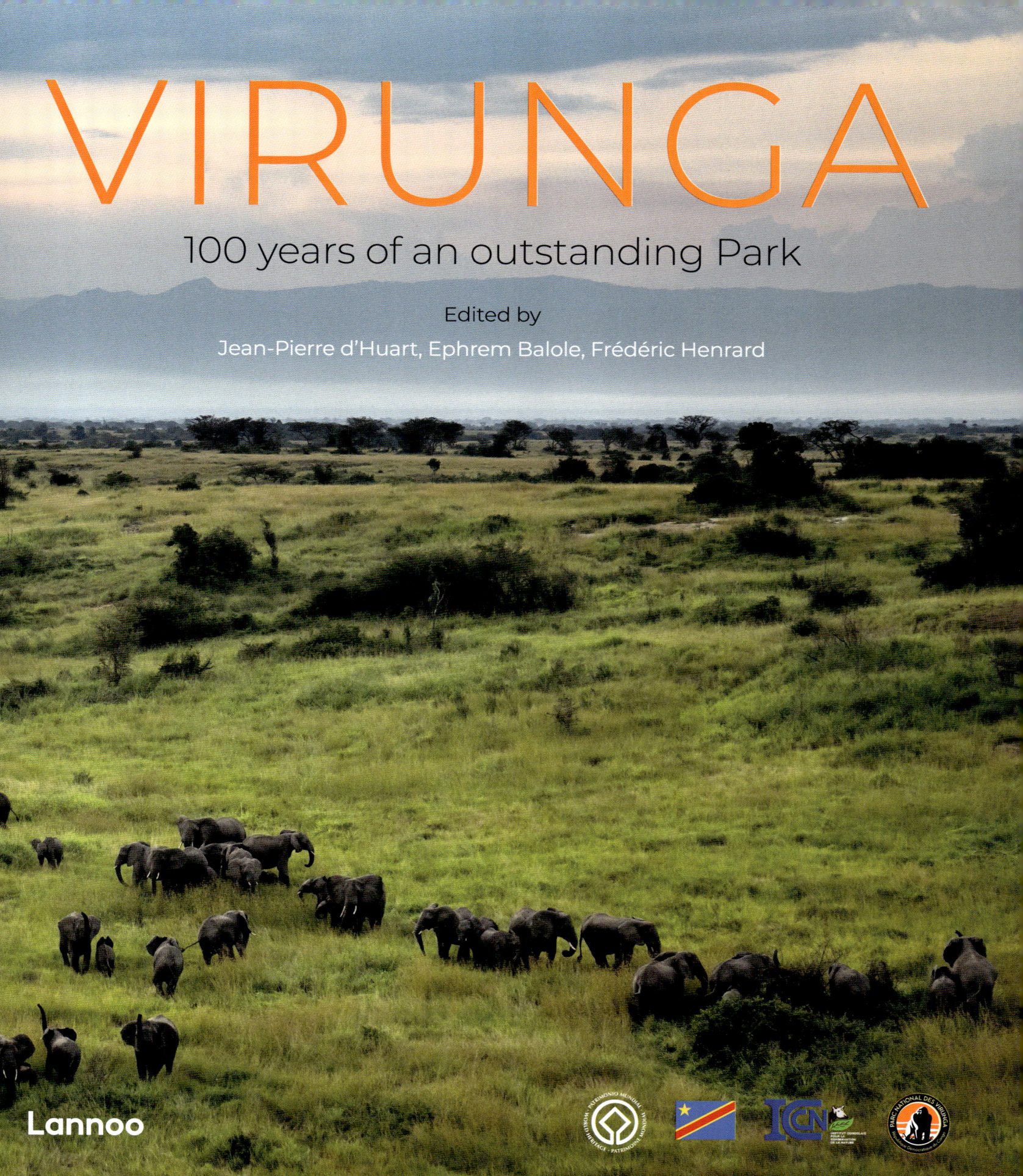

VIRUNGA

100 years of an outstanding Park

Edited by
Jean-Pierre d'Huart, Ephrem Balole, Frédéric Henrard

front endpaper
Map of the extinct volcanoes of the Virunga massif in 1933.

p. 1
Silverback gorilla watching over his family on Mount Mikeno.

p. 2-3
Cloudy sky over the Ishasha Valley in Lulimbi.

p. 4-5
Elephants in the savannahs near Uganda.

p. 7
View of Lake Edward from Ishango.

p. 8
Lake of bubbling lava in the Nyiragongo crater.

p. 10
Power line in the periphery of the Park near Mutwanga.

p. 12
Okapi in the Ituri forest.

p. 16-17
Some winding meanders of the Rutshuru River.

p. 58-59
Lenticular cloud at the summit of Mount Mikeno.

p. 138-139
Hippopotamuses in the Ishasha River.

p. 234-235
Dusk at the Nyakakoma fishery.

p. 318-319
End of day on the Rwindi–Rutshuru plain.

p. 324-325
Eroded cliffs at the edge of the Lulimbi plateau on the Great African seismic fault.

back endpaper
Provisional geobotanical map of the Albert National Park in 1929.

Disclaimers

The ideas expressed in this book reflect the opinions of the authors and are not binding on the organisations or individuals who supported its publication. Similarly, the content of each chapter is the sole responsibility of its authors, not of the authors of the other chapters or the publishers.

The international borders traced on the maps may be approximate and do not represent the publishers' or authors' beliefs regarding their exact location. The spelling of the names of certain places may vary according to local pronunciation.

The authors have used the most common and/or most recent taxonomy. However, it has not always been possible to apply the latest nomenclatural recommendations. Where this is the case, it does not imply any disagreement with the most recently introduced taxonomy.

This book is published in French and English. There may be some differences between the two versions. The French version is the original.

Requested citation:
Henrard, F. & J.P. d'Huart (eds.), 2025.
Virunga, 100 years of an outstanding Park.
Lannoo, Tielt, Belgium. 352 pp.

English translation: Anne Baudouin
Coordination for Lannoo Publishers: Ann Brokken
Graphic design: Studio Lannoo
Layout and typesetting: Keppie & Keppie

© Lannoo Publishers, Belgium, 2025
D/2025/45/98 - NUR 653/253
978-90-209-0000-2
www.lannoo.com

A newsletter about the new books and offers from Lannoo is available by registering on the website.

Any information on the content of the present publication can be obtained from info@virunga.org. Comments or questions about the publication can be sent to art@lannoo.com.

All rights reserved. No part of this book may be reproduced or transmitted in any form or by any means, electronic, mechanical or otherwise, without the prior written permission of the copyright owners and publishers.

Foreword

H.E. Mr President of the Democratic Republic of Congo

FÉLIX-ANTOINE TSHISEKEDI TSHILOMBO

Virunga National Park is part of our national consciousness. We live with the images of its landscapes and wildlife, including the emblematic mountain gorillas, and the wonder-filled tales of those lucky enough to have spent time there.

The inclusion of Virunga National Park on UNESCO's World Heritage List both honours us and entrusts us with a responsibility: to ensure its protection for ourselves, for the world and for the future. I would like to pay tribute to the men and women of the *Institut Congolais pour la Conservation de la Nature*, who work selflessly in difficult circumstances, sometimes at the cost of their lives. In the face of continuing threats, their efforts are crucial to passing on this national jewel to future generations.

A century after the Park's creation, the paradigms of nature protection have evolved: the Congo's protected areas are now lived by our people and for our people. In addition to its extraordinary biodiversity, Virunga National Park is an asset for the development of our country, thanks to the wide-ranging development programmes it drives for the benefit of the people of North Kivu Province. As a pioneer of a new approach, it demonstrates that nature conservation and human development are not contradictory, but complementary.

This community-oriented model is destined to be replicated elsewhere in the country. We have decided to apply it to the vast Green Corridor linking the Ituri forest to Kinshasa, along the Congo River, which has now been designated a protected area. This ambition will give concrete expression to the Democratic Republic of Congo's vocation as a 'solution country' in the global effort to combat climate change. In so doing, a century after the creation of Africa's first national park, we will continue to do our part to protect the environment and reduce poverty.

On the occasion of this hundredth anniversary, I am happy to say that Virunga National Park will continue to make the Congolese people proud for many years to come.

Foreword

Mr European Commissioner for International Partnerships

JOZEF SÍKELA

Virunga National Park embodies viable solutions to the major challenges of the 21st century: biodiversity loss, social and environmental injustice, and conflicts that affect the most vulnerable.

For over 40 years, the European Union has been working alongside the Democratic Republic of Congo to protect its ecological heritage, promote sustainable development to the benefit of local communities, and help reducing violence.

The partnership between the EU and the DRC is exceptional in more ways than one. Initially aimed at preserving the Park, it contributes to the sustainable exploitation of natural resources and the creation of economic opportunities for young people, helping to restore the dignity of populations who have suffered 30 years of unimaginable violence. A small symbol of the success of this partnership: today, the cafeterias of the European Commission serve customers Park-produced chocolate bars – a quality, sustainable product, made in Congo. And the ambition remains strong: as part of the dual Global Gateway strategy and the NaturAfrica programme, the next step is to establish a logistical and commercial link between the east of the country and Kinshasa.

The obvious must be highlighted: our superb achievements are made possible by the daily commitment of the men and women who work in a difficult and often dangerous environment. It is thanks to their dedication that our ambitious projects become reality. We express here our sincere gratitude to them.

Steeped in its remarkable past, and strengthened by the challenges it faces, Virunga National Park will continue to write the history of nature and people in the Democratic Republic of the Congo.

Foreword

Mr Director General of the Congolese Institute for Nature Conservation

YVES MILAN NGANGAY

On the occasion of the centenary of Virunga National Park, it is our duty to pay tribute to all those who, over the decades, have contributed to the preservation of this exceptional natural heritage. This book bears witness to the resilience and courage of our colleagues, past and present, who carry out their mission despite the challenges of war, insecurity and human pressures. Their sacrifice, sometimes at the risk of their lives, deserves our deepest respect.

Inspired by their illustrious predecessors, the ICCN staff members look to the future with determination and hope. The challenges are many, but the past teaches us that it is possible to reconcile conservation and development. Together, we will continue to protect the biodiversity of the Democratic Republic of Congo for the benefit of future generations.

This book is an expression of our gratitude to those who, yesterday, today and tomorrow, work tirelessly to protect Virunga National Park.

TABLE OF CONTENTS

Introduction

19   Preamble
M. LANGUY & E. DE MERODE

27   1 — Overview of Virunga National Park
M. LANGUY

A century of history

61   2 — The birth of the Park (1925-1960)
P. VAN SCHUYLENBERGH

75   3 — The life in the Park (1925-1960)
J. VERSCHUREN

89   4 — The new start (1960-1991)
J. VERSCHUREN & S. MANKOTO MA MBAELELE

103   5 — The transition years (1992-2005)
J. KALPERS & N. MUSHENZI

115   6 — The new challenges (2005-2025)
E. DE MERODE, F.X. DE DONNEA & R. MUGARUKA

131   7 — Prestige and fame
F. HENRARD & P. VAN SCHUYLENBERGH

100 years of dynamics

141   8 — The volcanoes
D. TEDESCO, G. BOUDOIRE, P.Y. BURGI, J. DURIEUX, P. MACUMU, G. MAVONGA & O. MUNGUIKO

155   9 — The habitats
S. DESBUREAUX, F. LANATA, M. LANGUY, L. PARKER & J. DE DIEU WATHAUT

175   10 — The wildlife
S. DESBUREAUX, J. KATUTU, M. LANGUY, L. PARKER, A.R. SHENGERI & J. DE DIEU WATHAUT

193   11 — Lake Edward
F. HENRARD, M. BAGURUBUMWE & G. SIVANZA

213   12 — Institution and governance
J.P. D'HUART, N. BAGURUBUMWE, S. BAKINAHE, F. HENRARD, J. KALPERS, R. LAIME, E. NGENDE & F. SARACCO

227   13 — Transboundary dimension
J.P. D'HUART, M. BAGURUBUMWE, A. LANJOUW, R. MUGARUKA, M. NSUBUGA & L. PARKER

Challenges and perspectives

237 14 — Social and environmental justice
E. BALOLE, J. GABRIEL & F. HENRARD

243 15 — Security and peace
F. HENRARD, L. MUNYANTWARI & E. NGENDE

255 16 — Boundaries and respect of limits
M. BAGURUBUMWE, J.P. D'HUART, F. HENRARD,
L.K. MUBALAMA & L. MUNYANTWARI

17 — The Virunga Alliance

269 Introduction
E. DE MERODE

273 Tourism
J. WILLIAMS, V. HARAKANDI, F. HENRARD & P. LIGOLI

282 Energy
J. GABRIEL, E. BALOLE, J. DUHA & F. HENRARD

295 Entrepreneurship
V. WEINAND, A. HAMULI & F. HENRARD

301 Agriculture
B. ALARD, M. KAMBALE BARAKA & F. HENRARD

311 Impact
E. BALOLE, F. HENRARD & M. VERPOORTEN

Conclusion

321 18 — One hundred years of effort and pride
E. DE MERODE, M. BAGURUBUMWE, E. BALOLE,
J.P. D'HUART, F. HENRARD & M. LANGUY

Appendix

326	Appendix 1	Acronyms
327	Appendix 2	Statement of limits
330	Appendix 3	List of senior managers
331	Appendix 4	List of mammals
335	Appendix 5	List of birds
341	Appendix 6	Authors' biographies
345	Appendix 7	Bibliography

351 Acknowledgements

352 Photo credits

INTRODUCTION

Preamble 19

1 —   Overview of Virunga National Park   27

0.1 Smoke rising from the summit of the Nyiragongo volcano.

Preamble

MARC LANGUY, EMMANUEL DE MERODE

Located in eastern DRC, Virunga National Park (*Parc National des Virunga* – PNVi) is the protected area of all superlatives. Not only is it the oldest national park in Africa, but it is also the richest in biodiversity and landscapes. Unfortunately, it is also the national park that faces the most pressures and challenges, holding the tragic record for the highest number of rangers who have lost their lives guarding a protected area.

These characteristics make the history of the Park unique, marked by cycles of construction and destruction, hope and despair, discoveries, mobilisations, desire and passion. Despite the challenges, 100 years after its creation, the PNVi still stands. It has retained its exceptional character and is increasingly contributing to the development and stabilisation of North Kivu, offering hope for its continued existence for the next 100 years, despite the troublesome context of its centennial. The survival of the PNVi, both past and future, is owed to the courage and dedication of its rangers and civilian staff, supported by many local, national and international actors. This book aims to pay tribute to their efforts and sacrifices.

The 100th anniversary of the PNVi is an opportunity to rediscover the biological and human treasures it holds, recall its history, document the challenges and the responses provided by its teams, and suggest pathways for its future. This book is therefore organised into five thematic sections:
- a factual description of the Park's habitats and biodiversity;
- an overview of 100 years of an extraordinary history;
- the evolution of dynamics affecting its biodiversity, landscapes and management model;
- the challenges posed in terms of security and politics, as well as the bold response of the Virunga Alliance to save the Park and transform it into a driver of sustainable development;
- lessons learned and perspectives for the next 100 years.

This book builds on a first edition published in 2006 (*Virunga. The Survival of Africa's First National Park*, Languy & de Merode), particularly concerning the history of the PNVi in the 20th century. The section on dynamics has been largely rewritten and fully updated with data collected up to 2024, while the chapters on current challenges and perspectives are entirely new.

In the same spirit as the 2006 edition, this work was written by over 50 authors, co-authors and contributors of 8 different nationalities, from various institutions, all with an intimate knowledge of the Park. Its coordinating editorial committee comprised Ephrem Balole, Méthode Baguru-

TIMELINE 1920-2025:

Some notable events marking the century of existence of Africa's first park

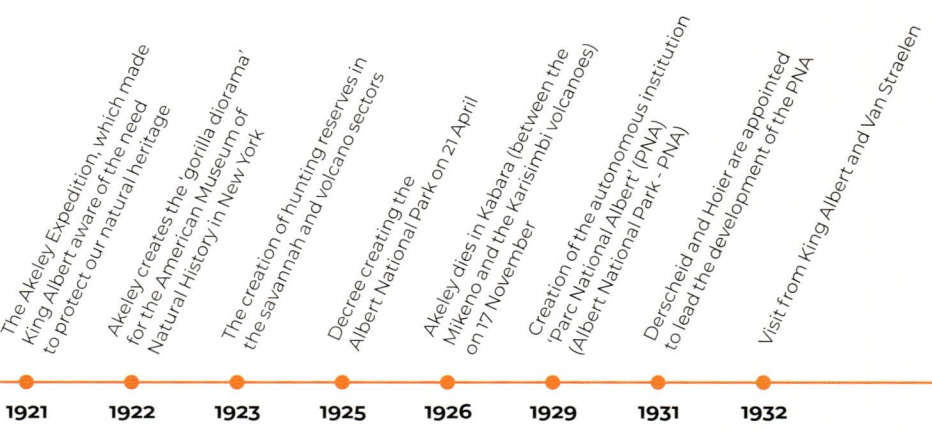

- **1920** — The Akeley Expedition, which made King Albert aware of the need to protect our natural heritage
- **1921** — Akeley creates the 'gorilla diorama' for the American Museum of Natural History in New York
- **1922** — The creation of hunting reserves in the savannah and volcano sectors
- **1923** — Decree creating the Albert National Park on 21 April
- **1925** — Akeley dies in Kabara (between the Mikeno and the Karisimbi volcanoes) on 17 November
- **1926** — Creation of the autonomous institution 'Parc National Albert' (PNA) (Albert National Park - PNA)
- **1929** — Derscheid and Hoier are appointed to lead the development of the PNA
- **1931** — Visit from King Albert and Van Straelen
- **1932**

bumwe, Jean-Pierre d'Huart, Emmanuel de Merode, Frédéric Henrard and Marc Languy.

Overview of the PNVi

The first chapter presents and summarises the key features of the Park. It is based on a review of the considerable quantities of scientific work carried out since 1925. Few parks attract as much interest from the scientific community, especially in the French-speaking literature, to the point that it is difficult to mention all publications. For this reason, a bibliography listing the main sources of information on the PNVi is appended.

100 years of history

The six chapters of the second section recount the history of the PNVi. They document the creation of Africa's first national park and the efforts to keep it alive through Congo's turbulent past.

In chapter 2, Patricia Van Schuylenbergh, drawing on her years of research devoted to Congo's national parks, reviews the historical sources from the early 20th century. Her analysis details the legal and social processes surrounding the creation of the PNVi, the establishment of its boundaries and its subsequent extensions.

Chapter 3 also draws on a review of the literature. During preparations for the first edition, it became clear that few people have as thorough an understanding of the events as Jacques Verschuren, who dedicated his whole life to the PNVi. This chapter recounts the personal experiences of a man who lived in the Park for over 50 years. As a young researcher, curator, chief curator and eventually Director of the Congolese Institute for Nature Conservation (*Institut Congolais pour la Conservation de la Nature* – ICCN), Verschuren tells the story and pays tribute to those who built the PNVi from its earliest days.

Verschuren also wrote chapter 4 on the post-colonial history of the PNVi during its golden age from 1960 to 1989. His co-author, Samy Mankoto Ma Mbaelele, had a remarkably similar professional career to his mentor's and succeeded him as Director of the Institute. Together, they provide a historical chapter that covers a generally prosperous period in the PNVi's history.

Chapter 5, written by José Kalpers and Norbert Mushenzi, describes the challenging years from 1992 to 2005. This was a transitional period, marked by changes in political regimes, the impact of the Tutsi genocide in Rwanda, and the wars of 1996–1997 and 1998–2002, in a country that had meanwhile been renamed 'Democratic Republic of Congo'. The authors were actively involved in efforts to ensure the survival of the PNVi during this pivotal period, the first as coordinator of a mountain gorilla protection programme and the latter as chief curator of the Park.

Chapter 6 traces the history of the PNVi over the past 20 years, with the emergence of new challenges related to armed conflicts that are still ongoing at the time of writing and the growing pressure exerted by local or displaced populations. This section also describes how, in parallel, the PNVi has created new conservation and development opportunities. No one was better placed than Emmanuel de Merode, Director of the PNVi since 2008, to write this chapter. François-Xavier de Donnea, Belgian Minister of State, member of the Virunga Foundation Board of Directors and well-acquainted with the Congolese politi-

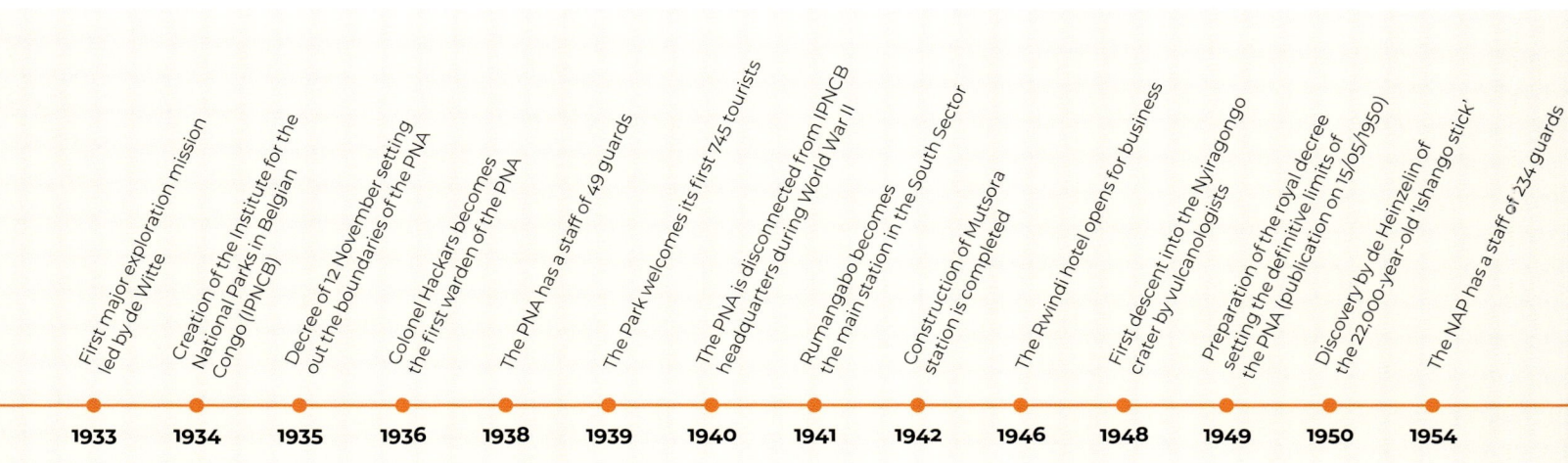

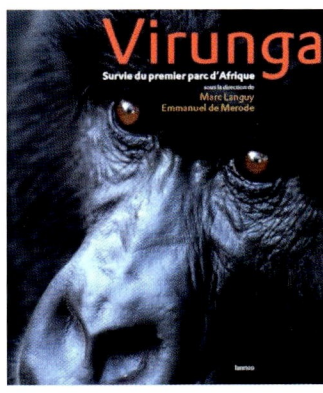

0.2 The first edition of the book, in 2006, highlights the key developments of the Park during the 20th century.

cal and security landscape, is his co-author, together with Rodrigue Mugaruka, the PNVi's Deputy Director.

Chapter 7 closes the historical section by highlighting the unparalleled prestige of the PNVi. In this chapter, Frédéric Henrard and Patricia Van Schuylenbergh recall the Park's renown from its creation to the present day. They explain how its resilience and vulnerability are intertwined, a paradox that becomes apparent when considering the incredible local, national and international support the PNVi receives, encouraged by significant media exposure. This chapter also discusses the notion of the Park's 'Outstanding Universal Value', justifying its inscription on the UNESCO World Heritage List.

100 years of dynamics

In this third section, the authors highlight the natural and human dynamics that have shaped the PNVi and how it has changed over the years. The Park has indeed undergone, and continues to undergo, multiple pressures to which successive managers have responded. By documenting these dynamics, the book describes the strong resilience of the PNVi, which is an essential element of its survival.

Ibirunga means 'volcanoes' in Kinyarwanda, and chapter 8 explores the Park's geology, focusing on the volcanological processes of the past 100 years. The PNVi is dominated by several extinct and two active volcanoes, largely responsible for the region's exceptional biodiversity. Dario Tedesco et al., complementing Jacques Durieux's 2006 text, trace the volcanic history, with a particular emphasis on the Nyiragongo and Nyamulagira volcanoes, and provide an overview of their future dynamics.

Climate change, in particular direct anthropogenic pressures (agriculture, charcoal production and fisheries) and indirect pressures (changes in elephant and hippopotamus populations), strongly impact the PNVi's vegetation. In chapter 9, Sébastien Desbureaux et al. document the vegetation dynamics since 1930 using photographs and satellite images. The Park's major habitats have been monitored for nearly a century and, remarkably, periodic photos from 1930 to the present offer unparalleled scientific documentation of the changes that have occurred.

The dramatic changes in large mammal populations are presented in chapter 10. For 60 years, censuses have been conducted regularly, though often using different techniques. Moreover, the wide variety of the PNVi's habitats requires techniques specifically adapted to each biotope. Despite these difficulties, building on Marc Languy's 2006 chapter, Sébastien Desbureaux et al. update the data and analyses on key large mammal species. The chapter describes the dramatic fate of many species, yet also the recovery, since 2018, of elephant, hippopotamus and mountain gorilla populations, which provides a strong

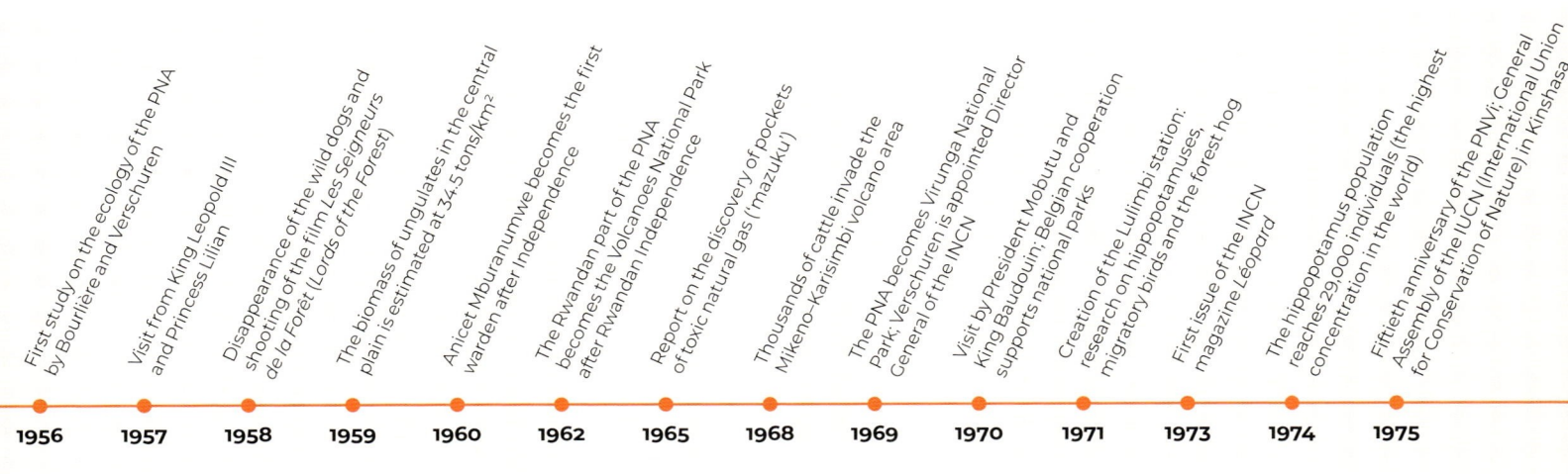

message of hope regarding the Park's potential for further rehabilitation.

The dynamics in Lake Edward are addressed by Henrard et al. in chapter 11. The authors consolidate and revisit the two chapters dedicated to the lake in the 2006 edition, trace its complex history – crystallising political, economic and environmental issues since the PNVi's creation – and document the pressure exerted on the lake by legal and illegal fisheries. Lake Edward is an integral part of the PNVi, but fishing is allowed, and nearly 100,000 people depend on it for their livelihood. However, the steep decline in hippopotamus numbers and the uncontrolled development of illegal fisheries in the early 2000s threaten its fishing potential. By putting these dynamics into perspective, the authors explain the PNVi's approach to establishing a governance framework that protects ecosystems and sustains the socio-economic benefits for local populations.

Its variety of habitats, the multiple pressures on the Park, the volatile political and security context, and evolving environmental protection paradigms all contribute to the rich dynamic in its management approaches. In chapter 12, Jean-Pierre d'Huart et al. explain how the mandate of the PNVi has radically evolved. During the colonial era, the objectives were almost exclusively centred on exploration, conservation and research, all of which entailed the complete separation of natural processes and human activities.

Starting in the 1990s, the PNVi became heavily dependent on external programmes and survived thanks to international funding that encouraged greater openness to the aspirations of local populations. The implementation of a public–private partnership in the 2010s represented a radical shift and positioned the PNVi as a societal and economic player within a sustainable economy approach. This approach, called the Virunga Alliance, is detailed in chapter 17.

The transboundary dynamics of natural resource management are described in chapter 13 by Jean-Pierre d'Huart et al. Located in the heart of the Albertine Rift, in the western branch of the Great African Rift, the PNVi is connected to five other national parks in Rwanda and Uganda, which are in turn directly adjacent to other protected areas. Its location makes the PNVi the backbone of a vast transboundary complex of protected areas. This chapter highlights the willingness of the authorities from the three countries to cooperate on ecosystem management and the shared challenges they face. While the threats are transboundary, the contiguity of the protected areas and the collaboration between their managers are also vectors for solutions.

Challenges and prospects

In their description of the tumultuous history of the PNVi and the various dynamics at work within its territory, the first sections of the book identify the challenges facing the protected area. The social, security and political context in which the PNVi's personnel operates is covered in this new section. It also describes the approaches used to meet these challenges.

Chapter 14 deals with a fundamental aspect of any future strategy: how can the PNVi ensure social and environmental justice in the context of the major socio-economic inequalities and growing demographic pressures that characterise North Kivu? Ephrem Balole – who wrote his doctoral thesis on the socio-economic value of the Park – and his co-authors show that the pressures and opportunity costs can be minimised if some conditions are met, including the restoration of the rule of law and improved governance. This

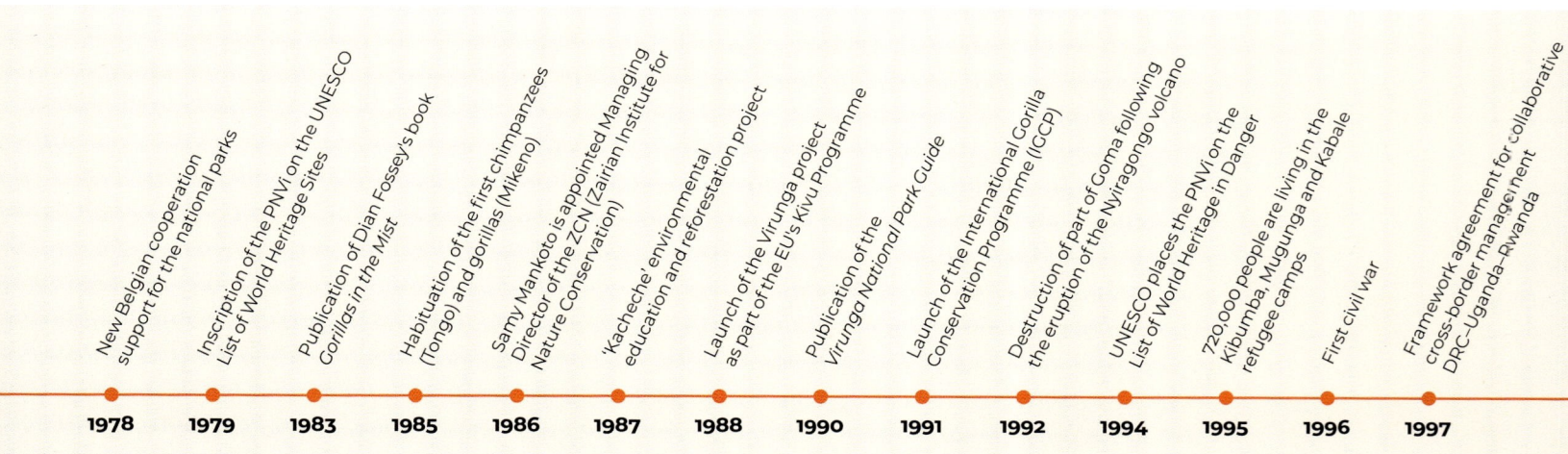

chapter provides the context in which the Virunga Alliance, the subject of chapter 17, was established.

In addition to its outstanding universal value, the PNVi is also known, sadly, for the armed conflicts that have been taking place in and around it for some thirty years. In chapter 15, Frédéric Henrard et al. tackle the complex subject of law enforcement interventions in the PNVi. They describe the landscape of armed groups, analyse the mandate of the ICCN and explain the security arrangements put in place to carry out interventions as per the law.

In chapter 16, Bagurubumwe et al. discuss the political and sociological context of the PNVi's boundaries. Far from being self-evident, the territorial determination of the Park results from a compromise between objectives: protecting ecosystems and granting legitimate access to natural resources to local populations, in particular access to land for farming. To be respected, the PNVi's boundaries must be recognised, understood and accepted by all stakeholders. The PNVi teams, building on the approach developed by WWF in the early 2000s, have developed a participatory demarcation methodology to achieve this objective.

Chapter 17 focuses on the Virunga Alliance, a vast programme to develop the PNVi's natural resources for the benefit of local communities. Based on the environmental and social injustice described above – an environmental wonderland declared a World Heritage Site that exists in a sea of poverty and violence – the Virunga Alliance aims to make the Park a lever for the development and stabilisation of North Kivu. The importance of the issue and the scale of the efforts made over the last 10 years justify covering the subject in several sections.

In section 17a, Emmanuel de Merode sets out the vision of the Virunga Alliance, its participatory working approach and its objectives: to protect and restore the Park, generate 1 billion dollars in annual economic activity, create 100,000 jobs and ensure the sustainability of the PNVi's funding.

In section 17b, Williams et al. revisit the history of tourism in the Park, its successes and setbacks, and analyse its impact on local communities, the public and staff. In addition to the income it generates, tourism is the visiting card of the PNVi, North Kivu and even the whole country.

The Virunga Alliance's Energy programme is covered by Gabriel et al. in section 17c. They explain how the PNVi rivers are sources of clean, high-quality and inexpensive electricity, produced by Virunga Energies. The arrival of electricity in towns and villages is transforming the economy and the daily lives of its inhabitants. Outstanding engineering and huge investments have turned the PNVi into the largest electricity producer in eastern DRC.

As a corollary to the arrival of electricity, the development of entrepreneurship, at the heart of the new economic fabric, is explained in section 17d by Weinand et al. The PNVi stimulates economic activity by providing entrepreneurs with financial loans – according to a unique model based on their electricity consumption – and industrial parks.

In section 17e, Alard et al. discuss the final pillar of the Virunga Alliance, agriculture, which remains the province's leading sector of activity. The PNVi promotes agricultural value chains by working on harvest improvements, the transformation of raw crops into value-added products, and their distribution on local, national and international markets. This integrated approach, made possible by electricity and the prestige of the 'Virunga' brand, contributes to food resilience and revives a sense of pride.

Finally, in section 17f, Balole et al. analyse the impact of the Virunga Alliance, drawing on data from the initial scien-

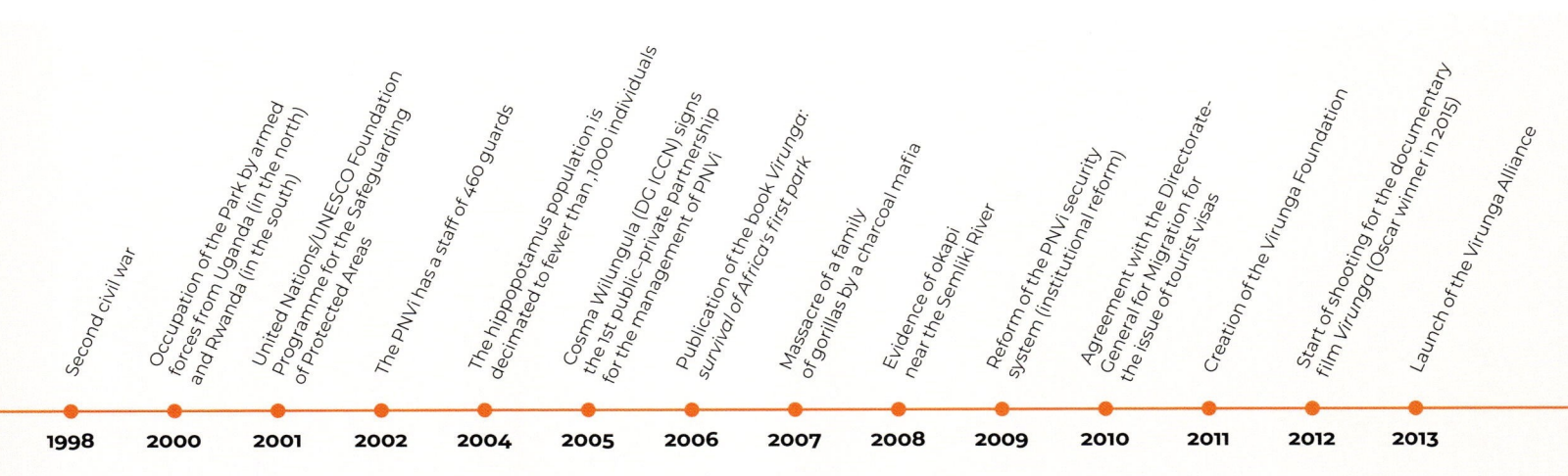

INTRODUCTION

tific research, and the impact of job creation on the reduction of violence and demobilisation of armed groups.

Conclusion

In chapter 18, the editorial committee collates the lessons learned over the first 100 years of the PNVi's history, from both its successes and unfortunate events. Based on this assessment, the book's authors highlight the conditions necessary for preserving the PNVi and discuss the conservation prospects for the next 100 years with optimism and realism. They also offer recommendations to achieve this long-term goal.

At the end of this volume, readers will find seven appendices, respectively: the acronyms used in the text; the Park's boundaries; wardens and directors; mammals; birds; biographies of authors and co-authors; and bibliographic sources.

The authors of this book have been careful to give an objective account of the history and evolutions of the PNVi. The successes will remain sources of pride for a long time, while the failures will remind us daily of the importance of resilience.

It is our firm belief that the texts in this anniversary book celebrating the centenary of Africa's first natural park will be a milestone and a historical reference for all who cherish this priceless jewel, the green heart of the Democratic Republic of Congo.

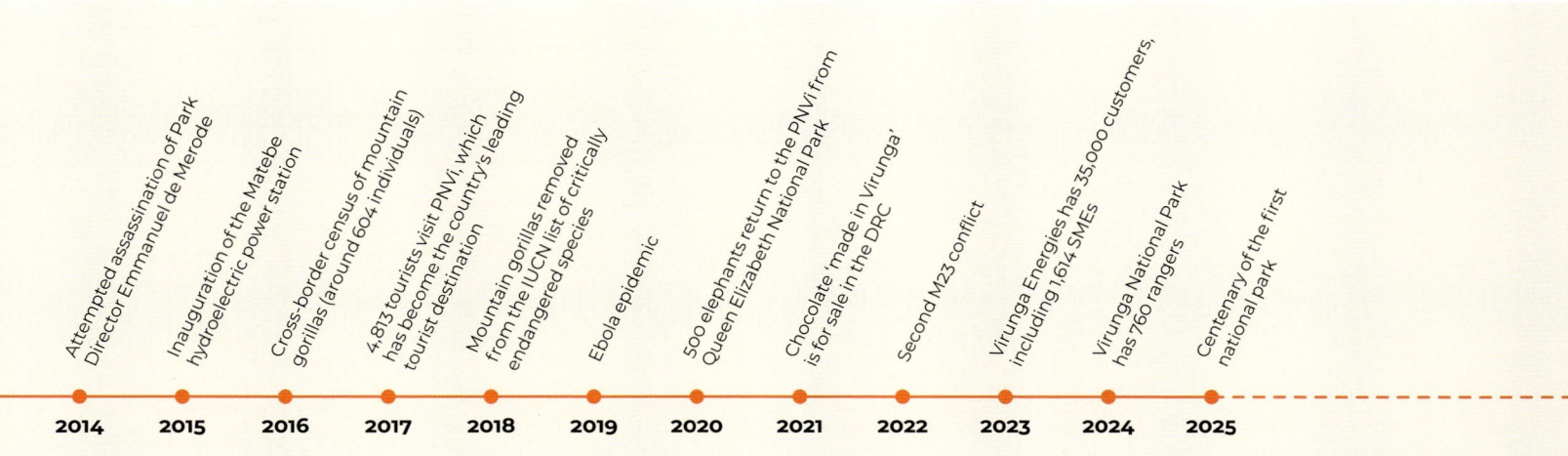

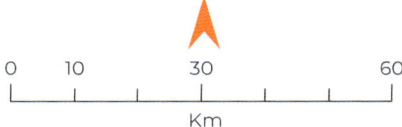

0.3 Virunga National Park, as seen from space.

Boundaries of the PNVi

Border

Road

Lake

Park sectors' HQ

Town

0 10 30 60

Km

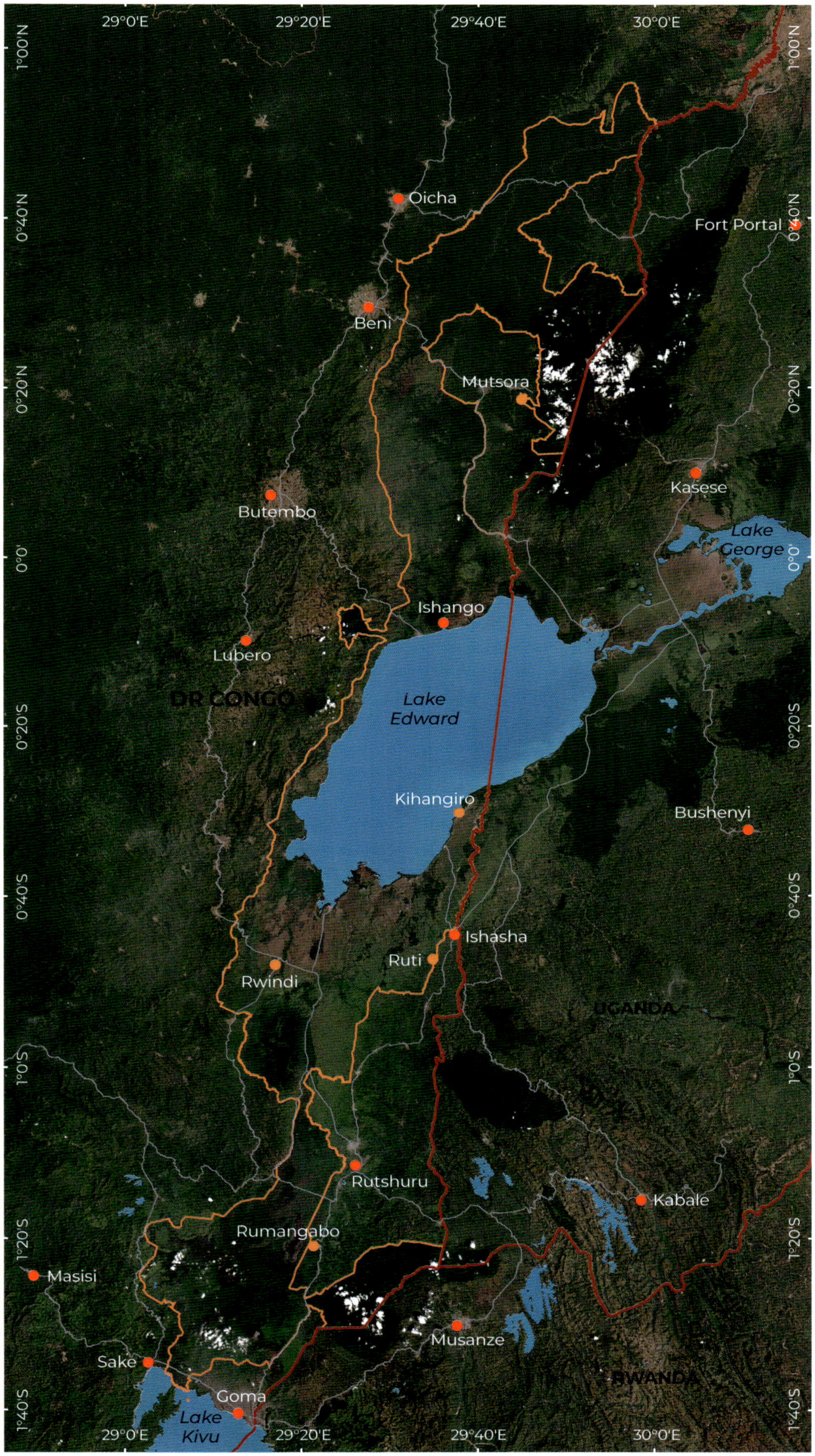

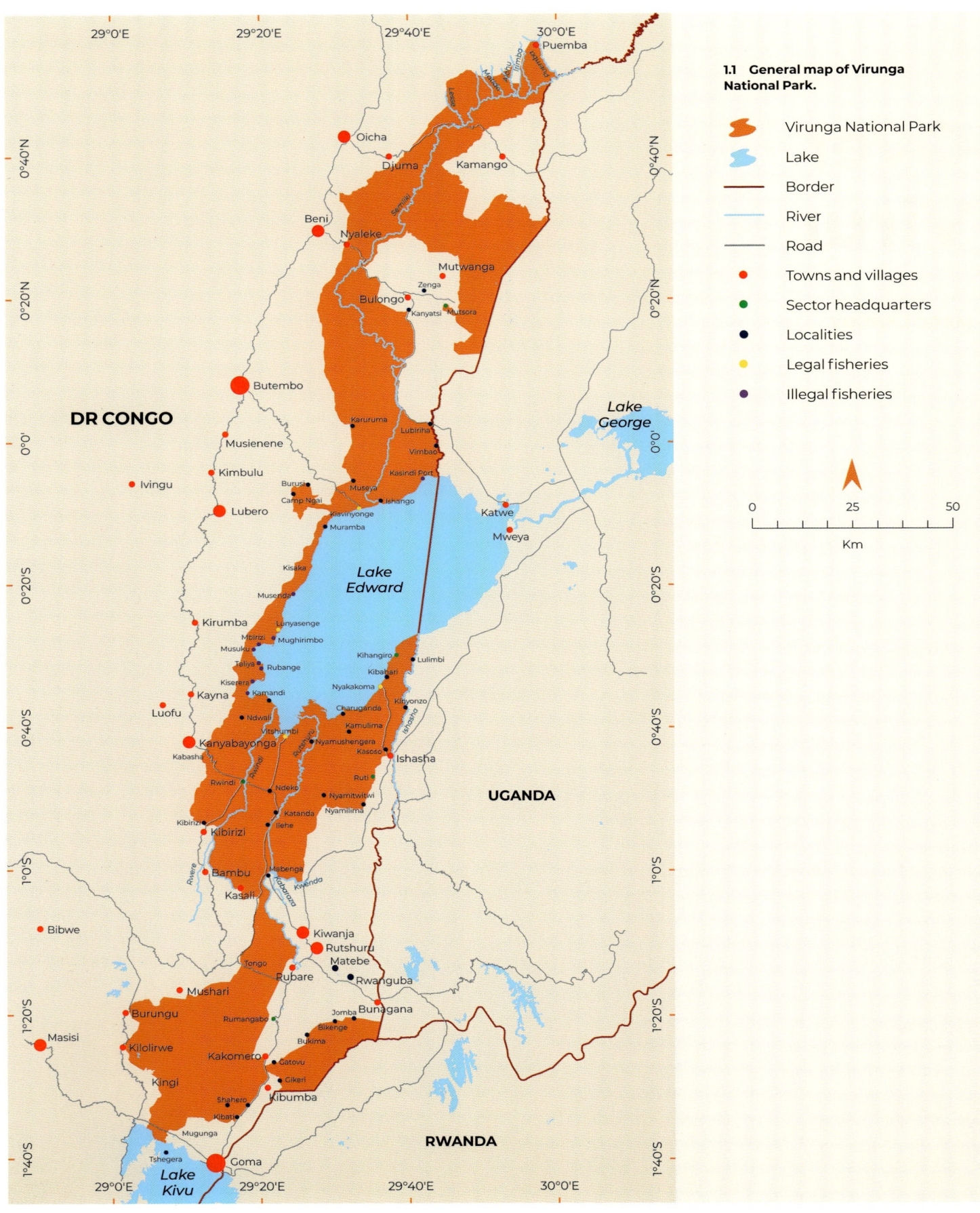

1.1 General map of Virunga National Park.

Overview of Virunga National Park

MARC LANGUY

The creation of the Park and its inscription on the World Heritage List are motivated by the protection of its exceptional fauna and its varied habitats. With more than 200 species of mammals and 700 species of birds, Virunga National Park is the richest protected area on the African continent.

1. Geography

Virunga National Park (*Parc National des Virunga* – PNVi) is located on the equator, in the eastern part of the Democratic Republic of the Congo (DRC), along its borders with Rwanda and Uganda. Its elongated shape along a north–south axis covers an area of 784,368 hectares. It is bordered to the north by the Puemba River at 00° 56' N and to the south by Tchegera Island in Lake Kivu, at 01° 39' S. Most of the PNVi lies at the bottom of the Albertine Rift, the western branch of the Great Rift Valley. From north to south, its maximum length is 300 km, and its average width is 23 km, with a minimum of just 2.3 km south of Mabenga. Due to its elongated shape and specific boundaries, the perimeter of the PNVi is exceptionally long at 1,150 km. Its maximum altitude is 5,109 metres (Margherita Peak on the Ruwenzori, the highest point in the country and the third highest on the continent) and its lowest 680 metres, at the confluence of the Puemba and Semliki rivers.

2. Climate

It is hard to determine the climatic characteristics of the PNVi as its habitats vary greatly over relatively short distances. It is, in fact, impossible to ascribe just one climate to the whole PNVi as the region is characterised by a multitude of microclimates. Ishango, the sunniest and least rainy site in the DRC, is situated 60 km from the least sunny and most rainy site, Ruwenzori, at an altitude of approximately 2,700 metres.

Basic weather stations have long existed in the localities surrounding the reserve (such as at Beni, Goma and Rutshuru), but these are far from indicative for the PNVi. Stations have, however, been established within the reserve (such as at Mutsora, Ishango, Rwindi, Rumangabo and Lulimbi). Many of these have remained operational despite the surrounding instability, and meticulous records have been kept.

Many authors, often in the distant past, have conducted in-depth studies into the global climate of Kivu (Bultot, Crabbé, Vandenplas), and numerous publications by zoologists or botanists begin by providing a general overview of the climate (Bourlière, Cornet d'Elzius, Delvingt, d'Huart, Lebrun and Verschuren). Caution is necessary, however, as instrument checks by specialists were often lacking. Rain gauges, for instance, often got clogged by hippopotamus faeces, while in other cases animals seem to have urinated into the instruments! Rain gauges were often torn off or damaged by hyenas, and

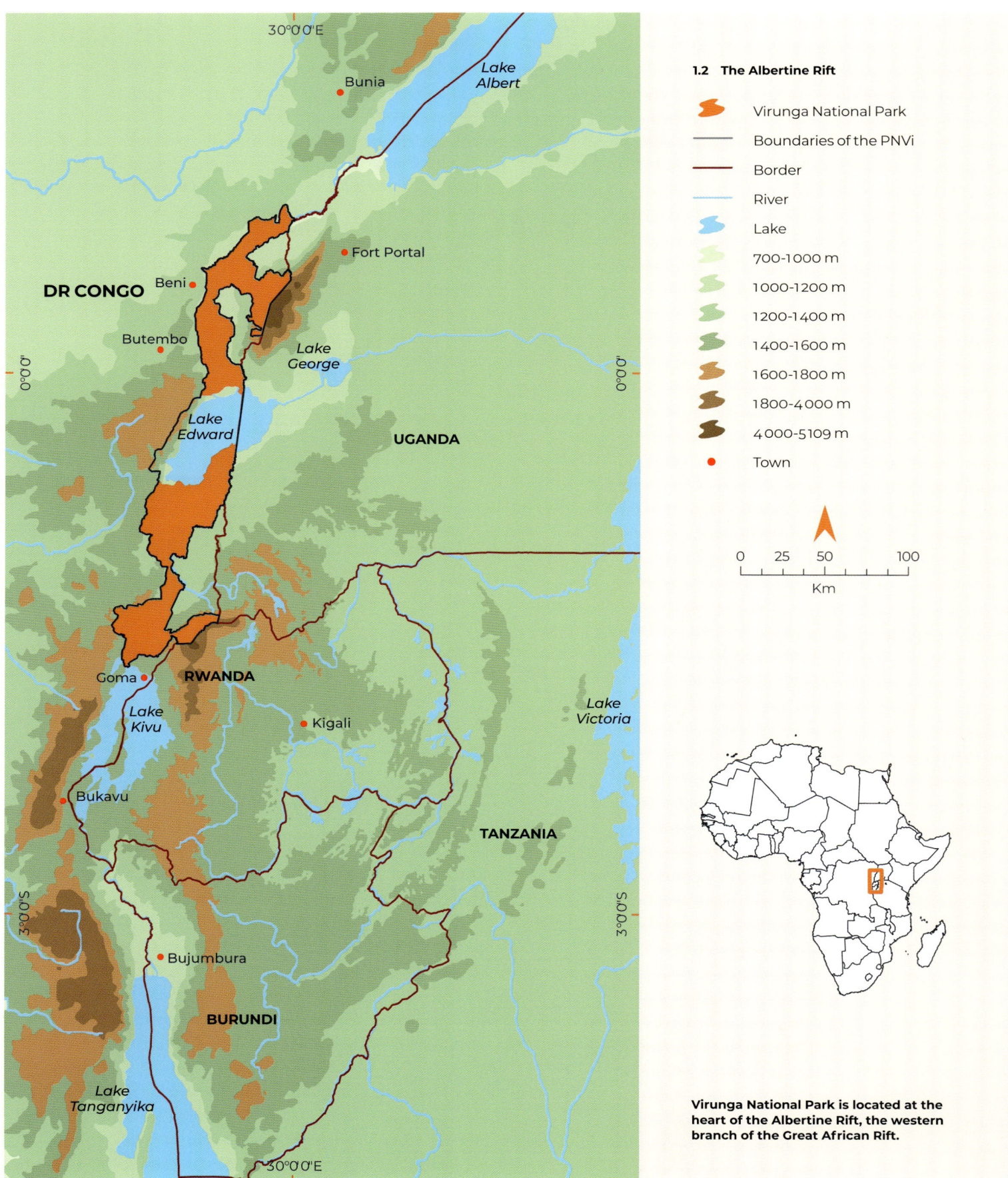

Virunga National Park is located at the heart of the Albertine Rift, the western branch of the Great African Rift.

elephants sometimes destroyed weather stations by rubbing up against them.

Recent crises in the PNVi have prevented the development of a monitoring system specifically dedicated to climate change in the Park. However, people who have remained on-site in recent decades report much more abundant rains in the gorilla sector, more severe and more frequent storms at Lake Edward, and higher flood levels in the Ruwenzori rivers. The rapid melting of the Ruwenzori glaciers is also well documented (see section 4.1.2).

2.1. Rainfall

Due to its position on the equator, the PNVi typically experiences two dry seasons and two rainy seasons, with significant local variations in total precipitation, but relatively few variations in the seasonal pattern. The examination of the monthly rainfall for the three main stations in the reserve (1955–1960) shows a peak in rainfall from April–May and September–October, with minimal precipitation in February and July.

The examination of the number of rainy days at Ishango (900 m), north of Lake Edward, and at Mutsora (1,200 m), at the foot of the Ruwenzori, confirms this seasonal rhythm but clearly reveals the difference between these two stations in relatively close proximity, with Mutsora counting nearly four times more rainy days compared to Ishango, and three times more precipitation.

Ishango and Nyamushengero (lower Rutshuru) seem to be the weather stations with the least rainfall in the PNVi (and in the DRC). Only the station at Banana, at the other end of the country, records similar levels of rainfall.

The dry seasons are, in general, relatively mild, both on the plains and in the mountains. Indeed, months without any rain are exceptional, as is the sight of a completely cloudless sky. On the other hand, rainy episodes lasting several consecutive days (like in Western Europe) are rare. Rain typically falls as showers, most often in the late afternoon.

The station at Rwindi provides 14 years of rainfall data, which suggests a relatively stable level of rainfall over this time period. The annual average rainfall for Rwindi, calculated over 14 years, is 930 mm. During those 14 years, the driest year had 783 mm of precipitation, compared to 1,203 mm (50% more) for the wettest year.

A comparison of these figures with those from before 1960 (average 885 mm of rainfall) and those from 1960 to 1970 reveals that there has been no marked drying of the climate in Rwindi, and the 1,000 mm mark was reached several times. A slight increase in precipitation may even be confirmed.

The Lulimbi station, southeast of Lake Edward, provides fragmentary data. Here, the average is 99 rainy days, with an annual rainfall of 701 mm. These figures can be usefully compared with those indicated by d'Huart (1978), which show relatively strong variations from year to year:
- 1972 – 988 mm
- 1973 – 585 mm
- 1974 – 755 mm
- Average – 776 mm

1.3 Monthly rainfall (mm) at the three main PNVi stations. Averages from 1955 to 1960.

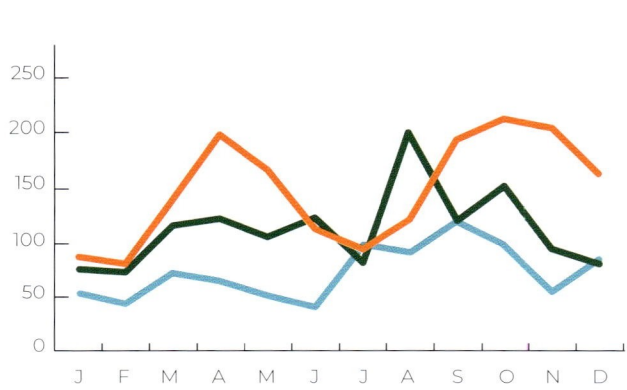

1.4 Evolution of the annual rainfall in Rwindi, from 1970 to 1983 (rainfall in mm).

The scientist Misonne points out that the envisaged rainfall figure of nearly 4,000 mm on the slopes of the Ruwenzori is incorrect. Rainfall and cloudiness are generally highest on the slopes of the Ruwenzori and the large volcanoes at around 2,700 m (tree heather).

The rainfall is much lower on the summits, as evidenced by old rainfall records. Records dated 1930 to 1957 from the totalising rain gauge installed at the top of Karisimbi at 4,500 m show an average annual rainfall of only 940 mm, but with significant variations between years: an annual minimum of 562 mm versus a maximum of 1,329 mm, more than double.

A study by E. Roche in the PNVi shows that rainfall increases with altitude up to around 2,500 m where it is maximal, then decreases sharply with altitude past that point. True drought periods are very rare in the Park, even if the southern and northern plains of Lake Edward sometimes give a marked impression of aridity. None of the rivers are ever completely dry.

The PNVi's severely degraded meteorological network should be reorganised as soon as possible. A network of thermometers and monthly totalising rain gauges should be installed at the stations. The Park has been much less studied in terms of climate than the Garamba Park, where Noirfalise has conducted in-depth research. Given the significant climate changes observed globally in recent decades, and particularly in recent years, monitoring climate parameters in different sections of the PNVi should be resumed as a matter of urgency.

2.2. Temperature

Like rainfall, temperature is extremely variable in the PNVi, as indicated by the following monthly average daily figures for the three base stations between 1955 and 1960. In the mountains, the thermal gradient is 0.7° C/100 m at the equator level.

At Rwindi, over 14 years of observation, absolute minimums are around 15° C in standard conditions and 12° C to 13° C on bare ground. A minimum record was reached in February: 9.4° C on grass. The annual average of around 23° C at Rwindi can also be determined by measuring the permanent temperature recorded in the soil at 1.5 m depth. It should be noted that increases in soil temperature due to fires, which are rarely severe in the PNVi, are extremely limited.

In Kiondo, the ground freezes every night. Misonne and Verschuren registered -8° C on bare ground here. At Margherita Peak, a fairly constant temperature of -3.5° C was recorded. Snow is quite frequent on the summit of the Ruwenzori. On Karisimbi, the summit is often covered with snow, but it does not last more than 24 hours. Analysis of various temperatures

1.5 Maximum and minimum daily temperatures on the Ruwenzori slopes.

HABITAT	LOCATION	TEMPERATURE (°C)
Semliki (lowland forest)	(730 m) Watalinga	19–32
Kalonge (mountain forest)	(2,200 m)	14.8–23.5
Kalindere	(2,700 m) bamboo	11–19
Mahangu	(3,390 m) heather	5–14
Camp des bouteilles	(3,820 m) heather	0–8
Kiondo (alpine)	(4,200 m) ragwort and lobelia	- 0.3–+ 8.1

1.6 Monthly daily temperature at the three main PNVi stations (six-year average, from 1955 to 1960).

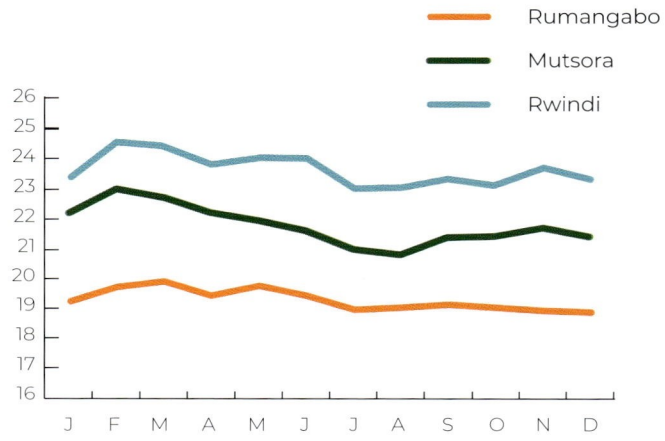

(average, maximum, minimum), both at low altitude and in the mountains, indicates that these have remained stable for several decades.

2.3. Sunshine

The data on sunshine hours at Rwindi over 10 years show that, on average, annual sunshine slightly exceeds 50% of the total possible hours (about 4,400 h) every other year. Despite subjective impressions, the number of sunshine hours is generally mediocre in the PNVi, even on the plains. At Rumangabo, sunshine hours do not exceed one-third of the total possible and can be compared to the number of sunshine hours registered in Brussels (1,400 hours).

An examination of winds, humidity, saturation deficit and evaporation would be superfluous as readers can refer to the studies of various authors, particularly Lebrun, for both the plains of the lake and the high lava plains. In general, with regard to the climate, it is to be noted that there is great spatial variety of climates within the PNVi, but also that the climate in each sector of the reserve has benefited from a certain temporal stability for several decades, at least until the end of the last century. The impact of global climate change on the Park remains to be determined.

3. The PNVi, the Albertine Rift and climate change

The great East African Rift, also known as the African Rift, extending from Mozambique to the Red Sea, was formed 30 million years ago. From south to north, the rift corresponds with the graben of Lake Malawi, at which point it splits into two branches.

The eastern branch traverses first Tanzania, then Kenya. It is in this Eastern Rift, sometimes called the Gregory Rift, that Lakes Natron, Magadi, Naivasha, Nakuru, Bogoria, Baringo and Turkana are located. The western branch, or Western Rift, is more commonly referred to as the Albertine Rift. It runs from the southern end of Lake Tanganyika to Lake Albert, passing through Lakes Kivu and Edward. The two branches of the rift then converge to form the Great Ethiopian Rift, which extends to the Red Sea.

At the heart of the Albertine Rift, which is 1,380 km long and rarely wider than 150 km, lies the PNVi. The Masisi massif, the Mitumba mountain range and Mount Tshiaberimu correspond to the western flank of the rift, while the extinct volcanoes of the Mikeno sector correspond to its eastern flank. The northern shore of Lake Kivu corresponds to one of the narrowest stretches of the Albertine Rift (less than 45 km), and as a result delights visitors with particularly striking landscapes.

The Ruwenzori massif, which is not of volcanic origin, does not correspond to the eastern flank of the rift. This huge massif rose from the bottom of the rift less than three million years ago.

The geological history of the PNVi is closely linked to that of the Albertine Rift. But the formation of the rift is still ongoing, and the two flanks of the rift follow the plate tectonics that are pushing East Africa away from the rest of the continent. The Nyiragongo and Nyamulagira volcanoes bear

1.7 The Ruwenzori, Africa's third highest peak, is a non-volcanic mountain that rose from the bottom of the Albertine Rift two to three million years ago. This enormous massif, also known as the 'Mountains of the Moon', dominates the entire North Sector of the PNVi.

INTRODUCTION

1.8 'Virunga' means 'volcanoes' in Kinyarwanda. Past and present volcanic activity in the PNVi is a key feature in the whole region. It bears witness to the dynamics of plate tectonics that separated East Africa from the rest of the continent, creating the Albertine Rift. It also explains the relief of the South Sector and the mountain forests that have developed forms of life unique to this massif. The Nyamulagira and Nyiragongo volcanoes are among the most active in the world and have become a major tourist attraction. Here, the eruption of Kimanura, an adventitious cone of Nyamulagira, in 1989.

witness to this evolution and are among the most active volcanoes on the planet.

This geological dynamism has always had a significant impact on the PNVi's habitats and plant formations. The Park's diversity has also been shaped by the succession of different climatic phases. It is now well established that Earth's orbital cycles induce significant climatic cycles. A very visible example is the current lower limit of glaciers, now 1,500 metres higher than it once was, as evidenced by the large U-shaped glacial valleys. These variations bear no relation to the climate change observed in recent years. The major climatic cycles responsible for the great glaciations in Europe are induced by a conjunction of cycles: the major cycles (of astronomical origin) that have prevailed for just under a million years are approximately 413,000 and 100,000 years – both linked to the eccentricity of the orbit – 23,000 and 19,000 years (these were due to the precession of the equinoxes and affected the formation of polar ice caps) and 41,000 years, linked to the obliquity of the Earth's rotational axis, which varies the length of the day and the intensity of the seasons.

These cycles have impacted regions of the planet in different ways. In the region of interest here, a humid, cool climate (pluvial period) induces an expansion of forests and a lowering of the altitudinal limits of mountain forests. However, during the last two million years, pluvial and arid periods have regularly alternated, continually changing the landscape of the future national park.

At the end of the Tertiary era – two million years ago – the prevailing humid, cool climate and the terrain as it was then created Lake Kaisien, which covered the future Lakes Albert, Edward and George. The subalpine level was then at 1,700 metres above sea level, compared to 2,600 metres today. A major climatic change occurred nearly a million years later, in the Middle Pleistocene, when a long period of aridity caused the retreat of the rainforest, raised the level of the mountain forests and allowed the development of savannahs and other non-forest formations. Meanwhile, volcanoes blocked the watercourses that previously flowed from south to north into Lake Kaisien, resulting in the formation of Lake Kivu and the repositioning of the crest separating the Congo and Nile rivers. With the drier climate, the dense humid lowland forest that had prevailed until then retreated and was replaced by xerophytic formations, savannahs or aquatic formations along the lakes that resulted from the division of Lake Kaisien.

Towards the end of the Pleistocene, the climate became more humid again, and the lowland rainforest gained prominence, yet without obliterating the drier formations. Then followed a particularly dry period, with some intermittent wetter episodes. The last 200,000 years have been characterised by numerous successions of pluvial and arid periods: extreme aridity occurred 200,000 years ago, very mild aridity 100,000 years ago, and high aridity again between 20,000 and 10,000 years ago. Between 10,000 and 5,000 years ago, the region's forests (and those of Central Africa in general) experienced full expansion with a warm and humid optimum around 6,000 years ago, then another recession with a peak of aridity (and thus the expansion of sclerophyll formations) around 4,000 years

1.9   The position of the PNVi, at the crossroads of the basins of Africa's two largest rivers and, above all, of different biogeographical regions, makes this protected area an ideal place for research.

1.10   The Wasolda plain at the foot of Nyiragongo was flooded with lava during the 1977 eruption. The highly fluid lava created a wave around the feet of the trees, leaving behind furrows of solidified lava that bear witness to the successive levels of the flow.

ago, and finally a short dry episode about 2,500 years ago. Currently, disregarding the effect of direct human action, the climate favours slow natural expansion of forests at the expense of savannahs. Understanding this geological history and especially the history of climates is essential for comprehending the mosaic of habitats and the wide spectrum of species.

Vegetation formations have responded to these numerous climatic variations with periods of forest expansion and recession, as well as a rise and fall of the limits of subalpine and mountain forests. The diversity of the PNVi is, therefore, due not only to the wide variety of current habitats and microclimates, but also to the past development – and subsequent maintenance – of sclerophyll formations, as well as the persistence of forest nuclei east of the Congo River basin, even during the driest periods. This persistence allowed for the recolonisation of savannahs by forest species and probably led to the formation of new species.

Another fundamental element has been the great altitudinal range of the PNVi's relief, which has allowed mountain forests to persist over time, ascending or descending the slopes to the rhythm of climatic variations. It is well established that these mountain forests were reconnected to other Afromontane forests, such as those in Cameroon, having been separated during periods of aridity. The Afromontane forests of the Albertine Rift, and of the PNVi, undoubtedly represent the richest entity of this biome on the entire African continent.

4. Description of the Park's major habitats

The PNVi is traditionally described as comprising four Sectors: North, Lake, Centre and South, corresponding to the administrative management divisions of the Park. The following pages describe the major habitats of the PNVi from north to south, without attempting to provide a comprehensive description of all habitats, as those are numerous and diverse.

The diversity of the habitats is exceptionally rich, ranging from the glaciers of the Ruwenzori to the grassy savannahs of Rwindi, including the large humid forest of Semliki, the montane forests, the dry forests of Tongo and a variety of aquatic habitats (high-altitude swamps, lakes, marshes, rivers, hot springs), as well as the lavas from active volcanoes. This landscape diversity is one of the reasons why the PNVi is included on the UNESCO World Heritage list.

4.1. North Sector: from the great humid forest to the snows of the Ruwenzori

Covering an area of 299,523 ha (22,324 ha of which are part of Lake Edward), the North Sector is the largest dry land area of the PNVi. It extends from the Puemba River to Lake Edward and is characterised by the Semliki River, the Ruwenzori massif and Mount Tshiaberimu.

4.1.1. Middle Semliki, up to its confluence with the Puemba

A major feature of this part is the large humid forest along the Semliki River, which feeds the waters of Lake

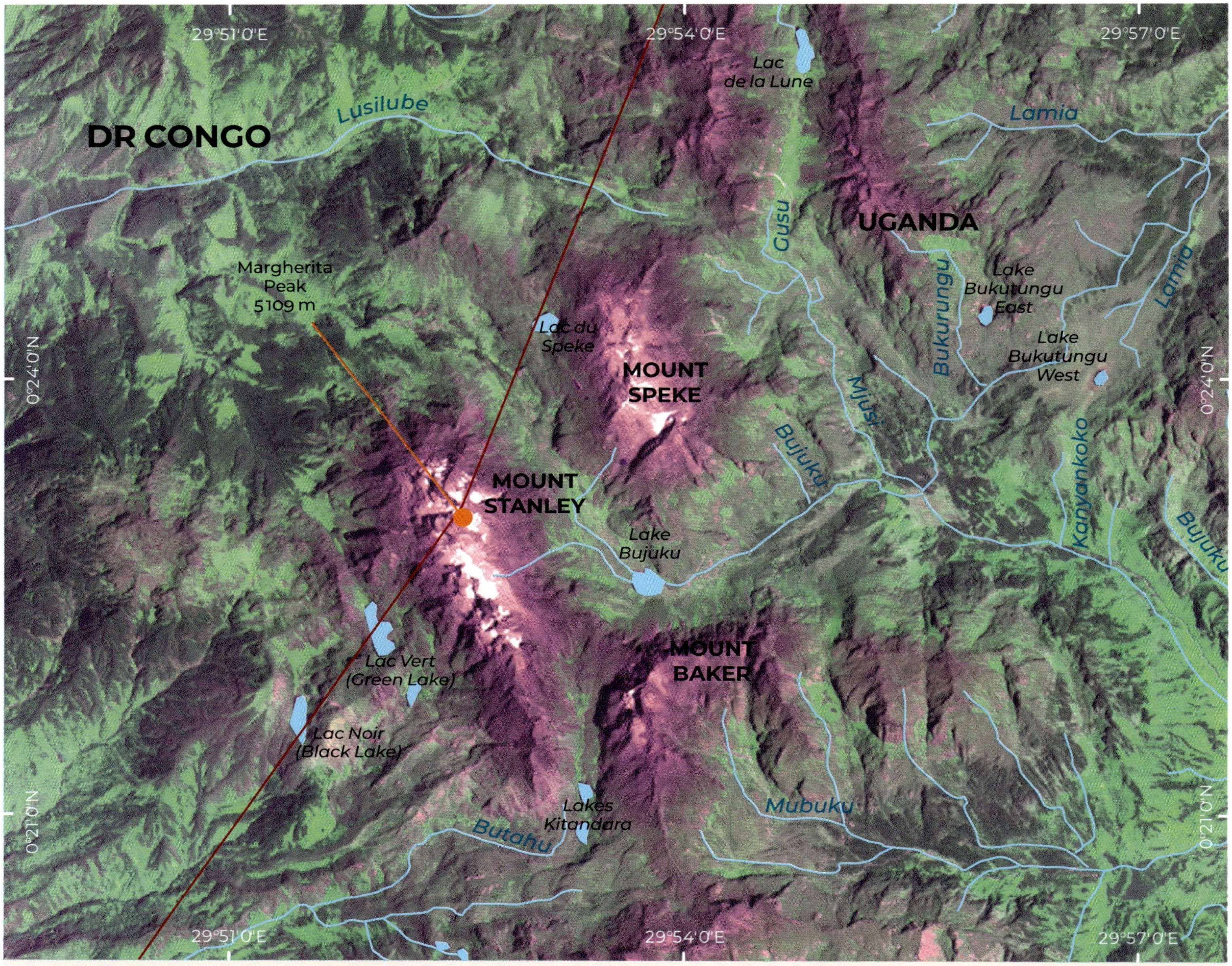

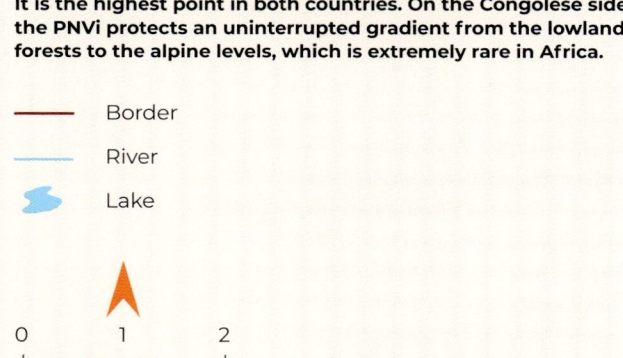

1.11 The Ruwenzori massif is shared by the DRC and Uganda. It is the highest point in both countries. On the Congolese side, the PNVi protects an uninterrupted gradient from the lowland forests to the alpine levels, which is extremely rare in Africa.

— Border
— River
— Lake

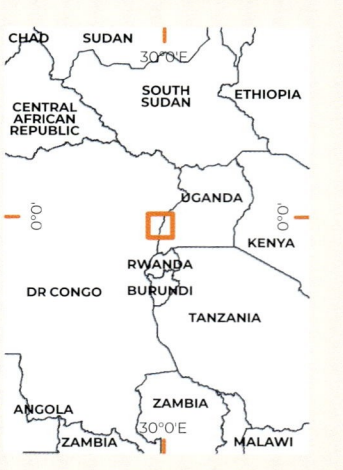

1.12 The many volcanoes and mountains have created an archipelago of Afroalpine vegetation from the south to the north of the PNVi. Here, a ragwort.

Edward into Lake Albert. The edaphic conditions, the altitude and especially the climate of this region, with an average temperature of 23° C and precipitation of over 1,500 mm spread over at least 10 months of the year, have allowed the development of its dense humid forest. Although the forest of the lower Semliki is part of the Nile basin, it shares many characteristics with those of the Congo basin. The vast majority of mammal, bird and plant species are typical of the Congo basin. Okapis and bongos, for instance, can be encountered near the Abia and Abatupi rivers on the left bank of the Semliki.

This area marks the edge of the great Congo basin forest, and true rainforest is found only in the lowlands of the major rivers, giving way to secondary forests on higher hills. It features stands of *Cynometra alexandri*, typical of non-rainforest. Unlike the Ituri forest extending to the PNVi's borders, no monospecific stands of *Gilbertiodendron* are to be found within the Park. Along the Semliki Valley, a pseudo-gallery of large acacias alternates with stands of *Cyperus papyrus*.

This low-altitude forest covers the northernmost part of the PNVi, from the Puemba River to the bridge at Vieux-Béni. However, grassy savannahs of a few hundred hectares are present in the extreme north, which are probably edaphic in origin.

4.1.2. Ruwenzori massif

The Ruwenzori massif is shared between Uganda and the DRC, together being protected as the Ruwenzori Mountains National Park in Uganda and the PNVi in the DRC. The massif covers an area of 4,800 km², of which 1,493 km² are above 2,000 m. It comprises a series of peaks, including the third, fourth and fifth highest peaks in Africa. Margherita Peak, at 5,119 m, marks the border and is the highest point.

The massif is geologically young, having risen from the Albertine Rift floor only two to three million years ago. This explains its height and still very rugged relief. During its formation, the massif separated the Semliki from Lake George: the rainwater draining the Ugandan side of the massif now flows east and then south, forming a long loop around the massif. Its waters flow into Lake Edward, before continuing their course as the Semliki River, to the west of the massif, to finally discharge into Lake Albert and feed the Nile.

This part of the PNVi has the greatest elevation difference: the middle Semliki (800 m) and the summit of the Ruwenzori (5,119 m) are only 30 km apart. Yet the main feature is that the forest is uninterrupted between these two extremes, forming a vast corridor presenting all types of transitional forest, a phenomenon now almost unique in Africa. The only other example of such a continuum on such an altitude gradient is Mount Cameroon.

This succession can be easily observed when climbing the Ruwenzori from the Mutsora station. After leaving the secondary mid-altitude forest, at around 2,000 m a dense montane forest will be reached. The upper limit of the montane forest is the bamboo forest. Unlike the situation in the extinct volcanic massif, the bamboo forest on the Ruwenzori massif is fragmented. It is better represented in

INTRODUCTION

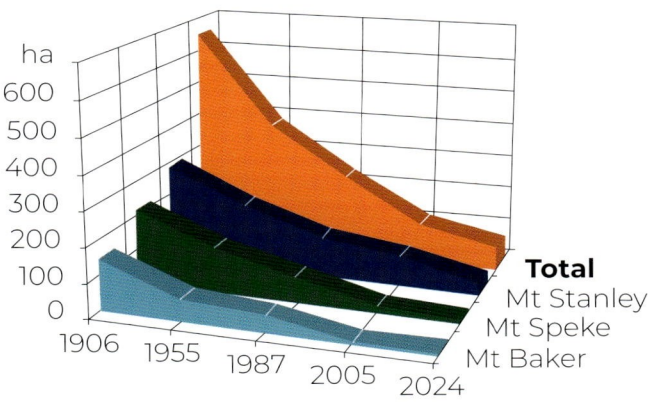

1.13 The retreat of the Ruwenzori glaciers was first observed at the beginning of the last century and has continued at a fairly steady pace ever since. Based on current projections, it is estimated that the glaciers will have disappeared almost entirely by 2050.

the northern part of the massif, the high Ruanoli. Near continuous bamboo stands occur from 2,150 m to 3,150 m, a record altitude for the region.

The *Hagenia abyssinica* forest is much less homogenous here than in the volcanic areas, and the species is often associated with *Rapine rhododendroides*, a Myrsinoideae. It is also less developed than in the volcanic areas and is quickly replaced, from about 2,600 m, by a forest of tree heathers that reach their full extent at just under 3,000 m and disappear at around 4,000 m.

The largest tree heather in the Ruwenzori is *Philippia trimera*. Jointly with *Rapine rhododendroides*, it dominates this zone, whereas on the extinct volcanoes it has been replaced by a congeneric species. It is easily recognisable by its twisted trunks, and its branches are typically covered with numerous lichens of the genus *Usnea*, which form full pale green beards. The ground is often covered with *Breutelia stuhlmannii* moss forming large yellow carpets.

As temperatures and precipitation decrease, the heathers gradually disappear, and just under 4,000 m, the first giant senecios and giant lobelias appear. The most typical species of the Ruwenzori are *Senecio johnstoni* and *Lobelia lanurensis*. From 4,500 m, Afroalpine formations dominated by mosses and lichens start to appear.

Testifying to the great expansion of ancient glaciers, the U-shaped valleys of the Ruwenzori often feature large peat bogs made up of *Carex monostachya* and *Carex runssoroensis*. These sedges form a carpet dotted with alchemillas, among which *Alchemia johnstoni* is the most common species. Another typical Ruwenzori landscape is the *Helichrysum* heathland growing on the rocky slopes and well-drained soils above the tree heather level.

Towards the top of the ascent are areas of rocks and glaciers. The retreat of the latter, noted as early as the 1950s by Heinzelin de Braucourt (1953), is unfortunately slowly continuing. The total area of glaciers has decreased from 650 hectares in 1906 to 350 hectares in 1955, 210 in 1987, 108 in 2005 and 66 hectares in 2024. It is very likely that the glaciers of the Ruwenzori will all have disappeared well before 2050.

4.1.3. Upper Semliki

Ascending the Semliki River upstream from the Vieux-Béni bridge to the Lusilube Falls, the valley is deeply entrenched, sometimes forming steep gorges such as those of Bomama. Spectacular waterfalls, like the ones at the confluences of the Butahu and Lusilube, alternate with calmer stretches.

Heading south from Vieux-Béni (at the level of the town of Beni and the Mutsora station on the western slopes of the Ruwenzori), the forest gives way to large woodland galleries. Stands of *Cassia siamea*, a species of

1.14 These photographs of the Ruwenzori peaks taken in 2004 (left) and 2022 (right) show the spectacular retreat of the glacier.

South American origin, are rapidly spreading here at the expense of the native forest.

The northern part of the upper Semliki is generally bordered by a very special gallery forest. Its banks are covered with strips of large *Acacia sp.* trees that are several hundred metres deep, growing on marshy soil. This is a nearly impenetrable environment for humans, but a refuge for elephants, buffaloes and bush pigs. The wildlife is much more abundant in this habitat than in the blocks of primary forest of *Cynometra alexandri*.

Further south, the upper Semliki plain north of Lake Edward is characterised by a *Cymbopogon* savannah with beautiful stands of the large *Borassus* palm tree. The southernmost part of this plain forms the north bank of Lake Edward and is dominated by a herbaceous savannah featuring, at Ishango, the Lake Edward spillway into the Semliki. Further to the east, the Lubilya delta constitutes a vast semi-marshy surface where lots of Mimosaceae bloom.

4.1.4. Mount Tshiaberimu

Mount Tshiaberimu is a true island of high-altitude vegetation connected to the PNVi by an extremely narrow strip called Mulango wa Nyama ('the gate of wild animals' in Kiswahili) along the Tumbwe River. The altitudinal gradient here is also steep, as the Tumbwe River flows at 916 metres while the summit of Tshiaberimu, less than 10 kilometres away, rises to 3,117 metres, representing an average gradient of 22%.

From the base of Tshiaberimu to its summit, successions of montane vegetation are to be found. However, the Afroalpine zone is minimally represented, with only the last few hundred metres covered with tree heaths, while bamboo is more widespread.

4.2. Lake and Centre Sectors: Lake Edward and its great plains

The Centre Sector of the PNVi, associated with the Lake Sector, includes the western and southern shores of Lake Edward and the plains of Rwindi–Rutshuru extending to Mabenga. This region also includes the Lulimbi area, along the Ishasha River forming the border with Uganda, a territory sometimes referred to as the Eastern Sector. The Centre Sector covers an area of 339,173 hectares, of which 144,548 hectares are part of Lake Edward.

4.2.1. Western shore of Lake Edward

At the level of Lake Edward, the western boundary of the PNVi roughly corresponds to the crest line of the Mitumba range, including a strip averaging a width of 3 to 5 kilometres between the Mitumba and the lake. This area is characterised by high-altitude forest vegetation at the summits and *Acacia sp.* savannahs at lower elevations, though significant recent anthropogenic modifications have greatly altered the natural habitat. The crests of the Mitumba range are covered with high-altitude grassy savannahs.

1.15 *Papilio lormieri semlikana* is a very rare subspecies, found in the far east of the Kivus, like this specimen photographed at the PNVi.

1.16   The Rwindi plain with the Kasali mountains in the background.

1.17   A typical landscape of the Centre Sector: the more or less wooded savannah of the Rwindi plain.

The riparian forest of Pilipili Bay, along the lower course of the Muyirimbo River, was until recently the most intact forest block along Lake Edward. It is a semi-evergreen forest consisting of very large trees. Further south, it features vast stands of *Aeschynomene sp.* ambach.

Although wildlife could move from the south to the north of Lake Edward along the western shore, until at least the late 1990s, the absence of topi antelopes (*Damaliscus lunatus*) in the north of the Park remains unexplained.

4.2.2. Lake Edward

Lake Edward is shared between the DRC and Uganda. It is important to note that all Congolese waters of Lake Edward are part of the PNVi, while the Ugandan part is excluded from the contiguous Queen Elizabeth National Park (QENP).

Situated at 916 metres above sea level, the lake covers a total area of 224,083 hectares, of which 166,872 hectares (74%) are part of the Congolese territory. Its average depth is 33 metres, but there is a significant depth gradient from west to east. The maximum depth (about 120 metres) is found in the extreme west of the lake at the foot of the Mitumba escarpment, gradually decreasing towards the east to less than 30 metres over almost all the Ugandan territory.

The climate in this region and the lake's shallow depth allow for a natural water mixing process at the end of each dry season, around August, thanks to the temperature change of surface waters cooling and sinking. Along with the input of 'green manure', from the excretion by thousands of hippos of large amounts of partially digested grass into the lake during the day after grazing at night in the savannahs, this process explains the lake's fertility and fish productivity.

The abundance of fish and the need to balance biodiversity protection with the protein demands of the local populations have led to the opening of three fisheries on the Congolese shores of Lake Edward: Vitshumbi in the south, Kyavinyonge in the north and later, though with a less clear legal status, Nyakakoma in the east. The context of their establishment is presented in chapter 11. More recently, two additional fisheries, Kisaka and Lunyasenge, have been recognised by the PNVi. Any other fisheries are considered illegal.

4.2.3. Plains south of Lake Edward

The area immediately south of Lake Edward is characterised by grassy and wooded savannahs, traversed by the Rwindi, Rutshuru and Ishasha rivers. This open landscape is complex, as evidenced by the vegetation (see chapter 9).

The grassy savannahs are of different types. There are lawns or scrubby savannahs, covered with various species of *Sporobolus* or *Cynodon*, depending on soil characteristics and grazing impact. Another type is the low savannah covered with *Sporobolus pyramidalis*, much preferred by animals, or, more locally, with *Themeda triandra*. Finally, the last type is the tall savannah covered with *Imperata cylindrica*.

There are also various types of wooded savannahs, mainly dominated by different species of Acacia. On shallow, rocky soils, *Acacia gerrardii* dominates, while on deeper soils *Acacia sieberiana* is found, which can reach 15 metres in height.

Other types of vegetation in the plains south of Lake Edward include xerophilous forests (where the dry season is most pronounced) dominated by *Euphorbia dawei*, the stag horn euphorbia, which forms dense forests locally, for instance near Lake Kizi. *Euphorbia candelabrum*, the candela-

The soils of the Rwindi–Rutshuru–Ishasha plain

MIREILLE VANOVERSTRAETEN

The soils of this region have been the subject of various studies, making it the part of the PNVi with the best-known pedology, which is presented here.

Soils, living elements that support biocoenoses, are part of a landscape unit. The landscape is characterised by a certain morphology. In the PNVi, this morphology results from the action of tectonics, which has created large structures as well as a hydrographic network and climate. The Rwindi–Rutshuru plains are part of a 'subsiding' geostructural entity, which means they form the floor of the western rift, which is dynamically sinking.

This rift valley opened following the collapse of a peneplain. At the same time, an orogenic phase generated the mountain range forming the western edge of the rift at an average altitude of 2,000 metres. In the region concerned, these are the Mitumba mountains. The average altitude of the plains below is 989 metres. In the middle of the plains rises the Kasali mountain horst, peaking at 2,220 metres.

Tectonics and climate have combined their actions over time. Their dynamic confrontation has resulted in a typical morphology. At the foot of the high slopes, glacis have formed from the accumulation of materials from the high reliefs. They form the transition between the reliefs and the central plains.

The plains extend over fluvial and lacustrine sediments that have gradually filled the rift valley. They stretch from the foot of the glacis towards the east, where the eastern slope of the rift gradually begins its descent into Ugandan territory. A change of scale allows the identification of compartments originally shaped by tectonic action.

From west to east:
- the Rwindi plain, separated from the Rutshuru plain by the Kasali horst;
- the Rutshuru plain, whose watershed is bounded to the east by the Kizi fault;
- the Rutshuru–Ishasha interfluve, limited by a tectonic step overlooking the Ishasha Valley;
- the Ishasha plain, the eastern boundary of the PNVi in Congo.

A detailed observation of the banks of the Rutshuru shows successive drop levels, sloping eastwards on the left bank and westwards on the right bank (8° to the Lulimbi–Ishasha plateau), confirming the combined effects of subsidence and tectonics.

The parent materials of the soils in the Rwindi–Rutshuru–Ishasha plains consist of fine sediments where variations in the proportion of clay and salts influence soil dynamics. The soils are composed of young clays with high proportions of exchangeable minerals, due to the fluvio-lacustrine nature of the deposits.

Radiocarbon dating indicates a lengthy occupation by savannah, long before these plains were protected in a reserve. The cartographic or morphopedological units called systems result from the confrontation of soil evolution regimes with vegetative and animal occupancy.

In marshlands, environments evolve in organic conditions. These unstable supports are subject to flooding. The littoral marshes are impractical, leaving large areas available for wildlife, safe from human incursions.

INTRODUCTION

1.18 The Rwindi river, upstream from the station of the same name, cuts through a ravine with vegetation typical of the forest galleries in the plains of Lake Edward.

bra euphorbia, is characteristic of the plain and can reach 8 metres in height. These very typical trees are, generally, more widely dispersed.

Finally, another type of tree vegetation in the Rwindi–Rutshuru plain found more locally, for instance near the Lulimbi camp, is characterised by a large number of *Rauvolfia vomitoria*.

A completely different type of vegetation in this sector are the numerous forest galleries. One of the most typical is the one along the Rutshuru River, stretching from Mabenga to its mouth in Lake Edward. This narrow gallery is dominated by the wild date palm, *Phoenix reclinata*, a relatively small palm (5 metres high) associated with *Sesbania sesban*, a papilionaceous plant, and with *Acacia kirkii*. More mature and taller formations (10 to 15 metres) are found on the middle Rwindi and middle Rutshuru. Here, the dominant species are the euphorbia (*Croton macrostachyus*) and the sausage tree (*Kigelia africana*). Locally, even taller gallery forests line the Rwindi and Ishasha rivers and are characterised by the sterculiaceous *Pterygota mildbraedii* tree, which can reach up to 25 metres in height.

The southernmost part of the Centre Sector also includes various types of sclerophyllous formations dominated by the *Olea europaea* olive tree, for instance along the middle course of the Rutshuru River, east of Mount Ilehe.

The famous hot springs, locally known as May ya Moto, represent a very unique habitat. They serve to remind us that the PNVi is located in a geologically active area, where magma rises close to the Earth's surface. The alkaline hot springs of May ya Moto can reach temperatures of up to 95° C at their source. A specialised microflora and microfauna have developed there, in association with algae and sulphur bacteria.

Finally, situated at the southernmost edge of the Centre Sector, the Kasali massif is another major feature. It is essentially a spur of the Mitumba mountain range extending into the PNVi to the south of the Rwindi camp. Stretching 15 km from north to south and covering an area of over 21,000 hectares, this massif reaches an altitude of 2,200 metres. It is covered with submontane forest and, locally, on certain ridges, with montane forest interspersed with large grassy savannahs.

4.3. South Sector: active and extinct volcanoes

The South Sector of the PNVi covers an area of 145,672 hectares, extending from the southern Kasali mountains to the northern shore of Lake Kivu. This sector includes the active volcanoes Nyamulagira and Nyiragongo, as well as the extinct volcanoes in the Mikeno sector.

The transition zone between the Centre and South Sectors is exceptionally interesting because of its highly varied habitats: Lake Ondo, the Kibuga Pond, swamps, the northernmost ends of lava flows and the sources of the Molindi River. In this topographically complex area, where numerous *Olea* trees grow, 'surgences' or pseudo-sources of the Molindi spring up everywhere. Apparently, nearly three-quarters of the downstream waters of the Rutshuru River come from the Molindi River. This significant flow brings back up to the surface the enormous quantities of water that fall on the lavas further south and are instantly absorbed. This area is located just north of the Congo–Nile Divide, which is actually underground.

4.3.1. Sclerophyllous forests of the northern slope of Nyamulagira

A significant part of the South Sector consists of sclerophyllous forests covering the geologically recent lava flows of Nyamulagira volcano. These flows reach and even surpass, to the north, the latitude of Rutshuru.

1.19 A forest gallery south of Lake Edward.

1.20 View of the Rutshuru River with its narrow gallery of characteristic small palm trees, the wild date palm *Phoenix reclinata*.

Due to the porous soil and the very thin humus layer on the most recent flows, these forests have had to adapt to xerophilic conditions. There is a very rich assemblage of these forests at different stages, due to the mosaic of flows of different ages. In just one or two years, lichens and then mosses establish themselves on the new flows. Next, ferns then fill the gaps between the various slabs or rocks, gradually producing humus on which, after 15–20 years, the first shrubs establish themselves. After about forty years, a sclerophyllous forest covers the ground, with various species of olives and figs, allowing mammals like chimpanzees to colonise the habitat. After 60 years, a forest corresponding to the paraclimax is established and characterised by *Bersama* and *Afrocrania*. These forests are typical of the 'Tongo Triangle' that, for obscure reasons, was not included in the Park at its creation.

4.3.2. Active volcanoes

The Nyamulagira (3,056 m) and Nyiragongo (3,470 m) volcanoes are among the most active in the world (see chapter 8).

This region forms the Nyamulagira sector of the PNVi. Since 1948, eruptions from parasitic cones in these volcanoes have occurred almost annually. On the slopes of the major volcanoes, the high altitude near the summits allows for the appearance of subalpine flora. As the prevailing winds at this altitude are from the east-northeast, the vegetation on this side of the Nyiragongo crater is often affected. Acid rains fall up to several tens of kilometres from the volcano when its plume of smoke (containing large quantities of SO_2) is blown away.

The eruptions of these volcanoes occur on their flanks or even at their bases, so the forest on these slopes, especially on Nyiragongo, is a mature forest on relatively deep and old soil. All stages of vegetation are therefore present at different altitudes.

A real bambusetum has sprung up in the extinct crater of Shaheru volcano. A particular flora, which includes 'sulfo-resistant' plants, also thrives in the vast craters of Nyamulagira.

4.3.3. Extinct volcanoes

The six main extinct volcanoes form an arc, commonly referred to as the Virunga massif. These are Mikeno, Karisimbi, Visoke, Sabinyo, Gahinga and Muhavura. Only Mikeno is entirely located within the PNVi and in the DRC. The Karisimbi, Visoke and Sabinyo volcanoes are partially located within the Park: the first two form the border between the DRC and Rwanda, the latter is shared between the DRC, Rwanda and Uganda. The Gahinga and Muhavura volcanoes are on the border between Rwanda and Uganda and not part of the PNVi. The PNVi's boundaries on the Congolese side are located a thousand metres lower (at around 2,000 m altitude) than in neighbouring Rwanda, ensuring greater diversity and habitat continuity.

The succession of mountain vegetation has been well described by Delvingt et al. (1990) in the PNVi tourist guide, and readers are encouraged to refer to this important publication for more details.

Afromontane forests develop at different altitudes in Africa, depending on latitude and local climates (especially the importance and above all the frequency of rains). In the PNVi, mountain forest develops from about 1,800 m.

1.21 The Nyiragongo volcano and the lava flow of January 2002 caused enormous damage in Goma and nearby villages.

1.22 The Nyamulagira volcano with one of the many recent lava flows cutting through the forest that covers its flanks.

1.23 The chain of extinct volcanoes, seen from Tshegera Island.

Dense humid mountain forest
This forest, typically growing at altitudes between 1,800 m and 2,800 m, comprises three main types.

The dense humid forest with *Ficalhoa* and *Podocarpus* is very diverse and rich in species. Its trees reach a height of 25 m and generally have smaller leaves than lower-altitude forests. *Podocarpus milanjianus*, the PNVi's only natural conifer, and tree ferns are found here. There is a great variety of epiphytes: orchids, ferns, mosses and lichens.

The secondary forest with *Neoboutonia macrocalyx* serves locally as a reminder that some areas of the PNVi were deforested before its classification. *Neoboutonia macrocalyx* is easily recognisable by its large, rounded leaves, often perforated with many small holes.

The Bamboo forest is generally found between 2,300 m and 2,600 m, on soft humus-rich soils. As noted earlier, bamboo can live above 3,000 m on the Ruwenzori and Tshiaberimu. This is a monospecific forest where the

1.24 In many places, the bamboo forest is monospecific and difficult to penetrate. Mountain gorillas dig up young bamboo shoots and eat them.

INTRODUCTION

1.25 The ragwort is a typical plant of the Afroalpine zone.

species is *Arundinaria alpina*. Bamboos are actually huge grasses with very rapid growth, and their young shoots are highly prized by mountain gorillas. Except in clearings, this type of forest does not support the development of a rich and diverse undergrowth, hosting only a few perennial plants or grasses, including *Viola abyssinica* and *Clematis wightiana*.

Afro-subalpine vegetation

From 2,600 m, precipitation decreases significantly, and the average temperature drops rapidly. The main type of vegetation at around 3,000 m is *Hagenia abyssinica* forest, an open forest dominated by this species of about 10 metres high. This results in a highly developed and diversified tall grass layer with *Peucedanum kerstenii*, a wild celery mountain gorillas feed on. The finest Hagenia forests in the PNVi straddle the hollow between Karisimbi and Visoke. They are associated with a very open undergrowth, dominated by *Hypericum revolutum* shrubbery.

At higher altitudes, a heather forest develops, mainly composed of *Philippia johnstonii* reaching up to 10 m and, on drier slopes, *Erica arborea*. The ground is typically covered with a thick layer of moss.

Afroalpine vegetation

At the upper limit of Hagenia and tree heathers, vast clearings appear at around 3,700 m altitude. The most typical species at these altitudes are giant senecios and lobelias, reaching a height of 8 m. Alchemilla thickets grow on the edges of depressions and crevices, while, in some places like the extinct Branca crater, giant peat bogs covered with Carex can be found.

The 'passes' between the volcanoes allow for a continuity of the various types of vegetation. At the summit of Visoke and Muhavura, small lakes resist freezing, unlike the high-altitude water bodies of the Ruwenzori. While the upper slopes of Mikeno are steep and accessible only to mountaineers, those of Karisimbi are much less so. At the summit of this extinct volcano (4,500 m), only

1.26 Above 3,000 m, the vegetation is dominated by tree heathers.

1.27 Endemic to the Virunga massif, this rare lamiaceous flower (*Coleus goetzenii*) is threatened by deforestation.

a few alchemillas and scattered grasses are observed among the rocks.

Finally, it is worth mentioning that, in 1957, a brief eruption (Mugogo) occurred in this so-called extinct volcano sector, accompanied by emissions of toxic gases, which were undoubtedly different from those of the mazukus in the active volcano sector. The 'extinct' volcanoes of the Mikeno sector are, in reality, geologically dormant.

5. Biological value of the PNVi

It is common to read that a particular protected area hosts exceptional biological diversity; indeed, many protected areas are unique. However, using superlatives too often may diminish their meaning. Still, the real biological and landscape value of the PNVi cannot be overstated, and neither can the extent to which it protects unique biological and geological processes.

In terms of biological richness, the PNVi is by far the most important of all protected areas on the African continent. It contains more than 700 bird species, twice as many as all Western European countries combined, and nearly 220 mammal species, also an African record. No other national park in the world has such a wealth of species.

This abundance of species includes a significant number endemic to the Albertine Rift: species that exist nowhere else in the world. Moreover, the PNVi hosts a large number of species threatened with extinction and listed in one of the categories of the International Union for Conservation of Nature (IUCN) Red List of threatened species.

1.28 Total number of species, endemic species and threatened species known to occur in the PNVi, based on the main taxa.

TAXON	NO. SPECIES	NO. ENDEMIC SPECIES	NO. THREATENED SPECIES
Mammals	223	21	13
Birds	713	25	11
Reptiles	109	11	0
Amphibians	78	21	10
Fishes	(100)	(71)	—
Butterflies	?	21	—
Higher plants	2077	230	10

5.1. Mammals

The PNVi is home to at least 223 mammal species, though it is very likely that about ten insectivores, an equal number of bats and almost as many rodents will be observed in upcoming studies, based on the distribution of these species and their habitats in the Park.

This exceptionally high number of species is due to the extreme diversity of the biotopes in the PNVi, which results from its significant variations in altitude and rainfall. Among these species, 13 are considered to be threatened with extinction. This puts the PNVi at the forefront of protected areas with the most threatened mammal species.

In general, though it possesses iconic species such as the lion (*Panthera leo*), the buffalo (*Syncerus caffer*) and the elephant (*Loxodonta africana*), the PNVi is relatively lacking in large savannah mammals. Their abundance is, however, unmatched in normal circumstances. As shown in chapter 10, the total weight of major ungulates in the savannahs south of Lake Edward (1,250 km^2) was estimated at 34,523 tons in the early 1960s, corresponding to a biomass of 27,619 kg per square kilometre, a world record density far exceeding that observed in the Serengeti. The main reason for this high biomass was the presence of the world's largest population of hippos (*Hippopotamus amphibius*), but this population was severely reduced in the 1990s and is recovering only very slowly.

Apart from this extreme abundance and unparalleled biodiversity, it should be noted that many of these species are endemic to the region, a fact that presents particular scientific and conservation interest. Notable examples include *Gorilla beringei beringei*, *Chrysochloris stuhlmani* and *Lophuromys medicaudatus*, all endemic to a small sector of the Albertine Rift. Species like *Pelomys hopkinsi*, very likely present in the PNVi, are extremely rare and endemic to the region's papyrus swamps. *Malacomys verschureni* is known from just five specimens in the world.

Among the large carnivores, the presence of lions has been noted in the savannahs of Lake Edward, along with leopards (*Panthera pardus*) and golden cats (*Caracal aurata*) throughout the PNVi. Camera traps have recently recorded the regular presence of golden cats in the Ruwenzori massif, up to over 3,000 metres in altitude.

Primates are undoubtedly a major attraction of the Park, and with 21 species their diversity is certainly a significant conservation target. These include species typical of the Congo basin like Dent's mona monkey (*Cercopithecus denti*), more widespread savannah species, and especially a set of species endemic or nearly endemic to the Albertine Rift, such as the golden monkey (*Cercopithecus mitis kandti*). The PNVi is also the only protected area in the world hosting three great ape taxa: the mountain gorilla

1.29 Number of known mammal species in the PNVi, based on order.

ORDER	CONFIRMED SPECIES	PROBABLE ADDITIONAL SPECIES
Tubulidentata	1	0
Hyracoidea	1	1
Proboscidea	2	0
Primates	21	0
Afrosoricida	2	0
Macroscelidea	1	0
Lagomorpha	1	0
Erinaceomorpha	1	0
Soriciomorpha	20	9
Chiroptera	45	8
Pholidota	3	0
Carnivora	25	1
Artiodactyla	26	0
Rodentia	71	7
Total	**223**	**26**

1.30 Servals are frequently encountered in the woodland savannahs around Lake Edward, tending to avoid denser forest.

1.31 The 24 primate species of the PNVi and their habitats.

SPECIES	SCIENTIFIC NAME	HABITAT IN THE PARK
Eastern Potto	Perodicticus ibeanus ibeanus	Montane forest (Mt Tshiaberimu), Primary and secondary forest
Demidoff's Dwarf Galago	Galagoides demidovii	Dry forest, lowland and montane forest
Thomas's Dwarf Galago	Galagoides thomasi	Primary lowland forest
Spectacled Lesser Galago	Galago matschiei	Primary and secondary montane forest
Senegal Lesser Galago	Galago senegalensis senegalensis	Secondary and montane forest
Silver Galago	Otolemur crassicaudatus monteiri	Montane forest
Red-tailed Monkey	Cercopithecus ascanius schmidti	Gallery forest, lowland forest
Dent's Monkey	Cercopithecus denti	Lowland primary forest (Semliki)
Owl-faced Monkey	Cercopithecus hamlyni	Montane and submontane forest
Golden Monkey	Cercopithecus mitis kandti	Montane forest
Blue Monkey	Cercopithecus mitis stuhlmanni	Gallery forest, lowland forest
Silver Monkey	Cercopithecus mitis doggetti	Lowland forest
De Brazza's Monkey	Cercopithecus neglectus	Lowland forest
Budgett's Tantalus	Chlorocebus tantalus budgetti	Savannah and dry forests
L'Hoest's Monkey	Allochrocebus lhoesti	Montane forest
Olive Baboon	Papio anubis	Savannah and dry forests
Angola Colobus	Colobus angolensis ruwenzorii	Montane forest
Western Guereza	Colobus guereza occidentalis	Gallery forest, lowland forest
Red Colobus	Piliocolobus semlikiensis	Lowland primary forest (Semliki)
Grey-cheeked Mangabey	Lophocebus albigena johnstoni	Humid primary and secondary forest
Agile Mangabey	Cercocebus agilis	Lowland primary forest (Semliki)
Mountain Gorilla	Gorilla beringei beringei	Montane forest (extinct volcanoes)
Eastern Lowland Gorilla	Gorilla beringei graueri	Montane forest (Mt Tshiaberimu)
Eastern Chimpanzee	Pan troglodytes schweinfurthii	Primary and secondary forest

(*Gorilla beringei beringei*), the eastern lowland gorilla (*Gorilla beringei graueri*) and the eastern chimpanzee (*Pan troglodytes schweinfurthi*). It is estimated that only slightly more than a thousand mountain gorillas remain in the world (1,063 in June 2024), of which nearly 300 individuals reside permanently or temporarily in the Park. This species, the subject of numerous scientific studies, holds significant media appeal and is a major source of the PNVi's tourism revenue.

Ungulates are obviously an important group for various reasons: tourism value, population reservoirs for neighbouring areas where hunting is allowed, and ecological processes.

1.32 The L'Hoest's Monkey, a very common species around the Rumangabo station.

INTRODUCTION

1.33 The hippopotamus is a flagship species of the PNVi. It has a major impact on savannah ecosystems, as well as on the local economy, by maintaining the high fish productivity of Lake Edward.

The most iconic ungulate of the PNVi is undoubtedly the hippopotamus, of which, until the late 1980s, the Park housed the largest population (up to 29,000 animals) and the highest densities in the world. The masses of hippos lounging in the muddy waters of Mwiga Bay are an unforgettable sight, as are their famous 'whinnies', which contribute significantly to the nighttime soundscape.

With over 20,000 individuals, the second most abundant ungulate, in normal circumstances, is the buffalo, found in all Sectors of the PNVi, both in savannah and forest, at low altitude and in the mountains. The current population, however, is much lower (between 1,000 and 2,000 individuals) due to intense poaching over recent decades. The Uganda kob (*Kobus thomasi*) is one of the most abundant mammal species in the plains of Lake Edward, both south and north. It remains common today. Other typical ungulates of the savannahs and thickets surrounding Lake Edward are the defassa waterbuck (*K. defassa*) and the bushbuck (*Tragelaphus scriptus*).

The PNVi is also renowned for its diversity in suids. It is one of the few protected areas hosting all three African suidae genera. The warthog (*Phacochoerus africanus*) is common, but limited to the savannah surrounding Lake Edward. Families with young can be observed in July–August. Though more widespread and inhabiting different forest types, the bushpig (*Potamochoerus larvatus*) is harder to spot, as it rarely leaves the undergrowth. The flagship species of this group, however, is the impressive giant forest hog (*Hylochoerus meinertzhageni*). It is relatively easy to observe when it leaves the forest galleries of the Rutshuru plain, in early morning or late afternoon, to venture into nearby grasslands.

Another highly symbolic ungulate species is the okapi (*Okapia johnstoni*), a relative of the giraffe. The okapi lives in the forest, is endemic to the DRC and has become a symbol of the Congolese Institute for the Conservation of Nature (ICCN). A small population exists on the left bank of the Semliki in the extreme north of the PNVi. A strictly endemic

1.34 The waterbuck is a common species in the savannahs south of Lake Edward.

1.35 With more than 10,000 individuals during periods of total protection, the Uganda kob is the most common antelope in the Park.

bovine species to the Ruwenzori massif is the Ruwenzori duiker (*Cephalophus rubidus*). This ungulate is confined to the upper strata of mountain vegetation: Hagenia forest, bamboo forest and Afroalpine zone. The PNVi is home to many other duiker species, including various subspecies endemic to the region.

Finally, two important groups that should not be overlooked are small rodents and shrews. These two groups include the species most endemic to the Albertine Rift. Some of these species are known only from the PNVi and/or Ruwenzori. It is likely that other species new to science are yet to be discovered, primarily in submontane and montane forests.

5.2. Birds

The PNVi is home to an exceptionally high number of bird species. With 708 species recorded to date, it is the richest protected area on the continent. As with mammals, this richness is due to its great variety of habitats and its geographical position at the intersection of several biogeographical regions. The Park is situated where the Central African avifauna – an extension of the Congo basin in the lower Semliki – meets the East African fauna, which is well represented in the Rwindi and Rutshuru plains. In addition to species from these two components, a host of Afromontane species, either endemic to the Albertine Rift or shared with the Cameroonian or East African mountains, are also present here. Finally, many Palaearctic migrants – raptors, passerines and water birds – winter in the Park or stop over in the area during their migrations from Europe and Central Asia.

The PNVi hosts 25 bird species that are strictly limited to the Albertine Rift, some of which are known from only two or three sites outside the Park, such as the Rockefeller's sunbird (*Cinnyris rockefelleri*). Eleven bird species in the PNVi are threatened with extinction.

Herons and storks are particularly well represented, with around twenty species. They are very visible in the PNVi, especially in the Centre Sector. Most of these, from the tiny little bittern (*Ixobrychus minutus*) to the impressive Goliath heron (*Ardea goliath*), are tied to aquatic systems. Among the multitude of rare and spectacular species, the strange-looking shoebill (*Balaeniceps rex*) is regularly observed, though it does not nest in the Park.

Raptors are also well represented, including numerous species of hawks, harriers, falcons, sparrowhawks, eagles and vultures. The African fish eagle (*Haliaeetus vocifer*) is a notable resident of Lake Edward and nearby rivers, recognisable by its large size, brown, black and white plumage, and distinctive far-carrying cry. Five vulture species share animal carcasses, while a wide variety of both resident and migratory eagles soar over the plains.

Passerines include many families that are impossible to review exhaustively here. Typically, forest-dwelling groups like bulbuls and robins are rarely seen, as they often hide in thickets, but their presence is easily betrayed by their charac-

INTRODUCTION

1.36 Regal Sunbird
Cinnyris regius

1.37 Ruwenzori Batis
Batis diops

1.38 Woodland Kingfisher
Halcyon senegalensis

1.39 Shoebill Stork
Balaeniceps rex

1.40 African Wood Owl
Strix woodfordii

1.41 Narina Trogon
Apaloderma narina

1.42 African Goshawk
Accipiter tachiro

1.43 White-starred Robin
Pogonocichla stellata

1.44 Greater Painted-snipe
Rostratula benghalensis

teristic songs. Others, swallows for instance, joined by Palaearctic migrants, patrol all PNVi areas.

One of the PNVi's ornithological interests is that it hosts certain species-rich bird families, such as bee-eaters (*Meropidae*) and kingfishers (*Alcedinidae*). Different species, very similar in appearance, coexist as they occupy the various ecological niches offered by the Park's numerous habitats. Ornithologists can easily spot eight bee-eater species in one day, which is a practically impossible feat in other protected areas.

Lake Edward is a significant wintering site for Palaearctic species, such as the black tern (*Chlidonias niger*), of which sometimes thousands are present, as well as many shorebirds. It is also, at times, an area of refuge for other species, such as the two species of flamingoes that have repeatedly, but unsuccessfully, attempted to nest near the Lulimbi, and the African skimmer (*Rhynchops flavirostris*).

Lake Edward's shores and the surrounding plains host many migratory waterfowl, particularly at the onset of the northern winter, before they continue southwards. This includes thousands of white storks (*Ciconia ciconia*) stopping briefly on their journey to southern Africa.

Overall, the PNVi hosts at least 108 Palaearctic migratory species, mostly waterfowl and waders, but also birds of prey and passerines. These birds are even more sensitive to habitat changes and disturbances.

5.3. Reptiles

The PNVi is home to a large number of reptile and amphibian species, but for these two groups, the number of species endemic to the Albertine Rift is particularly high (more than 30). The group of chelonians, the turtles, includes relatively few species. Most common in the Rwindi–Rutshuru plains is *Pelusios rhodesianus*. An aquatic species endemic to East Africa, *Pelusios williamsi*, is known from Lake Edward and adjacent rivers.

A very large number of lizards live in the PNVi. This group includes geckos, agamas, chameleons, monitor lizards, skinks and 'real' lizards.

Among the geckos, the omnipresent house gecko (*Hemidactylus mabouia*) cannot be ignored. This friendly neighbour to humans can be found in practically every home. At night, its clicks, a means of communication with its fellows, are often heard. Like many other geckos, this species can swiftly change its colouration depending on the surrounding environment. The four-striped forest gecko (*Cnemaspis quattuorseriatus*), found in the mountain forests of the Mikeno sector, is endemic to the Albertine Rift.

Agamas are well represented in the PNVi. One ubiquitous species is the black-collared agama (*Acanthocercus atricollis*). The males, which can grow to 30 cm, are easily recognisable by their very large blue heads. The species is common in many habitats, from tree trunks in the Rwindi plains to lava flows at about 2,400 metres in altitude. The diversity of chameleons is impressive, with no fewer than 12 species, of which two, *Chamaeleo carpenteri* and *C. xenorhinus*, are known only from the Ruwenzori.

Monitor lizards are very large lizards. The Nile monitor (*Varanus niloticus*) is a common species, frequently encountered along rivers and on the banks of Lake Edward. Its

1.45 The Uganda blue-headed tree agama lives in trees and on rocks. It is often seen on buildings, and is even found on lava flows at an altitude of up to 2,000 m.

1.46 The Ruwenzori three-horned chameleon is endemic to the Albertine Rift and can be found in montane forests throughout the Park.

INTRODUCTION

1.47 The chameleon species of the PNVi.

SPECIES	RANGE
Chamaeleo adolfifriderici	Albertine Rift
Chamaeleo dilepis	Widespread
Chamaeleo ellioti	Mountains of East Africa
Chamaeleo gracilis	Widespread
Chamaeleo ituriensis	Albertine Rift and Ituri
Chamaeleo johnstoni	Albertine Rift
Chamaeleo laevigatus	Widespread
Chamaeleo rudis	Mountains of East Africa
Chamaeleo xenorhinus	Ruwenzori Mountains
Chamaeleo carpenteri	Ruwenzori Mountains
Chamaeleo bitaeniatus	Widespread
Rhampholeon boulengeri	Mountains of East Africa

length can exceed 2 metres and it is an excellent swimmer and climber. It feeds on all kinds of invertebrates, as well as frogs, bird chicks and eggs. The monitor lays 20 to 50 eggs, most often in still-active termite mounds. It is very likely that its forest twin species, *Varanus ornatus*, inhabits the Semliki.

The PNVi is home to about ten skink species. These are lizards with typically atrophied limbs. Among them, *Leptosiaphos meleagris* is known only from the Ruwenzori and Ituri, while its counterpart, the Virunga skink (*L. hackarsi*), is restricted to the forests of Bwindi and the Virunga massif. This reptile's distribution is very similar to that of the mountain gorilla.

Some spectacular species from the snake group live in the Park, such as the python (*Python sebae*), which is found in most of its habitats, but especially in forest galleries and near the swamps lining Lake Edward's shores. This species can reach 7 metres in length and weigh up to 40 kg. Other impressive, but less frequently observed, species include the puff adder (*Bitis arietans*), the black-necked spitting cobra (*Naja nigricollis*) and Jameson's mamba (*Dendroaspis jamesoni*). These are all venomous species, none of which have, however, ever bitten a tourist. The egg-eating mountain snake (*Dasypeltis atra*) is endemic to the East African mountains. It is peculiar in that it feeds exclusively on bird eggs.

The Nile crocodile (*Crocodilus niloticus*) has always been known to live in the North Sector, but seems to have been confined to the north of the Semliki Falls for a long time. However, since June 1986, the species has been observed at Ishango on the northern shore of Lake Edward and has spread quickly. Nile crocodiles were noticed on the western shore of Lake Edward near Mosenda in 1989 and reached Rutshuru, near Nyamushengero, by mid-1991. Several individuals were observed downstream from May ya Moto in 2005. By 2024, the species was present in almost all its tributaries, including the Ishasha River.

5.4. Amphibians

At least 119 amphibian species are known in the Albertine Rift, representing one-fifth of the total for the African continent. Based on a study of 27 sites in the rift (Plumptre et al., 2003), the PNVi proves to be the richest area, with 78 species recorded, more than a quarter of which are endemic to the rift. These species belong to 10 families and subfamilies, distributed across 17 genera. Unlike the montane forests of eastern Tanzania, the PNVi does not harbour any Gymno-

1.48 The Nile crocodile population underwent a sudden, massive expansion of its range in the late 1980s. The species can now be found throughout Lake Edward and its tributaries.

1.49 One of many species of frogs found in the PNVi.

1.50 The fish from Lake Edward is a major source of protein and income for local communities.

phiona amphibians (formerly caecilians), which are limbless and beltless and resemble earthworms. Nor does it host any urodeles. The amphibian class is, until proven otherwise, represented solely by the Anura order (tailless amphibians). Frogs and toads belong to two suborders: archaic and tongueless frogs and modern frogs (*Neobatrachia*), of which toads are a subclassification.

The range of frogs includes archaic or tongueless frogs with claws and a characteristically flattened body, the *Pipidae* of the genera *Xenopus* and *Hymenochirus*, and the true toads of the Bufo genus, among which the very large, smooth-skinned *Bufo superciliaris*, listed in Appendix 1 of the Washington Convention. The PNVi also has very specialised toad species, such as the viviparous arboreal dwarf toad (*Nectophryne afra*). Canopy-dwelling tree frogs, the Rhacophoridae, are represented by *Chiromantis rufescens*, a species with a very unusual reproductive mode, as it builds a foam nest made of air bubbles.

The North Sector alone counts 50 amphibian species. Notable examples include *Hyperolius xenorhinus*, known only from Mount Teye on the slopes of the Ruwenzori, and *Rana ruwenzorica*, endemic to the Ruwenzori massif. With 47 species, including 16 that are endemic to the Albertine Rift, the Virunga massif – and the Mikeno sector – is yet another important area for amphibian conservation. Species like *Phrynobatrachus bequaerti*, known only from this massif, are also found there.

5.5. Fish

Fish are the least documented group of vertebrates in the PNVi. It is estimated that around a hundred species are present, several of which are endemic to Lake Edward and Lake Kivu. The ichthyofauna of these two lakes is relatively poor compared to that of Lakes Tanganyika, Albert or Victoria. The small number of species in Lake Edward (about fifty), which is compensated by the species abundance, may be due to its shallow depth and limited habitat diversity. A long dry period between two rainy periods during the Pleistocene may also have caused the lake to almost dry up, thereby eliminating a large number of species. A recolonisation occurred, but was limited, due to the lake's isolation from Lake Kivu (by volcanoes) and the Nile River downstream (by the Semliki Falls). As for Lake Kivu, the recent geological history of the lake explains the limited diversity of species (about thirty).

INTRODUCTION

1.51 Very few studies have been carried out on the PNVi's insects and other invertebrates. Their distribution, abundance and even their occurrence are often unknown. However, some species have important ecological value, for instance the Goliath beetle, which is unfortunately threatened by international trade.

OVERVIEW OF VIRUNGA NATIONAL PARK

1.52 The Park's wide variety of flowering plants, trees and shrubs, ferns and mushrooms arouses the interest of naturalists.

One of the most important species found in Lake Edward, given its economic role, is the tilapia (*Oreochromis niloticus*). Indeed, it is the primary target of fishing efforts on the lake, preceding the catfish (*Bagrus docmak*), the barb (*Barbus altianalis eduardianus*), the lungfish (*Protopterus aethiopicus aethiopicus*) and the catfish (*Clarias gariepinus*). See chapter 11 for additional details.

5.6. Plants

The PNVi is characterised by the great number of superior plants its supports, which number more than 2,000. As with the animals, its floristic richness is due to the great variety of biotopes and its geographical position. It includes elements from three major phytogeographical regions: the Guineo–Congolian region, the Afromontane region and the Central African Great Lakes region. The first region is represented by the low-altitude rainforest along the middle Semliki. The second is found in each of the three Sectors: Ruwenzori and Tshiaberimu in the North, Kasali in the Centre, and active and extinct volcanoes in the South. The third region is mainly represented in the plains of Lake Edward, both to the north and south of the lake.

More than 200 species, about 10%, are endemic to the Albertine Rift; these are mainly mountain forest species. The rate of endemism is exceptionally high, even reaching 13% in the Ruwenzori, where 75 species are endemic exclusively to this massif.

Most of the species characteristic of each region are mentioned in the preceding description. The WWF produced a

1.53 Surface areas of the major habitat types in the PNVi.

VEGETATION TYPES	SURFACE AREA (%)
Afroalpine floor	1.4
Afro-subalpine heather zone	2.8
Bamboo montane forest	2.4
Podocarpus and *Neoboutonia* montane forests	11.2
Sclerophyllous woodland and scrub	12.3
Hagenia forest	0.4
Lowland humid forests	11.8
Gallery forests	1.4
Grassland and wooded savannahs	35.7
Recent lava flows	2.3
Lakes and rivers	18.3

simplified vegetation map in 2005, based on high-resolution spot satellite images as well as the work of numerous authors. This map shows the approximate distribution of the main vegetation types.

1.54   Botanical inventories have revealed the existence of more than 2,000 higher plants. Here, a *Crocosmia* flower.

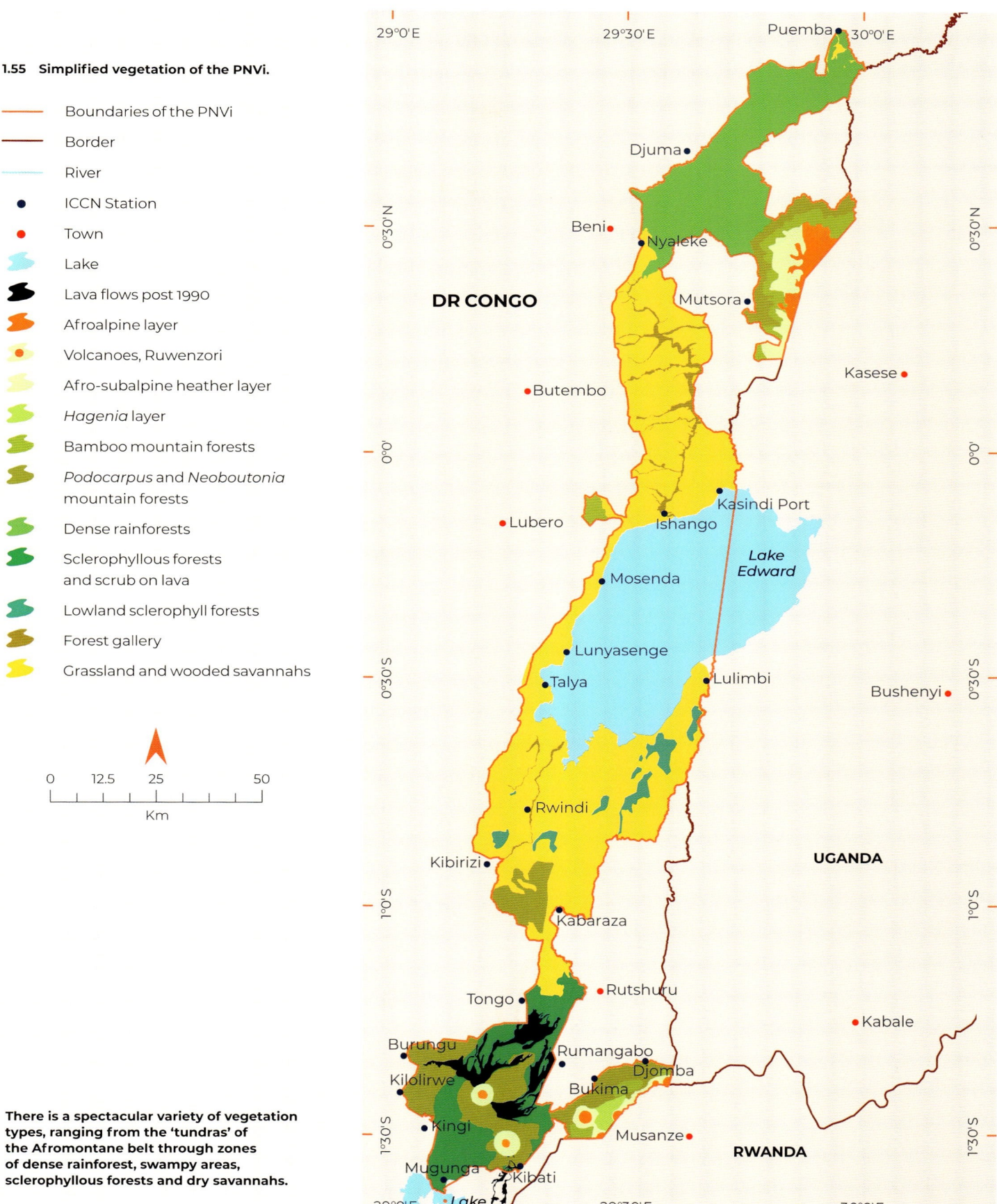

1.55 Simplified vegetation of the PNVi.

There is a spectacular variety of vegetation types, ranging from the 'tundras' of the Afromontane belt through zones of dense rainforest, swampy areas, sclerophyllous forests and dry savannahs.

A CENTURY OF HISTORY

2 — The birth of the Park (1925-1960) 61

3 — The life in the Park (1925-1960) 75

4 — The new start (1960-1991) 89

5 — The transition years (1992-2005) 103

6 — The new challenges (2005-2025) 115

7 — Prestige and fame 131

2.1 The very first tourist guide to the Albert National Park (PNA) was published in 1934. The gorilla on the cover is painted by James Thiriar.

2

The birth of the Park (1925–1960)

PATRICIA VAN SCHUYLENBERGH

The legal and institutional aspects that accompany the creation of the Albert National Park are rich and complex. Historical research explains the circumstances in which Africa's oldest national park came into existence and clarifies lingering misunderstandings about the relationship between customary rights and national law.

1. Towards the creation of the Park

A long, tumultuous human history characterises the territories that would form the future national park. Lithic pieces and fossil bones discovered on the shores of Lake Edward, and particularly at the Ishango site, date back to at least 20,000–25,000 years BC (Cammaert and Jadin, 2017) and probably two million years (Crèvecoeur et al., 2014). In an extremely rich natural environment, societies and cultures started to develop. These resulted from the multiple confrontations, encounters and economies based on numerous resources issuing from agropastoralism, fishing, and dense and diverse trading in plant products, salt, copper and iron (Chrétien, 2000).

During consecutive imperialist and colonial expansions, this region became a significant geostrategic concern and a source of territorial rivalries among the British, the Germans and the Belgians, as they discovered its enormous economic, aesthetic and scientific potential. From the second half of the 19th century, European exploratory expeditions in the region[1] gathered geographical, botanical and zoological knowledge, while intensifying the hunting of characteristic animal species. Wildlife trophies soon became coveted by individuals, as well as by museums in the western world.

In this context, during an expedition in October 1902, two mountain gorillas were killed on the slopes of the Sabinyo volcano by Robert von Beringe, a captain in the East African Imperial German colonial army. One of them, a large male, was sent to the Berliner Zoologisches Museum, where Paul Matschie categorised it as a *Gorilla beringei beringei*, a subspecies of the eastern gorilla group (which was known as *Gorilla beringei graueri*) (Van Schuylenbergh & de Koeijer, 2017).

This new discovery aroused such enthusiasm that it sparked a competition among envoys of colonising nations to be the first to have the honour of bringing back new specimens to their respective metropolises. At the beginning of the 20th century, frequent international requests for gorilla hunting permits were made to the Belgian Ministry of Colonies, the administrator of the Congo from 1908. These requests were strongly supported by museums and other foreign scientific institutions, especially American ones, for both scientific and commercial purposes. Sweden, for instance, organised an expedition in 1921, led by Prince William of Sweden, who was granted no fewer than 14 hunting permits by the Belgian authorities, which earned the latter significant international criticism. The Swedish prince did, however, report many details about the life of gorillas (William, 1923) and it was he who

2.2 In 1921, during a scientific hunting expedition in the region of the future PNA, Prince William of Sweden shot several mountain gorillas. He shared his wish with the Belgian authorities to see the Rwindi plain established as a nature reserve to protect its fauna, flora and soil.

2.3 Taxidermist Carl Akeley's expedition to Kivu on behalf of the American Museum of Natural History (New York) was decisive in informing the Belgian authorities of the precarious situation of the gorillas. He asserted that the gorilla was an 'amiable and decent' creature and called for the creation of a sanctuary to carry out scientific research.

drew the Belgian monarch's attention to the scientific interest of creating a reserve park in Kivu, to ensure the conservation of its exceptional fauna and flora, soils and overall environment.

In the same year, an expedition led by Carl Akeley, a renowned taxidermist and naturalist at the American Museum of Natural History (AMNH, New York) and a committed conservationist, marked another fundamental step towards the creation of the future national park. Akeley was tasked with bringing back the remains of several gorillas and a quantity of evidence to create a diorama presenting this subspecies in the museum hall dedicated to large African fauna. He was, however, deeply affected by these killings and, having observed the gorillas in their environment, become convinced that they were in danger of extinction. He advocated for preserving them safely in a space dedicated to their reproduction, where scientists would be able to study them in favourable conditions. He also demonstrated that they were gentle and rather fearful, contrary to older yet still prevalent literature that portrayed them as hideous, ferocious monsters.

After his stay in the region, Akeley returned to the United States, where he developed the idea of creating a Gorilla Sanctuary dedicated to their protection in their habitat formed by three extinct volcanoes: Mikeno,

Karisimbi and Visoke. Until 1925, he lobbied vigorously for this cause on both sides of the Atlantic, gaining support from the American and Belgian scientific, financial and diplomatic communities.

From 1922, the Belgian Ministry of Colonies also considered wildlife protection measures in response to increasing requests for gorilla hunting permits. These came from foreign scientific institutions as well as high-ranking hunters, so, for diplomatic reasons, refusal of these permits would have been embarrassing. To address this issue, two hunting reserves were created in the Kivu district by ordinance of the Vice-Governor General. In response to suggestions from Prince William of Sweden, the Albert Reserve was established between the Rutshuru River and the south of Lake Edward (24 February 1923). To the northeast of Lake Kivu, between Mount Sabinyo and the Tongres-Ste Marie catholic mission (now Rugari), a second reserve was created, dedicated to protecting rare animals, especially gorillas (23 November 1923).

The creation of hunting reserves by the colonial government was not unprecedented. The reserves reflected the continuation of a policy of protecting certain animal species, initiated in 1901 by the government of the Congo Free State and later continued by the Belgian Congo. The latter enacted legislative measures, in part to fulfil the wishes expressed at the first International Conference for the Protection of Animals in Africa, signed by several colonising nations (London, 19 May 1900), but mainly to meet economic and utilitarian objectives. Elephants, in particular, were protected not so much for their biological uniqueness but rather to maintain a stock of ivory producers, a significant source of income for the colony (Van Schuylenbergh, 2019b).

The support of King Albert I marked a decisive step in the establishment of the future national park. Influenced by American positivism, and by the role of private patronage in scientific research he had closely observed on his trip to the United States and Brazil in 1919, he favoured the role science could play in the development of the nation. Supported by a diplomatic entourage already sympathetic to this cause, he encouraged the emerging movement to protect nature in eastern Congo. After a crucial meeting with Akeley, having taken in the suggestions from Prince William of Sweden, and having read various American publications, the King gave his full support to Akeley's project. He did not limit it to the protection of gorillas but extended it to encompass all wildlife, flora and the entire 'natural beauty' of the Rwindi region, adding the term 'national' to 'reserve park'. The wildlife and flora reserve, named the 'Albert National Park' (*Parc National Albert* – PNA) was created by decree on 21 April 1925. It encompassed a region particularly remarkable for its fauna and flora and presenting specific scientific interest, including the dormant volcanoes Mikeno, Karisimbi and Visoke. The PNA, later renamed Virunga National Park (*Parc National des Virunga* – PNVi), became Africa's oldest national park, just months before the Kruger National Park was established in South Africa in January 1926.

2. Early developments

The delimitation of this first total reserve, as initially proposed by Akeley, was still inaccurate and rudimentary for lack of knowledge of its physical geography and its human and economic realities. In July 1925, an ordinance from the General Governor of Congo determined new limits and added the obligation to consider the needs of the populations. These were further specified during a second expedition by Akeley, who conducted research in the reserve, for the AMNH and as a special envoy of the Belgian Ministry of Colonies. He was accompanied by the zoologist Jean-Marie Derscheid. The two men were commissioned to undertake a complete study of the PNA, improve its topographical knowledge, lay the foundations for its organisation and gather data on the distribution areas of plants and animals. Akeley's unexpected death in November 1926 at the Kabara camp led Derscheid to take over. According to his instructions, the territory would consist of two distinct regimes. The first would be an 'integral nature reserve' dedicated to the strict protection of biotopes, where all human presence would be prohibited, save for scientific missions. This comprised the territories dedicated to the Gorilla Sanctuary proposed by Akeley, and the hunting reserve created in 1923, and was extended more widely to include the entire volcanic region.[2] The second would be 'annex territories' surrounding the integral reserve on the Congolese side, forming a vast buffer zone with neighbouring populations. The latter's gathering, hunting and fishing activities had been regulated by the colonial authorities, but were further restricted by this new allocation of their ancestral lands.

2.4 A monument to commemorate the creation of the PNA was erected near Rwindi station.

2.5 In 1926, a joint mission by the Belgian zoologist Jean-Marie Derscheid (pictured) and the American Carl Akeley contributed to implementing the royal decree creating a flora and wildlife reserve, known as the PNA.

2.6 Tomb of Carl Akeley, who died in the Kabara camp on 17 November 1926.

In addition to the decree of 18 August 1927, which extended the PNA reserve further to the southeastern slopes of the Visoke and Karisimbi mountains in the Rwandan territory under Belgian mandate, on 9 July 1929 a decree constituting the PNA was signed by the King. It defined the autonomous nature of the institution, which was granted legal personality, registered in Brussels but still financed and controlled by the Belgian Ministry of Colonies and governed by an Administrative Commission. This commission consisted of 26 Belgian and foreign scientific personalities appointed by the King, and a Management Committee of 7, later 9 members, for day-to-day and financial management. The decree further expanded the Park's area from 25,000 to 190,000 hectares, divided into four Sectors: Centre (core of the extinct volcanoes and Sabinyo); West (zone of active volcanoes, Nyamulagira and Nyiragongo up to the northern tip of Lake Kivu); East (zone of Gahinga and Muhavura volcanoes, in Rwanda, south of the Ugandan border); and North (former Kivu hunting reserve, south of Lake Edward). It also included some annex territories: a strip of land stretching around the Centre and East Sectors, and another one extending south of the North Sector with the same surface area, but densely populated and exploited by neighbouring communities.

The PNA Administrative Commission was initially entrusted to Prince Eugène de Ligne (president) and Derscheid (vice-president). This duo wished to see the founding of a federation of African nature reserves with the Park as its nucleus. They hoped that international scientific cooperation would become sufficiently important to justify financial support from abroad, mainly from the United States. Differences in views resulted in their replacement, in late 1931, by Prince Leopold, Duke of Brabant, who assumed the presidency, and one of his mentors, Victor Van Straelen, omnipotent new Director of the Belgian Museum of Natural Sciences and a confidant of King Albert. Unlike their predecessors, these men wished to free themselves from American influence and management and to prioritise national research in the Park grounds quasi exclusively (Van Schuylenbergh, 2019a).

After a trip to the PNA in 1932, they set out the principles for reorganising the administrative services. They stated their intention to create the Institute for the National Parks in Belgian Congo (*Institut des Parcs Nationaux du Congo Belge* – IPNCB) and to strengthen the Park's surveillance measures. They also expressed the wish to extend the territories of the reserve by incorporating the western slopes of the Ruwenzori mountains and a portion of the equatorial forest, where the okapi live.

The status of the PNA as an integral natural reserve was consolidated by its Directors' intention to safeguard the absolute integrity of the selected territories by restricting human intervention to a minimum. This was done not solely for reasons of aesthetics or tourism, but also because the Park was considered a natural heritage to be safeguarded for the sake of promoting scientific, economic and utilitarian

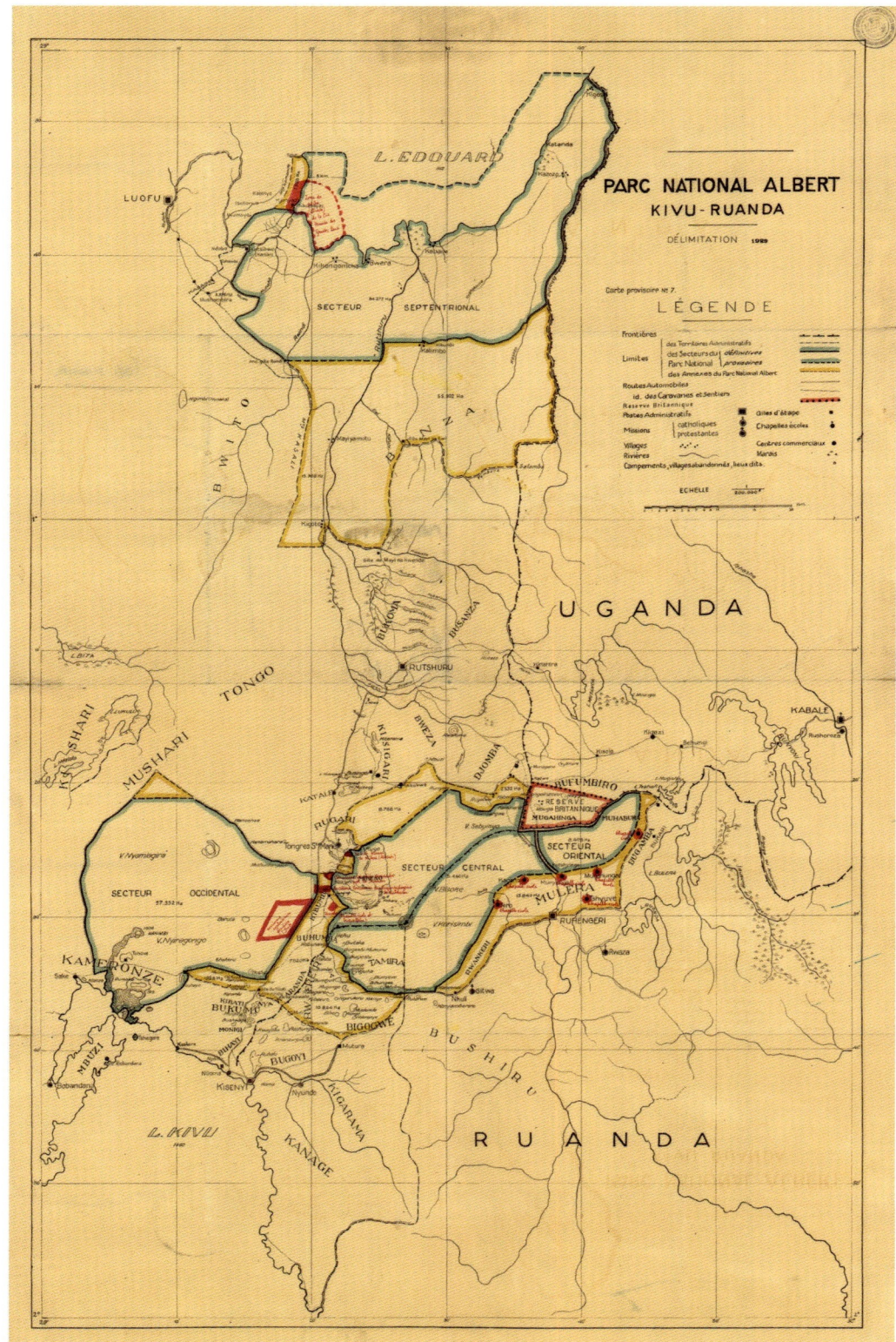

2.7   In 1929, the PNA, covering an area of 200,000 ha, was divided into four discontinuous Sectors, each one bordered by secondary territories. It was not until 1935 that the volcanoes and Rwindi plain sectors were united into a single block.

2.8 The Duke of Brabant, future King Leopold III, filming one of the active craters in the Nyamulagira sector – then known as the West Sector – in 1933.

knowledge. This mindset was widely advocated by the participants of the International Conference for the Protection of African Fauna and Flora (London, 1933), which defended the preservation of natural riches as 'common heritage of mankind' (IPNCB, 1935). In his remarkable speech at the African Society on 16 November 1933, Leopold of Belgium also insisted on the moral duty to safeguard this natural heritage 'of which we are temporary and accountable keepers' (de Brabant, 1933). This meant that the (current and future) national parks would hold a specific scientific function, as they constituted open-air laboratories where researchers were called upon to research natural environments shielded from human interference that were, consequently, either 'unspoiled' or regenerated in a 'natural' way.

Two main research areas were subsequently favoured. First, inventory making, descriptive studies and systematic collecting from a bionomic zone or a group of living organisms; second, the study of issues presenting a general scientific interest for which the national parks provided favourable and often uniquely suitable conditions. A call was launched from 1933 for scientific collaborations among scientific institutions and metropolitan universities. Scientific research would not now solely aim to accrue scientific knowledge by means of observation and on-site collecting. It would instead predominantly strive to offer practical solutions to ensure an ecological equilibrium in the future, as the natural balance was being disrupted by 'modern' man's anthropogenic activities. In this sense, Van Straelen may be considered the frontrunner of a new generation of researchers, whose main concern was the ecological perspective.

Between 1933 and 1961, 28 scientific missions were launched, composed of 87 Belgian and international researchers, who were granted the status of project managers. The IPNCB trained 13 naturalist explorers and subsidised 34 collaborators to carry out 15 exploratory missions, among which 11 involved the PNA. These missions resulted in 231 publications, featuring 323 internationally distributed, influential scientific studies. The PNA's first official mission was entrusted to Gaston-François de Witte, a herpetologist, head of the Zoology and Entomology Section at the Museum of the Belgian Congo. It was to carry out an ethological and taxonomic study of the region's herpetological fauna, as well as collect invertebrates, fish, birds and small mammals. The specimens were determined by many Belgian and international zoologists, who published the results between 1937 and 1956 in the IPNCB collection. This mission was followed by a hydro-biological mission (Hubert Damas, 1935–1936); a botanical mission (Jean Lebrun, 1937–1938); an anthropological mission (Peter Schumacher, 1933–1936); a volcanological mission (John Verhoogen, 1938–1940); and a stratigraphical and palaeontological mission (Jean de Heinzelin de Braucourt, 1950), all of which were milestones in Belgian scientific history.

3. Management by the colonial authorities

The decree of 26 November 1934 met the above-mentioned objectives and modified the constituting decree by founding the IPNCB, hoping to be further entrusted with the management of other national parks being founded at the time.[3] This broader institution wished to obtain greater operational freedom, vis-à-vis the Belgian Ministry of Colonies, and, in particular, the authority to appoint a special

2.9 Following field surveys, a proposal to draw the boundaries of the South Sector of the PNA was submitted to the Belgian authorities in 1934.

2.10   The Park boundaries were clearly signposted along the access roads.

2.11   The first PNA headquarters were a house assigned to the IPNCB by Jean Fontaine, the territorial administrator.

body of wardens and rangers, as these tasks had until then resided under the local colonial authorities. The decree also marked the development of a parks policy, divided into three main areas: the protection of fauna and flora, the development of scientific research, and cautious encouragement of tourism in certain zones of the Park. The latter activity was seen as a way of financing scientific research (Van Schuylenbergh, 2015 & 2017). Besides the subsidies provided by the Belgian Ministry of the Colonies for the management of the PNA, the creation of a 'Foundation to promote the scientific study of the Belgian Congo's national parks' helped to provide additional funding. The yearly donations from the industrialist Louis Empain to this foundation, for instance, were in part used to cover the costs of the scientific missions and to ensure that their results were followed up and valorised.

In 1934 and 1935, two other decrees reshaped the boundaries of the PNA. The first (26 November 1934) released certain zones within the Park to avoid land disputes with local populations and European companies. In return, it inserted into the integral reserve certain annex territories that were still occupied by local residents, as well as some new territories, increasing the surface area of the PNA to 390,000 hectares, a joined-up territory connecting, for the first time, the West Sector (Nyamulagira–Nyiragongo) with the North Sector (Lake Edward). The second decree (12 November 1935) introduced new boundaries that corresponded with the study reports of warden Hackars.

He increased the reserve area towards the north by 470,000 hectares, by incorporating all the Belgian waters of Lake Edward, the high and middle Semliki plains and the Belgian hillsides of the Ruwenzori and the Tshiaberimu.[4] The PNA was divided into seven Sectors corresponding with distinct geographical features[5] and clustered around two administrative and technical stations: Rutshuru–Rumangabo, managing the South and Centre Sectors, the African headquarters of the IPNCB, with a warden, a delegate for visits and a technician; and Mutsora, managing the North Sector, also with a warden.

From 1928 to 1934, the responsibility for monitoring the reserves fell to warden René Hemeleers, a non-executive agent of the colony. He was assisted by deputy Director Rasmus Hoier, a Danish colonel of the Public Force, and reported directly to the PNA Management Committee. The management of the Park was entrusted by the IPNCB to Henri Hackars (Mutsora station), who was instrumental in the new delineation of the northern sectors. He also played an important part in the negotiations for the repurchase of the rights of the indigenous people, who were to be expropriated as they were likely to encumber the expansion grounds. Colonel Hoier (Rutshuru station), warden of the South Sector, took an active part in organising the Centre Sector until 1946.

The war years disrupted the connections between occupied Belgium and its colony. The PNA found itself

2.12 The Dane Rasmus Hoier (1906–1955), a former colonel in the Danish army, was a warden in the PNA for over twenty years.

2.13 The first tourist caravan to visit the plains of Lake Edward in December 1934.

cut off from Brussels and the IPNCB, all decisions regarding it being made by the colony's general government, while warden Hoier held in-situ management power. During this period, the colonial administration showed much greater tolerance towards the numerous demands of local populations to return to their lands and exercise their essential rights. This relaxation threatened the provisions made in the IPNCB's organisational decrees and indeed the very existence of the Park, challenged by its numerous opponents. After the war, eager for the situation of the PNA to revert to its former more viable state, Victor Van Straelen undertook several inspection trips to the Congo to investigate the option of taking more radical measures in the field. He pressured the Minister of the Colonies to strengthen the Park's protection objectives at the expense of certain indigenous rights.

The overall decentralisation of power after the war – in favour of the general government and to the detriment of the Belgian Ministry of the Colonies, which favoured the Park authorities – exacerbated the confrontation with local populations. A tightening of positions among the parties involved resulted in increased resistance and acts of sabotage against the PNA by the local residents.

A decree by the regent (15 May 1950) revised the previous royal decrees (4 May 1937 and 17 May 1939). In response to the conclusions of an investigative commission established to attempt to settle indigenous rights, the decree readjusted the boundaries of the PNA by adapting the western and Mikeno sectors. The Park staff was strengthened to cope with the wardens' increasing number of tasks to be performed (administration, welcoming prominent visitors, expanding constructions, demarcation works) while being subjected to more rigorous IPNCB controls. At the same time, the number of indigenous guards ensuring the surveillance of the Park increased considerably (132 guards in 1947, 240 between 1954 and 1960), as did the number of artisans or workers assigned to subordinate tasks.

2.14 The PNA had 234 rangers in 1954. Here, ranger Ndabananye in Rumangabo in 1956.

4. Thorny issue of the rights of indigenous populations

The existence of the PNA during the entire Belgian colonial occupation was marked by the friction between two divergent, even contradictory, trends: a long-term vision marked by the desire to preserve parcels of wildlife at any local cost, and a short-term vision opposed to the Park, arguing that it constituted a major obstacle to the economic development of the region. However, this meta-analysis requires nuance. Other factors compromised the balance between, on the one hand, satisfying the needs of the indigenous people and increasing the agricultural productivity of the region, and, on the other, securing the integral nature reserve and its surrounding areas to maintain optimal protection and conservation of their various biotopes. Significant factors to be taken into account included the consequences of human and animal diseases, an unpredictable increase in population density and migratory flows, the gradual settlement of European colonists and the rise of increasingly demanding economic activities. As we cannot address all of these, we will limit ourselves to summarising the issue of indigenous claims on the PNA, a crucial topic then as now. It is both vast and complex as it considers other economic and political factors induced by colonial occupation, which have a huge impact on the lives of local populations.

The history of the PNA is marked by a series of legislative and legal entanglements concerning the fate of the original populations of the territories occupied by the Park and its surroundings. Unexpected and often problematic situations, in terms of respecting human rights, have cropped up. During its creation, it was the colonial administration's responsibility to set the boundaries of the Park while considering the needs of the local populations inhabiting areas constituted as reserves. These populations had essential subsistence rights, recognised by colonial legislation. To best respect the notion of an 'integral nature reserve' where all human activity is prohibited, the Park's authority decided to have the local administration evacuate the populations and prohibit all circulation in the reserve. Only a group of 300 Twa pygmies, considered 'harmless' and suitable for anthropological studies, due to their perceived closeness to the 'natural' state, remained. Two solutions were considered: expropriation of the populations outside the Park and the buyout of their traditional land rights, which were practices rigorously monitored by the colonial government based on the existing legislation.

The procedures for expropriation were established by the decree of 26 November 1934 and modified by the decree of 28 July 1936: populations were compelled by the colonial authorities to leave their lands, in exchange for fair compensation and the provision of land of at least equal size, or value to, those they previously occupied. These measures were dictated by a colonial government whose role as 'tutor of the natives' included protecting them with a minimum of care and guarantees. Consequently, it adopted the solution of buying out rights, conditional on obtaining the consent of the populations concerned, essential for validating the land transfer.

While hunting, fishing, gathering and wood cutting practices theoretically posed no problem, since the Park territory was emptied of humans, these activities were also prohibited or strictly limited in the Park's annex territories, except for the rights to satisfy the basic needs of the indigenous people and to meet requirements prescribed by customs and admitted by the colonial authorities. However, imprecisions regarding the definition and variety of 'acquired rights', and 'basic and customary needs', and the resulting restrictions, also became a thorny issue for the Park managers.

In 1929, for example, the extension of the PNA territories had not sufficiently taken the populations' need for arable land, firewood and construction timber into account. An administrative commission headed by Colonel Hackars was set up to consider these local claims. Its conclusions resulted in a revision of the Park boundaries in 1933 and restitution to the population of the most heavily occupied annex territories, mainly in Rwanda, Kibumba and Binza. In exchange for this revision, other territories (west of Lake Edward, Semliki Valley and the Ruwenzori massif) were included in the Park area. The latter territories, mostly occupied by Nande and Lendu populations who were dispossessed in turn, became a major source of conflict between the Park and local colonial authorities. The Nande-north issue in the Ruwenzori massif is exemplary, as it shows the tension between two divergent political visions. On the one hand, the necessity for the primary forest of the massif to remain 'inviolable', as its ecosystem is linked to the large Ituri tropical forest; on the other hand, the need to provide the Nande with protein resources obtained from fishing activities in the Semliki, thereby preserving them as the sole labour reservoir in the Stanleyville province. The 1934 decree, based on the commission's work, did eliminate other points of friction by recognising fishing rights (in the Rutshuru River upstream of May ya Moto); kerere liana cutting and ubuzi plant rights (between the Molindi River and the Mabenga to Tongo path); and unrestricted circulation rights on the Ngoma–Irumu roads (in the central Rwindi–Rutshuru sector) and Ngoma–Sake (in the Nyamulagira sector), which are important communication and trade routes.

When the decree of 12 November 1935 planned to once again extend and incorporate new territories into the PNA, the execution of the procedures inherent to the transfer of indigenous rights was crucial to the IPNCB, as this would allow it to acquire 'free disposal of its domain'. However, the local administration had tolerated new settlements to enlarge the indigenous villages still present in the Park. Fisheries that had been prohibited since 1925 were reopened, when the populations living along the Semliki and Lake Edward were progressively displaced due to trypanosomiasis[6] (Van Schuylenbergh, 2016). Implementing the 1935 decree on the ground proved impossible, so the situation remained as it was before 1934.

Under Hackars' direction, a new commission was assigned to determine the PNA's new delimitation and tasked with resolving the rights transfer. It obtained the populations' abandonment of the rights they had wanted to retain in 1934 – the recovery of lands they had to leave due to trypanosomiasis, hunting rights, access to and exploitation of salt marshes – in exchange for guarantees that they would not be displaced and for fishing rights in the Semliki and Lake Edward (at locations to be determined in agreement between the IPNCB, the local population, territorial authorities and hygiene services). However, medical authorities overrode these wishes: in 1937, they ordered the evacuation of villages in the Semliki plain and along Lake Edward, as well as the closure of a fishery belonging to the African Great Lakes Mining Company, which harvested significant quantities of fish to be consumed by its workers.

Prior to 1937, the procedures related to land vacancies and the transfer of certain indigenous territories to the PNA, which required an agreement between the indigenous people and the colonial authorities, were not carried out by the latter, despite having been prescribed by the 1934 decree. This slowness in implementing the conditions requested by the IPNCB reflects both the colonial government's hesitations regarding the PNA extension, and structural delays due to the fact that newly engaged personnel in the territorial administration were unfamiliar with previous agreements between the indigenous people and the investigative commission.

In the Centre and South Sectors of the PNA, displaced populations finally received compensation in 1937, as recorded in the colony's budget in 1938, from which date the conventions had force of law. However, the situation remained unresolved for the lands targeted by the 1929 decree that were never subjected to any land vacancy and rights transfer investigation, as well as for the extension lands provided for by the 1934 decree. The urgency of the matter necessitated the organisation of preliminary investigations into the rights transfer acts. In 1939, the new commission in charge of these investigations noted a significant change in the attitudes of local populations. They refused

2.15 Colonel Henri Hackars in 1937. As PNA warden in 1933–1934, he compiled most of the data that formed the basis of the royal decree of 12 November 1935, delimiting a large part of the Park until today.

to cede their rights, especially bamboo cutting, claiming that the Park encompassed almost all bamboo forests, while felling them increased the area under cultivation. They also demanded grazing rights for livestock in the dry season (in the Rugari, Bukumu, Bweza and Jomba territories), fishing rights (in lower Rutshuru and Lake Edward) and fishing rights in exchange for ceding their hunting rights (to Bwito and Ngezi), as well as lands for setting up habitats and crops in Vitshumbi (on Lake Edward) and Kashwe (on the Rutshuru).

This inextricable situation led the IPNCB to consider outright expropriation of the recalcitrant populations, as no amicable rights transfer acts could be obtained. This decision was frozen by the onset of war. By late May 1940, the indigenous rights issue in these sectors had not been resolved. Governor Pierre Ryckmans expressed the viewpoint of the colony's general government, which had acquired authority over the Park, when he asserted that the populations' claims were justified, particularly regarding the fishing activities on Lake Edward and the Semliki and Rutshuru rivers that were of great economic and social interest. Land retrocessions were also granted in the Kigeri and Rugari–Kishigari regions in Rwanda.

Throughout the war period, the PNA structure wavered due to the intrusion, circulation or return of local communities, with the reopening of indigenous fisheries, the re-establishment of fishing villages with crops and banana plantations, deforestation (bamboo), but also the gathering of rubber plants to support the war effort, iron ore extraction and salt exploitation. At the same time, the claims of the populations, freed from constraints during these four years, had multiplied, as had those of the Europeans. Taking advantage of the commercial boom, they pushed the indigenous people to occupy volcanic lands to develop pyrethrum plantations and to deforest the lands retroceded in the mid-1930s to the PNA, which benefited colonial enterprises. Higher prices for game meat also stimulated the hunting of game and protected species that were seeking refuge in the Park.

After the war, the inevitable conclusion was that the concept of an 'integral nature reserve' had become indefensible, for social and economic reasons. In the following years, reconciling both biological and zoological interests, and demographic and economic interests, became increasingly difficult. The Lake Edward sector was particularly sensitive as the limits on fishing imposed by the PNA sparked a strong public reaction. As fishing activities represented a crucial commercial stake for the region's profitability, public opinion deemed it unacceptable that the complete protection of the lake on the Congolese side in fact favoured fishing on the Ugandan side, at Katwe, which was not subject to this limitation (Van Schuylenbergh, 2016).

The IPNCB saw its room for manoeuvre dwindle, and encouraged the Belgian Ministry of Colonies to define more clearly the legal status that protected the PNA from successive encroachments threatening its survival, while seeking solutions to reduce the Park's attractiveness. This included providing populations with the necessary food resources for their subsistence. Victor Van Straelen saw the problems encountered in the Park as consequences of the colonial occupation and management of these territories. These had caused a disruption of the Congolese agricultural economies that, combined with a demographic boom, resulted in a steep increase in needs, and a decrease in available resources. The IPNCB also highlighted the colonial government's hostility to the implementation of the 1929, 1934 and 1935 decrees that determined the existence and sustainability of the PNA. Meanwhile, the Belgian Ministry of Colonies called on the IPNCB to comply with colonial legislation and refrain from overstepping its prescriptions. This was a stand-off, with each side firmly entrenched.

In 1947, a new commission of inquiry into indigenous rights, presided by Louis De Waersegger, the King's prosecutor, managed to obtain several agreements. The PNA grounds would be recognised, free of every servitude and dispute, in exchange for compensation paid to the concerned populations, and the indigenous people would abandon their fishing rights in the Rutshuru and Semliki in exchange for the creation of two indigenous fishing cooperatives at Vitshumbi and Kyavinyonge, under the supervision of the Cooperative of Lake Edward Indigenous Fishermen (COPILE), as well as an indispensable right of passage for local populations. The establishment of these fisheries responded to the increasing food needs of local populations and the local authorities' desire to intensify the commercial exploitation of fish resources around Goma and Costermansville (Bukavu).

In the early 1950s, the COPILE's activities gradually exceeded the limits assigned to them: continuous circulation, harvesting of construction wood, operation of a stone quarry, introduction of domestic animals, non-compliance with fishing-prohibited areas and exceeding the cap on tolerated fishing. The IPNCB's frustrations grew in 1957 when,

2.16 The fishing village of Kiavinyonge in 1946.

2.17 The rangers at Rumangabo station in the 1930s. They carried spears but no firearms. The Nyamulagira volcano looms in the background.

at the request of local authorities, the institute had to authorise the opening of several markets on the western shore of Lake Edward, which led to excessive circulation within the Park.

During this decade, other activities deemed illegal were on the increase in the North and South Sectors of the PNA: bamboo cutting, poaching, fishing by Ugandan populations, and cattle grazing with bush fires by Hema herders. However, thanks to the 15 May 1950 decree, legislative measures were introduced to abolish a series of rights previously acquired by local populations: fishing rights in the Semliki River, cutting rights for vines and ubuzi plants, salt harvesting rights on the Rumoka volcano, palm nut harvesting rights on the right bank of the Semliki and wood cutting on Mount Bukuku. In return for these restrictions, the Park proactively addressed existing and potential problems by organising bamboo distributions in the Rumangabo sector and building water tanks in the Rutshuru sector. Similarly, with the support of local leaders, awareness campaigns were launched among residents about nature conservation and the missions of the IPNCB.

Other problems continued to emerge in the years preceding Independence, the most concerning of which was related to the population density in the Jomba and Rugari regions, in Rutshuru territory, oversaturated with people and cattle since 1955. While the colonial authorities anticipated a doubling of the population in the next 25 years, the PNA officials could only establish the facts: a tense situation and a shortage of arable and pastoral lands they had already reported in 1940. In response, the general government adopted a strategy of relocating populations from these regions to Mushari and Bwito, and planned an irrigation programme in the Rutshuru plain, along with the establishment, in late 1953, of an agricultural settlement comprising 350 plots.

In 1956, the Park's personnel reported the presence of several thousand heads of cattle during the dry season in the protected forests covering the slopes of the extinct volcanoes, particularly Mikeno. American scientist George Schaller, on a mission to study the ecology and behaviour of mountain gorillas (1959), could only note a reduction in their numbers in this refuge area. Two trails in this area were also regularly used for smuggling various goods between Rwanda and Uganda. This was a politically dangerous situation, with herders limited to two alternatives: entering the Park or losing their cattle. The intervention of Jean-Paul Harroy, the governor of Ruanda-Urundi, a former PNA warden (1937–1938) and former member of the Administrative Commission and the IPNCB's board of directors, proved crucial. New grazing areas urgently had to be found. In 1958, pending a new decree to resolve the situation, and with the agreement of the IPNCB, herders were temporarily authorised to graze their cattle in a 6,000-hectare area in the Ruhengeri and Kisenyi territories.

On the eve of Independence, frustrations ran high among residents deprived of part of their lands and rights. This situation posed a serious threat to social and political peace in the region. The following years would unfortunately testify to this. The resentment and hostility towards the PNA that had alienated local populations since the 1920s increased, as did tensions related to land, the basis of social rural order, and became decisive factors in conflicts and violence in this region that persist to the present day.

The PNA, this exceptional creation in an equally exceptional setting, struggled for its survival throughout its colonial history, facing sometimes questionable political and economic interests, but also human rights that must be considered. The Park can be seen as a metaphor for the issues induced by the challenges of conserving a 'cloistered' natural and human environment.

1 The Europeans 'discovered' the region from the 1860s. The Englishman Speke, who was looking for the sources of the Nile, glimpsed the Virunga region in 1861. The German Stuhlmann wrote the first precise description of what was then called the 'Mfumbiro mountains' in 1892 (Stuhlmann, 1894), while Count von Götzen explored these in 1894 (von Götzen, 1899).

2 This area stretches, on the Congolese side, to include the entire region of the volcanoes, which encompasses the northern part of Lake Kivu up to the boundaries with the '*Réserve de chasse Albert*' and, on the Rwandese side, to the zone that extends the PNA to the southeast.

3 The Kagera National Park (Rwanda) on 26 November 1934, the Garamba National Park (Uele) on 17 March 1938 and the Upemba National Park (Katanga) on 15 May 1939.

4 Surface areas somewhat modified by the royal orders of 4 May 1937 and 17 May 1939.

5 Six sectors formed a long stretch of land extending between the southern part of Lake Kivu and the Ruwenzori (Nyamulagira, Rwindi–Rutshuru, Lake Edward, higher Semliki, lower Semliki and Rwenzori) while the seventh, the Mikeno sector, was almost isolated due to the presence of the major Goma–Rutshuru road.

6 The evacuation of the population had been carried out by the medical authorities of the Eastern Province in order to eradicate the sleeping sickness raging in the Semliki plain and on the shores of Lake Edward. Between January and March 1934, the evacuation of 17 villages in the North Sector and one in the West Sector was the culmination of a gradual relocation by the colonial authorities of the population of the region affected by the epidemic in 1927 (7,000 infected individuals). There were three population relocations in all: 1929, 1932 and 1934, the latter in the context of the PNA.

3.1 The mountain gorilla was discovered by science in 1902. The large primate soon attracted the attention of many American and European researchers. Though still little known in the 1920s, the population was one of the main reasons for creating Africa's first national park. Here, the first photo of mountain gorillas in their natural habitat, taken in Kabara in 1960 by J. Verschuren.

3

The life in the Park (1925–1960)

JACQUES VERSCHUREN

(This chapter is a first-hand historical account written in 2006. The testimony of Jacques Verschuren (1926–2014) tells the story of his own life and depicts the life of rangers in the field from the early years until Independence.)

The management principles of the Albert National Park evolved up until the country's Independence. Yesterday, like today, the expertise, creativity and courage shown by the staff made it possible to meet the daily challenges. The strategic choices made at the time shaped the face of the Park for decades to come.

1. Written sources

The first five-year report for the years 1935–1939 by the Institute of National Parks of the Belgian Congo (*Institut des Parcs Nationaux du Congo Belge* – IPNCB) (IPNCB, 1942) is a remarkable source of data. Not a single annual report was published after this first document, except for a text dated 1976. Some archives exist, but analysing them is cumbersome. Also, the hundreds of individuals who contributed to the preparation of the first report all died before 2006. A great number of publications on the status of the parks of the Belgian Congo were produced up until 1960, but apart from my own writings, almost nothing has been published on the crucial period from 1960 to 2006.

2. Issue of claims: perspectives from the field

How were the apparent claims by certain populations regarded in the field? First of all, let us not confuse the Albert National Park (*Parc National Albert* – PNA) and its modest problems with the Upemba National Park, where certain claims were indeed made that were still not settled in full by the end of the last century. A large part of the grounds in the south and the centre, some of which were volcanic or not inhabited by humans, were offered by Mwami Ndeze, a large landowner, to his 'brother and friend' King Albert I. Very locally, in the southwest of the southern sector, some minor land disputes with the Wahunde arose, but these were swiftly settled.

In the North Sector, *in tempore non suspecto*, before the creation of the Park, large areas were willingly evacuated by the Nande people when trypanosomiasis (sleeping sickness) was decimating the population. This is how some annexes of the important Beni post came to be evacuated spontaneously. In the early 2000s, remnants of the Vieux-Béni lazaret were still visible in the northern part of the savannahs of Semliki River. Thorough land surveys were conducted in the North Sector of the Park; these areas (Ruwenzori, ombrophilous forest) were devoid of human inhabitants. The rare opponents to the move were relocated with the utmost diplomacy to better lands, without any pressure from the authorities, and received substantial indemnities as compensation. No survivors from this period have remained; their descendants have forgotten about these events. Most of the documents certifying these financial transfers were destroyed during the turmoil of 1960. The main regions concerned were the lower slopes of the Ruwenzori and the eastern base of the northern Mitumba graben (Kasaka, Museya, Karurume, etc.). At this level, the boundaries of the Park were drawn along the base, not the ridges, of this mountainous massif.

Between 1950 and 1960, land claim issues were the last thing on the wardens' minds, except for matters relating to fishing poaching. The few areas in the north that were inhabited, such as the Watalinga enclave, were not included in the reserve. Over many years of roaming the Park, my Congolese colleagues never raised these issues. Not one native ever said to me: 'This is the land of my ancestors, with their graves, *Awa, adjali kabouli na tata na tata na bisu*,' (in Lingala). 'The Park has robbed us.' Never.

With hindsight, we should admit that we failed to find a definitive solution for the extreme south of the Park, where it borders on Lake Kivu. Its populations were perpetually contentious towards all authorities, regardless of who they were. The existence of remnants of a very ancient presence of a small number of temporary inhabitants within the Park's boundaries cannot be denied, evidenced by graves, trapping pits, names of localities in the forest, caravan tracks and citrus trees. These traces were left by Bantu, who were hardly sedentary at all: after a few years of exploiting and exhausting the lands, they abandoned them to migrate elsewhere. This means the existence of ancient names proves nothing, except that temporary settlements existed there in the past. Many forest regions were *terrae incognitae* – even the best local trackers got lost there. It took me a great deal of patience to find the vernacular name of a vast pseudo-unknown pond, a former cove of the Semliki, Lake Bwirina.

As a biologist I had, in 1958, at the request of the Brussels management committee, prepared a detailed report on the reserve areas that could be retroceded because they were of less interest in ecological terms. Fortunately, this report has been preserved, unused, in the archives. The few Congolese

3.2 Mwami Daniel Ndeze, Grand Chief of the Bwisha sector in the Rutshuru territory, with several dignitaries. He promoted a positive vision of the Albert National Park within his chiefdom and raised awareness of environmental protection among the local population.

who were shown this report, much later, exclaimed: 'Never! The Park must keep its 800,000 hectares!'

3. Personalities and historic events

The first notable personality was the American Carl Akeley, true founder of the reserve, who passed away in 1926. He died in Kabara, the heart of the Hagenia forest, 'the most beautiful place on Earth', where he was eventually buried. A tombstone will remind us of him for a long time to come. During the mutinies, robbers broke into his coffin to seize his remains. The other true founder of the PNA is Victor Van Straelen, also a Director of the Institute of Natural Sciences, known for his strict adherence to integral conservation. Let us remember that King Albert I, who had at one point attempted the extraordinary 4,400 m ascent of Mikeno, was reluctant to give his name to the reserve. Still, unlike King Leopold III who, when polled on the expediency of lending his name to the Garamba Park, refused to highlight a second member of the dynasty in the naming of the reserves of the Belgian Congo, he did accept. The sovereign, who presided over the IPNCB, assisted by vice-president Victor Van Straelen, stepped down in 1934 upon his inauguration as King of the Belgians. Let us recall some excerpts from the speech he held in London on 16 November 1933:

'If a single subject embodies greatness surpassing human horizons, it is the protection of nature's eternal assets, of which we are temporary and responsible custodians. Do we have the right to modify the natural state of things at will, considering only the consequences our current knowledge of phenomena allows us to foresee? (…) If we consider the scientific aspect of the question, we notice that nature reserves are the indispensable extension of laboratories. Until now, the progress of natural sciences has been due to laboratory work and study; only a small proportion was the result of direct observation of nature… We want to escape our bustling cities, where we feel imprisoned. We demand pure air, light, space, earth, water and greenery: our generation has reconciled itself with nature. (…) Possessing this unique heritage bequeathed to us by nature entails, for us, a threefold duty. Firstly, we must ensure its integral conservation with the utmost vigilance. But while ensuring the achievement of this fundamental goal, we should also pursue a methodical and scientific exploration of our remarkable domain. Thus appears our

3.3   Exploration of the central channel of a Nyamulagira lava flow by J. Verhoogen's volcanological mission in 1938.

A CENTURY OF HISTORY

3.4 On 18 April 1956, a commemorative ceremony marking the death of warden Rasmus Hoier was held in Rumangabo.

3.5 H.M. Queen Elizabeth, widow of H.M. King Albert, on an official visit to the PNA in 1958. On her left, Dr Jacques Verschuren, the park biologist.

3.6 Major Ernest Hubert, warden at the Rwindi camp in 1937, with two rangers, presenting the tusks of an elephant found dead after a fight with another elephant.

second duty: to have our institution contribute actively to the progress of knowledge. To this end, specialists' missions should undertake the study of scientific problems. Finally, without in any way compromising the principle of absolute conservation, we will open parts of our reserve to visitors, as we cannot deprive humanity of so many sources of emotion, joy and splendour.'

Clearly, Belgium was interested in conservation in the Congo long before any modest efforts were launched in the metropolis. The evolution of the PNA, which he visited on many occasions up until 1956 and 1958, remained of great interest to Leopold III until his dying days in the early 1980s.

Queen Elisabeth visited PNA extensively in early 1958. She was particularly impressed by the indescribable beauty of the bird songs. I will always remember the Queen's reaction in Ishango in February 1958, at the top of the cliff overlooking one of the most beautiful sites on the planet. When I told her I wished to place rangers by her side to prevent lion attacks, she replied: 'But risk, young man, is the joy of life.'

Among the other personalities who played a crucial role on the ground is the brilliant warden Hackars, who passed away in 1940. He established the Park's boundaries by walking thousands of kilometres, an adventure I repeated a quarter of a century later. Also noteworthy is the Dane Hoier who, left without directives from Brussels during the war, just kept the work going. At a certain point he was forced, against his convictions, to yield to the pressure to tolerate the Vitshumbi fishing ground.

We must mention Hubert, an excellent populariser and, like de Witte, an outstanding photographer, and finally Harroy, Vice-Governor General and an effective park manager before the war, who succeeded Lippens, the warden who would go on to create the Zwin (in Belgium). Other figures inextricably linked to the history of the parks are

3.7 Gaston-François de Witte (1897–1980) was a Belgian zoologist attached to the Tervuren Museum who led the first major exploration mission to the PNA between 1933 and 1937.

3.8 Claude Cornet d'Elzius, PNA warden from 1957 to 1959, with Brigadier Vukoyo in Rwindi in 1973.

Verhulst (Kagera), Ory (Kagera and Garamba), Bouckaert, Heine, Kint and Rousseau, who were all so very passionate about their activities as wardens. I remember several other wardens who left their mark: Major Van Cools, future chief general of the Belgian army, and Donis, who had the foresight to envision the creation of new parks. More recently, Micha, chief warden and a renowned cartographer, supervised the Kagera National Park in Rwanda, and Count Claude Cornet d'Elzius was an energetic president of the Foundation for the Promotion of Scientific Research in Africa (*Fondation pour Favoriser les Recherches scientifiques en Afrique* – FFRSA).

4. Management and functioning

One point of criticism regarding the staff should not be evaded: the absence of any Congolese warden before 1960. This was a fairly widespread policy in various sectors during the colonial period. Two or three months before Independence, the future leaders of the region were invited to visit the nature reserve. However, one official was sternly reprimanded by the Brussels management committee for having invited the elites of tomorrow to his home in Rutshuru to explain the reasons why the nature reserve was so important.

This Brussels committee was theoretically all-powerful, but had little knowledge of African issues, despite the prestigious titles of some of its members. The actual management-from-a-distance was the work of president Van Straelen and commissioner van der Elst. They were assisted by three or four executives, primarily the brilliant De Saeger, driving force of the IPNCB, known for his formidable efficiency, who passed away in 1994 at almost one hundred years of age. We should also mention Nuyten and especially Houben, who, after a lifetime of managing paperwork regarding the Park, finally realised his lifelong dream by visiting the PNA in 1974. Five people, at most, directed the activities of thousands of wardens, rangers and other field workers. Later on, some fifty to sixty officials supervised the parks from Kinshasa, sometimes with mixed results, though there were exceptions, for instance Biwela, a man from Kinshasa, who did very well. Also worth noting was the existence, for a while, of a financial committee, a local body in Kivu consisting of high-ranking provincial personalities, colonists and planters.

How were the parks organised in practice? When I arrived at the reserve in early 1948, as a student collaborating

3.9 Victor Van Straelen, Chairman of the IPNCB, in conversation with wardens J. de Wilde and H. De Saeger at the Mutsora ranger camp in 1953.

A CENTURY OF HISTORY

3.10 Brigadier Kanzaguhera in Rutshuru in 1956. All the Congolese staff were recruited from the local population and trained in various support functions to the Park management.

3.11 The PNA administration building in Rumangabo nearing completion in February 1945.

3.12 The exploration of the Ruwenzori mountains has been the subject of numerous scientific missions organised by the IPNCB.

with the ethologist Hediger, my first impression was that everything worked impeccably: the organisation was just perfect. Things were directed admirably from Brussels, including our interview with the General Governor in Léopoldville, who told us: 'You are lucky men: not only are you about to visit a biological paradise, but – even if it's something of a state within a state – you will get to see the best-functioning organisation in the Belgian Congo.'

The PNA was divided into three Sectors: the South, home to active and extinct volcanoes, with its base in Rumangabo; the Centre, including the southern plain of Lake Edward, with its base in Rwindi; and the North, protecting the upper Semliki, the equatorial forest and the Ruwenzori, managed from Mutsora. This structure has never changed. To include the stations in the Park, its boundaries were stretched here and there to form some strangely shaped 'appendices'. One of these marks the boundary at Tshiaberimu. The Rutshuru station, an old management base built in 1927, remained the property of the IPNCB, but it aroused some jealousy in overcrowded North Kivu. The official documents proving the land rights of the IPNCB were destroyed in 1960.

Each sector was managed by a warden, assisted by a deputy and often a station manager. Many were former officers, while others were agronomists or reserve officers. These managers spoke the local vernacular language well, which, in the PNA, was Kiswahili, quite different from that of East Africa. Some decisions were announced in French, but Kiswahili, or sometimes Lingala, was usually favoured. Each warden was a Judicial Police Officer with general authority over the entire Park area. This, sometimes, caused issues with the territorial administration. Courteous relations were maintained with these officials. The wardens' main activities were strict surveillance and law enforcement.

Each warden spent two to three weeks a month in the field (camping and moving around too often in 4x4s, not often enough on foot). The wardens also had various administrative tasks, for the execution of which they were supported by collaborators known as *karani*, high-level local employees.

Aside from building lodges and bridges, wardens drafted reports. Each month, they had to send a detailed report to Brussels, including accounting records and biological observations. Initially, European wives were rare; the Park was a bachelors' den. But over the years, the presence of women gradually became tolerated, then accepted. Some of the women collaborated in their husbands' conservation activities, particularly Marie Huguette Ory in the Garamba National Park. Others, who were just married and had seen their journey as a honeymoon, were frightened and dreamt of fleeing after two weeks in the depths of the bush.

In most cases, relationships among wardens and their equivalents were harmonious. Each expatriate manager served uninterrupted terms of 36 months without returning to Europe. They often performed their duties at one and the same station throughout this period. The advantage was that they became thoroughly familiar with local issues. The disadvantage was that some of them were entirely ignorant of other reserves. There was no such thing as a 35, 40, or 80-hour working week for wardens or rangers: they worked non-stop, on duty almost day and night. Once or twice a year, they prepared for an inspection visit by big boss Van Straelen. There was no tangible separation between PNA sectors in Congolese or Rwandan territory. The PNA was a single unit, located in two future different countries.

One of the wardens' missions was to receive high authorities from within the country or from abroad. In the Park,

3.13   The Mabenga bridge (shown here in 1954) on the road from Goma to Beni spans the Rutshuru River and connects the South and Centre Sectors.

3.14   IPNCB field sheets report the observation, by G.F. de Witte, of two young Nile monitor lizards along the Rwindi River in 1956.

3.15 The garage workshop at Rumangabo in January 1947.

this task fell to the 'visits delegates' Hubert and Baert. Another, perhaps even more important, activity was to establish friendly relations with the locals, various chiefs and others, living around the Park, though vast areas contiguous to the reserve were almost uninhabited at the time. Relations with customary notable neighbours were cordial, despite claims to the contrary made decades later. Some *mwami* were proud to be the first to report poachers.

The PNA's neighbouring residents benefited from numerous advantages such as well-paid jobs, free transportation, admission to certain schools or dispensaries and sometimes the opportunity to hunt any excess animals straying from the Park.

The major human infrastructure within the Park? This was, without any hesitation, the rangers. Their numbers evolved considerably, at times exceeding 250 people. The PNA was completely self-sufficient. In addition to the rangers, the workforce included workers of all levels. The following list reflects their diversity:

- Armourers
- Assistant drivers
- Assistant rangers
- Biologist preparers
- Blacksmiths
- 'Boys'
- Canoeists
- Carpenters
- Catechists
- Cobblers
- Conservators
- Cooks
- Detached military personnel
- Drivers
- Electricians
- Ferrymen
- Guides
- Laundresses
- Long sawyers
- Lumberjacks
- Masons
- Meteorologists
- Mountain porters
- Nurses
- Orderlies
- Ordinary porters
- Ordinary workers
- Painters
- Plumbers
- Prison guards
- Radio operators
- Rangers
- Road workers
- Shopkeepers
- Station managers
- Tailors
- Taxidermists–stuffers
- Teachers
- Telephone operators
- Trackers
- Trail cutters
- Trainee rangers
- Visits delegates
- Water carriers
- Welders
- Wood carriers

All these workers were housed, fed and equipped by the Park.

Let's move on to the rangers. A base team was stationed in each of the major stations to carry out the heavy patrols, meant to intimidate illegals. The basic principle was to scatter patrol posts all along the boundaries, each housing four or five rangers, including a brigadier. They lived with their families and children in houses built by the national park authorities and their autonomy was sometimes almost absolute. The supervisors patrolled their sector almost daily. Initially, the presence of the families posed no problems; later on, threats from poachers or other criminals forced the authorities to keep one, or even two, rangers on-site to ensure the families' security. The role of the itinerant brigadier, accompanied by one or two porters, was crucial. He visited all the camps in his sub-sector at least once a month.

On-duty brigadiers provided the isolated rangers with repaired equipment, as well as with food and wages. The

3.16   Among the thousands of field sheets and photographs documenting the Park's wildlife and habitats, this one shows a photograph of wild dogs taken by warden E. Hubert in 1938. Unfortunately, this species was exterminated at the end of the 1950s. This is the only species ever to have disappeared from the PNVi since its creation.

3.17   Among the scientific missions to the PNA, the one executed by F. Bourlière and J. Verschuren (1957–1959) marked a significant development, as it was the first to focus on the ecology of large fauna. In particular, their research established the importance of mammal populations and their impact on natural habitats.

3.18   Preparations for one of many field missions in the 1950s. These lengthy expeditions in often difficult terrain required major logistical efforts. They provided many local jobs and benefited from the skills and local knowledge of the Congolese collaborators.

3.19 Sampling parasites from a dead elephant in the Rwindi plain in 1945.

rangers were rotated regularly. Most of their camps were located along the boundaries, so the supervisors could buy supplies in nearby villages. Some of the wives cultivated a small plot and raised some domestic animals such as chickens and goats. However, abuses had to be prevented.

Wild animals sometimes lived in commensalism near patrol posts and were respected by the rangers: baboons in Mosenda, warthogs in Lunyasenge, buffaloes in Rwindi and Lulimbi and even elephants in Vitshumbi and Rwindi.

Unannounced heavy surveillance patrols were conducted at random hours. To ensure that the rangers were actively controlling their sector, they were required to punch a service card attached to tree trunks at various locations in their zone of activity. Each ranger had three sets of equipment: one for parades and two for the bush. Rapid wear and tear of uniforms was appreciated, because this indicated that they were constantly active in the forest, where outfits were easily torn. At first, the supervisors had only machetes and spears; later they were given rifles. When surveillance posts were distributed, the aim had been to mix ethnic groups, to prevent collusion and potential corruption. However, rangers were very seldom 'bought off' and very seldom killed animals for food or for resale. When supervisors caught poachers or illegals, they transferred them to the central station. In principle, rangers spent three weeks in the field each month. They were well-paid, equipped and fed, and they were regarded as a bit like the aristocrats of Kivu. Criminals were terrified of them.

They managed 'their' sector as if it were their personal property. They had tents, waterproofs, boots and backpacks, as well as notebooks to record their findings. The percentage of total illiterates was low. Great importance was attached to veterans: Brigadier Bavukahe, who joined when the Park was first created, died there at nearly a hundred years of age. Widows, especially those of men who died in combat, were privileged. Old rangers were very often allowed to remain living in their house until the end of their days. Many rangers and equipment porters accompanied me on hundreds of walking safaris in often wildly different and totally unknown sites. Without these valuable auxiliaries, our scientific research or surveillance expeditions would have been impossible. Particularly, the remarkable tracker Senkwekwe, rangers Joachim and Lubutu, and captains Kissa and Kasiwa spring to mind as invaluable companions.

The lives of wardens and zoologists were both paradisiacal, because of the environment, and hellish due to the Spartan conditions. The relationships between rangers and wardens were harmonious. Strict military discipline prevailed, and the surveillance style was somewhat police-like. Capturing illegals, poachers and other criminals, sometimes at the risk of your and their lives, is, however, pointless if justice does not follow. Too often, offenders were released immediately after their arrest. Many instances of poaching went unpunished. What sometimes – albeit rarely! – happened was that some members of the judiciary opposed the existence of the national park, because they did not understand its purpose. Others enforced the law energetically, like Fontaine, the brilliant substitute from Goma, whose support for the PNA was always invaluable.

5. Funding and logistics

A question arises regarding the PNA as well as other reserves. In addition to the limited staff in Brussels, the IPNCB funded about twenty wardens or equivalents, 700 rangers and 700 workers, at a low estimate. Operating costs and the cost of supplies, subsidies for investments and transportation were high. Building costs were considerable.

After 1960, financial support was provided initially by the Ministry of Agriculture in Léopoldville, then by the Presidency, and later by the State Commissioner for the Environment, Nature Conservation and Tourism. Some revenue was generated from visitors. Before 1960, foreign cooperation had been non-existent, except with the Foundation for Promoting Scientific Research in Africa (*Fondation pour Favoriser les Recherches scientifiques en Afrique* – FFRSA) and the Royal Belgian Institute of Natural Sciences (*Institut Royal des Sciences Naturelles de Belgique* – IRSNB). Later on, Germany intervened, followed by the United States, Switzerland and the Netherlands. Subsequently, official and private international cooperation came into play.

Meanwhile, in the field, three solid basic stations had been erected, built to last 100 years (which indeed they have), and a number of ranger camps, also solid but more basic.

Solid buildings guarded the access barriers (Kasindi, Mabenga and Kakomero). Gites were constructed on the mountains (three on Nyamulagira, four on Ruwenzori, one in Kabara). Other types of buildings served as ranger posts

3.20 The Mutwanga hotel (shown here in the 1950s) was for a long time a favourite starting point for climbing the Ruwenzori.

3.21 Thanks to their exceptional solidity, the buildings constructed in the PNA survived without major repairs for almost 100 years. Here, the covered terrace of the North Sector's headquarters in Mutsora.

3.22 In 1945, the State ran the dispensary at the Vitshumbi fishery.

3.23 Fishing in Vitshumbi and the other fisheries was small-scale but Lake Edward provided the local chiefdoms with an important source of fish protein. Here, a fisherman with his catch of the day in 1933.

3.24 The Ishango pavilions were renovated in February 1957 for the visit of H.M. King Leopold III.

near the lake, to control fishing. The lake rangers proved to be excellent navigators because Lake Edward can be deceptive. I had gites on Nyiragongo, Rukumi and Lulimbi built during the 1970s.

Houses for subordinate personnel were provided at a hundred metres from those of the authorities, as were temporary housing and tents. Garages, dispensaries ('lazarets') and schools were also built on-site, but the population living outside the reserve also, on occasion, benefited from these services.

Regarding traffic routes: no paved roads were built. Unfortunately, several major roads not under the control of the IPNCB did cross the Park: the Goma–Beni road and its various branches and later on some illegal roads. The number of tourist trails scattered throughout the PNA had also been kept deliberately limited. After 1960, these were unthinkingly allowed to multiply, often for reasons having nothing to do with tourism. In the mountains, some well-maintained footpaths were established. But, most often, there was not the slightest trail, and teams moved around just anywhere across the entire area.

Transportation was a major problem. At the time, movement was made on foot. Each station had about two trucks and two to three all-terrain vehicles, plus a prestige vehicle for important visitors. The local drivers were highly skilled and capable, as mechanics, of repairing the worst wrecks. Surveillance stations had small garages that were independent from the larger facilities (Salvi, Schalbroek) located in Rutshuru and obviously in Goma. Some drivers had a bad habit of transporting illegal passengers for a fee and required strict supervision. But let us also note the efficiency of technicians like Boné and Mazowa, who were expert drivers.

Multiple boats were deployed to patrol Lake Edward and catch illegal fishermen or other poachers. The Vitshumbi–Ishango lake route avoided the endless road between Kayna and Beni via Butembo, which was of no interest to naturalists anyway. Shipwrecks were not uncommon on these deceptively calm waters. Occasionally, boats were capsized by hippos, which cost human lives. The use of inflatable boats was rare. Two side-mounted pirogues were used to descend the middle and lower Semliki River. The expedition I conducted in 1958 with Xavier Misonne was a somewhat perilous 'first', as it opened access to some grandiose unknown sites, such as the extraordinary Sinda gorges. Downstream of the Semliki, the crocodiles were at times threatening, but they had not yet moved up the river to Ishango. Let us not forget that the use of aeroplanes, already common in East Africa by the mid-century, was prohibited over the PNA in the name of ecological purity. Taking integral conservation to the extreme!

Communication between surveillance stations was a major problem because there were no telephones back then.

Messages were transmitted by couriers and by 'drum radio'. But this weak point was compensated by the very high quality of the postal services and their Congolese technicians. In this regard, the PO Box 18 in Rutshuru has remained legendary. Sending a letter from the depths of Kivu to Europe took only three to four days.

6. Last days under Belgian control

How did events unfold in the PNA in the years and months leading up to Independence on 30 June 1960? Apart from very calm elections, where I was an assessor in the bush, nothing happened. North Kivu enjoyed almost absolute political tranquillity until the end of colonisation. The region was to pay for this 30 to 40 years later. I was never confronted with rioters. Law enforcement functioned perfectly. No stones were thrown at the authorities, as was the case elsewhere in the Congo. The local populations were hardly politicised at all and made virtually no demands.

The wardens were, at the time, more concerned with the shameful retrocession of the Tamira zone, in the Rwandan sector of the PNA, and the early preparations for the creation of the Salonga National Park. Some of the rangers were delegated to the 1958 Brussels Exhibition, where they made quite an impression. No significant resurgence of poaching, hunting or fishing was reported until the end of June 1960, with just one exception. I remember with emotion how I swam across the torrential upper Rutshuru River – leading several rangers who were not accustomed to water – to capture a gang of poachers seemingly determined to eliminate giant forest hogs from the reserve. Scientific research continued unhindered until 29 June 1960, when some gigantic thermal springs were discovered. Some wardens' wives left the area of their own accord but it would be inaccurate to say that 'panic-stricken' managers sent their personal belongings and scientific collections overseas. Life went on, peacefully, and surveillance was maintained. The PNA remained intact.

To conclude this description of the first stage of life at the PNA, I would like to remind the reader of the reasons behind its creation. No financial objective whatsoever was sought. The only target was Kivu's ecological future:
- the conservation of its exceptional fauna and biotopes;
- the advancement of scientific research;
- of secondary importance, tourism.

3.25   Collection of scientific works on the Park in the library of the Royal Belgian Institute of Natural Sciences in Brussels. Between 1933 and 1972, out of a total of 328 publications issued by the IPNCB, 202 studies were devoted to the PNA alone.

4.1 After Independence, the PNVi was managed from its main station in Rutshuru by the first staff of the IPNCB. Here, warden B. Munyaga with his senior brigadier and a team of rangers.

4

The new start (1960–1991)

JACQUES VERSCHUREN, SAMY MANKOTO MA MBAELELE
(based on the original 2006 text)

As in many former colonies, Independence had a major impact on the management of national institutions, including the ICCN. Virunga National Park survived this tumultuous period before experiencing a gradual recovery. The decline in State support was mitigated by the growing interest of the international community.

1. Transition to Independence

On 30 June 1960, the Congo gained its independence. At that time, the Albert National Park (*Parc National Albert* – PNA) had existed for 35 years. How would it evolve? Predictions were not optimistic. According to a French journalist, '…the first achievements to disappear in the Congo will be the national parks.' This was a clear error of judgement. Up until the final days of the colonial period, the park had not faced any major problems: alongside a little poaching and minimal hostility towards the existence of the reserve, the scientific research was well developed and tourism was expanding. The reserve was located in a region that was politically calm. When the flags were lowered on 30 June, the wardens remained at their posts without any major incidents. The rangers kept working efficiently. The assaults from outside the region began on 10 July with the mutinies of the Public Force soldiers. These soldiers had assumed the rangers would follow suit, but that did not happen.

The mutineers forced the rangers to leave, yet the Kivu population remained calm. A turning point came on 27 July 1960: even the rangers in isolated posts suddenly realised that all authority had evaporated. On that day, between 200 and 300 rangers from across the reserve, some armed with rifles, gathered at Rwindi. A minority questioned the survival of the Park. Accompanied by Habarukira, the new Rutshuru territory administrator, I took the risk of intervening, facing these armed men. I delivered a speech in Lingala, translated into Kiswahili by the territory administrator, concluding: 'The Park will not die. Long live the natural reserve of independent Congo.' That was the moment the rangers understood that the PNA would be reborn.

Had the vast Congolese protected area been lost entirely in the wave of Independences sweeping the continent, foreign reserves might have followed suit. The conservation of nature and national parks in the new States might have collapsed. This did not happen, the Congolese rangers quickly resumed work, and it seemed the Park had been saved. The first official act of the new district commissioner of Goma, Ruyange, was to appoint the agronomist Anicet Mburanumwe as the first Congolese chief warden.

Following this, three national wardens were appointed (1962–1967): Munyaga, Bakinahe and Kajuga, who served the Park for over 45 years. The representative of the President of

A CENTURY OF HISTORY

4.2　The Park's first Congolese chief warden, Anicet Mburanumwe, pictured with his daughter in 1963 in Rumangabo.

4.3　The rangers' colonial uniform (left) was changed several times after Independence.

independent Congo, Miruho, the new governor of Kivu province, made the appointments. Soon after, the Department of Waters and Forests in Léopoldville formalised the revival of national parks.

Let us pay special tribute to Biwela, the head agronomist, who sustained the parks for a decade from a distance, from the General Directorate of Parks in Léopoldville, alternating with his colleague Mokwa. It was only logical that the Brussels Directorate gradually faded and lost all authority. At this level of power, the transition was smooth. It is worth mentioning the death in 1964 of Victor Van Straelen, president of the parks from 1934 and Director of the Royal Belgian Institute of Natural Sciences. His dynamism contributed greatly to making the PNA a prestigious institution.

In 1960, 1961 and 1962 the rangers continued to work with equal conviction. However, starting in 1960, they began to 'die for the elephants' in outright battles against poachers, mostly Ugandans. Allow us to mention Brigadier Sauswa, the first to die while defending nature, and his colleague Saambili.

When new mutinies erupted, Buni, the warden of Mutsora, faced with his assassins, declared: 'I will die for the Park, but the reserve will never disappear.' The attacks were not aimed at the PNA itself: all authority was being chal-

4.4　Some of the Park's senior wardens in Goma during a mission led by J-P. d'Huart in 2001. From left to right: Alexandre Wathaut, Stanislas Bakinahe, Anicet Mburanumwe, Déogratias Kajuga and Muhindo Mesi.

lenged. This continued to be the case in the following decades. The staff's lives were tough, especially as a financial issue added to the problem: Brussels was no longer sending funds and the local budget was much reduced.

In 1961, an operation was mounted to transfer funds, released by Director Biwela in Léopoldville, to even the most isolated sectors of the Park, supplemented with private support from Belgium. An official 'smugglers' caravan managed to sneak through to the volcanoes to pay the employees, who felt abandoned. Malaysian and Indonesian UN bodyguards assisted the participants in this venture. At the time of departure, a new rebellion broke out in Kivu. It was a close call for Mburanumwe, and I would have been sentenced to death for 'selling the Park to the UN'.

Three rangers died in combat or in service against poachers: Buni in Mutsora, Mburanumwe in Rumangabo and, on 23 October 1975, Bilali, the warden of the Centre Sector. A monument was erected in his memory at May ya Moto.

2. External relations and influences

In 1960, it was illusory to count on any of the officials of the general Belgian administration outside the PNA: they had all left the country. Could we rely on neighbouring Uganda? This country immediately wanted to rename the reserve 'Kivu Park', while also providing the largest contingent of poachers. Some colonists and planters were valuable auxiliaries because they cared about 'their' reserve. Rwanda, still a Belgian colony until July 1962, remained on the sidelines but protected the Kagera National Park, where the new young warden, De Leyn (1929–1962), would nevertheless be assassinated. The modestly sized Rwandan part of the then Parc National des Virunga was later named 'Volcanoes National Park'.

At the end of 1961, an international conference took place in Arusha. The global scientific community solemnly congratulated the Congolese authorities for preserving the Park, even at the cost of many human lives, and especially for maintaining its policy of integral conservation. The role of Professor Grzimek, from the Frankfurt Zoological Society, would prove crucial for the PNA's future.

We should also acknowledge the positive contributions of Dr Harold Coolidge, a prominent American environmentalist. The illustrious British biologist Julian Huxley, brother of Aldous, was also interested in maintaining the reserve, which he visited in 1961. He made the fatal proposal to end its integral conservation. In 1961, the rebirth of the Congo's parks had become a fact. No land was retroceded, and poaching remained within acceptable limits. Nevertheless, the Park struggled until 1968, primarily due to a lack of financial resources. That was when it became a department of the Directorate of Waters and Forests of Léopoldville-Kinshasa's Ministry of Agriculture.

3. Towards a revival of the PNA

In 1968, an inspector discovered a deplorable situation: the rangers no longer had uniforms or any transport, though basic surveillance remained. The wardens and many rangers had remained at their post and courageously defended the reserve. While the PNA remained a priority in Léopoldville-Kinshasa, local political pressures weakened it. This was evidenced by the blatantly illegal installation of a large-scale fishery at Nyakakoma, which destroyed the only xerophilous forest bordering the lake. All attempts to dislodge this fishery were unsuccessful. The invasion of fishing canoes, even into spawning grounds, was to have dramatic consequences. At the time, fish poaching was essentially the work of semi-militarised gangs of fishermen from Uganda.

Also in 1968, field investigations yielded disheartening findings: thousands of cattle from Rwanda had invaded the gorilla sector (Mikeno–Karisimbi). However, it must be acknowledged that the herders did not irreversibly damage the forest. Nevertheless, the absence of any official contact between the Congo and the authorities of Rwanda's Volcanoes National Park was a serious shortcoming. In the Centre Sector, elephant poaching continued, though not at the levels observed in 2000. In July 1968, I counted 5,272 hippos in the Rutshuru River alone (Centre Sector), 1,300 more than 10 years earlier. The poorly controlled North Sector was the major victim of the reserve's deterioration. Thousands of hippos were exterminated, though this slaughter was not comparable to the 'hippocide' of 1995–2005. The Ruwenzori and the equatorial forest were completely unsupervised at the time. In 1969, despite everyone's efforts, especially those of the directors and wardens, things went from bad to worse. Reports were sent to the Head of State of Congo, who reacted energetically: by Ordinance 69/041 of 22 August 1969, the President confirmed the authority of the National Institute for the Conservation of Nature (*Institut National pour la Conservation de la Nature* – INCN). This ordinance was later supplemented by a new official document, 72/02, dated 21 February 1972, specifying certain elements.

The new manager enjoyed almost dictatorial powers. He reported directly to the Head of State, with first Kayenga Onzi Ndal and then Dr Muema acting as occasional intermediaries. Mobutu's chief of staff, Bizengimana, played an ambiguous and sometimes harmful role regarding the principle of integral conservation. The Congolese Presidency

4.5 From 1971, all ICCN staff members were issued an official service card. This showed the hierarchical dependence of the Institute on the Presidency of the Republic.

4.6 In 1970, a Special Agreement between Congo and Belgium enabled President Mobutu to appoint Dr Jacques Verschuren as the new director of the Congolese Institute for Nature Conservation (ICCN). This appointment was accompanied by a support programme to revive the national parks.
Extract from the newspaper Le Soir, 11 June 1970.

financed the new institute almost entirely, and also supervised environmental issues through a Ministry (State Commissariat) of Environment: a first in Africa. Madame Lessedjina was appointed as its head, by an ordinance of 1972.

Penalties for poaching were increased significantly. Hunting dogs were culled, as they sometimes carried rabies. Another highly effective measure was implemented: henceforth, rangers no longer had to prove they were acting in self-defence when using their weapons against poachers. They were authorised to shoot after three warnings. The positive consequences were immediate. Rangers who had been imprisoned for capturing poachers were released and commended.

The headquarters of the institute were officially located in Kinshasa (rue Dreypondt, then Avenue des Cliniques). They were supplemented by several, often superfluous, regional directorates. Such localisation seemed inadequate, even with their radio communication – another first. I would have preferred a headquarters in Rumangabo (Kivu), at the heart of the oldest protected area, rather than 1,300 km away. In 1969, I started a campaign against bureaucratic waste. Salaries absorbed a third of the total budget, and many tasks were useless for conservation. I prioritised the fieldwork, decreeing that 90% of the staff had to be active in the field. The staff were given strict instructions, with regular checks and, if necessary, demotions.

Conversely, wardens knew how to reward those who performed their duties rigorously and bravely, by increasing their monthly bonuses. I also recommended that rangers gather together villagers, with the help of the traditional chiefs, to explain the purpose of the PNA and to remind them that the reserve also had benefits for them. It was necessary to be tough on illegal acts while remembering the need to live harmoniously with the Park's neighbouring communities.

Management was implemented through widespread direct action. For instance, when a damaged bush dispensary needed repairs, the Director General advanced the money without delay. This method allowed for a rapid recovery of the reserve. The rangers were re-equipped, tracks were restored and the transport fleet increased tenfold. Aircraft became a part of the Park's operational structure, as did boats.

From 1969 to 1972, the sole decision-maker was the Director General. Starting from 1973, he was assisted by a management committee. This seemed a commendable initi-

THE NEW START (1960–1991)

4.7 Brigadier Vukoyo and his family in Rwindi in 1962. He took part in numerous field explorations with Dr J. Verschuren.

4.8 One of the many priorities in the 1960s was to organise the management and to train the rangers, at a difficult time when poaching was rife. Here, an inspection of the rangers stationed at Mutsora in August 1961.

4.9 A special grant from the Foundation for Promoting Scientific Research in Africa (FFRSA) allowed the purchase in 1972 of a light aircraft – a Piper SuperCub – piloted by W. Delvingt (here with ranger Kambale). It was invaluable for mapping, monitoring and counting large mammals.

ative, but it had the effect of slowing down this direct action. It signalled the return of tenders, endless debates, and agreements with bureaucrats. In short: classic red tape. A certain inertia replaced direct management. At the end of 1969, my deputy Mokwa and I participated in the International Union for Conservation of Nature (IUCN) General Assembly in New Delhi where, as in Arusha eight years earlier, the Congo was praised for its positive actions towards nature conservation and for maintaining the principle of integral conservation, the basic objective when the reserve was created. Like other reserves, the PNA, now renamed Virunga National Park (*Parc National des Virunga* – PNVi) experienced a resurgence of activity for five years, coinciding with successive prosperous years for the Congolese economy. In 1972, Deputy Director General Gahuranyi Tanganyika collaborated in the management activities. Despite some opposition, the revival proved to be real and effective.

Except for the incidents in July 1960, no land claims were raised by PNVi's neighbouring populations between 1960 and 1976. The Park's most energetic supporter, the great traditional chief Daniel Ndeze, who had offered his lands to King Albert, lived for several years in Belgium, just a few metres from the Tervuren Museum. During the 1960s, 1970s and 1980s, measures were taken to oppose the construction of new roadways in the PNVi. However, two illegal roads had to be tolerated: the so-called 'route de Monseigneur', descending from the heights of the Nande regions towards the upper Semliki, near the Kasaka and Museya rivers; and, worse, the subsequent construction of an east–west road, splitting the reserve right across the lava plain, just south of the latitude of Rutshuru.

A CENTURY OF HISTORY

Au Zaïre, les parcs nationaux retrouvent leur splendeur d'avant l'indépendance

[Extract from La Libre Belgique newspaper article]

4.10 After three years of hard work, Belgian–Zairian cooperation made it possible to launch a vast rehabilitation project for the national parks, regarding management, infrastructure, research, equipment and training.
Extract from the newspaper La Libre Belgique, 9 August 1973.

4.11 The abundance of giant forest hogs in the Lulimbi sector triggered the first research into the ecology of this little-known species. Here, Brigadier N. Bagurubumwe crouches in the shelter (the 'bauge') of a family of giant forest hogs underneath some thorny bushes in *Capparis*.

4. First Belgian cooperation agreement

In 1970, a Special Cooperation Agreement was signed with Belgium, which contributed somewhat to the operating and investment costs of Virunga National Park and other reserves. This agreement financed the Director General as project leader and allowed the hiring of five foreign experts, each a renowned specialist in his field: Willy Delvingt, future professor of agronomy at the University of Gembloux; Jean-Pierre d'Huart, scientific researcher; Alain Jamar, pilot; André Letiexhe, an indispensable technician familiar with the Congo since 1950; and Jean-Pierre von der Becke, manager. Each collaborated with one or more national counterparts and was integrated into the ICCN's organisational chart. Among this project's numerous achievements were the launch of the magazine *Léopard*, with five issues

4.12 The PNVi tourism revival in the 1970s owes a great deal to J-P. von der Becke, a passionate protector of the Park's gorillas. He died prematurely in 2011.

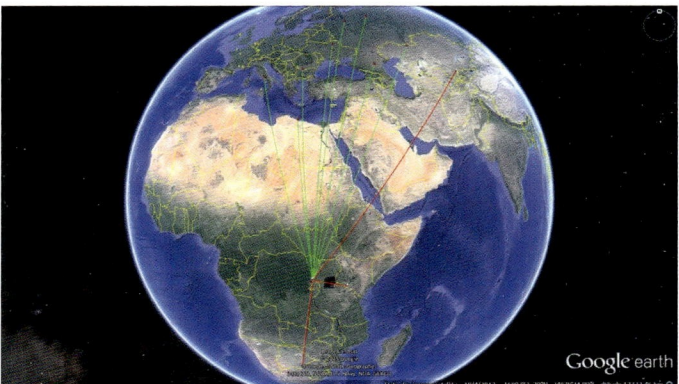

4.13 Representation of some migratory birds' captures at Lulimbi (in red) and recaptures abroad (in green). More than 12,000 migratory birds of Palaearctic origin were ringed between 1971 and 1975, representing 36% of all birds caught, including 287 African species.

4.14 The ringing of migratory birds on the shores of Lake Edward was one of the priority programmes of the Lulimbi research station. In the presence of W. Delvingt (right), N. Bagurubumwe, the brigadier in charge of ringing, hands over a captured bird to Dr Verschuren.

published between 1971 and 1977; the construction of infrastructure in all parks thanks to André Letiexhe (including tourist lodges, Lulimbi research station, airstrips, patrol posts, trails and bridges); original studies on hippopotamus ecology (Delvingt); giant forest hog ecology (d'Huart); integrated park management (Mankoto); tourism organisation (von der Becke); the banding of migratory birds (Delvingt, Bagurubumwe and d'Huart); periodic large mammal censuses; the creation of a reference herbarium; and the training of Congolese colleagues. Samy Mankoto Ma Mbaelele became a researcher at Lulimbi, where he prepared a thesis on 'Ecological Problems in PNVi', before presenting it at Laval University (Québec), returning as scientific and technical director, and eventually becoming CEO of the Zairian Institute for Nature Conservation (*Institut Zairois pour la Conservation de la Nature* – IZCN) in 1985.

The project ran until 1975. Partly due to the Zairianisation of 1973, it encountered some problems, though these did not compromise the final result. Even if this earlier agreement was a limited initiative, it was exemplary for subsequent national and international cooperation. I have to mention another, albeit regrettable, initiative. A manual ferry, originally intended for visitors, was installed on the lower Rutshuru, providing easy access to the eastern plains.

In 1972–1973, the station and laboratory at Lulimbi were built on a site that would frequently be submerged by violent floods and subjected to regrettable human degradation. Following the ransacking and deterioration of the station and laboratory over the past 30 years, this site has been transformed and now serves a tourist function.

Many Congolese specialists, including Norbert Mushenzi, were sent to Garoua (Cameroon) and Mweka

(Tanzania) to attend the International College of Wildlife Management, where they garnered accolades. By the end of 1976, 19 Congolese rangers had received this additional training. Let us not forget the attendance of Congolese delegates at the IUCN General Assembly in Banff, Canada, and the second World Parks Congress in Yellowstone (September 1972). The Congo invited the global organisation to its general assembly in Kinshasa and Rwindi in 1975, which was a success. The PNVi was celebrating its half-century of existence at the time.

Let us go back a few years. In August 1970, the President of the Congo invited Baudouin, King of the Belgians, and his wife Fabiola to the Park. The two Heads of State spent nearly a week in the reserve. They were dazzled by the exceptional floral and faunal richness. This visit was followed by several visits from the President, who decided to improve the Rwindi lodge.

The issue of the pygmies was re-examined between 1970 and 1975. They had once been tolerated in the reserve as part of the forest ecosystem, but some unfortunately evolved from gatherers to poachers. The authorities had decided to relocate them, but this never happened. Furthermore, the management of the Rutshuru Hunting Domain was entrusted to PNVi by departmental decree 024 of 14 February 1974.

5. Zairianisation period

In 1974, following Zairianisation and widespread indiscipline (though not among the rangers), the general management was forced to make several trips to the north to quell revolts, while continuing its scientific research missions. Violent clashes took place in middle Semliki. Without decisive action it would most likely have been the rangers who sacrificed their lives.

In 1974, 714 rangers were employed to monitor the Congolese parks, spread across the country's 22 zones (territories). The cooperation agreement with Belgium was interrupted in 1974–1975, yet this did not deter national and foreign scientists from continuing their activities. No one, at the beginning of the 1980s, could foresee the extent of the deterioration that lay in store for the PNVi. Several General Directors succeeded one another. Only one proved mediocre and even engaged in blatant poaching on an industrial scale. This individual was arrested and imprisoned. Apart from this sad period, the rangers never allowed themselves to be corrupted and tirelessly continued their surveillance. The result was that, in 1975, the PNVi commanded overwhelming respect and recognition throughout North Kivu.

6. Second Belgian cooperation agreement

Due to various delays in signing the agreement between the Belgian General Administration for Development Cooperation (*Administration Générale de la Coopération au Développement* – AGCD) and the Zairian government, the second phase of the project financed by Belgium only started in 1978. New technical experts based in Lulimbi were to support the management and research in the Park: Jan Van Gysel focused on the dynamics of the vegetation on the plains south of Lake Edward; Mireille Vanoverstraeten on

4.15 The ferry on the Rutshuru River at Nyamushengero links the Rwindi and Lulimbi sectors.

4.16 The creation of the first permanent scientific research station at Lulimbi in 1970 has, over 20 years, occasioned major studies of the Park's flora and fauna.

the soil in the same region; while Hadelin Mertens documented ungulate population sizes and dynamics.

All these support programmes aimed to obtain scientific data on which to base the PNVi's first management and development plan. This objective was, unfortunately, never achieved. The project's third phase was never carried out because relations between Zaire and Belgium had cooled.

Still, the two phases of the AGCD support project did allow for significant advances in the PNVi's scientific knowledge. Local capacities were developed by training numerous Zairian researchers and technicians. With significant financial support, and thanks to the development of infrastructure, tourism also resumed and the potential of the Park fully revealed itself. The presence of numerous film and television crews, inter-university exchanges and visits from internationally renowned personalities helped elevate the Park's international profile. This was evidenced in 1979 by the recognition of the Park as a UNESCO World Heritage site. This recognition indicated that tourism could generate significant revenues for the Park's operation and the whole network of protected areas in the country. However, Zairianisation hampered foreign investment and prevented the full development of certain aspects of tourism.

7. FZS/WWF/IUCN programme

After the difficult period for the General Directorate in Kinshasa, and the ending of Belgian support, there was a need to turn the fortunes of the PNVi around. This was achieved by combining two elements: the implementation of the Frankfurt Zoological Society (FZS)/WWF/IUCN project, negotiated in 1983 and effective from April 1984, and some changes in the IZCN management. The FZS project, supported by the WWF, facilitated great strides in gorilla and chimpanzee tourism. The project developed the framework for such activities and multiplied the revenues generated by this sector.

In 1985, the PNVi celebrated its 60th anniversary, shortly before Garamba National Park's 50th. To mark the occasion, major ceremonies were held in Kinshasa and Rwindi. Once again, the Head of State declared that this protected area was vital for the country.

The increased number of tourists restored the PNVi to its deserved place on the national and international scene, and the significant financial potential of this type of tourism became a decisive factor for the future. With over 6,500 visitors a year – for the gorillas alone – and the shift from the Zaire to the US dollar as its currency of revenue, the IZCN was given a breath of fresh air. Moreover, this potential would prompt the European Union to incorporate the Virunga Program into its broader Kivu Program in 1988.

In 1987, the FZS/WWF/IUCN Gorilla Program added a chimpanzee component, with the habituation, funded by the FZS, of a group of chimpanzees in Tongo for tourism, and also an educational component. This was the WWF's Virunga Education Program (PEVI, renamed the Environmental Program around Virunga in 1996), which has continued to remain active to this day. While the future International Gorilla Conservation Programme was being developed by the African Wildlife Foundation (AWF)/Fauna and Flora Preservation Society (FFPS)/World Wildlife Fund (WWF) trio, the development of gorilla tourism was included in the Kivu Program from 1988 onwards.

4.17 With private investment, the refurbishment of the Rwindi camp provided tourist agencies with a flourishing business. The many visitors on safari were accompanied along the network of tracks by excellent Park guides. Here, Joseph Paluku, the very popular chief guide.

4.18 1960. The security offered by the Rwindi station long encouraged old buffaloes to stay close to the homes.

4.19 A visit from an elephant around the home of a warden at Rwindi in 1972.

8. European Union's Kivu Program

The vast Kivu Program, funded by the European Union, got underway in 1988. It covered various development areas, including road infrastructure, agricultural revival and health, but one component focused specifically on the PNVi building on the achievements of the FZS/WWF/IUCN project and previous support from the AGCD and extending them to the entire Park. The Virunga Program was supported by four international experts, including Conrad Aveling, its principal technical advisor. With funding equivalent to seven million euros over four years, the main impact areas were the development of infrastructure, such as lodges and trails, equipment, including vehicles and patrolling equipment, and support for surrounding populations, the latter in partnership with the WWF's PEVI project, focused on agricultural services and water supply, among others.

This programme allowed the IZCN to maintain and develop the international image of PNVi, with tourism becoming prosperous again. The numerous personalities visiting the Park enhanced its reputation. President Mobutu continued to invite his counterparts and other VIPs to visit his 'favourite park'. He remained a major supporter until the early 1990s.

The publication of significant studies and reference documents was another achievement of this programme. Notable examples include the hippopotamus census by Mackie (1989), the elephant and buffalo census by Aveling (1990), the famous PNVi Guide (Delvingt et al., 1990), and the study of the fishery potential of Lake Edward by Vakily (1989).

The early 1990s nevertheless marked the end of an era and the beginning of a decline from which the country would struggle to recover. The inflation rate of 3,000% per year, repeated looting by the army and growing corruption caused the socio-economic and political situation to deteriorate inexorably. September 1991 is a significant date in the history of the country and of PNVi: the Kinshasa riots marked an end to the cooperation with many countries and multilateral donors. This led to the premature withdrawal of the Kivu Program and its Virunga component. The dramatic events that marked neighbouring Rwanda and the Kivu war at the turn of the 2000s prevented the celebration of both the 75th and 80th anniversaries of PNVi.

9. Institutional factors influencing the Park

9.1. Context

In the early 1980s the morale among the field staff, particularly the rangers, was at its lowest, and for good reason: at the General Directorate, the Director of the IZCN had just been arrested and imprisoned for illegally selling ivory to the son of an influential politician. Furthermore, poaching was rampant in the protected areas. The poorly equipped, underpaid rangers did their best to curb the scourge but were unsuccessful, as the magistrates tended to release poachers after sham trials. Further north, in the Garamba National Park, the population of northern white rhinos plummeted: their numbers fell from a thousand individuals to 250 in 1971, and to just 11 in 1984. Faced with this catastrophic situation and following a resolution of the IUCN General

Assembly in Madrid, a high-level delegation led by Professor Jean-Paul Harroy, the first Secretary General of the IUCN when it was created in 1948, and further composed of Professor Jeffrey Sayer, Charles Mackie and Dr Kai Curry-Lindahl, met with President Mobutu in Kinshasa, in the presence of Victor Njoli Balanga, the Minister of Environment and Nature Conservation. The President declined the Madrid resolution's offer of translocation and promised to do everything possible to ensure the survival of the rhinos *in situ*. It was in this context that Samy Mankoto was appointed head of the IZCN in April 1985. At 38, he became the youngest President of the Board and Director General of the Institute, which earned him remarks that were as inappropriate as they were malicious.

9.2. Institutional review and reorganisation

Upon taking office, Samy Mankoto immediately undertook significant reforms. In October 1985, he organised the celebration of the 60th anniversary of the PNVi in Goma, marked by a parade of rangers in new uniforms and equipped with modern weapons. The ceremony mobilised the entire city of Goma, and the day was declared a public holiday with paid leave by Vice-Governor Koya Gialo Basete Gerengo. Many notable figures were present: ministers from the Central African Republic, Congo-Brazzaville and Zaire, as well as ambassadors from various countries and the European Union. I was present as a former Director General of the Institute, along with Professors Jean-Paul Harroy and Alexandre Prigogine, Dr David Kabala Matuka, an international civil servant at UNESCO, the Director General of the ORTPN (Rwandan Office for Tourism and National Parks), and all the members of the IZCN's Board of Directors and General Directorate staff.

Prior to this, an important national conference was organised in Kinshasa, with the participation of experts from many countries. Under the high patronage of the President of the Republic, the conference was opened by Kengo wa Dondo, the Prime Commissioner of State (Prime Minister). The discussions were lively and facilitated an examination of the fundamental issues related to conservation in Zaire and the sub-region, and the formulation of recommendations and strategies. Subsequently, nearly 150 people were transported by plane to Goma and then to Rwindi. This complex logistical operation was carried out successfully from start to finish. The CEO's General Services and Protocol team, coordinated by Simon Sivi dia Yamba N'Suka, who was affectionately known as the 'bulldozer', performed wonderfully well and in perfect harmony with the protocols of the State and the supervising ministry.

The celebrations for the PNVi's 60th anniversary in 1985, and the Garamba National Park's 50th anniversary in 1989, along with the extensive media coverage of these major events put the spotlight on the country's national parks, four of which were already UNESCO World Heritage sites (Virunga, Garamba, Kahuzi-Biega and Salonga). This marked the beginning of a new era of rehabilitation of the rangers and the IZCN's brand image.

The results followed swiftly: the rhino population tripled to 33 individuals by 1995. Garamba National Park was removed from the World Heritage in Danger list in 1994. In the PNVi, notorious poachers like Mzee Tembo were arrested and transferred to Kinshasa's central prison, far from their home environment, after a legal battle waged by the General Directorate with the support of the supervising Minister and the Prime Minister, himself a renowned lawyer and university professor. Mzee Tembo's relocation caused a stir among the other poachers in the region. A surreal phenomenon ensued: Mzee Tembo's teammates converted and furtively handed in their weapons, depositing them in churches, notably in Mutsora.

At this point, CEO Mankoto felt the need to step up his efforts. He decided to commission an institutional audit of the IZCN to restructure and strengthen it. With backing from Jean-Pierre d'Huart and Roseline Beudels, he contacted the European Commission. He presented his project to Enrico Pironio, whom he had met in Rwindi in 1987, and desk officer Tincani. Following a field consultation mission, an institutional study of the IZCN was conducted between 1990 and 1991, in two parts: an institutional study, looking at the organisation, its management and human resources, financed by the World Bank; and a study of the IZCN's accounting and financial organisation, and the capitalisation of revenue-generating activities, including ecotourism and management of the IZCN's hotel assets, including the Rwindi hotel, financed by the European Commission.

9.3. A few results

At the General Directorate level
- In 1986, the launch of ecotourism, with the collaboration of various partners (WWF International, WWF Belgium, WWF USA, PICG, GTZ, WCS, UNESCO–IUCN–SZF Consortium, European Union), in particular for great apes (gorillas in the PNVi and Kahuzi-Biega, and chimpanzees in Tongo). The General Directorate introduced an innovative policy of foreign currency revenue collection and, to this end, created, by agreement with the National Bank, 'foreign currency resident' accounts, coupled with a revenue-sharing policy (granting incentive bonuses to guides and rangers, implementing village microprojects for populations living near the parks, and

4.20 The Rwindi station, developed in the 1970s as a strategic camp at the heart of the Park, was equipped with a comfortable tourist lodge, much appreciated by travellers.

establishing a policy of authorisation and taxation for filming in the parks).
- The strengthening of the management capacity of technical and scientific personnel by getting donors to finance scholarships for young researchers to study abroad, and providing systematic training of conservators, assistants and senior ranger officers at the Garoua Wildlife School in Cameroon.
- The recruitment of young university graduates (researchers and accountants, particularly from the Higher Institute of Commerce), computerising services for efficient financial management and timely production of reliable financial statements. These organisational improvements earned the IZCN a donation of two minibuses from the FZS meant for transporting General Directorate staff in Kinshasa.

At the regional level and in the field
- The implementation, in 1991, of a policy of decentralisation, by creating Regional Directorates, and the retrocession of revenues to the parks based on a 60% (parks) versus 40% (General Directorate) split, as decided by the Board of Directors.
- The appointment of Regional Directors, to whom the Board of Directors delegated certain powers in 1991, such as managing operational staff.
- The launch of a major training programme for rangers, by establishing a training camp at the Lulimbi scientific station. A training manual covering numerous aspects was developed. The first training session, in 1986, lasted three months and included, among others instructors, park wardens, a team of senior officers from Rumangabo and the Zairian Armed Forces (*Forces Armées Zairoises* – FAZ) top brass from Kinshasa. This significant training effort was coordinated by Colonel Kalume Numbi, who later became a General and Minister of Planning in the Third Republic. The training session concluded with an official diploma ceremony at Lulimbi, presided over by the Commander-in-Chief of the FAZ. From Lulimbi emerged the elite mobile unit of Kabaraza, commanded by Lieutenant Fofolo.
- The establishment of a policy of dialogue with local communities, youth and traditional authorities through the Virunga Education Program, a large-scale reforestation project involving local populations, and the launch of the *Kacheche* magazine (WWF–GTZ) that was highly appreciated by the public. The donation by the WWF of an audiovisual vehicle to Goma had a psychological impact and was highly successful in North Kivu: it was greatly envied by Mobilisation, Propaganda, and Political Animation of the MPR-State Party (MOPAP).

At the national level
- With revenues of about 650,000 dollars per year, primarily generated by Virunga and Kahuzi-Biega National Parks, the IZCN moved from the E category of public enterprises to the C category of commercial enterprises and was congratulated by the government.
- The signing of the programme contract between the IZCN and the Superior Portfolio Council in 1994, stating performance indicator criteria.

At the international level
- The internationalisation of the IZCN, recognised by the IUCN as a model to follow and replicate elsewhere in Africa, particularly in Madagascar.
- The signing of the first Headquarters Agreement between the DRC and WWF, and appointing Dr Hadelin Mertens as the first WWF Resident Representative in Zaire on 1 March 1990. This far-reaching agreement gave a significant boost to international cooperation with the IZCN. Following his participation in the celebrations for the 25th anniversary of the WWF in Assisi (Italy) in September 1986, the CEO managed to have Zaire included among the priority countries for WWF actions in Africa.
- The arrival of new donors and partners, such as the World Bank's Forests and Environment Project, the European Union, UNESCO, IUCN, WWF, GTZ, SZF, NYZS (now WCS), PICG, GIC, Milwaukee Zoological Society, helped to enhance the visibility of the IZCN and to mobilise substantial extra-budgetary funds to

support the PNVi and other parks and reserves.
- The presence of major donors at the IZCN fostered a climate of trust and collaboration. This enabled the IZCN to organise international meetings in Kinshasa and elsewhere within the country and in the PNVi. Notably, in August 1989, the Sub-regional Workshop Seminar on Training and Refresher Courses for National Park and Protected Area Wardens was held at Rwindi, presided over by the Secretary of State for the Environment. It attracted over 60 experts from Burundi, Congo, Uganda and Zaire.
- As a body governed by public law, the IZCN was admitted to membership of the IUCN.

10. Conclusion

This chapter gives an overview of the fortunes of the Park from Independence to the early 1990s. It outlines how, thanks to the determination of certain individuals, either in the field, in the capital or even outside the country, the Park managed to overcome major threats. Apart from this human aspect, another decisive factor was the financial and political support lent by both the central government and donors. Subsequent successes, such as the recovery of illegally invaded land and the stabilisation, or even growth, of the animal populations, resulted from the commitment of new players on the ground and in Kinshasa.

5.1 The forests in the South Sector and the neighbouring areas suffered extensive damage with the search for fuelwood to supply the Rwandan refugee camps between 1994 and 1996.

5

The transition years (1992–2005)

JOSÉ KALPERS, NORBERT MUSHENZI

Virunga National Park suffered head-on from the regional wars and ongoing crises that began in the early 1990s. They had a destructive effect on the ecosystems and undermined the work of the ICCN. The courage and resilience of the rangers enabled the Park to get through these years of chaos.

1. Managing protected areas during armed conflicts

In times of peace, managing protected areas is a challenge across most of the African continent: fragile or even corrupt institutions, lack of support from national authorities, demographic pressure and the poverty of rural populations constrain sustainable conservation activities. When a crisis emerges, such as an armed conflict or a natural disaster, the difficulties become almost overwhelming for managers of protected areas, as well as their institutions and partners. The impact of armed conflicts on protected areas can be classified as follows (Blom, 2000).

Direct impact on biodiversity
- The conflicting parties directly and deliberately affect the environment. This destruction is generally aimed at a strategic objective, such as clearing, deforestation or defoliation to limit or prevent ambushes and the passage of infiltrators.
- Natural resources, such as ivory and rhino horn, are used to finance military operations.
- Movement and settlement of refugees or displaced persons near protected areas, and resource extraction by these populations for survival.

Indirect impact on institutions
- Logistical constraints: The conflict greatly hampers conservation activities and often leads to significant human losses among surveillance personnel.
- Financial constraints: Donors and partners become reluctant to continue their support, and tourism revenues are significantly affected.
- Shifting priorities: During a conflict and its accompanying humanitarian crises, national authorities and supporting agencies no longer primarily focus their attention on environmental aspects and biodiversity conservation.

Prior to 1991, Virunga National Park (*Parc National des Virunga* – PNVi) had already been experiencing serious structural problems (Kalpers, 1996). The institutional weakness of the official semi-State agency responsible for managing and conserving protected areas in Zaire was an issue. This weakness was evident at the Zairian Institute for Nature Conservation (*Institut Zairois pour la Conservation de la Nature* – IZCN) headquarters in Kinshasa and in the field stations. It was mainly due to a lack of technical and logistical resources and was further exacerbated by the country's socio-economic and political crises. In September 1991, the worsening sociopolitical climate led to the withdrawal of most development projects in the field of biodiversity conservation and imposed a new series of constraints.

2. Beginning of unrest in the North Sector (1986–1994)

The North Sector was the first to be affected. Disturbances involving bands of poachers in the foothills of the Ruwenzori region first occurred in 1986. When President Mobutu installed a three-party system, and later a multi-party system in 1990, rebel groups based in Watalinga and Mount Hoyo gathered in the region. Patrol posts were attacked, several rangers and their associates were killed, and the number of lootings increased rapidly. Simultaneously, there was a sharp increase in poaching to supply the rebels and finance their activities. Elephants and buffaloes were massacred and, in Ishango, the hippopotamus population was nearly wiped out. A trade in elephant and hippopotamus meat and ivory developed locally and towards Uganda.

In 1991, the first weapons of war appeared on the scene, and a succession of attacks hit the IZCN and the Park. After a relative lull, the situation deteriorated again in 1994, with several raids targeting the Mwalika and Vimbao patrol posts and the Ishango substation. Dr Simon Lulengo, Technical Director of the IZCN, died in an explosion when his vehicle hit a mine.

The IZCN gradually lost control of the extreme north of the Park, which was taken over by various rebel groups scouring the region. This marked the beginning of a long period of insecurity for the North Sector. Further south, the IZCN retained control, but the socio-economic fabric, particularly the governance, degraded. Repeated cases of external poaching ensued, as well as instances of internal poaching within the IZCN, resulting in severe direct threats to wildlife. Contrary to popular belief, most hippopotamus losses (18,000 animals killed) occurred in the period before the armed conflicts (Languy, 1994a).

In October 1993, UNESCO sent a mission to assess the worsening situation. Its conclusions prompted the inclusion of PNVi on the undesirable list of World Heritage Sites in Danger. This inclusion was largely based on findings established before the Rwandan genocide and the refugee crisis, though the formal decision was not made until the end of 1994 (UNESCO, 1995).

3. War in Rwanda (1990–1994)

Not only did the war in Rwanda cause enormous harm to biodiversity conservation and protected habitats in the

5.2   An elephant skull poached for its ivory.

Virunga massif region, but it also had severe consequences for the neighbouring areas. Starting in January 1991, with the first offensive by the Rwandan Patriotic Front (RPF) in the north-west of Rwanda, and the first attack on Ruhengeri, the Virunga massif became the theatre of military operations. Military leaders quickly grasped the immense strategic importance of this region, the only forested area between Rwanda, Uganda and Zaire. As such, it offered armed groups dense cover and secure retreat routes. The soldiers realised they could move freely in the region without attracting attention. In 1991, the eastern part of the Volcanoes National Park in Rwanda and the entire Mgahinga Gorilla National Park in Uganda were affected by military operations. The RPF soon adopted a strategy of skirting around Mount Sabinyo (a place bordering the three countries). As a result, its military operations impacted the Mikeno sector of PNVi on Zairian territory. Between 1991 and 1994, the Virunga massif experienced significant infiltration movements by RPF troops, as well as patrols and sweeping operations by the Rwandan Armed Forces (FAR), due to increased military presence in this vast forest, with both the rebel forces and the regular army intensifying their activities. The FAR established permanent positions at strategic locations, such as the forest's edge and in the cavities between the volcanoes in the eastern Virunga (Sabinyo, Gahinga and Muhavura). Several hundred mines were laid in the forest massif, particularly on the trails leading to the forest and along the Rwandan–Zairian border.

Despite the monstrous impact of the 1994 genocide on the Rwandan population, the environment as a whole, and protected areas in particular, were not severely affected during the 100 days of massacres. During the final RPF offensive in July 1994, however, the thousands of people who sought refuge in Zaire, using the trails and paths of the Virunga massif, brought a significant portion of their livestock with them. This massive exodus triggered one of the century's most acute humanitarian crises and had a significant environmental impact on the Park.

4. Rwandan refugees crisis (1994–1996)

Within just a few days in July 1994, two million people left Rwanda and sought refuge in neighbouring countries, notably Zaire. On 15 July alone, 500,000 people crossed the border and arrived in Goma. They were joined by 300,000 more in the following days. The refugees hoped Goma would be able to meet their needs for water, firewood and food, all of which were available in and around the southern part of PNVi. In July 1994, three camps were constructed in Kibumba, Mugunga and Katale, where the refugees settled. Refugees from Rwanda continued to arrive, so humanitarian organisations built two additional camps in late 1994 and early 1995: Lac Vert and Kahindo. By late 1994, the refugee population was estimated at 720,000 people (Delvingt, 1994). The refugee camps in the Goma region remained in place on the border of the Park for over two years. They only dispersed when the area was directly affected by new conflicts.

Deforestation

Deforestation was one of the most visible and best-documented consequences of the refugee crisis. The refugees were provided with shelter and food by the humanitarian agencies, but they had to cook for themselves. Collecting and cutting firewood quickly became a significant threat to the environment. Trees were felled for firewood, construction or even commercial purposes – large-scale charcoal production, for example, became a thriving business. Early in the crisis, an average of 40,000 people entered the Park daily in search of wood (Tombola & Sanders, 1994) and deforestation subsequently intensified even further. On certain days, up to 80,000 people entered the Park, cutting up to 1,000 tons of wood daily (Languy, 1995; Henquin & Blondel, 1996). During the 27 months of the refugee camps' presence on the border of the PNVi, deforestation kept intensifying, particularly in the Nyamulagira sector (an active volcano sector). The impact is illustrated by the figures and data from Henquin & Blondel (1997): two years after the refugees' arrival, 105 km² of forest had been affected by deforestation. The area that was completely cleared totalled 35 km².

The total deforestation was equivalent to clear-cutting 63 km². It is estimated that most of the deforestation (two-thirds) concerned the lava plain forests, which were relatively low in biodiversity compared to, for example, the subalpine virgin forest in other northern parts of PNVi. Moreover, at least 50% of the areas cleared or severely affected by refugees were young forests composed of pioneer species at the initial stage of recolonising the lava flows.

5.3 One of many Rwandan refugee camps established in 1994 at the immediate edge of the Park.

The longest-lasting damage was observed in the Mikeno sector, the area impacted by the Kibumba camp, where significant areas were deforested. The mountain forest's *Podocarpus milanjianus* was particularly affected. Around the Katale and Kahindo camps, which housed 290,000 refugees in total, deforestation remained relatively limited, probably because humanitarian agencies implemented Park protection programmes when the camps were established. In contrast, the wooded areas near the Kibumba camp experienced intensive deforestation during the first year. Considerable resources were mobilised the following year to protect the significant ecosystem in the area. By 1996, the damage had practically ceased.

Deforestation was particularly severe in the areas surrounding the Mugunga and Lac Vert camps, which housed around 200,000 refugees. Refugees collected large quantities of firewood for personal use and established a vast commercial enterprise selling wood and charcoal to Goma (Languy, 1995). As there were no security forces to protect the forest, the deforestation rate increased during the second year. A study conducted over two years (Henquin & Blondel, 1997) extrapolated the total deforestation caused by refugees in the Park over the two years and three months of the camps' existence:

- Areas affected by deforestation in the PNVi: ± 113 km²
- Areas completely cleared: ± 71 km²
- Areas equivalent cleared: ± 75 km²

Bamboo cutting

Illegal bamboo cutting was primarily organised and carried out by refugees from the Kibumba camp (Bremer, 1996). South of Lake Edward, bamboo, *Arundinaria alpina*, is found only in the Mikeno sector, part of the gorilla habitat, at higher altitudes. Refugees used the bamboo for various purposes, such as basket-making, mat weaving and constructing shelters. An international NGO even launched a project encouraging refugees to produce handicrafts, but it was abruptly halted when it was discovered that the bamboo was being sourced from the Park. In total, 192 hectares of bamboo were 50% exploited in the Mikeno sector, meaning half the affected area was cleared (Henquin & Blondel, 1996).

Poaching

Poaching intensified during the two years of refugee presence in the region, in both southern sectors of PNVi (Biswas & Tortajada-Quiroz, 1996). Poachers primarily targeted two antelope species, the bushbuck and the duiker, but also hunted forest buffaloes and elephants (Wathaut, 1996).

5.4 The reduced surveillance capacity during the crisis years encouraged the local population to enter the Park to produce charcoal. The rangers destroyed a large number of 'makala' kilns.

5.5 The Park defenders had to witness, often helplessly, an unprecedented upsurge in poaching. Here, thousands of snares found on the slopes of extinct volcanoes are destroyed by rangers.

In July and August 1995, poachers killed four mountain gorillas, including three silverback males and one adult female (Cooper & Cooper, 1996) – the first gorilla massacres in the Virungas in 10 years (Weber, 1989). This type of poaching was not necessarily linked to the presence of refugees but was more likely a consequence of the general state of disorder and insecurity at that time (Werikhe et al., 1998).

Disruptions caused by refugees movements
Among the refugees fleeing Rwanda in July 1994, several thousand crossed the Virunga massif to reach Zaire. Some lived in the forest for several weeks before emerging on the Zairian side. Many travelled with livestock, including cows, goats and sheep. This activity likely affected the forest ecosystem and increased the risk of disease transmission to wildlife.

Medical waste disposal
During the first year the camps were in operation, particularly in the early months, many refugees required emergency medical care, which produced significant quantities of medical waste. Several organisations working in the medical sector disposed of this waste by simply dumping it in the Park. Used syringes, human waste and materials containing human blood were found (Biswas et al., 1994). By the second year, these dumping practices had largely ceased.

Security
In Zairian territory, security deteriorated significantly due to the presence of tens of thousands of former Rwandan army soldiers. These soldiers brought modern weapons with them, greatly reducing the effectiveness of the IZCN ranger patrols. Armed groups of former soldiers sometimes confronted and threatened IZCN field agents. The IZCN completely lost control of two areas in the southern PNVi: one near the Mugunga–Lac Vert camps in the Nyamulagira sector, the other in the heart of the Mikeno sector (between the Mikeno, Karisimbi and Visoke volcanoes).

General disorder
The deterioration of security in the region exacerbated illegal 'opportunistic' activities in which local populations sometimes engaged. Previously mentioned examples are the intensification of poaching and charcoal production (Werikhe et al., 1997).

Decline in tourism revenue
Tourism was severely impacted throughout the crisis, though the gorilla tours never ceased. At Djomba, an excellent access point for tourists to the Park, some visitors continued to observe gorillas.

Shortage of natural resources for local populations
The deforestation during the refugee crisis occurred mainly within the Park (Werikhe et al., 1997) but tree plantations outside the Park were also gravely damaged. In a region where firewood was already scarce before the crisis, the arrival of refugee camps worsened the situation and threatened the local populations' long-term energy needs.

5. Mitigation measures and conservation strategies

Mitigation measures were undertaken by various humanitarian, development and conservation agencies to halt the dramatic environmental degradation recorded during the refugee crisis.

Wood supply
Wood supply operations (Henquin & Blondel, 1997) were primarily funded by the UN Refugee Agency (UNHCR), in collaboration with several implementing agencies (including the *Deutsche Gesellschaft für Technische Zusammenarbeit* – German Development Cooperation, or GTZ). The quantities of wood provided to refugees in the camps tripled between July 1994 and July 1996. On average, 50% of the camps' energy requirements during the second year were met. Available data suggests that, during this period, environmental programmes implemented by various partners, including a WWF project to plant three million trees, saved at least 4,000 hectares of forest over two years. Without these interventions in support of the Park, deforestation would have been 1.65 times greater than observed (Blondel, 1997).

5.6 Throughout the wars and the occupations, organising surveillance patrols proved very complicated.

Coordination meetings

From the onset of the crisis, the GTZ set up a collaboration with the Technical Unit of the UNHCR to create a pilot environmental unit (the Environmental Information Office) in Goma, capable of collecting and disseminating information on the environment (Delvingt, 1994). In early 1995, the UNHCR established a new official structure by creating a position for an environmental affairs coordinator (Leusch, 1995).

Improved stoves and energy-saving techniques

Several agencies, including the GTZ and the International Federation of Red Cross and Red Crescent Societies (IFRC), promoted improved stoves and energy-saving practices in some refugee camps (Delvingt, 1996). Aware that using improved technologies would not automatically reduce energy consumption, the GTZ also disseminated other energy-saving techniques. GTZ staff taught the local populations how to dry and store wood, as well as efficient food preparation and cooking methods.

Educational and awareness measures

Education campaigns targeting refugees in camps surrounding the South Sector were conducted with the assistance of numerous international and local NGOs.

Protection and surveillance measures

The IZCN, the organisation responsible for managing the Park, had been relatively weakened before the crisis. Initiatives such as strengthening IZCN operations in the South Sector enhanced the institute's visibility, especially its capacity to enforce laws and carry out general surveillance. The Zairian Presidential Special Division (DSP) provided several hundred soldiers. The cost of surveillance operations, including employee bonuses, means of communication and transportation and operating expenses, was covered by the UNHCR.

Rehabilitation phase

When the Rwandan refugee camps were closed in November 1996, various agencies launched rehabilitation programmes. The UNHCR undertook an ambitious plan for

5.7   During the wars from 1996 to 2003, the rangers were sometimes disarmed by the armed groups controlling the PNVi. Negotiations initiated by UNESCO and a coalition of NGOs resulted in the organisation of joint surveillance patrols.

the North Kivu province in several sectors, including the environmental sector. Many local organisations assisted the UNHCR in implementing its programme, notably reforestation operations and the creation of nurseries. The UNHCR also contacted two conservation projects and long-term IZCN partners: the Virunga Education Program and the International Gorilla Conservation Programme (IGCP). They jointly planned and implemented rehabilitation activities until October 1997, when the new political authorities forced the UNHCR to stop all operations in the Goma region. The large-scale rehabilitation programme was not completed. Projects to rehabilitate numerous hospitals, roads and markets had to be abandoned practically overnight. Despite these difficult circumstances, the IZCN (which had since become the ICCN) and the IGCP (funded by a trio of NGOs: AWF, FFI and WWF) managed to find alternative funding and continue their activities.

Furthermore, the Virunga Education Program, a WWF project, received funds from the UNHCR to intensify its reforestation activities around the South Sector and continue its education and awareness activities for local populations. Thanks to this support, the WWF project was able, through various partnership mechanisms, to produce and plant nearly one million trees in 1996 alone.

The International Gorilla Conservation Programme, meanwhile, focused its rehabilitation efforts on the Park and notably on restoring the management capacity of the ICCN. This project had several components (Kalpers, 1998) and was aimed primarily at monitoring and strengthening institutional capacities (Kalpers & Lanjouw, 1998).

6. Civil wars in Congo-Zaire (1996–2003) and uncontrolled groups (2004–2006)

Following the end of the Rwandan refugee crisis in October 1996, Congo-Zaire experienced a period of civil wars that directly impacted the PNVi. The 'first liberation war' culminated in the capture of Kinshasa by the Alliance of Democratic Forces for the Liberation of Congo (AFDL) in May 1997. After a period of calm, a second war broke out in August 1998 that continued until November 2003 and particularly affected the North and South Kivu regions and Ituri. The ICCN staff suffered greatly from these wars. Many agents were killed or injured by armed groups on all sides (Mushenzi, 1996). In the South Sector, the infrastructure (Rumangabo station and patrol posts in the Mikeno sector) was heavily damaged (Werikhe et al., 1997), either by local populations seeking building materials, or by armed bands freely roaming the region, causing systematic destruction. Several gorillas were killed by armed groups or poachers (Cooper & Cooper, 1996). Considering the severity of the crises in this region, it is almost a miracle that not more gorillas were lost during this period. The animals may owe their survival to the fact that local populations generally do not eat gorilla meat and that their economic value for tourism is often recognised. Various military forces in the region – rebels, government troops, and allied forces from other countries – practised illegal activities such as wood cutting and poaching. In the Mikeno sector, military units, together with several thousands of refugees, engaged in agriculture, cultivating exotic plants like potatoes, tobacco, wheat and hemp (Rutagarama, 1999).

Some of the deforestation was perpetrated for strategic purposes. The ecological corridor of Mwaro, connecting the Mikeno and Nyamulagira sectors, suffered the most severe impact. Several animal populations, including elephants, used to migrate from the extinct volcanoes to the rest of PNVi through this corridor. To limit the risk of ambushes, the military forces controlling the region cleared the sides of the Goma–Rutshuru road, thereby altering the landscape. The cleared area had initially been 20 metres wide, but the road was swiftly widened (up to 50–70 metres in some places) by local populations, sometimes with the support of military officers. This had detrimental consequences, as this ecological link was crucial for elephant populations and other animals using it for seasonal movements. Armed rebel groups freely used certain forest areas, particularly around the Mikeno volcano and patrol posts in Gatovu, Kibumba, Bukima and Bikenge. The weakening of the ICCN was another consequence of this near anarchic state. The drastic decline in revenue from tourism, as well as military control over the Park,

5.8 The infrastructure was severely affected as it was repeatedly looted and sometimes destroyed. Large quantities of equipment and documents were lost. Here, buildings in Rwindi after years of occupation by the military.

A CENTURY OF HISTORY

5.9 Poaching is mainly carried out by armed groups, rebels from various factions or, as in this case, the regular army, when, in May 2005, elements of the FARDC shot five elephants in the Rutshuru hunting reserve.

5.10 The temporary loss of control over the Park has resulted in a worrying increase in the resident population at some sites. Here, an aerial view of Vitshumbi at the beginning of the 2000s.

significantly contributed to the weakening of its official mandate and operational capacities.

In the North Sector, an already precarious situation worsened significantly with the arrival of the AFDL in February 1997. All ICCN staff were disarmed, ambushes and lootings occurred regularly, and a rebel army training centre was established in Nyaleke. In January 1999, a car park was cleared for vehicles crossing the international border between the DRC and Uganda, which had a severe impact on the Lubilya site, as did the clearing for cultivation in many parts of the Park. From December 2000, the North Sector faced constant threats to its integrity. Its boundaries were violated by the population in many places (Kyavinyonge, Kanyatsi, Bulongo, Balombi, Lume, Mayangose, Mavivi, Lubilya, Kasindi and Tshiaberimu). Hima herders settled in the Karuruma River area with several thousand cattle, and various poaching gangs remained active throughout the sector. The problems with invasions were resolved only in April 2006.

Mitigation measures and conservation strategies

In April 1999, representatives of many organisations working in conservation gathered in Naivasha, Kenya, for a seminar on World Heritage Sites in Danger in the DRC. Participants included governmental organisations, such as the ICCN; NGOs like WWF, WCS (Wildlife Conservation Society), GIC (Gilman International Conservation Foundation), IRF (International Rhino Foundation); and development sector groups including UNESCO and the GTZ. This seminar enabled participants to define precise conservation strategies and develop a common action plan (ICCN, 1999). It also helped to gain the international community's attention and formulate an emergency funding proposal, which was sent to the United Nations Foundation by UNESCO (UNESCO, 1999). This proposal was accepted in November 1999, but the project only officially started in June 2001. Named UNF/UNESCO/DRC, this project provided essential logistical and institutional support to the five World Heritage Sites in Danger in the DRC, including the PNVi.

The goal was to mobilise financial and diplomatic support and draw international attention to these five sites, whether for their protection or to allow scientists to study the environmental consequences of armed conflicts. The funding for the first phase amounted to more than 4 million dollars, with approximately 2.9 million dollars provided by the United Nations Foundation (Bishikwabo, 2000). The second phase received 5.6 million dollars of funding over four years. This project enabled all ICCN partners to join

5.11 Fishing on Lake Edward was anarchic. Here, fry have been caught in spawning grounds using mosquito netting.

issue is the tension between the conservation sector and emergency aid organisations. Humanitarian agencies, such as the UNHCR, ICRC, Oxfam and MSF, are increasingly willing to incorporate environmental components into their intervention programmes. Sharing common goals, however, does not necessarily equal collaboration on the ground, as is particularly evident during acute crises.

In the early stages of the refugee crisis in Zaire, the lack of coordination between the various environmental protection organisations was obvious (Languy, 1995). Collaboration was gradually organised around a common partner, the ICCN. Regular meetings ensured that the different actors involved in the environmental sector could discuss strategies and coordinate their actions to improve efficiency. Additionally, the UNHCR established an environmental coordination unit, which helped to limit damage on the ground. The European Union set up a similar structure for the period of the refugee camps. During the rehabilitation phase in eastern DRC, the UNHCR ensured collaboration with various organisations by drawing up contractual agreements. These partners were chosen based on their technical expertise and credibility. The IGCP and the Virunga Education Program (WWF-PEVi) implemented rehabilitation programmes financed and coordinated by the UNHCR.

In a crisis, it is important to not only coordinate activities on the ground but also exchange information and knowledge. These exchanges, whether through training seminars, conferences or more informal contacts, are crucial because they allow different sectors to present their methods, requirements and respective mandates.

Transboundary collaboration and emergency situations

The PNVi is part of a vast transboundary block comprising nearly a dozen contiguous protected areas, a characteristic that has played, and continues to play, a major role in efforts to protect the region. Maps and satellite photos clearly show the insular nature of protected areas in the Great Lakes region, particularly in the Virunga volcano area, where forests are the only natural habitats, entirely isolated in an essentially agricultural human landscape. The Virunga forests are the only areas where vegetation cover allows armed groups to move freely without attracting attention. The fact that it is also a transboundary habitat significantly increases its strategic value for military forces. All these regional characteristics explain why the Virunga massif attracts military forces operating in the region.

This transboundary nature has also played a buffering role. During periods of intense fighting, for example, animal populations, such as elephants or gorillas, could migrate to safer areas. As the combat zones shifted, conservation pro-

forces in a dynamic collaboration, by managing parts of the allocated funds, coordinating technical interventions or mobilising additional funds for specific sites.

7. Looking back on 15 years of armed conflict

Security concerns

The greatest threat was undoubtedly the particularly high level of insecurity observed in and around the PNVi. This insecurity prevented the ICCN from exercising control over the entire Park during various crises. Efforts to mitigate the environmental impact of refugee camps, for example, were hampered significantly.

Mechanisms for intersectoral collaboration

Under normal circumstances, it is relatively easy to initiate collaborations between the development sector and conservation organisations. In the Great Lakes region, several projects quickly implemented these basic principles. However, these initiatives were taken almost exclusively in stable situations, without armed conflicts or emergencies. Collaboration between emergency aid organisations and the development sector has traditionally been good. The main

5.12 The need for agricultural land compels the local population to clear wooded areas to create new fields. Only a few remnants of submontane forest remain in the valley bottoms.

jects like the International Gorilla Conservation Programme could focus their activities in the less secure areas of Virunga. Cross-border collaboration between agencies managing protected areas in the three countries dates back to the early 1980s. Chapter 13 of this book examines these transboundary aspects in detail.

8. Conclusion

Throughout the crises that shook the Great Lakes region from 1992 to 2005, the international community often missed opportunities to play a positive role in resolving problems. When crisis struck, the United Nations conservation agencies mobilised too slowly – if at all.

Neither the United Nations Environment Programme (UNEP) nor UNESCO seemed to act on recommendations made to them, specifically during the refugee crisis in Zaire (Biswas et al., 1994). It was not until after a decade-long crisis, in June 2001, that UNESCO developed a project providing much-needed support to the ICCN, in collaboration with all active partners in eastern DRC, as well as high-level political and diplomatic support. Another issue was the vulnerability of conservation projects funded by official donors. As a political or military situation looks unfavourable, donors suspend or halt interventions. This happened in Zaire in 1991–1992 when the European Union and USAID each cancelled a major project in and around the PNVi. By contrast, we should highlight the role played by conservation NGOs active in the region. Unlike official donors, these NGOs have few or no political constraints. They can fully dedicate themselves to their mandate and have the flexibility to adapt to current conditions and redirect their actions if necessary.

Despite sometimes limited financial resources, conservation NGOs can have a very positive impact, by providing material and financial support, albeit minimal, to the agency responsible for protected areas, as well as technical and even moral support to field agents sometimes disoriented by the events. Finally, conservation NGOs have an important role to play in communication. By serving as a relay for their partners on the ground, they can convey appropriate messages to the international community, identify and solicit funding sources, coordinate sometimes disorganised actions, and pressure Western governments and international institutions.

Unsurprisingly, the weaker the institution responsible for protected areas, the more difficult or non-existent coordination between partners from different sectors becomes (Languy, 1995). Institutions that were strong before a crisis are more apt to manage a crisis. Efficient collaboration with military personnel is also very useful in emergency conditions. In cases of armed conflict, classic consequences include the sudden takeover of protected areas by the military, isolation of conservation agents, by denying them access to the protected area or confiscating their weapons, and exploitation of resources by some military personnel. In this context, it may be in the interest of protected area managers to develop close contacts with military officers in the region. These can enable them to explain the reasons for their actions, the role of conservation agencies and their political neutrality, but also help to develop codes of conduct for the military, convincing them that field personnel, thanks to their extensive knowledge of the area, represent a valuable asset.

6.1 Nine mountain gorillas were killed between June and September 2007. The massacre prompted a thorough review of the PNVi strategy. No gorillas have been killed since.

6

The new challenges (2005–2025)

EMMANUEL DE MERODE, FRANÇOIS-XAVIER DE DONNEA, RODRIGUE MUGARUKA

The last decades have been marked by chronic insecurity and conflict-related upheavals. Despite difficult circumstances, the partnership between the ICCN and the Virunga Foundation opened a new era in the management of the Park. The new institutional set-up made it possible to rebuild the institution, strengthen the ecosystems and initiate a vast economic development programme.

1. A new start shattered by the gorilla killings (2005–2007)

The opening years of the 21st century were a period of overwhelming weakness in the conservation community's capacity to preserve Virunga National Park (*Parc National des Virunga* – PNVi). The Congolese Institute for Nature Conservation (*Institut Congolais pour la Conservation de la Nature* – ICCN) was crippled by political divisions defined by the succession of rebellions, and international NGOs were competing for access to the Park's most valuable assets, in particular the mountain gorillas. Vast areas of the PNVi, such as the centre and north, were effectively abandoned by all except the ICCN's under-resourced staff. Wildlife numbers in all areas, with the remarkable exception of the mountain gorillas, plummeted during this period.

Several important developments in the mid-2000s positively affected how the Park was managed. The UNESCO/United Nations Foundation programme instilled a level of coordination among partners that started to take effect by 2005. From 2003 to 2006, the creation of a government of national unity allowed the reunification of all government administrations, including the ICCN. This put an end to the challenge of managing the Park under two separate administrations separated by the lake, with the RCD–Goma in the south and the RCD–K/ML and MLC in the north. Within the Park, a further strengthening of a unified, coherent management was made possible with the coordination committee among partners under the leadership of the ICCN, which, though somewhat unwieldy in its decision-making abilities,

6.2 The investigation on the killing of gorillas revealed that the goal was to facilitate the production of charcoal. The Park rangers responsible for their protection prevented free access to the forest.

A CENTURY OF HISTORY

allowed for significant improvements in the support given to the ICCN and enables the institution to operate during crisis times. This also began to be felt on the ground with radio communication systems implemented, an aircraft deployed and regular salary supplements and rations offered to ICCN staff. Consequently, the PNVi once again began to be managed as a single entity, after 10 years of deep division at almost every level.

These positive improvements were curtailed in 2007 by a huge blow to the ICCN's core mission of protecting the Park's most valuable resources. A succession of violent attacks on the mountain gorilla population unfolded between June and September 2007. These saw the unprecedented killings of nine gorillas, some of whom were eaten, but the majority were left untouched, often with baby gorillas alive in the vicinity. This drew extensive global media attention, especially following the publication of the photos by Getty photographer Brent Stirton, which produced cover editions of *Newsweek* and *National Geographic*. There followed a very intense reappraisal of the PNVi's management led by the Director General of the ICCN, coupled with a legal enquiry into the causes of the gorilla killings. The investigation will reveal that the gorillas were killed to facilitate charcoal exploitation as the rangers responsible for their protection prevented free access to the forest. The process provoked the suspension of the PNVi Director, and the nomination of a new management team within what was to become the public–private partnership between the ICCN and the Virunga Foundation.

2. CNDP occupation (2008–2009)

2.1. Destruction and exile from Rumangabo

The new management team became operational in August 2008 and was almost immediately confronted with a second major crisis: the emergence of the National Congress for the Defence of the People (CNDP) rebellion. By mid-September, a nascent CNDP militia, under the mutineer general Laurent Nkunda, launched an offensive across Rutshuru, which culminated in a large-scale bombardment of the headquarters at Rumangabo. Staff and their families, who had never experienced violence on this scale, immediately fled with little or none of their possessions. As the Rumangabo headquarters were looted, they dispersed through the forests and lava fields, embarking on a long, painful journey on foot to Goma. The presence of hostile militia and the absence of food and water exerted a terrible toll on them. Six of PNVi's staff lost their lives during this journey.

The weeks that followed were chaotic and painful but created a cohesion and a team spirit within the personnel that would last for years. For weeks, staff members would travel every morning to Rusayo, on the northern outskirts of the Park, and penetrate the forest in an effort to recover their colleagues and families on the final stages of the 50 km foot journey. By late October, the trickle of exhausted and dehydrated rangers appearing in Rusayo stopped altogether. However, in Goma, an unexpected component of humanitarian law created an additional challenge: because the PNVi rangers were part of the State security

6.3 The conflicts in Kivu are marked by periods of fighting and lulls. Here, an exchange of fire during the first M23 war in 2013.

6.4   The Armed Forces of the DRC (FARDC) have a key role within the PNVi territory and in the periphery.

6.5   The United Nations deployed a peacekeeping operation in eastern Congo in 2000 (MONUC initially, MONUSCO later on).

agencies, they were refused access to the internally displaced people's (IDP) camps overseen by the UN. A local member of parliament lent a hectare of land at Kisutu, and a fundraising campaign was launched to buy the tarpaulins and mattresses to settle the 900 PNVi-related refugees into a makeshift camp. For two months, the management learned the skills of managing an IDP camp, fighting off malnutrition, a cholera epidemic and appalling living conditions. An elderly man and a young girl died during this tumult, while four births were registered. Through it all, an extraordinary morale was maintained under unfathomably difficult living conditions.

2.2. Work of the ICCN during the conflicts

Within a few days of the exodus to Goma, the CNDP announced that all State administrations had been driven out of Rutshuru, and the rebellion would appoint an independent civilian administration. This was deeply problematic for the Park's senior management, as a significant proportion of the staff was blocked in Goma, and the prospects of a new CNDP administration overseeing the PNVi. This perilous situation placed the institution on the verge of bankruptcy.

This impossible situation led the Park Director to travel to Kinshasa to seek a meeting with the then Minister of the Environment, Jose Endundo. Several hours were spent examining the multiple risks and opportunities of trying to negotiate a return of the ICCN personnel into the rebel-controlled territory. Issues relating to political risk, national and international law, and to the security staff on the ground, were explored in great detail. Ultimately, the Minister assigned the highest level of importance to the country's international commitments, in particular the World Heritage Convention that requires all parties to protect the PNVi's exceptional resources beyond the political priorities of the moment, and emphasised that both parties to the conflict had to adhere to this commitment. Following that decision, the PNVi's Director was cleared by the office of the Head of State to enter into negotiations with the CNDP to secure their adherence to the same guiding principles. Discussions were held at a local level and messages were sent to the CNDP leadership through intermediaries. Within days, feedback was received that the CNDP leader, General Nkunda, was willing to meet.

On the morning of 2nd November, a small team of rangers crossed the Congolese army's frontline up to the CNDP positions. After a brief check, the vehicle was permitted to drive to Rumangabo. There followed a series of meetings with CNDP political officers, and on the 9 November, the team were cleared to meet with General Nkunda. The meeting lasted about an hour, and General Nkunda agreed to the terms that all ICCN staff could return and resume their work unhindered. The ICCN team returned to Goma and consulted with the Governor of North Kivu Province, who confirmed the Government's position on redeploying Park rangers into the rebel-controlled territories. Within days, a little over 200 rangers loaded their few possessions onto a convoy of flatbed lorries, and, after an hour of checks, crossed into the rebel-controlled district of Rutshuru. In Rumangabo, they were greeted by thousands of local community members in what became one of the most powerful moments in the PNVi's recent history.

Significant challenges still lay ahead. The Mikeno sector had been under CNDP occupation for over 15 months, and the status of the mountain gorillas was a mystery. Securing access was the highest of priorities, but obtaining clearance

6.6 The conflicts are violent. Here, the abandoned police station in Vitshumbi and drawings of soldiers on the wall of the ruined Rwindi lodge.

to enter the area proved challenging as it contained the CNDP's most important supply lines with Rwanda and Uganda. After a few weeks, a small team of officers was allowed to leave by foot as the roads had become impracticable. They managed to conduct a preliminary inspection and returned to Rumangabo, after getting lost within rebel-held territory, arriving exhausted in the early hours of the morning. This first exploration was followed by a sequence of trips into the gorilla sector, the establishment of a camp at Bukima, and a census of the habituated groups that yielded the extraordinarily encouraging news that these populations, instead of a much-feared decline in numbers, had shown a remarkable increase of 8%.

For two months, the Park's rangers maintained their politically sensitive position in Rutshuru. Regular contact was maintained with the Director General and with the Minister of the Environment to seek guidance on the sensitive issues. Several diplomatic missions, including the European Union, the Belgians and the UN, used the Rumangabo headquarters during that period, which were a safe haven from which to manage the multiple negotiations that were taking place.

On 23 January 2009, an extraordinary series of events unfolded. General Nkunda was summoned to Gisenyi by the Rwandan authorities and was promptly arrested. A procession of several hundred Rwandan troops walked past Rumangabo on 25 January and met with their Congolese military counterparts. This signalled the beginning of the Amani process, aimed at pacifying the eastern provinces of the DRC, focusing specifically on the Democratic Forces for the Liberation of Rwanda (FDLR) units in North Kivu. The international community, and in particular the UN, having been sidelined in the negotiations, were taken completely by surprise. So too were several Congolese politicians who protested the presence of Rwandan troops in Congo.

These events led to the CNDP troops being rounded up into reintegration camps or 'camps de brassage', with a view to integrating them into the Congolese army. Several CNDP commanders were given senior officer ranks in the Congolese armed forces, the most notable being Bosco Ntaganda, a notorious leader who had been indicted by the UN for war crimes in the Ituri Province in 2003. This policy of Disarmament, Demobilization and Reintegration (DDR) added additional complexity to the situation to be dealt with by the ICCN.

3. Internal reforms (2009–2012)

3.1. Addressing the root causes of poverty and violence

The period of uneasy peace opened the doors for a transformative reappraisal of the PNVi's strategy, especially with respect to its collaboration with community institutions, and the process of creating economic value for the local populations. From this was born the Virunga Alliance, which sought to boost three sectors of the economy – tourism, energy and agriculture – and transform them into an instrument for the reduction of poverty and violence (see chapter 17 for additional details). The European Union expressed a strong interest in supporting this approach, with the goals of protecting biodiversity and making the Park a vector for peace and development.

Tourism was relaunched a few months after the end of the war. A flow of tourists from Uganda and Rwanda began to arrive almost immediately and signalled an instant boost for the Park's reputation as a viable economic actor. In 2010, the infrastructure department began working on a high-end lodge in Rumangabo. In 2011, a major breakthrough was achieved under the auspices of the Ministers of the Environment and Interior, with the inter-ministerial decree for the establishment of a tourism visa that could be administered at the level of the PNVi. This cleared the way for a dramatic increase in the number of visitors in 2012.

As regards energy provision, significant efforts were made to find alternatives to charcoal, with the somewhat unsuccessful effort to launch briquettes, which were not well received by local consumers. In contrast, new funding from the European Union was secured to build a first hydroelectric plant, which came online in 2013, generating 380 kilowatts off a river in Mutwanga. It provided the basis for the development of the PNVi's first joint venture with local actors and international partners into relaunching agro-industry: the construction of the Sicovir soap factory, for the local market, which drew its energy from the Park's rivers.

The experience in Mutwanga yielded evidence of the link between local development and the reduction of armed conflicts: a megawatt of electricity, once delivered to the community, would create between 800 and 1,000 jobs, and many were taken by young men from the militias. The impact of electrification in Mutwanga provided the basis for a broad two-year analysis of the entire Park's watershed. It was established that six sites from rivers flowing from the Park's ecosystems could generate a total of 105 megawatts. This energy had the potential to create up to 100,000 jobs in the surrounding communities, driving a new green industry capable of industrialising the agricultural sector and, through that, having a GDP impact that could overcome the enormous opportunity cost of the PNVi on the local economy. The drive towards large-scale development sought to compete with the armed groups on the labour market, by providing better paid, safe and dignified employment to a young Congolese generation. It also sought to create new value chains for natural resources that were free of violence, where previously they were part of illegal trafficking networks. With the Virunga Alliance, the invisible hand of the market was making its entry into the PNVi landscape.

3.2. Rebuilding a strong and legitimate institution

There are obvious conceptual contradictions to offering a classical liberal economic model as a solution to the problems caused by an illegal militia-led economy. Indeed, the very absence of regulation, rule of law and State authority could correctly be perceived as a primary reason for the dominance of coercive non-State actors. Arguably, the non-State actors were also, to some extent, a cover for State officials acting in a private capacity. There is little doubt that the success of the Virunga Alliance would rely on a careful balance between the opportunities offered by the sustainable and legal development of natural resources for economic value and the constraints of a legitimate State regulating authority. With respect to the PNVi's resources, the legitimate institution was, of course, the ICCN. However, in 2009, with over 1,000 demoralised and underpaid rangers, it was in no fit state to fulfil that role.

A full reform process involved a vast array of programmes, including training, human resources restructuring, strategic reappraisals and the redefinition of the institution's culture and ethics, alongside overhauling equipment, infrastructure and management systems. This was an overwhelming prospect if only for the PNVi alone, but it could not succeed without the support of the ICCN leadership in Kinshasa, which also needed effective support for its own reform process.

6.7 230 Park rangers have died violent deaths in the last 20 years.

Once again, the European Union committed to providing both the funding and the technical support for the process. A team was established in Kinshasa to work with the ICCN's headquarters, and to support the process on-site in Rumangabo. The rigour of the reform process, which lasted for three years, brought several measures that lifted the dignity and the living conditions of the rangers. Among many results, the programme delivered a retirement support for ageing staff (from over 1,000 rangers to 230), the recruitment of a younger generation of rangers, disciplinary and performance-based appraisal systems, stable wage conditions and critical security support instruments. The programme represented the first phase of an ongoing performance-oriented and improvement effort that continues today (see chapter 15 for additional details).

4. New low-intensity conflicts (2009–2014)

4.1. Rise of political pressures

The incredible optimism of the post-CNDP war period heralded extraordinary developments. It contributed to establishing the PNVi as a pioneer in developing innovative conservation approaches in Africa. Unfortunately, those early years also saw rampant insecurity deepen its roots in North Kivu. The Park rangers increasingly became the target of violent attacks by militias on an unprecedented scale. In 2011, six rangers were killed in a single ambush near Rwindi. This incident was sadly the first in a long series that anxiously accompanied the daily work of the teams on the ground.

This period also marked the beginning of significant political pressures on the PNVi, with a combination of powerful interests with links to armed groups and illegal activities seeking to destabilise and exploit the Park's resources, and increasingly vocal campaigns and a torrent of misinformation targeting the PNVi for political ends. As an example, in 2011, one local politician in particular delivered a succession of inflammatory speeches as part of his electoral campaign. One notorious event took place during a public rally in Kyavinyonge, during which he called on the population to

6.8   The partnership between the ICCN and Virunga Foundation is the cornerstone of the Park's new management model. From left to right: Atamato Madrandele (ICCN Warden), François-Xavier de Donnea (co-founder of the Virunga Foundation), Emmanuel de Merode (Director) and Norbert Mushenzi (Deputy Director) in Mutsora in 2009.

6.9   The ICCN has demonstrated great institutional creativity in pursuing its mission despite the State's shortcomings. From left to right: Atamato Madrandele (ICCN Warden), Cosma Wilungula (ICCN Director General), Emmanuel de Merode (Director), in Ishango in 2008.

6.10   The reconstruction of the PNVi required the recruitment of a new generation of motivated, efficient and honest rangers. Here, a parade at the end of training in 2008 at the Ishango training centre.

6.11 In 2014, an elephant found refuge at the ICCN patrol post in Mabenga (Centre Sector) after poachers had slaughtered two members of its herd.

attack any rangers. The same evening, a small nearby patrol post was attacked, a ranger was killed and another was seriously injured. The PNVi management pressed charges against the Member of Parliament, but these were unsuccessful because of parliamentary immunity. A dispute with this politician remains to this day.

6.12   Illegal landing of a SOCO oil company helicopter in a Lake Edward fishery in 2012.

4.2. Threat of oil exploitation

In 2009, a concession agreement for Bloc 5, which covered the heart of the PNVi, was assigned by the Ministry of Hydrocarbons to SOCO, a UK-listed oil company. There had been no prior consultation with the Ministry of the Environment or with the ICCN over the legal incompatibility of the PNVi's status with that of an oil concession. In fact, the World Heritage status compounded this incompatibility: under the DRC constitution, an international law that has been ratified by Parliament has precedence over any other law, including a concession signed by a Minister. Facing a dilemma, the PNVi's senior management opposed the plans based on the certainty of this legal position, which triggered five years of intense confrontation between the institution and the oil company.

The PNVi's response was depicted in a documentary filmed between 2009 and 2014. The film investigated SOCO's activities in relation to suspected acts of human rights violations and corruption. The material became so compelling that it eventually won an Oscar nomination and captured the world's imagination. The two years that followed the launch of the film in April 2014 saw an intensification of the campaign: local civil society groups became more engaged, UNESCO and legal advocacy groups mobilised in defence of a World Heritage Site, and international media converged on the issue. SOCO, with their annual general meetings in London drawing unwelcome attention, faced growing criticism from some of its institutional investors, such as Investec, which chose to divest their funds and support a campaign in defence of the Park. Others, such as

6.13   Three national reserves are attached to the PNVi: Sarambwe, Lac Vert (picture) and Mont Hoyo. In the past, the PNVi also supervised some provincial reserves that have now fallen into disuse (picture: Mount Goma on the shores of Lake Kivu).

the Church of England, maintained their investments, choosing to use their stake to voice their protest against SOCO's actions. On the ground, the confrontation became violent: three fishermen who had objected to SOCO activities were found floating in the lake (the third survived and volunteered the evidence), the PNVi's Deputy Director was illegally detained and tortured for 17 days, and the Director was attacked by unknown assailants after delivering compelling evidence to the State prosecutor in Goma (he sustained severe gunshot injuries but was rescued by two young farmers). The breaking point came when a local activist was able to obtain irrefutable evidence of bank transactions between SOCO and a senior Congolese army officer identified in Human Rights Watch's report on the assassination attempt on the Director. These events and the media outcry ultimately lead to the withdrawal of SOCO from the PNVi in 2015, leaving a sad feeling of victory as the struggle was intense and brutal.

Memories of an encounter: the Park and its people

EMMANUEL DE MERODE

The PNVi's unique and extraordinary story is built on the shoulders of generations of deeply committed civil servants who grew attached to its wildlife and people, to the point of knowingly risking everything, and in so many cases, losing their lives.

For my part, I arrived at the Park in the latter stages of this century-long story. My work with the ICCN rangers began in the early 1990s in Garamba, an extraordinary savannah park on the border with South Sudan. From there, I watched from a distance the collapse of Mobutu's regime, and the upheaval in the Kivus, as it descended into a terrible battlefield. The information that filtered back to Garamba was of the efforts of the PNVi's rangers in the midst of the civil war, and the sheer number of deaths to keep their struggle alive.

The intense appeal of an impossible challenge drew me to this unique place, and I arrived at the PNVi in 2001, on a motorbike purchased in Kampala. I was met in Beni by an old friend from Garamba, Atama Madrandele. Together, we met with the North Sector warden, Norbert Mushenzi, and the three of us took stock of the perilous state of the rangers force. Uniforms and basic equipment were long gone, and rangers were receiving less than 5 dollars a month in remuneration. Within six months, a number of donors stepped in. The UN Foundation, with UNESCO, provided basic pay and a political framework to manage the PNVi while under rebel control. Soon, the Zoological Society of London offered an institutional platform, the European Union reinitiated its long-term support to the PNVi, and the Darwin Initiative and US Fish and Wildlife Service mobilised emergency support.

Atama and I undertook a training in Kruger Park with South African military trainers, then returned to set up a training centre in Ishango. Robert Muir, with the Frankfurt Zoological Society, joined this effort in 2004, and began placing the building blocks for an effective, motivated team of rangers. It was at that time that the European Union asked me to advise on the relaunching of their development support programmes in eastern Congo. To assist with that work, I was joined by Ephrem Balole, who grew to become the key figure in developing the Virunga Alliance over the next twenty years. Another consistent support was Filippo Saracco, at the European Union, who provided critical advice to navigate an increasingly complex political and institutional environment. The PNVi's new Deputy Director, Innocent Mburanumwe, also had a key role in assisting me with leading the ICCN rangers.

A constant frustration was our inability to structure the institutional support to the PNVi. Donors were struggling with financial procedures that were near impossible to implement effectively in a remote, conflict-affected environment, coupled with the reluctance of large conservation organisations to place the needs of the rangers on the ground as the highest priority. In response, we established a not-for-profit structure, WildlifeDirect, designed to provide direct and tangible support to field rangers. Francois de Donnea and Jan Bonde Nielsen were instrumental in creating this new organisation, later renamed the Virunga Foundation.

In 2007, the gorilla massacres in the Mikeno sector highlighted the failure of classical nature protection policies, calling for a new approach. A debate on how to rescue the PNVi became the subject of intense discussions between Eulalie Bashige, the then ICCN Director General, her successor Cosma Wilungula, Francois de Donnea and myself.

The idea of a public–private partnership that could deliver a critical mass of support, not just to rebuild and manage the Park, but also to support the needs and aspirations of local communities, became the centre of discussions. In 2008, the partnership with the ICCN was completed and, soon after, the Virunga Alliance would come to life.

5. First M23 conflict (2012–2013)

Alongside the tensions provoked by the oil company, a new conflict started with the first rebellion of the March 23 Movement (M23). In April 2012, a mutiny took place at the small army camp at Kiseguru in Northern Rutshuru. The rebels made their way south of the Mikeno sector. As they approached the Rwandan border, it became increasingly clear that they were the residual units of the earlier CNDP rebellion that ended in 2009. For several months, they vacillated between the Mikeno sector and Masisi, using the Park's forests for cover. They settled eventually in the high-altitude saddle known as Kabara, between the Mikeno and Karisimbi volcanoes. In the months that followed, a succession of violent confrontations gave them control of the entire region.

The M23 offensive culminated in the seizing of Goma on 20th November 2023. Most of the international humanitarian community withdrew, including many of the UN agencies, leaving the city population in a state of extreme vulnerability. The most acute threat, beyond the risks caused by the fighting, was that the high-voltage powerlines from the Ruzizi power plant in South Kivu were destroyed during the fighting, which left the city without power. This meant that the pumping stations supplying water to over a million people could no longer function due to lack of electricity. If water wasn't restored within a few days, massive cholera outbreaks were likely. The PNVi's infrastructure team, being one of the only development actors remaining in the city, started a race against the clock to bring a megawatt of power to the pumping stations. They were helped by the Howard G. Buffett Foundation, which proved to be a uniquely effective actor for unusual responses to major crises. In less than 36 hours, the team was able to design the plans, to install the generators and to get the water flowing. This approach marked the beginning of the strong partnership between the PNVi, the Howard G. Buffett Foundation, the European Union and the Schmidt Family Foundation.

In May 2013, the M23 rebellion ended almost as quickly as it began. M23 forces were driven back into the Mikeno sector and took refuge in Rwanda and then Uganda. As in 2009, the PNVi management took stock of the losses suffered during the war and revised its plan for post-conflict development. Drawing on lessons from the past, an ambitious agenda took shape. A name was chosen – the Virunga Alliance – to reaffirm the inseparable link with the natural resources of the PNVi. Its launch was formalised during a forum – the first in a long series – with provincial authorities, security forces, representatives of civil society, environmental and human rights associations, and the private sector. The objective was twofold: protecting the Park and fostering peace through large-scale job creation, and bringing young men and women away from the armed groups that caused so much damage to Congolese society. Practically, the new vision would focus on relaunching tourism, producing energy and developing agricultural transformation.

6.14 Two champions of the PNVi revival after the conflict years: Innocent Mburanumwe, Deputy Director of the Park, and Ephrem Balole Bwami Lubala, driving force behind the Virunga Alliance and Director of Virunga Energies.

6. Relaunch during the calmer years (2014–2018)

In the years that followed the end of the first M23 conflict, six lodges were built and tourism numbers soared. The 13-megawatt Matebe power plant was inaugurated by the Head of State in December 2015. The PNVi built three additional power plants in subsequent years to become the biggest supplier of electricity in eastern Congo. It also became a major actor across a range of agricultural value chains by developing products such as coffee, cocoa, palm oil and chia seeds. On the conservation side, the Park began to

6.15 Many schools visit the PNVi headquarters in Rumangabo. Here, a guard of honour before an official ceremony in 2009.

recover from poaching and land invasions. The mountain gorillas population continued to grow, the restoration of the Ishasha Valley was started to restore the savannah corridor, and the numbers of large mammals, including elephants, were increasing sharply. Additional information on the extraordinary results during this booming period is available in chapters 10 to 17.

7. Resilience during a new degradation phase (2018–2022)

7.1. Responding to hazards and crisis

Regrettably, a sequence of unfortunate events unfolded and challenged the new optimism. In 2018, two British tourists were attacked by a faction of the FDLR, the ranger attempting to protect them lost her life and the driver was wounded. The visitors were kidnapped and held in the forest for several days. Courageous members of a local civil society group volunteered to act as negotiators, and by deploying rangers to seal off the kidnappers' position, it became possi-

6.16   Within 10 years, the Virunga Alliance has brought electricity to many areas of North Kivu.

ble to exert pressure and secure the release of the victims. Following this tragic event, all tourism activities were suspended for a year to review and overhaul security protocols.

In the same year, North Kivu succumbed to the second most devastating Ebola epidemic on record. The PNVi responded with the recruitment of health workers and the construction of control stations at the locations where the roads crossed the rivers inside its territory. All people leaving the Ebola-affected areas were tested for symptoms and their contact registered so that subsequent outbreaks could be traced. This set-up proved to be most effective because of the inability to circumvent the control points and the Park was referred to as 'a natural firewall to the spread of the disease'. However, following the end of the Ebola outbreak, the Covid-19 pandemic brought tourism activities to a lasting standstill.

The most recent eruption of the Nyiragongo volcano occurred on 21 May 2021. Late in the evening, earth preceded a vast lava flow towards the city of Goma. At about 1 am the following day, the lava entered the city, causing 32 deaths and burning 800 homes as well as 9 km of high-voltage power lines and water pipelines. The destruction of these services suspended water supply to over 800,000 people, creating an exponential risk to lives in the city. Virunga Energies and the PNVi's infrastructure department were immediately mobilised. They worked non-stop for seven days, on the still hot lava, and restored the water and electricity distribution. This success aroused multiple expressions of gratitude from the authorities and the general public.

7.2. Increasing violence

From 2008, the threats to the rangers steadily increased, with a succession of violent attacks led by a growing number of small or well-structured armed groups throughout the province. 2020 and 2021 were exceptionally bad years, with the worst attack on 24 April 2020, when 13 staff members were killed on the road outside the Park's headquarters in Rumangabo, in an incredibly violent FDLR ambush, as they were trying to assist civilians who had themselves come under attack. To this date, in the South Sector, the FDLR remains one of the most active armed groups that gains profit from the illegal charcoal production from the Park's forest. This vested business interest, which the rangers frequently counter, is an underlying cause of the violence against PNVi representatives.

In the Centre Sector, another casualty saw six of the rangers killed on 10 January 2021. Several rangers survived these attacks but were severely maimed. Civilians were also targeted, with a particular increase in the number of kidnappings, many of which ended in the killing of the victims.

6.17 Reviving tourism requires long-term efforts. Here, the start of work on Bukima lodge (2009) and the completed Kibumba lodge (2022) in the gorilla sector.

At the request of the Governor, the PNVi rangers stepped up the escorted convoys on Route Nationale 2 through the Park, leading to a drastic decrease in the number of kidnapping incidents.

In the North Sector, the Allied Democratic Force (ADF) began perpetrating unspeakable and indiscriminate violence against civilian communities. This led to several thousand deaths and the displacement of vast numbers of people. When the violence hit the Ruwenzori area, where the North Sector's headquarters are located, the PNVi established an early warning system with the support of civil society groups, faith groups, the civilian administration and the FARDC, to allow the rapid deployment of security services in the event of an alert of an imminent attack. Several protected positions housing up to 60 security agents were built, with the PNVi providing construction materials,

6.18 Ambition and hard work pave the way for beautiful results in unlikely environments. Here, a view from Route Nationale 2, which leads to the Matebe business centre.

vehicles, communication equipment and training. Since April 2021, no victims of militia attacks have been registered in the towns around Mutwanga. The approach has been expanded to other towns to further reduce attacks on communities.

This succession of tragic events, resulting in the violent and unjust deaths of young men and women performing their duties, led the PNVi to develop support structures to heal those injured or suffering mental trauma. The assistance programme also extends to their families. To date, it provides livelihoods, as well as medical, school and social support, to 113 widows and 243 orphans. This voluntary support policy is a moral obligation of the PNVi towards its past, present and future employees.

8. Second M23 conflict (2022 onwards)

In the long series of security incidents across the province, one specific attack occurred on 21 November 2022 at Bukima, on the flanks of Mount Mikeno. Unexpectedly, this proved not to be a Mai-Mai or FDLR attack, but a M23 offensive on a PNVi position, marking the start of the second M23 conflict. As in 2012–2013, the group took control of the Rutshuru territory by first controlling the gorilla sector, then the strategically critical border town of Bunagana, followed by a sequence of battles leading to the taking of Rutshuru town, and subsequently a move towards Goma. During that expansion phase, several PNVi positions, as well as the sub-region of the Matebe power plant and the Rwanguba power plant construction site, and eventually the headquarters in Rumangabo, came under the control of rebels.

Similarly to the policy adopted during the previous CNDP and M23 rebellions, the non-uniformed staff were evacuated to Goma and a small team of rangers with their senior command remained in Rumangabo, digging trenches as protection from the repeated artillery fire. The senior management, including the Director, remained in Rumangabo for five months to mark the continuous presence of the ICCN. They initiated a long and protracted negotiation to establish the terms by which the ICCN could continue operating, as during the first conflict in 2012–2013. Although there was very limited contact with M23 and Rwandan Defence Force officers, their presence became controversial, with senior politicians in Kinshasa, as well as some local activists, accusing the PNVi's personnel of collaborating with M23. Their accusations were blind to the fact that the electricity infrastructure was maintained, providing a lifeline to Goma when the city was effectively under siege, the PNVi's headquarters were preserved, and the monitoring activities of the mountain gorillas were resumed. However, both the rebels and the Government forces, at the highest level in Kinshasa, showed a remarkable willingness to support the ICCN in its efforts to maintain a neutral stance during the conflict and carry on the PNVi's protection activities. Politics aside, due to the intensity of the clashes, the headquarters, including the aviation department, had nevertheless to be transferred to Rwindi in November 2022.

Outside the occupied zone, the Park's protection and development programmes were continued at an accelerated pace to keep staff morale up and preserve the good image of the PNVi in the neighbouring communities. Among many initiatives, Virunga Energies and the Park's infrastructure department supported the humanitarian actors to establish the pumping stations and the water infrastructure for the

A CENTURY OF HISTORY

6.19 The Senkwekwe sanctuary is home to gorillas that survived the 2007 massacre and to those that cannot survive in the wild.

IDP camps around Goma. The 28-megawatt Rwanguba power plant was built under battlefield conditions, within budget and its tight deadline (a remarkable achievement). Headway was also made on the agricultural value chains, with more farmers selling their crops at a higher price.

In April 2024, the M23 rebellion launched a large-scale offensive into the Centre Sector. The temporary headquarters in Rwindi came under attack, and once again, a team remained on-site to retain control. It had to withdraw two weeks later because of the overwhelming artillery fire and the inadequate protection, but their two-week resistance made it possible to withdraw all staff and equipment safely, thereby minimising losses.

Two months later, the offensive extended to the towns of Nyamilima Ishasha, on the Ugandan border. The ecologically critical Ishasha Valley became the frontline between the M23 rebels and the FDLR and Mai-Mai militias. M23 forces swept through the militia positions, forcing them to retreat into the Park, and, in early August, a brief battle took place on the outskirts of the fishing settlement of Nyakakoma, which came under M23 control. FDLR and Mai-Mai militias were dispersed into the Park, and within days poaching incidents began to spike. The ICCN rangers remained active in the combat zone to protect the herds of elephants and large savannah mammals, dramatically increasing the frequency of armed contact between rangers and the militias. The struggle was in vain because the armed groups were significantly stronger in terms of firepower and political weight. Made aware of this perilous situation that threatened years of ecological restoration work, the US, EU and Belgian embassies exerted strong diplomatic pressure in support of the PNVi, and following a week of tension, both the Government forces and M23 agreed to withdraw from Nyakakoma, on the understanding that the ICCN and the traditional authorities would administer the area. To date, this fragile balance has

6.20   The PNVi assists the families of rangers who have died in the line of duty. Here, widows display their latest sewing creations.

been preserved and poaching has effectively been brought under control.

9. Looking back

This chapter sweeps through 20 extraordinary years in the PNVi's history, trying to capture a few of the extraordinary moments experienced by the men and women who work tirelessly to protect its treasures. More than anything, it is important to honour the memory of the more than 230 staff members who have lost their lives since 2005 and to assist those who bear the scars of the extreme violence that accompanied their work.

Yet this difficult period is also characterised by remarkable achievements. Despite the onslaught of civil wars and conflicts, a volcanic eruption and two major epidemics, the PNVi's ecosystems are healthier than they were 20 years ago. The experience acquired with the ICCN neutrality policy during conflicts enabled the PNVi rangers to continue their work in all circumstances, even on the battlefield. Last but not least, the Virunga Alliance has become a powerful lever for reducing poverty and violence, nurturing the hope of a better future for the Park and the populations of eastern Congo.

7.1 Mountain gorillas have fascinated the general public since the creation of the Park. Legend has it that a man who meets the gaze of a gorilla is changed forever.

7

Prestige and fame

FRÉDÉRIC HENRARD, PATRICIA VAN SCHUYLENBERGH

The riches of Virunga National Park alone do not explain the fascination it exerts in the DRC and throughout the world. Its prestige is nourished by the involvement of major personalities. Subject of countless books, films and publications, the Park is engraved in the hearts of millions of people.

1. Long-standing fascination

The fame of Virunga National Park (*Parc National des Virunga* – PNVi) dates back to the discovery of mountain gorillas by the German army captain Robert von Beringe in 1902. The announcement caused a sensation and led to the dispatch of several international expeditions tasked with providing European and North American museums with a supply of specimens. One such expedition was led by the sculptor and taxidermist Carl Akeley, who created a 'gorilla diorama' – a display of naturalised specimens – at the American Museum of Natural History in New York in 1921. Deeply moved by his close encounters with the animals when filming them in their environment, Akeley launched a campaign to create a Gorilla Sanctuary to protect the species from hunters. He organised conferences, published articles and

7.2 Moved by his encounter with mountain gorillas, Carl Akeley campaigned for a sanctuary to protect gorillas in the early 20th century. His efforts resulted in the creation of the Albert National Park, the forerunner of Virunga National Park.

7.3 Since the 1930s, the Albert National Park has been the subject of numerous documentaries, presenting its natural riches to lovers of the great African landscapes in Europe and the United States.

A CENTURY OF HISTORY

7.4 'Ishango sticks' are prehistoric engravings on bone, discovered in the 1950s on the northern shore of Lake Edward. They are 20,000 years old and are often described as 'mankind's first calculator'.

publicised his advocacy in the United States and Belgium, gaining support from various personalities. His efforts helped raise the awareness of the King of the Belgians, who was keen to replicate the American model of national parks in the Congo. The Albert National Park (PNA) was established in 1925 – a first on the African continent. Carl Akeley, who died during a new expedition in 1926, now lies buried on one of the slopes of Mount Mikeno, within the PNVi.

The years following the creation of the Park saw American, British and even Japanese researchers conducting scientific expeditions in the region. Despite prohibitions issued by the Institute for the National Parks in Belgian Congo and Ruanda-Urundi (IPNCB), which sought to prioritise national (i.e. Belgian) research, international interest in the Albert National Park and its gorillas remained strong, especially in the USA. In the 1930s, studies became rarer due to the deteriorating political situation and limited budgets for hosting scientists. However, a major archaeological discovery occurred in the 1950s: the Belgian geologist Jean de Heinzelin de Braucourt discovered the Ishango bones, also called 'Ishango sticks', at the eponymous site (north of Lake Edward). These 20,000-year-old artefacts attest to an unprecedented practice of arithmetic used by the inhabitants of that time. They are nicknamed 'mankind's first calculator'.

7.5 The cover of *National Geographic* in January 1970 brought international fame to Dian Fossey – who stayed at Rumangabo – and fuelled public sympathy for the mountain gorillas.

7.6 H.M. King Baudouin and Queen Fabiola are welcomed by H.E. President Mobutu Sese Seko and his wife in Rwindi in 1970. Also present (left to right): J. Verschuren, A. Mburanumwe and A. (Safari) Prigogine.

In 1959, just before Congo became independent, the zoologist George Schaller mounted an expedition, at the end of which he promoted a new methodology for observing gorillas. This was later replicated by primatologist Dian Fossey in the Rwandan part of the park, which became the Volcanoes National Park after Rwanda became independent in 1962. A new generation of researchers emerged, who used new media to disseminate their research findings. Schaller's doctoral thesis (1963) provided the basis for the popular science book *The Year of the Gorilla* (1964), which put a definitive end to the legend of gorillas as woman snatchers, and demonstrated the species' social nature, peacefulness and intelligence. In January 1970, *National Geographic* dedicated its cover to Dian Fossey, giving her international recognition. In 1983, her book *Gorillas in the Mist* became a bestseller translated into several languages. Her murder in 1985, and the release of the eponymous film starring Sigourney Weaver in 1989, which went on to win several Academy Awards and Golden Globes, cemented the iconic status of mountain gorillas.

The ravages caused by the 1994 genocide in Rwanda and the subsequent wars in eastern Congo had a severe impact on both parks (Virunga and Volcanoes). During this troubled period, gorillas continued to appear regularly on the cover of *National Geographic*, with writings by Schaller and photographs by Michael Nichols, while the duo Mark Jenkins and Brent Stirton regularly documented the threats posed by poachers, military personnel and trophy sellers. From 1995, Anglo-Saxon documentary films on the subject also experienced a resurgence, with the increasing involvement of Hollywood celebrities.

The PNVi's international fame has fuelled the pride of the Congolese since the country's Independence. As early as 1960, its ecosystems were prominently featured in primary, secondary and university textbooks. In the 1980s, television nurtured the collective imagination of middle-class households with documentaries that promoted the Park as a tourist destination. Frequent visits by President Mobutu Sese Seko – nicknamed the 'Warden in chief' – and numerous foreign dignitaries further reinforced the prestige of the site. Locally, the comic strip *Kacheche* – named after a wagtail ('Kacheche' in Swahili), considered a lucky bird in villages – captivated its readers, both children and adults. This environmental education magazine was distributed free of charge, primarily to teachers in North Kivu, but copies were eagerly requested in rural households everywhere. Conversely, the wars and conflicts that have occurred over the past 30 years have associated the Park with the tragedies experienced by millions of Congolese and fuelled suspicions about the motivations of armed groups seeking to establish themselves in its territory. More recently, the successes of the Virunga Alliance – particularly its energy programme, which has made North Kivu one of the best-electrified regions in the country – have sparked growing public interest.

2. Box-office successes

Several cinematic missions have drawn significant attention to the Albert National Park, starting in the 1930s. Commissioned by the Ministry of Colonies, Italian-American filmmaker and novelist Attilio Gatti made a promotional film aimed at the North American public. In a similar naturalist approach, the Belgian-American filmmaker Armand Denis produced the feature film *Dark Rapture*. The film was warmly received in the United States, where the *New York Times* said that if it was not 'the best film about Africa ever made, it is certainly the most beautiful and most richly documented production of its kind ever to achieve general release in this country.'

Before the Independence of Congo, the IPNCB produced several educational and propaganda documentaries. The message conveyed was that nature was generous here, a unique heritage the Belgians had inherited and managed as good stewards. Two feature films stood out and were box-office successes. *Lords of the Forest* (1958), edited from tens of thousands of metres of film, produced by Henri Storck and directed by Henry Brandt, showcased the wildlife and local populations. A grand project, due to its scale and the quality of its scientific contributors, the film was translated into 22 languages, with international distribution handled by 20th Century Fox. The English version's voice-over, narrated by Orson Welles, elicited additional acclaim. King Leopold III of Belgium – who had frequently visited the Park over the years – supported the project from its inception and contributed to its promotion. *No Room for Wild Animals* (1956), released two years earlier and directed by the German zoologist Bernhard Grzimek, depicted wildlife leading a free existence, while hunting and population growth posed increasing threats. The film criticised the Malthusian imbalance between space and resources and fuelled the discourse advocating a preserved African nature where human presence was to be prohibited. Awarded two Golden Bears at the Berlin International Film Festival, it was shown in 63 countries, including the Soviet bloc, China and Japan. In 1958, the workings of the national parks were also highlighted during the Brussels World's Fair.

Fifty years later, in a dramatically different context – the struggle for the survival of the PNVi during the Congo wars – *Virunga* (2014), a feature film by the British director Orlando Von Einsiedel, became a prime example of media

A CENTURY OF HISTORY

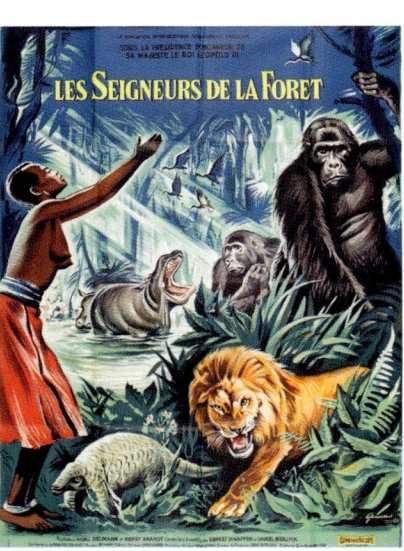

7.7 The 'Kacheche' magazine has fascinated generations of Congolese schoolchildren in North Kivu.

7.8 The film *Lords of the Forest* was a resounding critical and popular success in the late 1950s.

7.9 The documentary about the fight against illegal oil exploitation sparked international support for the Park.

advocacy for the preservation of a protected area. Initially conceived as a compilation of visual evidence for legal proceedings against the abuses committed by an oil exploration company (SOCO), the film blends documentary and investigative journalism: on the one hand action, suspense and psychodrama unfolding in a region traumatised by violence; on the other emotions evoked by magnificent landscapes, courageous yet sometimes powerless human heroes and touchingly fragile gorillas, both orphaned and endangered. The environmental heroism depicted in the film garnered widespread media and public interest – especially after its release on Netflix – and its success made a decisive contribution to the fight against unscrupulous oil exploitation. The film received numerous awards, including at the Tribeca Film Festival, and was nominated for Best Documentary at the Academy Awards (Oscars) in 2015. A fictional adaptation, directed by Barry Jenkins and co-produced by Leonardo DiCaprio, is being prepared.

3. Global media coverage

The PNVi arouses the interest of individuals, media and celebrities all over the world. Many officials have stayed there, including President Mobutu Sese Seko, who had a camp built for him and his family on the banks of the Rutshuru River, and President Joseph Kabila Kabange, who inaugurated the Matebe hydroelectric plant and visited the Rumangabo lodge. Numerous international celebrities have visited the Park, such as actors Anna Friel, Ben Affleck and Leonardo DiCaprio, as well as royals including Queen Elizabeth, Prince Leopold, King Baudouin and Queen Fabiola (Belgium), Prince Bernhard (Netherlands) and Prince Henrik (Denmark).

In recent years, besides its promotion of biodiversity, the environmental justice championed by the PNVi has also received extensive media coverage, with regular reports in newspapers and across TV channels worldwide (BBC, Le Monde, CNN, Deutsche Welle, The New York Times, The Guardian, Nikkei, China Daily, etc.). The Park has also an extensive online profile, with nearly half a million followers on social media (X/Twitter, Facebook, Instagram) and more than a million people visiting its website since 2020. In the Congolese press and social media, threats from armed groups and the violent deaths that have resulted from their activities, oil exploitation, economic development driven by hydroelectric plants and biodiversity extinction are among the most debated issues. But the Park also fosters national pride, as it is regularly promoted as one of the most prestigious sites in the country.

Aside from this media coverage, the PNVi and/or its representatives have also received numerous international awards, including the Goldman Environmental Prize, the Tusk Award for Conservation in Africa, National Geographic Explorer of the Year, the Biodiversity Award from the Albert II Foundation of Monaco, the Albert Schweitzer Award, the Conservationist of the Year Award from the Zoological Society of London and the Freedom from Want Award from the Franklin D. Roosevelt Foundation. The challenges faced by the Park and its work to secure its future have been the

PRESTIGE AND FAME

7.10   H.E. President Joseph Kabila Kabange inaugurates the Matebe hydroplant in December 2015.

H.E. President Félix-Antoine Tshisekedi Tshilombo meets the Director General of the ICCN in July 2024.

subject of numerous debates, including in the National Assembly in Kinshasa, the European Parliament, the U.S. Congress, the United Nations Security Council and the Davos Economic Forum.

4. Resilience and renown

In many ways, the renown of the PNVi is linked to its long history of vulnerability. Its precarious survival touches a nerve in millions of people as it relates to their commitments to similar causes close to home. Emmanuel de Merode, appointed PNVi Director by the Congolese government in 2008, highlights the Congolese men and women who drive its resilience.

The mountain gorilla population symbolises the Park's strengths and weaknesses. Once threatened with extinction, the species has rebounded and its population is growing again, thanks to the unwavering commitment of the Park rangers. Many of them have lost their lives in the line of duty, and their sacrifice commands the respect of people near and far.

The values of optimism, innovation and justice associated with the Virunga Alliance – which aims to turn the Park into a lever for promoting development and stabilisation in North Kivu – also generate public enthusiasm. The arrival of electricity in North Kivu, chocolate bars on shop shelves and the establishment of the first Bitcoin mine operated by a

7.11   The Goldman Environmental Prize is handed over to Rodrigue Mugaruka Katembo, Deputy Director.

A CENTURY OF HISTORY

7.12 André Bauma, keeper of the Senkwekwe sanctuary for orphaned gorillas, bonds with Maïsha, a survivor of the gorilla massacres in 2007.

7.13 Emmanuel de Merode, Director since 2008, is the face of the efforts to protect Virunga National Park ecosystems.

national park, to name but a few examples, are rays of hope that inspire admiration both in the DRC and beyond.

The emotions stirred by the PNVi – whether they touch institutional or private partners, public figures or anonymous individuals, in the DRC or around the world – in conjunction with the significant media attention it receives, go beyond its cause. The ongoing efforts to ensure its survival, and utilise the Park's resources to establish the conditions for a better future for the local populations, have become a flagship of environmental protection efforts in Africa and the world. A hundred years after its creation, the destinies of the Park and the inhabitants of North Kivu remain inextricably linked, and worldwide interest in their shared future shows no sign of waning.

7.14 The sacrifice made by the Park rangers has earned them the esteem of the general public worldwide.

7.15 A monument commemorating the 60th anniversary of the Park and its inclusion on the World Heritage List (in 1979) was inaugurated in Rwindi in 1985 by Samy Mankoto, General Manager of the IZCN.

UNESCO

GUY DEBONNET

The Convention for the Protection of World Heritage was adopted by UNESCO in 1972. It aims to identify, protect and preserve the world's cultural and natural heritage by promoting the premise that certain sites have outstanding universal value, which justifies their preservation as elements of humanity's common heritage. It also stipulates that the international community must participate in protecting this shared heritage. Ratified by 194 States Parties, the Convention is now nearly universal. The Democratic Republic of Congo was among the first countries to ratify the text in 1974.

The prestigious World Heritage List includes 1,199 sites in 168 countries (as of 2024). Among these, 227 natural sites can be recognised as meeting at least one of four criteria: their importance in terms of biodiversity and the conservation of threatened species (criterion x); outstanding examples of ecological and biological processes in the evolution and development of ecosystems (criterion ix); outstanding examples of major stages of Earth's history, such as geological processes (criterion viii); and areas of exceptional natural beauty and aesthetic importance (criterion vii).

Listed as a World Heritage Site in 1979, the PNVi is among the first natural sites recognised by the Convention, alongside the Galápagos Islands (Ecuador), Yellowstone National Park (USA), the Ngorongoro Conservation Area (Tanzania) and Bialowieza Forest (Poland). It is the third natural site listed on the African continent and the first World Heritage Site in the Democratic Republic of Congo.

The inscription of the PNVi is justified by its exceptional biodiversity (criterion x), its geological importance (criterion viii) and its natural beauty (criterion vii). The characteristics of these three criteria are detailed in the Annex to the Convention. The Park is distinguished by its chain of volcanoes (both extinct and active) and its habitat diversity, which surpasses that of any other African park. These habitats range from steppes, savannahs and lava plains to swamps, lowlands, Afromontane forest belts, unique Afroalpine vegetation and the ice fields of the Ruwenzori mountains, with peaks rising above 5,000 metres. This great habitat diversity supports exceptional biodiversity, including endemic species and rare endangered species such as the mountain gorilla.

The PNVi is also recognised under the Ramsar Convention as a wetland of international importance.

The PNVi has been on the World Heritage Sites in Danger list since 1994. The purpose of this list is to alert the international community to any threats faced by the sites and to encourage the adoption of corrective measures. At the time of its listing, the Park was threatened by the arrival of refugees fleeing the Rwandan genocide, leading to large-scale deforestation and poaching. These threats have since evolved but remain significant. The other four World Heritage Sites in the DRC (Kahuzi-Biega, Garamba and Salonga National Parks, and the Okapi Wildlife Reserve) are also on the World Heritage Sites in Danger list.

The fact that the Park is featured on this second list has contributed to the international mobilisation for its conservation. During the war, in 1998, UNESCO initiated an emergency programme to maintain surveillance operations in the five World Heritage Sites, notably by paying the rangers' salaries. In 2004, an international conference mobilised donors to favour the DRC's natural heritage. In 2010, the World Heritage Committee called for the cancellation of oil exploration and exploitation permits, deeming them incompatible with World Heritage status. This stance significantly influenced decisions by the public authorities and private companies involved in this sensitive issue.

The UNESCO World Heritage Committee continues to focus on the PNVi, hoping that its restoration will eventually allow the Park to be removed from the World Heritage Sites in Danger list, which is also one of the goals of the partnership between the Congolese Institute for Nature Conservation (*Institut Congolais pour la Conservation de la Nature* – ICCN) and the Virunga Foundation. The mobilisation of the DRC government, the determination of local populations and the continued support from the international community will be necessary to ensure the future of this extraordinary common heritage.

100 YEARS OF DYNAMICS

8 — The volcanoes   141

9 — The habitats   155

10 — The wildlife   175

11 — Lake Edward   193

12 — Institution and governance   213

13 — Transboundary dimension   227

8.1 A lovely lenticular cloud has formed at the summit of Mikeno. This cloud (an altocumulus lenticularis) forms and deforms continuously as it is shaped by the wind blowing over the mountains. Even if the wind is calm in the valley or on the mountainside, the presence of a lenticular cloud indicates that there are strong currents aloft.

8
The volcanoes

DARIO TEDESCO, GUILLAUME BOUDOIRE, PIERRE-YVES BURGI, JACQUES DURIEUX, PATRICK MACUMU, GEORGES MAVONGA, OLIVIER MUNGUIKO

A major feature of Virunga National Park is its collection of active and extinct volcanoes. They shape the relief and allow the development of exceptional flora and fauna. The city of Goma, clinging to their flanks, is continually threatened.

1. East African Rift

The East African Rift is one of the largest geological faults on the planet: astronauts tell us they can see it with the naked eye from the Moon. Stretching nearly 4,000 km, it extends from the Red Sea to Mozambique and probably Madagascar. Geologists consider this giant relatively young: it formed 30 million years ago and continues to evolve.

Thirty million years ago, the African tectonic plate was much larger than today: its eastern flank included present-day Arabia. Pulled at its edges by large movements due to plate tectonics – for nearly 150 million years, the Atlantic Ocean had been opening on its western flank – this African plate had managed to maintain its integrity. However, a plume of hotspots – upwellings of hot, light mantle material – struck the African plate. This plume exerted vertical pressure on the lithosphere, heating and thinning it, and causing it to bulge and swell. Pierced by magma upwellings, cut by fractures, thinned and heated, which means softened, the African plate could no longer resist the forces acting upon it. It tore apart under the impact of the plume of hotspots initiating the rupture. This tear was not continuous but split into three branches: one to form the Gulf of Aden, the second to become the Red Sea Rift, and the third to tear the African plate over a long distance to become the East African Rift, extending southwards.

The opening of the East African Rift had repercussions on the landscapes and climate of the entire eastern continent. In some places, the bulging of the African plate raised the average ground level to nearly 1,600 m. At the summit, the soil fractured into the huge crevasse that is the rift, several kilometres wide and sometimes several hundred metres deep. This long scar and its elevated margins created a climatic barrier separating the western and eastern slopes, diversifying landscapes between tropical forests and savannah, and influencing the evolution of animal species in these new landscapes. At the bottom of this trench, where the thinned lithospheric plate is very frail, numerous fractures opened, allowing the underlying magma to rise and form various volcanic massifs on the surface, some of which are very famous, like Ol Doinyo Lengai or Kilimanjaro. Further south, the rift divides into two parallel branches, east and west. The Virunga chain formed in the western branch, the Albertine Rift.

The tear of the rift is not always regular. At times, large blocks detach from its walls. The Ruwenzori massif, also called 'Mountains of the Moon' since Ptolemy located the source of the Nile there, is a 120 km long and 40 km wide massif. It peaks at 5,109 metres and is covered with glaciers. This is the third highest peak in Africa and the highest point in the DRC. It is composed of ancient metamorphic rocks – mainly granitic gneisses and Precambrian quartzites from the African continental basement – and contains an ancient volcanic series. About ten million years ago, the bottom of the rift collapsed, forming an uplifted horst, the great Ruwenzori block: a block that was fractured, compressed and then lifted more than 3,000 metres by the tectonic forces acting across the entire continent as the rift was opening. Intense erosion of this block has led to a thick layer of sediment accumulating in the adjacent rift.

8.2 Virunga National Park is located on the western branch of the Great African Rift, also known as the Albertine Rift.

2. Virunga chain

North of Lake Kivu, which occupies the entire width of the western branch of the East African Rift, several fractures allowed large volumes of magma to rise. Of these fractures, some are oriented north–south, along the rift axis, and others east–west, almost perpendicular to the rift. These various fractures and their intersections are the origin of the Virunga chain volcanoes. The oldest volcanoes are located just east of the rift (Muhavura, Gahinga and Sabinyo), or right on the rift's edge (Karisimbi, Mikeno and Visoke). Finally, deep in the rift, we find Nyiragongo and Nyamulagira. The entire chain is oriented east–west, roughly perpendicular to the rift. Nyiragongo and Nyamulagira, located within the rift axis, in the watershed area of the Congo and Nile rivers, are the only two volcanoes that have been active in historical times. The other volcanic structures are said to be dormant, despite a brief eruptive episode (24 hours) of the Visoke in 1956.

The build-up of the Virunga chain has had significant consequences for the hydrographic network of the entire region. It is generally considered that in the Middle Pleistocene, the waters of a series of primitive lakes (Tanganyika, Edward and Albert) flowed northwards and probably fed the Nile. However, in the Late Pleistocene, less than a million years ago, the build-up of the Virunga volcanoes created a large barrier across the rift. Waters accumulated behind this barrier and flooded the pre-existing relief, forming the current Lake Kivu, whose shores are marked by numerous bays and peninsulas, remnants of flooded valleys. The water level of Lake Kivu, finding no outlet in the volcanic barrier, then rose to more than 100 metres above the current level. Between 10,000 and 20,000 years ago, the lake began to overflow towards the south, carving out the Rusizi threshold, and lowering its level by feeding the present-day Lake Tanganyika and Congo River.

The Nyiragongo and Nyamulagira volcanoes are among the most active in the world. In recent years, their eruptive activity was primarily concentrated on the summit craters. These create temporary lava lakes and lava flows, either from lava overflows or from eruptive fissures. Lava lakes are relatively rare on the planet, and the presence of two in a single region is exceptional. In 2024, only five volcanoes in the world are considered to exhibit such a phenomenon: Erebus in Antarctica, Kilauea in Hawaii, Masaya in Nicaragua, and Nyiragongo and Nyamulagira in the DRC. These volcanoes are marked by so-called 'lateral' eruptions, which occur on their flanks and are characterised by the opening of eruptive fissures and the propagation of lava flows extending over several kilometres. The morphology of these two volcanoes, punctuated by numerous cones on their flanks, attests to this eruptive activity. Given the very fluid nature of the emitted lavas due to their exceptional chemical composition (nephelinite at Nyiragongo and

8.3 The six great extinct volcanoes (or better: dormant volcanoes) are the oldest in the Virunga chain. They are located east of the rift (Muhabura, Gahinga, Sabinyo) or on the very edge of the rift (Karisimbi, Mikeno, Visoke). Apart from Mikeno, which lies entirely in the DRC, their peaks mark international borders. Mountain gorillas live on their forested slopes.

8.4 The agronomist and geologist Haroun Tazieff on the small Kituro volcano (between Nyamulagira and Nyiragongo) during a 1948 mission.

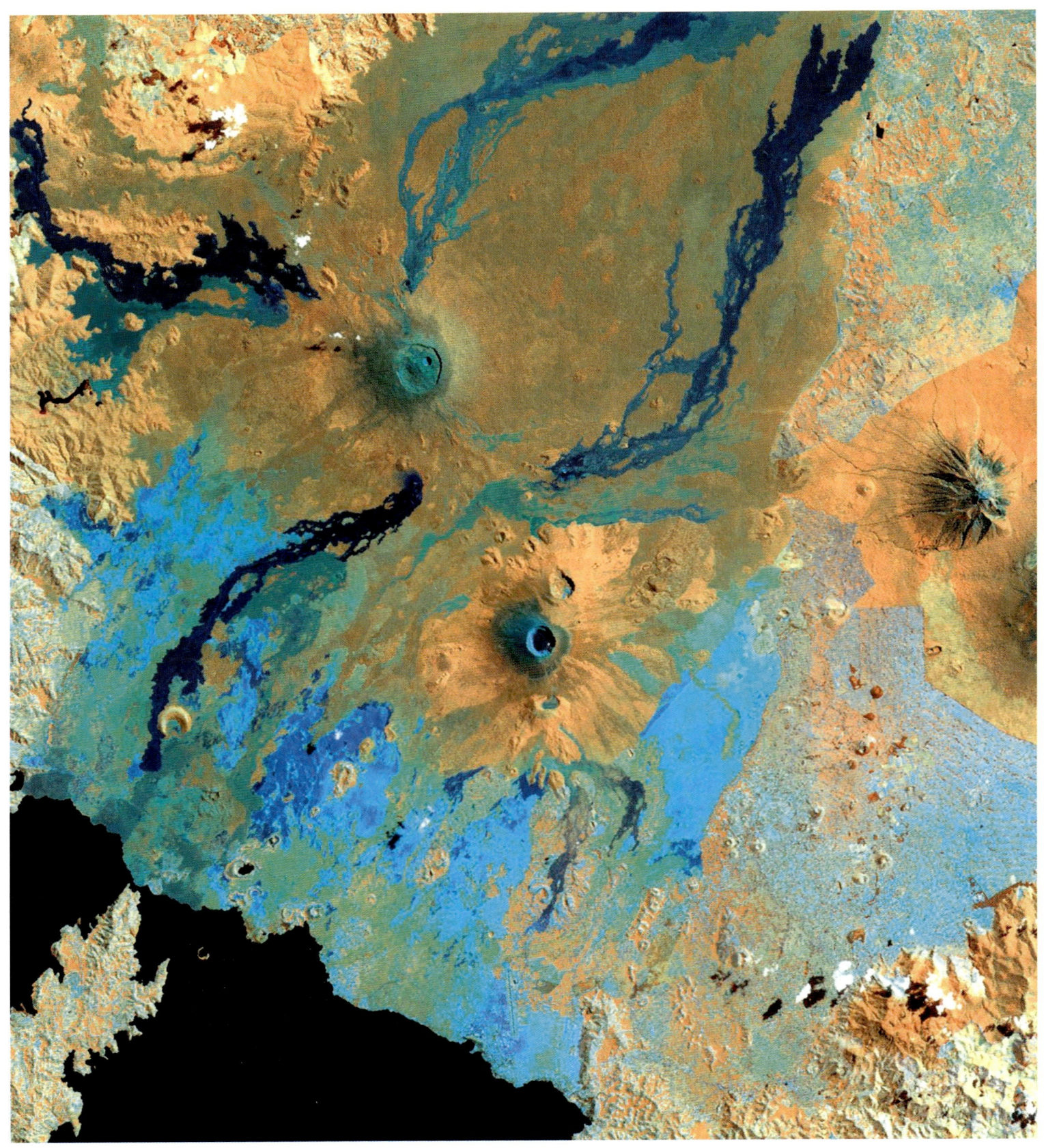

8.5 Relief image based on a satellite image, showing the actual relief of the ground in the Virunga range. Nyiragongo and Nyamulagira are located at the bottom of the rift.

basanite at Nyamulagira), these lava flows can propagate at high speed (up to 100 km/h on the very steep slopes of Nyiragongo), posing a significant risk to inhabited areas near these volcanoes. Despite their proximity (less than 13 km apart), the Nyiragongo and Nyamulagira volcanoes are considered separate entities, with different magma reservoirs, distinct dynamics and differently composed magmas. Although these two volcanoes are marked by historical effusive eruptive activity, the numerous peripheral cones near the shores of Lake Kivu remind us of the possibility of explosive eruptive activity. These cones are linked to phreatomagmatic eruptions, which are explosions caused by the sudden vaporisation of lake water or groundwater coming into contact with rising magma.

3. Nyamulagira and Nyiragongo volcanoes

3.1. Nyamulagira

Nyamulagira is a prime example of a 'Hawaiian' or 'shield' volcano. Peaking at 3,053 metres, it covers a large surface area, crowned by a caldera over 2 km in diameter. Repeated lateral eruptions with long flows of fluid lava have given Nyamulagira broad, gently sloping flanks. Frequent lateral eruptions characterise this volcano's activity. A lava lake appeared in the active part of the caldera in 1921 but drained during the major Tshambene eruption (1938–1940), one of whose flows marks the eastern boundary of the PNVi near Sake. The caldera floor collapsed and it has since been slowly refilled by lava flows from various eruptions.

Since the lava lake drained in the mid-1900s, lateral eruptions have occurred more often, once every one to four years. Each eruption builds up one or more new cones aligned with tectonic fractures in this western branch of the East African Rift. These eruptions produce significant volumes of lava (50 to 80 million cubic metres) in powerful flows capable of reaching 10 to 30 km in length. Most of these flows remain confined within the Park's boundaries, posing minimal risk to inhabited areas. Still, complaints about the damage these incandescent flows cause to the ecosystems of the Park are frequent. Indeed, each eruption burns large areas of vegetation, replacing them with extensive lava fields and forcing the local wildlife to flee. Nonetheless, volcanic eruptions are part of a natural cycle, and national parks must also protect mineral resources. Despite its apparent brutality, the volcanic environment is extremely fragile.

3.2. Nyamulagira recent activity

The last fissural eruption began in November 2011 and ended in 2012. Since then, Nyamulagira's typical eruptive activity has evolved significantly: it has primarily occurred within its crater. Between 2013 and 2015, a new lava lake formed inside a collapsed crater in the northeast part of the caldera. In 2015, several small scoria cones appeared close to the lake, producing minor lava flows. As the crater filled, the activity decreased until it almost ceased, with occasional appearances of a small active lava lake. The crater floor collapsed by several hundred metres and activity gradually resumed, refilling the crater. From 2015 to 2021, three cycles

8.6   Lava flows in the Nyamulagira caldera, eruption in May 2020.

of filling and collapsing were observed (Burgi et al., 2021). In the spring of 2024, some thermal and seismic anomalies indicated a new phase of intense activity, as a significant amount of lava filled most of the caldera, even causing intermittent overflows, while creating a new lava lake.

3.3. Nyiragongo

Nyamulagira's neighbour Nyiragongo also produces very fluid lavas but has a very different morphology. Peaking at 3,470 metres, it is made up of a main cone with steep slopes, flanked by two large lateral cones: Baruta to the north and Shaheru to the south. The current summit is composed entirely of a vast crater with an average diameter of 1,200 metres, whose depth varies with volcanic activity. This volcanic activity consists of an active lake at the bottom of the crater, which makes it one of the most remarkable in the world. The lava lake was officially discovered in 1928 when the crater was first described, but likely existed long before, as gas plumes and red glows had been previously reported. The lava lake disappeared in 1977 due to the collapse of the inner crater following the first recorded lateral eruption. It reappeared in 1982, quickly raising its level within the crater. After remaining inactive for 12 years, it resumed activity in 1994–1995, then disappeared again until the January 2002 eruption. A new lava lake appeared in November 2002 and remained active until the last lateral eruption in May 2021.

3.4. Recent Nyiragongo eruptions

It was long believed that the eruptive activity of Nyiragongo was limited to the lava lake within the crater. Attracted by the fertile volcanic soils, a dense population consequently settled around the volcano, including the growing city of Goma, which is currently home to around two million inhabitants. Three recent historical lateral eruptions are drastically challenging this scenario.

January 1977

On 10 January 1977, a north–south oriented fracture system caused the volcano to split in two, accompanied by a series of region-wide earthquakes. Lava was vigorously expelled from multiple points at the foot of the volcano. The entire magma column from the lava lake was injected into the fractures, rapidly producing voluminous flows. A veritable wave of lava swept the area, leaving traces on some tree trunks at heights of up to 3 metres. According to various accounts, the flows reached inhabited areas within minutes, at speeds ranging from 20 to 60 km/h. Roads, villages and farmland were quickly covered in lava, resulting in between 70 and 400 fatalities, depending on the source. The eruption, which lasted no more than 60 minutes, emitted nearly 20 million cubic metres of lava, the highest basaltic flow rate ever recorded. After the lava lake drainage, the structure of successive terraces and pits on the crater floor collapsed, forming a wide, 800 metre-deep pit. Five years later, in June 1982, a new lava lake appeared at the bottom of the pit and rose over 400 metres within the crater by September. A new phase of activity began in July 1994 and ended

8.7 The eruptions of the Nyamulagira and Nyiragongo volcanoes are constantly changing the surrounding landscape. Within 30 to 40 years a new forest reappears, becoming mature at around 60 to 80 years, creating a mosaic of forest blocks of different ages.

8.8 The Nyiragongo lava lake, bubbling at the bottom of the crater, in February 2019.

in August 1995, which raised the level of the lava lake by an additional 90 metres.

January 2002

In 2002, announced by a few precursor seismic shocks, the fracture system that had opened up in 1977 reactivated and extended southwards to Goma. As per the 1977 scenario, magma was injected into the fractures, producing multiple lava emission points. The highest emissions, at Shaheru (around 2,600 metres), devastated the forest covering the volcano's slopes. Lower flows invaded several villages at the foot of the volcano, severing the Goma–Rutshuru road in multiple places. The final flows were ejected just above Goma airport, destroying the upper third of the runway and preventing all aircraft access. The combined flows crossed Goma from north to south, ending in Lake Kivu. The city's destruction extended to 17%, leaving about 120,000 people homeless in one of the region's most densely populated areas. The administrative and commercial centres were demolished, which affected nearly 80% of the regional economy. The population spontaneously evacuated the city. Approximately 40 direct casualties from the eruption were registered.

May 2021

Following the January 2002 lateral eruption, in May 2002 a new lava lake appeared that was steadily filling Nyiragongo's crater. In February 2016, a unique eruptive phenomenon disrupted this filling, with the appearance next to the lava lake of a scoria cone inside the crater. This cone, fed by an independent conduit (a 'dyke') from the lava lake, continuously produced lava, which poured into the crater and even

8.9 The active Nyiragongo volcano above the city of Goma. During a few months after the eruption on 22 May 2021, its activity changed significantly. The lava effusions inside the crater were intermittent, the plume was no longer visible, and neither was the lava lake.

the active lava lake. This combined activity continued until the 2021 lateral eruption, five years later. On 21 May 2021, at 6pm, without any apparent change in recorded activity, the lava lake drained like an emptying sink. Minutes later, the lava re-emerged along a fracture 400 metres down the southern flank. The lake's 10 million cubic metres of lava rapidly flowed towards Goma's outskirts. A tourist at the summit of the volcano during the eruption reported the event. The final toll included nearly 1,500 homes destroyed, 30 to 50 deaths (with some persons missing to this day) and several hundred people injured. Over 50,000 people lost all of their possessions. In the case of many volcanoes, eruptions are preceded by seismic, geodetic and chemical signals due to magma ascent, but Nyiragongo's situation is unique. The fact that the lava already present in the lava lake spreads through pre-existing fractures means that there is almost no warning before a lateral eruption occurs. However, the Goma Volcano Observatory did note some unusual seismic activity along a fracture zone linking Nyiragongo and Nyamulagira in the month before the eruption, and a

8.10   During the eruption of the Nyiragongo volcano on 17 January 2002, a residential part of Goma was destroyed by lava flows.

8.11   After a devastating lava flow in Nyiragongo, this woman salvages sheet metal from the roof of her destroyed house.

8.12 Parallel fractures from the eruption of Nyiragongo on 22 May 2021 near the village of Mudja.

8.13 In January 2021, the Nyiragongo lava flow cut off the national road, blocking all traffic for several days. The road had to be levelled and tons of earth spread to re-establish communications between Goma and the north.

significant increase in CO_2 emissions from the ground earlier in the year. As with many other volcanoes, only post-eruption analysis can help identify potential precursors for future eruptions.

3.5. Latest observations

The weeks following the eruption on 21 May 2021 were marked by intense seismic activity, felt by the population and causing significant damage to infrastructure in the border towns of Goma and Gisenyi. Fears of a potential eruption in Goma and the accompanying panic, fuelled by imprudent reports and statements in local and international media, led the Goma authorities to evacuate the entire central part of the city – around 400,000 residents – to the Sake–Bulengo–Lac Vert area for three weeks, in precarious conditions. Since the eruption and until the spring of 2024, no permanent lava lake has been detected in the Nyiragongo crater. Significant activity peaks related to the arrival of magma and the occasional emergence of lava at floor level in the crater have been observed (via satellite measuring and image recognition). Still, this magmatic activity is currently insufficient to guarantee the formation and stability of a new lava lake.

3.6. Landscape and biological diversity

The activity of the two volcanoes in the southern sector of Virunga National Park (*Parc National des Virunga* – PNVi) is remarkable. The aesthetic, landscape and scientific value of these volcanic phenomena were among the criteria for selecting the Park as a UNESCO World Heritage site. The rapid succession of eruptions and lava flows – geologically speaking – is also the basis for unique forest successions. Delvingt et al. (1990) have well described and illustrated the different stages of forest colonisation on lava flows, where a sclerophyllous forest develops in about forty years and may, in the lava regions east of Tongo, become a paraclimax where *Bersama* and *Afrocrania* grow, after sixty years.

Given the youthful character of these forests and their perpetual renewal (on an evolutionary scale), these forests are poor in endemic species. They are, however, like the waters of the hot springs associated with volcanic activity, of unparalleled scientific value, as they serve as a living laboratory where scientists and biologists can continuously observe the colonisation of different life forms and the evolution of ecosystems. The conservation of forests and geological landscapes on the slopes of Nyiragongo and Nyamulagira volcanoes must, therefore, remain a priority for the Congolese Institute for Nature Conservation (*Institut Congolais pour la Conservation de la Nature* – ICCN). Moreover, these landscapes and phenomena represent a significant source of income thanks to the tourism they generate.

3.7. Goma Volcano Observatory

Initially established in 1986, the Goma Volcano Observatory (*Observatoire Vulcanologique de Goma* – OVG) is an offshoot of the Department of Geophysics at the Natural Sciences Research Centre (CRSN) in Lwiro (Bukavu). It was looted several times before 2002, preventing it from fulfilling its role of monitoring and forecasting due to the lack of adequate equipment.

After the eruption on 17 January 2002, the international community mobilised to re-equip the OVG. This structure, based in Goma, received the support of several international actors. From 2006 to 2013, it was supported by a European Union project and by the United Nations inter-agency 'Volcano Risk Reduction' programme. From that time, until 2022, a Belgian–Luxembourg consortium collaborated closely with the OVG.

The missions of the OVG are multiple but complementary: monitoring the Virunga volcanoes, forecasting eruptions, risk management, communication and education. The active volcanoes are monitored using a seismological network of more than ten automated stations installed around the Nyamulagira and Nyiragongo volcanoes. The stations transmit the data live via the internet to the OVG. A second network focuses on ground deformation measurements and monitors specifically the active fractures of 1977 and 2002. Lastly, geochemical monitoring of the gas plume is carried out using ground sampling and spectrometer (DOAS) measurements or satellite data acquisition. The data is processed and summarised in weekly reports at the OVG.

Special emphasis is placed on communication and education: warning signs have been installed in the city and the surrounding communities, and regular information sessions are being held. An educational programme on volcanoes and their risks is taught at all the schools in the region.

Finally, contingency and evacuation plans have been drawn up, a collaborative effort of the OVG, the provincial authorities, the city of Goma and various humanitarian actors.

3.8. Mazuku

In April 1958, a remarkable discovery was made in the Albert National Park. A biologist prospecting the extreme north of the lava plain, a densely wooded, close environment, discovered some vast rocky clearings (over 50 metres long) scattered with ancient lava blocks (Verschuren, 1965). In these trenches, he found dozens of carcasses of elephants, hippos, lions and monkeys in various stages of decomposition. The researcher descended into the pit – cautiously, roped. After a few moments of euphoria, he suddenly lost consciousness. Fortunately, he could be evacuated safely. Subsequently, more pits

8.14 The volutes of gas released by volcanic cones are a constant reminder of the dynamism of the rift and the danger they represent. These spectacular fumes can also cause health problems for populations too close to the volcanoes.

(around fifteen) were discovered in the same area, at the junction of the southern and central sectors. These pits were located near the crystalline resurgence of the Molindi River, a major tributary of the Rutshuru (80% of its downstream flow). Simple homemade methods were used for sampling the toxic gases, which were analysed in Bukavu at the Mining Service. It turned out that these gases were composed of 60–65% carbon dioxide (CO_2).

Experiments with domestic animals resulted in almost instantaneous but reversible anaesthesia in high-metabolism vertebrates, followed by lethal anoxia. The animals observed during the test constituted a perfect sample of local fauna: rodents, hyraxes, instantly falling birds, reptiles, amphibians and a host of small invertebrates, particularly lepidopteras. In the victims' abdomens, larvae swarmed, apparently insensitive to the gases. A succession of animal deaths was observed: a dead warthog attracted a hyena that attracted another hyena, then a jackal... and they all died eventually. Some human carcasses were also found, which were attributed to hunters searching for ivory.

The higher frequency at which young elephants were found dead, compared to adult populations, raised questions. The phenomenon is due to the variation in the upper level of the CO_2-rich gas layer (denser than air) contained in these depressions, which hovers quite close to the ground during the day but sometimes reaches several metres in height at night due to daily barometric variations. These phenomena are related to the local volcano-tectonic context, though their precise origin cannot be explained. A recent study (Tedesco, 2010) on the gaseous emissions of the mazuku throughout the PNVi has determined the origin of these gases. It is a deep-origin gas, not issuing from superficial magma, but very likely coming directly from the mantle, through a series of regional fractures resulting from the

8.15　All vertebrates can fall victim to the gases (over 65% CO_2) released by the natural gas pockets known as mazuku. Their corpses attract scavengers, like this hyena that has also succumbed to asphyxiation.

8.16　Having abandoned their village on 17 January 2002 during the eruption of Nyiragongo, the people of Munigi returned home treading on the still-warm lava flow.

development of the rift and the communication of deep layers with more superficial layers.

Most of these gas-filled pits, 'mazuku' in the local terminology, are situated at a height of around 1,200 metres. However, mazuku have been discovered between Goma and Sake (1,500 metres) and even in the mountains at over 2,000 metres. The phenomenon plays a major role in regulating the number of vertebrates in the plain. No adaptation to this phenomenon is perceptible, as almost sedentary hippos (Lake Ondo, Lake Kibuga) are just as much victims as migratory birds from the far north (sandpipers and plovers).

Tourists need not worry, as the mazuku are located outside the areas accessible to them and finding them would require several hours of walking through dense vegetation. However, they constitute a significant risk for local populations, which may be caught up in urban expansion and migratory flows, especially refugees, who tend to settle in areas marked by the occurrence of mazuku, such as along Lake Kivu between Goma and Sake.

9.1 Often associated with ragworts, giant lobelias are characteristic of altitudes above 3,500 metres.

9

The habitats[1]

SÉBASTIEN DESBUREAUX, FRANCESCA LANATA, MARC LANGUY, LAURA PARKER, JEAN DE DIEU WATHAUT

Virunga National Park is home to nine ecosystems with exceptional biodiversity. Its habitats adapt to the climate, react to the evolution of key species and resist anthropogenic pressures. Human invasions remain the most significant threat.

1. Evolution of the habitats

Between equatorial forests and high-altitude forests, mountains and glaciers, savannahs and wetlands, the ecosystems of Virunga National Park (*Parc National des Virunga* – PNVi) show unparalleled diversity, recognised by UNESCO (see chapter 7 for additional details). Various pedestrian and motorised observations, aerial photographs by the Military Geographical Institute (1958) and the Park's aviation team, along with recent satellite images, have documented the changes since 1925.

1.1. Equatorial forest

At the Ituri border, the PNVi connects the East African ecosystems with the equatorial forest of the Congo basin. Within the Park, the forest has remained unchanged since its creation. Outside its boundaries, data collected by the explorer H.M. Stanley in the late 20th century shows a retreat of vegetation, as it is replaced by landscapes altered by human activity. The continuity between the Ruwenzori mountain forests and the large western forest is characteristic of the PNVi and a rare situation on the African continent. The forests in the extreme north of the Park contain vast, scattered grassy meadows, called *Esobe*, and numerous *Borassus* palms. On the ridges, savannah mammals, such as waterbucks and lions, evolve largely undisturbed.

1.2. Ruwenzori massif

In the north-west of the Park, the Ruwenzori range features three of the last glaciers on the continent: Baker, Speke and Stanley. All three are on the slopes of Africa's third highest peak, Mount Stanley, which rises to 5,109 metres. In the early 20th century, the surface of glaciers and snowy zones was likely over 600 hectares. Regression was noted in periodic photographs starting in 1937. By the 2020s, satellite imagery suggested that the total surface area of the three glaciers was under 100 hectares.

The tree heather zone appears to have been preserved on the Congolese slopes, to the north and the west, and the alpine zone has remained intact. The lower slopes of the massif, up to about 2,000 metres, have been disrupted by sporadic cultivation. The mid-altitude mountain forest, characterised by giant *Cyathea* ferns, is discontinuous in the valleys. The Mutsora area, at the foot of the Ruwenzori mountains, was once covered by low-altitude forest, which had largely been cleared even before the Park's creation. The establishment of the PNVi allowed for forest recolonisation, which led to the growth of the tall *Pennisetum*.

1.3. Upper Semliki plateau

Towards Lake Edward, the forest gives way to savannahs, extending to Ishango. Human activity is sporadic as the population has deserted the area to escape trypanosomiasis (sleeping sickness). Many rivers, bordered by gradually retreating gallery forests, originate west of the Park. The Semliki River, lined with cliffs, remains intact. This area is where archaeological excavations unearthed 'Ishango Man' and the famous 'Ishango bones' (see chapter 7).

The Bukuku hills, east of the Semliki spillway – presented as one of the sources of the Nile – are covered

9.2 In the alpine area of the Ruwenzori, the characteristic rosette of a young giant lobelia. At an altitude of more than 3,000 metres, it will take years before the plant reaches its adult height of 5–6 metres.

9.3 High-altitude landscape on the slopes of the Ruwenzori, with its characteristic vegetation of ragwort and giant lobelia. The climate is getting warmer and the snow cover is inevitably receding year after year.

with grasses. They overlook the Lubilya River plain, once filled with vast expanses of marshland, often with papyrus, alternating with acacia woodlands. The plain is one of the areas most degraded by human presence, mostly due to the growth of the Kasindi settlement. The savannahs between the left bank of the Semliki, near Kyavinyonge, were once exclusively grasslands. By 1988, they were covered in xerophilic bushes because the elephants had nearly disappeared.

1.4. Mount Tshiaberimu

The geographical appendage of Tshiaberimu is the habitat of the eastern lowland gorilla subpopulation. The mountain has been surrounded by cultivation for several decades, but the local populations respect the Park area. This is also true for the very narrow Tumbwe River valley. Until the 1960s, vast bamboo expanses covered the graben ridges, up to around Kabasha (75 km to the south). After 1958, except on Mount Tshiaberimu, nearly all the bamboo was cleared.

9.4 A landscape characteristic of the Semliki Valley downstream from Ishango.

9.5 Both on the slopes of the Ruwenzori and of the extinct volcanoes, the bamboo zone consists of a monospecific forest that is not conducive to the development of undergrowth. It is found between 2,300 and 2,600 metres on the volcanoes and as high as 3,000 metres on the Ruwenzori and the Tshiaberimu.

9.6 Two elephants on the coastal strip between the Mitumba and Lake Edward. This ecological corridor between the North and Centre sectors of the Park has disappeared as a result of human encroachments on the west coast of the lake.

1.5. West coast of Lake Edward

The steep western shore provided ecological continuity between the North and Centre Sectors. At the mouths of the Mosenda and Kisaka rivers, small plains were covered with grassy vegetation, dotted with large tree species.

The residents of the Park were allowed to buy fish from Vitshumbi on the shore, but in the late 1980s, fishing settlements became permanent. The savannahs around the fisheries were converted into fields, which destroyed the ecological corridor. Until 1988, at the mouth of the Talya River, a splendid primary forest protected by the local microclimate had remained intact. Bushpigs and elephants lived in this forest until it was destroyed in the 1990s.

The shores of Kamandi Bay, south of the ecological corridor, used to be covered by a densely wooded savannah, damaged by elephants in 1957. The shores harboured vast, impenetrable stretches of ambatch (balsa wood, *Aeschynomene elaphroxylon*). The mouth of the Lula River was covered in abundant papyrus.

The Mitumba mountains overlook Lake Edward to the west and the plain to the south-west. The slopes are covered with vegetation, preserved for several decades, alternating bushes and grassy strata and, higher up beyond 2,000 metres, also eagle ferns. The twin-peaked mountain with its characteristic ridge was once covered by vast areas cultivated since the early 2000s. The bushy vegetation bordering the Kabasha escarpment road shows a tendency towards reforestation. This main road is an obstacle to fires as the difference in vegetation between both sides of the road is striking.

1.6. Savannah plains

As fires cannot penetrate it, the Rwindi gallery forest south of Lake Edward has undergone very few changes. The shores of Lake Edward, between Kamandi and the mouth of the Rwindi River, have dramatically evolved, with the formation and subsequent disappearance of many small, isolated ponds that communicated with the lake. The vegetation is dominated by short grasses that are not susceptible to fires and, towards the east, an acacia invasion is apparent. The presence of candelabra euphorbias (*Euphorbia dawei* and *Capparis tomentosa* bushes), especially near Vitshumbi, has varied little in decades.

Aerial observations show that the numerous convolutions of the middle Rutshuru have remained identical over the years. The boundaries of the modest gallery forests, featuring *Phoenix reclinata*, have also remained unchanged, and the Rutshuru delta has been covered in large papyrus for several decades.

East of the Rutshuru River, several 'crest' ponds, such as Lake Kizi, were covered with Nile lettuce (*Pistia*) and offered refuge to hippopotamuses. Vast stands of *Euphorbia dawei* surrounded the lake. The progressive drying of the ponds, and the drastic decline of elephant numbers between 1990 and 2020, have profoundly altered this habitat. Acacias invaded the crests, but the recent return of elephants may well restore the original landscape.

The course of the Ishasha River is characterised by a wide gallery forest, with *Croton* and *Pterygota*. Chimpanzees and migrating herds of elephants live in this closed habitat.

9.7 The Rutshuru River develops local meanders that change the landscape and diversify its vegetation cover.

Towards the lake, the river marks the border between the DRC and Uganda. Its course has varied significantly since the Park was created, to the point of causing confusion as to the actual location of the border between the two countries. Vast bare beaches characterise the habitat between the river and the plateau.

The savannahs east of the Rutshuru remained intact until the 1970s. Access to these savannahs, which used to be very difficult, was made easier by the installation of a ferry at Nyamushengero. The development of the Nyakakoma fishery also increased human presence. Population pressure on the Park border, between the Ishasha and Nyamilima villages, grew significantly in the 1990s. Vast stretches of farmland have developed over 55 km² within the Park. In 2019, participatory demarcation of the Park boundary, and the construction of a fence, ended the invasions and allowed for the gradual restoration of habitats (see chapter 16). The situation is the opposite in the Rutshuru Hunting Domain – adjacent to PNVi but lacking the operational protection to support legal texts – where almost all the savannahs and the splendid forest near the Kwenda and Evi rivers have disappeared over fifty years.

1.7. Kasali and Ilehe mountains

With its gently sloping western flanks, the Kasali massif forms a mountain island that connects the South and Centre Sectors. In 1958, a vast remnant of humid forest persisted on the ridge, fully exposed to the winds. Towards the east, the steep slopes are covered with bushy savannah and a few closed forest islands. From the summit of the steep Ilehe hill, the plains east of the Rutshuru River are visible.

South of Mabenga, the narrow gallery forest downstream of the Rutshuru River was extended by vast stands of *Phoenix* palms. The south–north road near Mabenga, which used to cross an open environment, has gradually become covered in *Olea*. West of Rutshuru town, small, wooded areas border the banks of the numerous springs. Their waters are lost downstream in the gaps between lava flows. The crys-

9.8 On the Rwindi–Rutshuru plains, vast savannahs are punctuated with various forest areas and forest galleries enclosing rivers. In the background, the Kasali mountains.

tal-clear waters of the Molindi alternate with mazuku, areas of toxic gas emissions that are deadly to wildlife, including elephants.

Since 1960, the vast decline in elephant populations has initiated a spectacular vegetation transformation. The savannahs have been invaded by bushes, mainly small acacias. The deterioration of security conditions over the last thirty years has been associated with numerous highly destructive farmland invasions. The last sightings of elephants in the Mabenga region, before they migrated to the north-east, date back to 2021.

1.8. Active volcanoes

The Rumangabo sub-region, which houses the Park headquarters, was once covered by a mountain forest (1,700 metres). The 400 hectares of the station that were completely cleared before being incorporated into the PNVi have benefited from 70 years of protection, having seen the emergence of tree species, including many figs. This secondary forest is now home to several monkey species, including a population of chimpanzees.

Beyond Rumangabo, the plain rises towards the two major active volcanoes: Nyamulagira and Nyiragongo. The great variety of plant formations, created by the different lava flows, was studied in detail by Lebrun (1947). On the eastern slope of the Nyiragongo, where rainfall is high (Kibati), volcanic rocks disintegrate rapidly. Trees may emerge from the lava soil just a few months after an eruption, whereas this disintegration is slower in the north, where rainfall is less abundant.

On the southern and eastern slopes of the Nyiragongo, and almost all of the slopes of the Nyamulagira, the establishment of Rwandan refugee camps in 1994, and the expansion of the city of Goma, have led to the disappearance of the forest ecosystems. Livestock farming and agriculture in the Masisi territory have also destroyed the forest cover of the lower slopes of the Nyamulagira. A new setback occurred in 2023, due to the ongoing conflict with the March 23 Movement (M23), which displaced over a million people. In a few weeks, the previously intact slopes of the Nyiragongo were deforested to meet the energy needs of displaced populations. Some mountainside plots have been transformed into farmland up to high altitudes.

1.9. Extinct volcanoes

The former secondary forest of the Mwaro corridor – traversed by the main road from Goma to Rutshuru – ensures territorial continuity between the sectors of the active and extinct volcanoes. Elephants were frequently encountered there, but gorillas never used the corridor and have remained completely absent from the slopes of the active volcanoes. The Mwaro corridor forest is now heavily degraded and large wildlife has completely disappeared.

Of the four western extinct volcanoes – Mikeno, Karisimbi, Visoke and Sabinyo – only Mikeno (4,437 metres) is in the DRC; the others are shared with Rwanda. They host a montane forest type characterised by a significant *Hagenia abyssinica* layer at around 3,100 metres altitude. The slopes of Mikeno are home to the only population of mountain gorillas in the world.

Human activities also have an impact on the forest in this area. During the 1960s and the 1990s, the forest was invaded by livestock, but the herders never cut down any trees. The

9.9 Senecios, often associated with giant lobelias, are typical of the Afroalpine zone at around 3,700 metres in altitude.

9.10 The heather floor on the Mikeno slope.

9.11 It takes a few years for pioneering plants to appear after a lava flow, and several decades for the complete vegetation cover to regenerate.

initial vegetation quickly regenerated when pastoral activities ceased. In 2003–2004, the area near the border with Rwanda suffered significant deforestation. The demarcation of the border between the nations and the edge of the Park, by building a stone wall, ended this disaster.

Tshegera island

The small volcanic island of Tshegera (11 hectares) in Lake Kivu is the only part of the PNVi located in the south Kivu province. Its crescent shape, with an inner lagoon, is due to the collapse of an ancient volcanic caldera. Decades of agriculture and livestock farming have had detrimental effects on the island's soil and the original vegetation. The Park is implementing an ecological restoration programme to re-establish the former forest cover (see below).

2. Photographic monitoring of habitats

Photographic archives help to document vegetation changes in eight sites over nearly a century. The oldest photos, by G.F. de Witte, date from the 1930s. The aerial photographs by the Military Geographic Institute in 1958–59 provide a second reference point. Thirty years later, J. Verschuren set up a photographic monitoring system. Finally, the photos taken in 2024 were captured during foot and aerial patrols. Each site is numbered based on Verschuren's original work (1986).

9.12   The succession of types of mountain vegetation on the slopes of the Ruwenzori and the volcanoes is typical of Afromontane forests. Their floral and faunal composition includes many endemic species that have been described by numerous authors.

2.1. Rutshuru river valley

In 1934, the Rutshuru River was bordered by a gallery forest, and the plain to the east was a grass savannah. Reforestation became visible in 1959, intensified in 1983 and was confirmed in 2005. Numerous trees, including acacias, now dominate the plains. The formerly open landscape has become almost completely closed in. This rapid change is due to the near-extinction of elephants between 1960 and 2000.

2.2. Rwindi river plain

In 1934, the plain was dotted with many trees, particularly *Albizia* and large acacias. At that time, there were few elephants. Photos from 1959 show almost total deforestation, due to the increase in pachyderms. By 1983, typical recolonisation by small acacias was underway, indicating a reduced elephant presence. These two successive changes were therefore both caused by changes to the elephant population.

9.13 Rutshuru valley (S1)

9.14 Rwindi plains (S4)

9.15 Location map of photographic monitoring sites.

2.3. Kasali massif

In 1939, the eastern slopes of the Kasali massif were covered by an extensive savannah, dotted with acacias. Only the high summits were wooded, apart from a large, clearly visible forest triangle extending broadly into the valleys. In the photos from 1988 and 2005, an increase is visible, first in the bush layer, then in the tree layer. The forest triangle with its high canopy is still discernible, but less clearly because the surrounding savannah has considerably closed in. The disappearance of the elephants, which fed on young trees, is the cause of the disappearance of the savannah in favour of reforestation.

G.F. de Witte (May 1956)

Gilliard (May 1939)

J. Verschuren (April 1988)

J. Verschuren (April 1988)

P. Banza (March 2005)

P. Banza (March 2005)

Fondation Virunga (2024)

9.16 Kasali mountains (S15)

9.17 Mitumba mountains (S16)

THE HABITATS

2.4. Mitumba ridge on the Kabasha escarpment

In 1956, the Mitumba slopes were entirely deforested, except for the gallery forests at the valley bottom. In 1988, this situation largely remained, though some sparse woodlands were visible on the slopes. The 2005 photo shows an increase in shrubs and trees, especially acacias, and this situation has remained unchanged 20 years later.

2.5. Rocky peak on the west shore of Lake Edward

Few changes occurred between 1959 and 1988, except for slight shrub recolonisation of the peak. The slopes were covered with shrubs and trees that reached the lake shore. A gallery forest in the valley bottom was also visible. The 2005 photo shows a striking change: the peak was almost entirely deforested and burned off. The slopes were nearly bare, the gallery forest was reduced to patches, and there were fields extending to the lake shore. The 2024 photo, intentionally framed wider, also illustrates the cultivation on the west shore of Lake Edward. The invasion of the Park by fishing populations explains the vegetation changes.

9.18 Rocky piton on the west bank (S18).

9.19 Kisaka (S19)

9.20 Mwiga bay (S20)

THE HABITATS

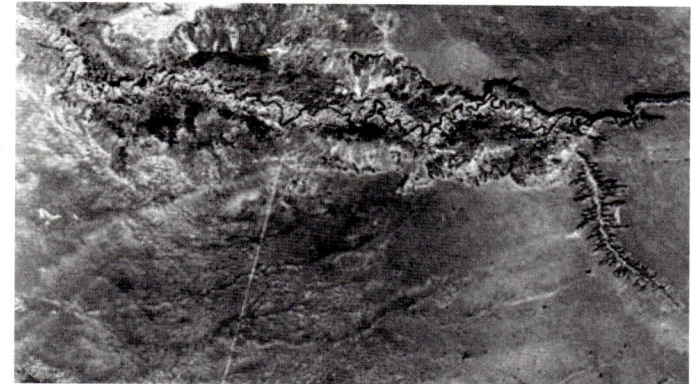
IGCB (1958)

J. Verschuren (April 1988)

Image satelite SPOT (July 2004)

M. Languy (July 2004)

9.21 Rwindi valley (S23)

2.6. Kisaka settlement on the west shore of Lake Edward

In 1957 and 1988, the hill slopes were covered with savannahs and trees grew in the valley bottoms and at the foot of the escarpment. This part of the Park was well-protected and free of agriculture and fishing. The 2005 and 2024 photos show a radical change: an almost total loss of forest cover due to the establishment of an initially illegal fishery, which was later recognised by the ICCN–COPEVI convention in 2020. The surrounding hills were burned off and used as farmland. The boundaries of the inhabited area exceed the photo frame.

2.7. Mwiga Bay on Lake Edward

The limits of Mwiga Bay and the bare salt flats were apparent between 1958 and 1988. The 2005 photo shows increased vegetation at the expense of the bare areas. This trend continued between 2005 and 2024. This may be the first documentation of a significant vegetation change related to the near-disappearance of hippopotamuses, which were abundant in the area. The same phenomenon is observed in other bays of Lake Edward, and along the banks of the Rutshuru River.

2.8. Rwindi valley near the ICCN station

Few changes are observed between 1958 and 1988, except for a slight increase in the gallery forest. The area south of the Congolese Institute for Nature Conservation (ICCN) Rwindi station (on the right in the photo) was entirely covered with grass savannah. In 2004, shrub cover was present in several places. The situation remained identical in 2024.

Human encroachments

Since the late 2010s, landscape degradation has been analysed using aerial surveys and satellite imagery. In 2024, 14.2% of the PNVi area was degraded by a significant human presence (fluctuating between 12 and 15% in recent years). Conversion into cultivated areas represents the greatest habitat loss, with 692 km² in March 2024, or 10% of the Park area. Other degradation causes include grazing (especially in the Masisi) and deforestation for charcoal production. Threats often overlap: an area deforested for charcoal production becomes farmland and sometimes even an urban settlement (24 km²). This has been the case for illegal fisheries, localities in the north (Kasindi and Kasindi Port) and west of Goma in the so-called Nzulo area.

There is less human pressure within the Park than there is outside, where all habitats have given way to fields and eucalyptus plantations. By comparing satellite images taken between 2000 and 2020, Desbureaux (2021) establishes statistically that there is two times less destruction of tree cover inside the Park than in comparable areas outside (same distance from roads, same distance from urban centres, same topography). Without the continuous efforts of the ICCN rangers, the loss of natural habitats would be much greater. However, each security or humanitarian crisis reshuffles the deck, and the ongoing conflict (M23) will likely have an impact on the landscape dynamics for decades to come.

9.22 Encroachments into the Park, situation in March 2024

TYPE OF ENCROACHMENT	COLOUR	SURFACE
Crops		692.3 km²
Pastures		144.2 km²
Degradations		92.1 km²
Urban agglomeration		25 km²
Deforestation		24.4 km²
Total encroachments		**978.1 km²**
Total Park		**6,894 km²**
% of encroachments		**14.2 %**

9.23 The fight against charcoal production within the Park remains a major challenge.

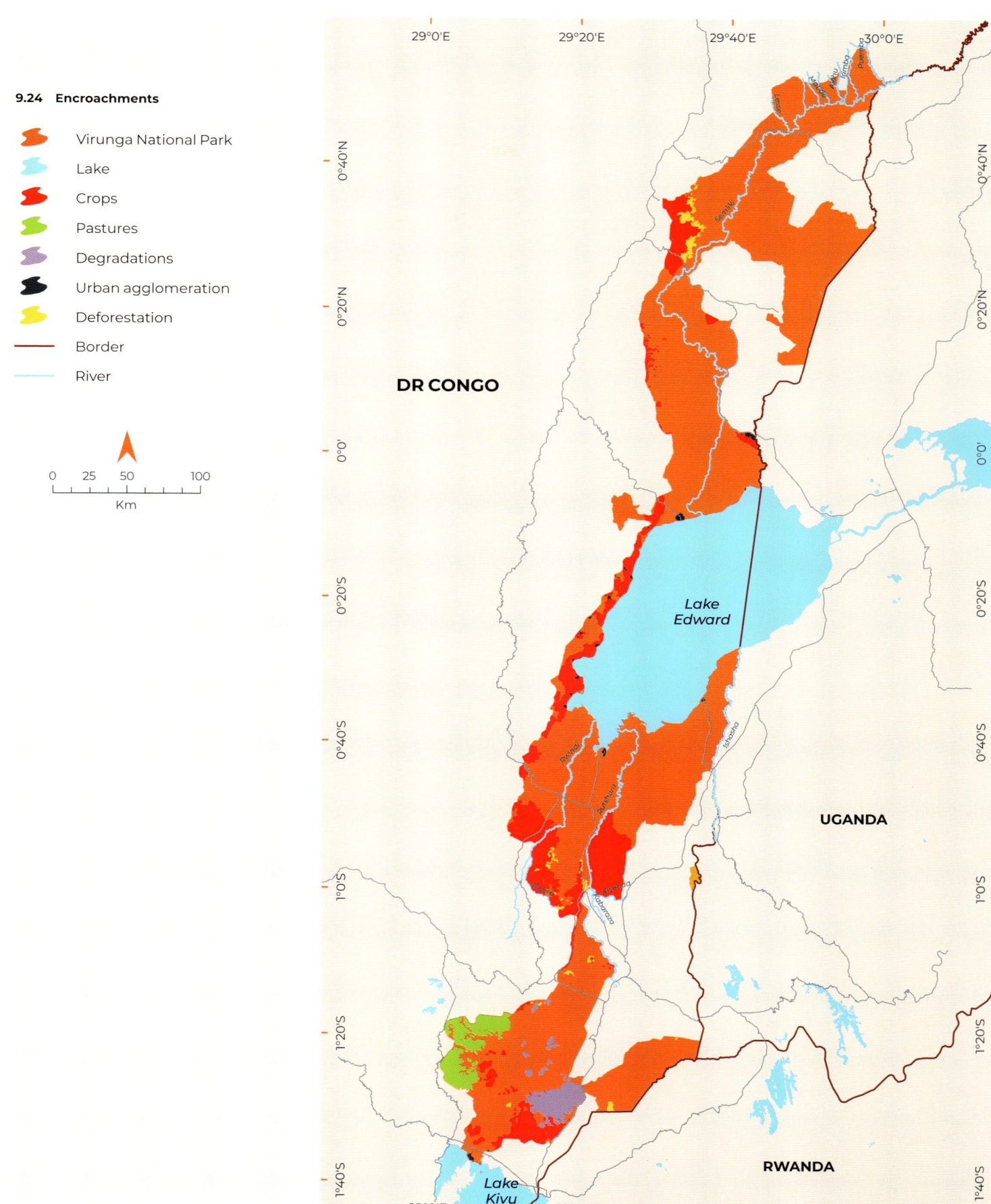

9.25 In December 1955, following heavy rains and the melting of the Ruwenzori snowpack, the Talya River experienced exceptional floods that eroded its banks and destroyed numerous infrastructures in Mutsora.

3. Challenges and perspectives

The review of landscapes and periodic site monitoring show significant vegetation changes over short periods. Various factors, which may have combined, drive these changes.

Weather and climate variations have an impact on landscapes. No specific weather study in the PNVi is available, but empirical observations report several changes. This is particularly evident for the Ruwenzori glaciers, which will inevitably disappear in the coming years.

Human activities are the main cause of habitat disruption. There are two types: on the one hand, soil and forest conversion (deforestation, charcoal production and agriculture) which affects habitats directly; and on the other hand, poaching, which leads to a significant decline in mega-herbivore populations, inducing slower but profound vegetation change (especially in savannah areas).

3.1. Threat of invasive species

The invasion of non-native plants has posed a major threat to the savannah ecosystems of the PNVi – and of Queen Elizabeth National Park (QENP) in Uganda – since the 2010s. Exotic shrubs that are quite common in the savannahs, such as *Lantana camara* and especially *Opuntia*, have destroyed vast areas in the QENP. In the PNVi, the two species are spreading more slowly.

Three species pose a particular danger: *Dichrostachys cinerea*, a shrub from the acacia family; *Maerua subcordata*, a small shrub from the Capparaceae family; and *Eichhornia crassipes*, the water hyacinth. While *Dichrostachys cinerea* and *Eichhornia crassipes* are native to the region, historically the three species have not been present in the PNVi. The collapse of savannah wildlife, the disruption of fire and climate cycles, and the soil degradation also favour the expansion of these species.

In the Ishasha Valley, the spread of *Dichrostachys cinerea* is a problem, due to its ability to regenerate by suckering and abundant seed production. The species is fire-resistant and can only be eliminated by mechanical means. Efforts undertaken in the QENP to prevent its spread have been ineffective and may even make the problem worse.

Maerua subcordata is also spreading rapidly in the Ishasha Valley. This small shrub, little known to scientists, has a tuber that makes it difficult to control its expansion, and using fire to eradicate it seems, on the contrary, to facilitate its development. Initial uprooting campaigns were undertaken in 2022.

At Lake Edward, water hyacinths are spreading at the expense of *Pistia* (water lettuce) in the shallow bays where they suffocate the water and threaten the lives of hippopotamuses and fish (as seen in Lake Victoria). Their presence was first documented in 1989. They are particularly prevalent on the southern shore around Nyakakoma and to a lesser extent on the northern shore near Kyavinyonge. Other invasive species might also pose a problem in the future, notably *Ludwigia peploides* (creeping water primrose), observed in several wetlands, though its frequency is currently unknown.

To address the invasive plant problem, the PNVi has established 38 observation plots where various control

9.26 To prevent encroachments and limit crop damage, the PNVi had to install fences in some densely populated areas.

9.27 The illegal occupation of Tshegera Island has utterly destroyed the natural vegetation of this ancient volcanic crater. Local species are being planted to restore the original forest cover.

methods are being tested. Monitoring is also ensured in the field by taking weekly aerial photos. The PNVi teams exchange information with QENP teams to develop a cross-border strategy. This approach involves managing teams of residents who convert the biomass into an energy source for the villages. A test is underway using *Maerua* and water hyacinth to produce biogas. The wood density of *Dichrostachys cinerea* makes this species another potentially interesting fuel.

3.2. Restoration of degraded areas

Tshegera Island is one of the first to benefit from the reforestation efforts by the PNVi, showing tangible results in less than 10 years. The island had been illegally occupied until 2014 and was covered with fields, shrubs, vines, banana plantations and fast-growing trees.

Tshegera Island was returned to the PNVi in 2015, and restoration works were launched in partnership with the Meise Botanic Garden (Jardin Botanique de Meise, Belgium – JBM). Bibliographic and iconographic research, as well as remnants of the original vegetation, have helped to identify the original cover (the sclerophyll species *Cussonia holstii*, *Myrica salicifolia*, *Erythrina abyssinica*, *Acanthus polystachyus* and five Ficus species). The restoration of the ecological structure began with eliminating eucalyptus, shrubs and vines. 1,940 plants of 21 local species were subsequently replanted, cultivated with seeds and cuttings collected from surrounding forests. Ten years later, the previous forest component is developing again. The number of returning birds is also spectacular.

9.28 Reforestation efforts involve a strong component of awareness-raising within local communities. The restoration of degraded natural habitats requires planting millions of native tree species.

Reforestation usually includes a strong educational component, including awareness-raising in schools, community nurseries and public debates. Two WWF programmes, '*Kacheche Tupande miti*' and '*EcoMakala*', have facilitated the planting of 12 million trees of local species since 1988. The '*Muti Karibu Yetu*' ('tree by our side') programme, still in partnership with the JBM, initiated the planting of 100,000 trees in the Bwisha territory, to embellish public spaces and combat heat. The 'CLiMA VIRUNGA' (Climate Mitigation and Adaptation in Virunga National Park) programme took over in 2020, with 1,500 hectares planted in a dozen surrounding communities to produce firewood and develop agroforestry. A new 240-hectare community forest, adjacent to the PNVi headquarters in Rumangabo, has made it possible to expand the chimpanzee habitat.

Among the species planted, particular attention was given to *Prunus africana*, the bark of which is used in traditional medicine and the Western pharmaceutical industry. This 'African cherry' is a species listed in Appendix II of CITES. The plantations contribute to its conservation and generate income for local populations.

9.29 With the cooperation of farmers, bamboo clumps are being planted at the edge of the Mikeno sector. Once grown, the bamboo will expand the gorillas' habitat and provide the local population with new incomes (firewood and processed products).

1 The first two sections of this chapter are based on sections of the first edition (2006) of the book by Jacques Verschuren, Jan Van Gysel and Marc Languy. This edition included a detailed, species-level study of the flora of the plains surrounding Lake Edward.

Electric cookers to combat deforestation

SÉBASTIEN DESBUREAUX, LARA COLLART

Nearly all the inhabitants of Goma, some two million people, depend on charcoal to purify the water from Lake Kivu – which carries cholera – and for daily cooking. The average household consumes 50 kilos of *makala* every month, equivalent to 160,000 tons a year for the whole city, or 3.2 million bags. Half of the charcoal is produced illegally by cutting down the PNVi forests. A study (Morisho et al., 2022) estimates the turnover from makala trafficking at 23 million dollars a year, 26% of which goes to armed groups (mainly the FDLR) and 18% to close intermediaries.

To stop this negative spiral, viable alternatives for the people of Goma must be found. The increasing availability of electricity in the city, added to the emergence of new energy-efficient cookers, may proffer a solution. However, the cooker manufacturers are reluctant to expand their activities outside the continent's major cities, as the purchase price of the equipment remains prohibitive for many rural households (though it significantly reduces their energy bills in the medium term). This is the reason that, five years after the arrival of hydroelectric power in Goma, only 5% of households connected to the Virunga Energies network are using electricity to prepare their meals. This situation – which prevails throughout Africa – is similar to that in Europe and the United States in the 20th century, where it took more than 50 years to get rid of coal.

Accompanied by economic researchers, the PNVi and Virunga Energies are promoting a transition to electric cooking in Goma. In 2011, 1,000 households received a cooker worth 70 dollars (a model developed in Tanzania) as part of a commercial operation. Of the beneficiary households, 90% also received advice on how to use the new equipment. One year later, 85% confirmed that they use the cooker to prepare half their meals. This change has led to a 30% reduction in charcoal consumption, equivalent to 10 dollars a month. At the same time, electricity consumption increased by just 2.5 dollars a month. Given that cookers have a lifespan of four to six years, the savings for households are likely to be substantial. Opinion polls also show that the families involved feel more strongly motivated to help protect the PNVi.

The success of this pilot project means the scheme can be expanded on a large scale. Institutional donors and private companies are being approached to distribute the cookers and promote their use to a large proportion of the population. This initiative will strengthen the combined objectives of reducing poverty and protecting the forests of the PNVi.

10.1 The elephant symbolises the tranquil strength of pachyderms but also the fragility of a species hunted by human greed.

10

The wildlife

SÉBASTIEN DESBUREAUX, JACQUES KATUTU, MARC LANGUY, LAURA PARKER, AUGUSTIN RWIMO SHENGERI, JEAN DE DIEU WATHAUT

The Park's wildlife experienced a dramatic decline during the war years but no species disappeared, with the exception of the wild dog. Populations can return to previous levels if responses are found to poaching, encroachments and deforestation. The recovery of mountain gorillas and savannah mammals in recent years gives reason for cautious optimism.

1. Mammals censuses

Virunga National Park (*Parc National des Virunga* – PNVi) has hosted numerous expeditions by national and international researchers since its foundation in 1925. The main ones are:
- General studies in the savannah: Cornet d'Elzius (1959–60, published in 1996), Mertens (1981), Verschuren (1988), de Merode et al. (2003–05), Kujirakwinja et al. (2006), Plumptre et al. (2010), Wanyama et al. (2014), Lamprey (2024)
- Surveys and censuses of hippopotamuses and elephants: Delvingt (1978), Mackie (1989), Aveling (1990), Languy (1994), Kujirakwinja et al. (2013, 2015), Shamavu et al. (2018), Wathaut et al. (2017, 2018, 2019, 2020, 2021, 2022)
- Mountain Gorillas: Harcourt & Groom (1972), Groom (1973), Weber & Vedder (1983), Harcourt et al. (1983), Vedder & Aveling (1986), Kalpers et al. (2003), Gray et al. (2013), Hickey et al. (2019)

The works of Cornet d'Elzius, a warden in Rwindi in the late 1950s, provide the most detailed census regarding the savannahs. It is based on thousands of days of foot patrols that allowed the collection of 69,603 'contacts' and 976,952 observations.

From the 1970s, wildlife counts progressively became aerial surveys, with field observations used to refine the findings. Routine patrols by rangers have remained essential, as they yield frequent and precise indications about the state of the wildlife. This methodology is not always consistent, but the rangers' observations are recorded on-site, reported to the operations centres by radio and compiled into a database via SMART software. Between 2014 and 2023, 28,683 ecological monitoring patrols on foot, covering 206,193 km, were conducted. These patrols recorded 97,480 contacts with wildlife and observed 1,324,501 animals.

Among the savannah species, the hippopotamus (*Hippopotamus amphibius*) was the most frequently surveyed. Monitoring efforts were particularly significant for the mountain gorilla (*Gorilla beringei beringei*).

2. Population trends

Nine inventories were conducted sufficiently rigorously and comprehensively to track the populations of five savannah species: the buffalo (*Syncerus caffer*), elephant (*Loxodonta africana*), Uganda kob (or Buffon's kob – *Kobus kob*), defassa waterbuck (*Kobus defassa*) and topi (*Damaliscus lunatus*). Though not all studies used the same methodology,

10.2 The Cape buffalo is one of the large ungulates characteristic of the Park's savannahs. In the high-altitude forests, the PNVi is also home to the forest buffalo.

10.3 The defassa – commonly known as the waterbuck – is a species typical of the Park's savannahs, where it is usually seen in small family groups.

they shared a common goal: to ensure the census using the most accurate methods available in each period. Figures 10.4 and 10.5 present the total population results for the Semliki savannahs (North Sector) and the plains south of Lake Edward (Centre Sector). The data from 1959, cited by Mertens (1983), was revised by Verschuren (1993).

These surveys concern only the savannahs to the north and south of Lake Edward. For Uganda kobs, defassa waterbucks and topis, whose habitat is confined to savannahs, the population counts correspond to the entire PNVi. For buffaloes and elephants, however, they only represent part of the total population, as these two species also live in the forest.

The populations of large mammals suffered a significant decline between 1959 and 2018. The PNVi had over 20,000 buffalo in 1959; by 2018, only 732 remained, a decrease of 97%. In this period, elephants declined from 3,425 individuals to 133 (-96%), defassa waterbucks from 2,223 individuals to 45 (-98%) and topi from 5,939 individuals to 439 (-93%). The population drop was particularly steep between 1981 and 2003, mainly due to successive regional conflicts around and within the Park. Poaching was a direct cause of the population decline, as these species were targeted for their meat and ivory.

Uganda kob was a long-standing exception, with its population remaining stable, at nearly 13,000 individuals, from 1959 to 2006. It is likely that this species, the smallest of the five, was not a preferred target for poachers. However,

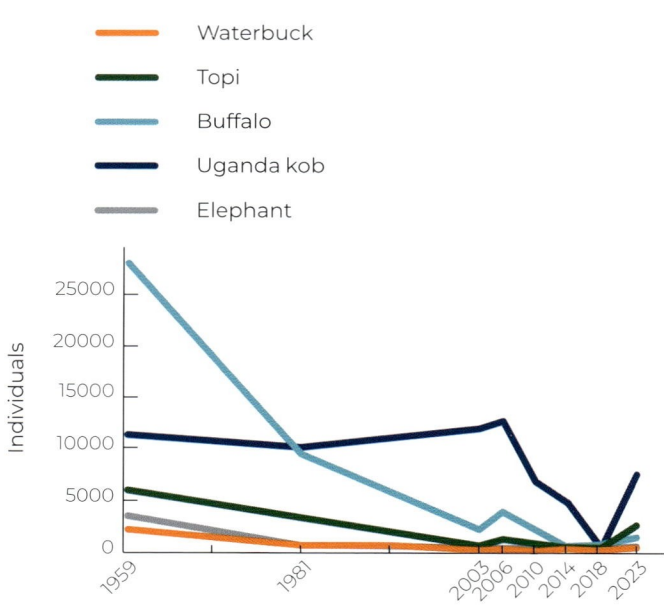

10.4 Population trends of five species of large savannah mammals.

10.5 Evolution of large mammal populations

SPECIES	SOUTH							
	1959	1981	2003	2006	2010	2014	2018	2023
Buffaloes	23,678	8,916	2,240	3748,	,505	551	697	1,535
Elephants	2,889	621	265	298	296	19	122	404
Uganda kobs	10,731	9,750	11,588	12,399	3,307	1,904	318	6,840
Waterbucks	1,531	570	169	368	85	47	45	401
Topi	5,939	3,460	855	1,353	1,040	672	439	2,743
SPECIES	NORTH							
	1959	1981	2003	2006	2010	2014	2018	2023
Buffaloes	4,629	799	52	74	649	61	35	0
Elephants	536	130	21	50	51	15	11	140
Uganda kobs	487	550	533	583	3,647	2,441	257	1,037
Waterbucks	692	210	42	6	84	168	0	17
Topi	0	0	0	0	0	0	0	0
SPECIES	TOTAL							
	1959	1981	2003	2006	2010	2014	2018	2023
Buffaloes	28,307	9,715	2,292	3,822	2,154	612	732	1,535
Elephants	3,425	751	286	348	347	34	133	544
Uganda kobs	11,218	10,300	12,121	12,982	6,954	4,345	575	7,878
Waterbucks	2,223	780	211	374	169	215	45	418
Topi	5,939	3,460	855	1,353	1,040	672	439	2,743

this exception did not last, as the Uganda kob population also collapsed to 575 individuals by 2018. Habitat conversion into agricultural zones, changes in savannah ecosystems caused by the collapse of other large mammals, and the arrival of invasive plants are possible explanations for this sharp decline.

After decades of decline, the trend drastically reversed between 2018 and 2023. The buffalo population doubled from 732 to 1,535 individuals; the elephant population quadrupled from 133 to more than 500 individuals; the topi population increased sixfold (from 439 to 2,743 individuals), the defassa waterbuck population ninefold (from 45 to 418 individuals) and the Uganda kob population thirteenfold (from 575 to 7,877 individuals). The fight against encroachments and poaching, coupled with the savannah landscape restoration that began in 2019, explains the return of these populations, some of which had found refuge in the contiguous Queen Elizabeth National Park (QENP). While the trend is encouraging, numbers still remain lower than before the 1980s.

10.6 In 60 years (1960–2020), the buffalo population has been reduced by 97% due to out-of-control poaching. As protection measures are strengthened, the population is gradually recovering.

100 YEARS OF DYNAMICS

10.7   The Uganda kob is, in normal times, the most common antelope in the Park's savannahs.

10.8   The mountain gorilla is the flagship species of PNVi. The Park is home to half of the cross-border populations. The population in the Park increased fivefold in 40 years.

3. Evolution of flagship species

3.1. Mountain gorilla

The transboundary Virunga massif – the PNVi in the DRC, the Volcanoes National Park in Rwanda and the Mgahinga National Park in Uganda – as well as the Bwindi-Sarambwe transboundary reserve, located about fifty kilometres further north, are the last refuges of mountain gorillas. The two subpopulations are evolving separately.

The first censuses estimated the Virunga massif subpopulation at 274 individuals in 1971, and 254 individuals 10 years later. Among these, 58 individuals were established in the PNVi. Their tiny population, low genetic diversity and rising insecurity led the International Union for Conservation of Nature (IUCN) to classify the species as 'Critically Endangered'.

Considerable efforts in the three countries have reversed the trend. In 2003, the number of individuals in the Virunga massif was between 359 and 395, including 131 in the PNVi. By 2010, the estimate rose to 480 individuals, including 186 in the PNVi. The latest census in 2015–2016 reported a population of 604 individuals, including 286 in the PNVi, distributed in 41 family groups and 14 solitary males. Among the four national parks that house mountain gorillas, the PNVi saw the most significant population increase (fivefold in 40 years). The individuals in the PNVi are also the healthiest. In the absence of a new transboundary census – partly due to the ongoing conflict with the March 23 Movement (M23) in the mountain gorilla sector – an extrapolation estimates the PNVi mountain gorilla population at over 400 individuals, based on an assumption of continuous growth for habituated groups and zero growth for non-habituated groups.

Habituated individuals are identified by their nasal prints. Their families have been visited by observers since the 1960s, initially for scientific purposes and later to develop ecotourism and strengthen conservation efforts. The PNVi had six habituated families between 2003 and 2012. In 2013, one family (Kabirizi) split, creating the Bageni family. In 2014, the Humba family split, creating the Nyakamwe family. From 2018 to 2021, two new families were habituated (Baraka and Wilungula), bringing the total to 10 groups. Families are often named in honour of people who have worked for their conservation, such as Baraka,

10.9   Population trend of the mountain gorillas in the PNVi.

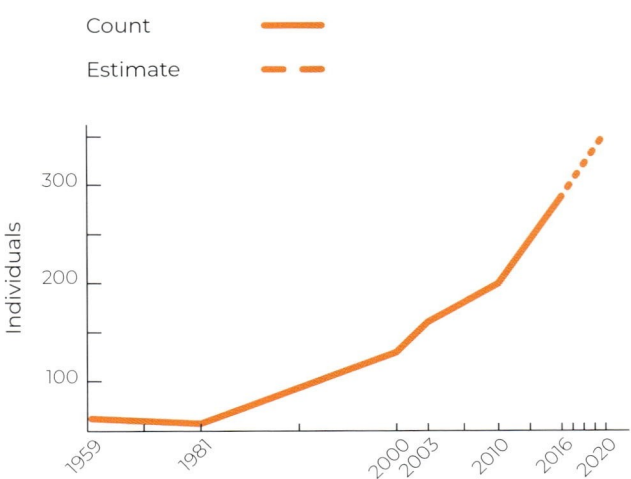

10.10 The Gorilla Doctors vets are invaluable when sick or injured animals need treatment. Here, a young orphan gorilla is being cared for at the Senkwekwe sanctuary in Rumangabo.

Kabirizi, Lulengo, Munyaga, Humba, Nyakamwe and Wilungula. The history of each silverback is also considered, such as Mapuwa ('nose'), whose nose was damaged during an interaction with another group, Bageni ('visitor'), first observed with tourists, and Rugendo ('traveller'), a gorilla who used to exhaust the teams monitoring his family.

Habituated populations experience higher demographic growth than non-habituated groups, partly thanks to the veterinary care they receive. Between 1994 and 2021, Gorilla Doctors' veterinarians treated 22 gorillas caught in traps, and saved 21. The habituated population of the PNVi recorded 78 births and 20 deaths between 2017 and 2022, increasing the population from 176 to 234 individuals. The marked dip in the Mapuwa lineage is explained by a silverback leaving his original family to create a new one in 2018. A few individuals followed him. Eight months later, the original family had been reconstituted.

Intense field monitoring is crucial for restoring the population. Between 2010 and 2022, rangers and community trackers (often former poachers) conducted 23,063 patrols and covered 185,292 kilometres to monitor habituated families and protect their habitat. Between 2014 and 2023 they made 490,053 observations. Unusually, the IUCN reclassified the species from 'Critically Endangered' to 'Endangered' in 2018.

Many threats remain. A major trap-dismantling operation in 2020 removed 1,275 traps (1.3 traps/km) meant for other mammals, such as buffaloes and antelopes, that may also be fatal to gorillas. The last poaching attack on gorillas was in July 2007, when seven individuals were killed, including the silverback Senkwekwe, leaving behind the infant Ndakasi, for whom an orphanage was subsequently established in Rumangabo.

10.11 Evolution of mountain gorilla 'habituated' families (i.e. accustomed to visits).

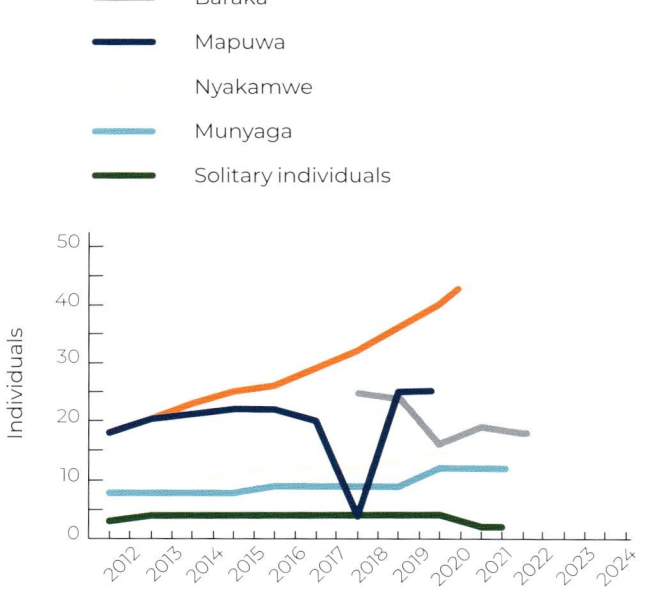
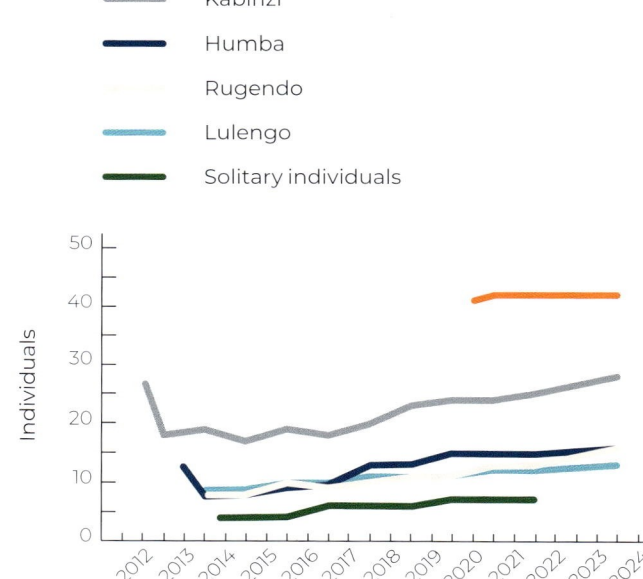

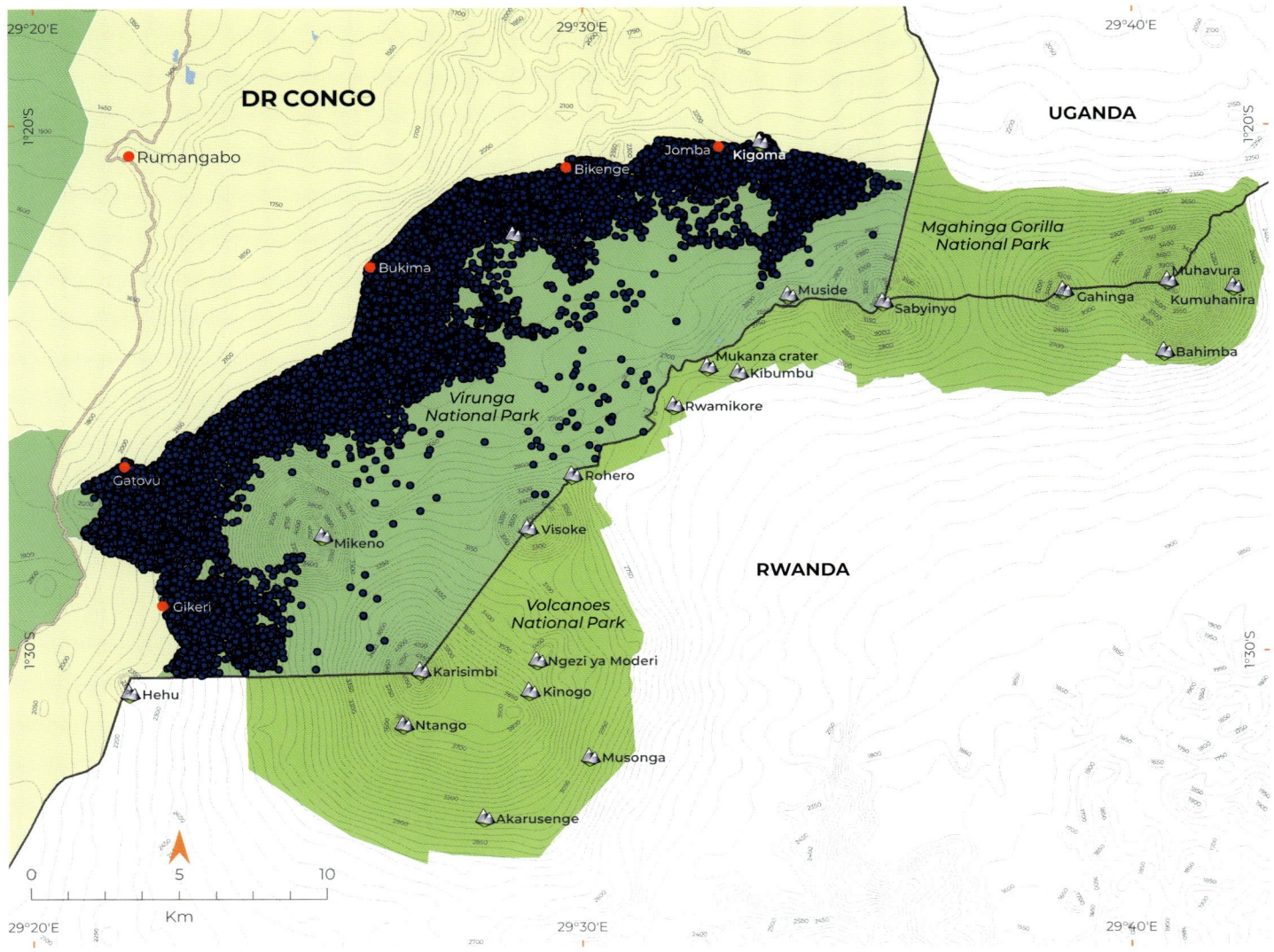

10.12 Observation points by the ranger patrols monitoring 'habituated' gorilla families (2015–2021).

3.2. Eastern lowland gorilla

The eastern lowland gorilla (*Gorilla beringei graueri*) lives in the PNVi on Mount Tshiaberimu, north-west of Lake Edward. The first population estimate was made by Cornet d'Elzius (1996), who mentioned a group of 31 individuals discovered in 1958. In subsequent years, various authors provided rough estimates with similar counts. In 1986, Aveling identified several groups totalling 25 to 30 individuals. Inventories conducted in 2001 and 2006 reported 19 and 21 individuals respectively.

The trackers' collective memory indicates that a significant group split in 2001 to form the Kipura group (4 individuals) and the Lusenge group (11 individuals). In September 2003, four individuals left the Lusenge group to form the Katsavara group, led by an eponymous dominant male. Since the death of the silverback of the Lusenge clan, its members have either become solitary or joined the Kipura or Katsavara group.

Between 2008 and 2017, militias repeatedly attacked the PNVi rangers, resulting in one death at Burusi. The area had to be evacuated. Militias have settled and mining has developed there. Only the intervention of the Gorilla Doctors' veterinarians allowed the monitoring of the individuals to continue. They numbered six in 2010 and five in 2018, distributed between the Kipura (2 individuals) and Katsavara (3 individuals) groups.

A close monitoring programme launched in 2021, involving rangers, community trackers and Gorilla Doctors, increased the population to seven individuals in 2022. However, it remains non-viable, especially genetically, as only introducing an external population could ensure its long-term survival. This prospect motivated the decision to transfer two to four females from the GRACE sanctuary near Butembo. Enclosures integrated into the natural environment were built on Mount Tshiaberimu to allow the gradual release of the captive gorillas into the wild population. Grauer's gorillas have never been successfully reintroduced, and the risks associated with translocation are high. A committee of scientists and practitioners (Gorilla Doctors, GRACE, Wildlife Impact, IUCN) accompanies this project with analyses and recommendations.

3.3. Chimpanzee

The PNVi is home to many small populations of chimpanzees (*Pan troglodytes schweinfurthii*), but information about past and current numbers is scarce.

An indication of population changes is provided by a distribution map dating from 1958–1960, produced by Verschuren (1972) and reissued by the WWF in 2006. The inventory was based on numerous surveys and land patrols:

- In the South Sector, almost all known observation sites in 1960 still housed chimpanzees: the slopes of Mount Nyiragongo, Maroba (north of Mushebele, with 26 individuals), the Rumoka volcano near Tongo, the area from Katwa and Mulalamule to upper Rutshuru. There was also a population outside the Park at Muhungezi (18 individuals).
- In the Centre Sector, chimpanzees were still found at all sites: the Mabenga to May ya Moto area, the Kasali mountains, upper Ishasha and Lunyasenge. Also, chimpanzees were sighted at Kitiriba (8 individuals) and between Talya and Kamandi (9 individuals). The latter population and that of Lunyasenge were severely threatened by human encroachment on the west coast of Lake Edward.
- In the North Sector, the 2006 observation areas corresponded with those of 1960. They showed an apparent absence on the north shore of Lake Edward at Nyaleke, but a presence further north, at the foot of the Ruwenzori (Balegha, Kikingi and Bamundjoma) as well as in the Semliki forest (Bahatsa, Lesse).

As a census comparable to those of 1958 and 2006 is lacking, observations by the Park rangers serve to provide the current status of subpopulations:

- In the South Sector, around fifty individuals are present in Tongo forest. These were accustomed to human presence between 1980 and 1987 (habituated for tourism) and despite the presence of armed groups,

10.13 Special operations to defuse traps and remove snares set by poachers are carried out.

10.14 As well as treating gorillas, the Gorilla Doctors' vets also take care of other injured species. Here, a tranquillised elephant is being treated for a leg injury.

10.15 Chimpanzees live in small populations, scattered across the Park. Some have disappeared due to human encroachments. The exact number of individuals of this emblematic, fragile species is difficult to assess.

the rangers are maintaining close monitoring with community trackers. The population suffered from the presence of refugee camps between 1994 and 1996, and remains threatened by deforestation. For these reasons, a group of 10 individuals migrated to the PNVi headquarters in Rumangabo in 2013, where their number has since increased to 18. In 2024, chimpanzees are no longer observed on the southern and eastern slopes of the Nyiragongo volcano (around Kibati), where militias and refugees have destroyed their habitat. Some individuals have, at times, been observed in the Mwaro corridor linking Nyiragongo to the Mikeno sector. The north-eastern slope of the Kitsimbanyi volcano has not been covered for many years, which makes it impossible to determine the population status in this area.

– In the Centre Sector, the entire population recorded by Cornet d'Elzius (1996) on the west coast of Lake Edward (between 200 and 230 individuals spread over the escarpment near the Lunyasenge River) has beyond doubt completely disappeared due to human encroachment. East of the Rwindi River, the groups that are spread throughout the savannah forests are doing well, but those near Mabenga are threatened by habitat destruction for charcoal production.
– In the North Sector, patrols confirm the presence of groups in the same areas as the ones identified in 1958 and 2006.

3.4. Elephant

The PNVi hosts two taxonomic groups: savannah elephants (*Loxodonta africana*) and forest elephants (*Loxodonta cyclotis*). The Park is one of the few areas where both species coexist and cross-breeding has been observed (Mondol et al., 2015).

The forest elephants live on the slopes of the Virunga massif and in the Semliki Valley forests, and some intermittent populations have been observed in the gallery forests of the Centre Sector. Regular monitoring is not possible due to the density of the canopy and the inaccessibility of the site. Cameras confirm their presence and population stability.

The savannah elephants reside around Lake Edward, notably in the Rwindi plains, the Ishasha Valley and the Kasindi plains. Verschuren (1993) recalls that, except in the savannahs, the species was ubiquitous in the Park, especially in the Kasali mountains and the lower and middle Semliki (tropical forest). The population was also regular, albeit in smaller numbers, in the extinct volcanoes (up to 2,000 m). It never settled in active volcano areas, nor in the Congolese part of the Ruwenzori massif, though some sightings have occurred in mazuku and in the Nyamulagira crater.

10.16 Beyond large primates, the PNVi hosts many species of smaller monkey, including (from left to right and top to bottom) the Angola colobus, the olive baboon, the L'Hoest's monkey and the blue monkey.

10.17   The elephant is a flagship species and an important asset for tourism. It is also a key species for maintaining the habitats and dynamics of the Park's natural ecosystems.

10.18   It is estimated that there were nearly 8,000 elephants in the PNVi in the 1960s. In the early 2000s, there were fewer than 400 but some of the population fled to the Queen Elizabeth National Park in Uganda. The troubles of the 1970s in Uganda led to the opposite situation. With the return to calm in the DRC and a reduction in poaching, elephant herds returned en masse to the PNVi. By 2024, their population is estimated at 400 to 750 individuals.

In 1960, Verschuren (1993) estimated the elephant population in the PNVi at 8,000, though a census counted only 3,000 individuals. In contrast, in 1981 their number was estimated at 750 individuals (Mertens, 1983), 350 in 2006 and between 100 and 200 in 2018. This dramatic decline entirely correlates with the success or failure of anti-poaching efforts. The decline began in the 1960s with the development of the ivory trade, leading to the slaughter of 'big tuskers'. In the 1970s, the rangers' interventions succeeded in stabilising and even increasing the population. A second decline followed in the early 1980s, linked to institutional difficulties affecting the rangers' work on the ground. Finally, the sociopolitical degradation and the wars of the 1990s–2000s paved the way for the near-disappearance of the species.

Fortunately, elephant movements are frequent between the PNVi and the QENP. In the mid-1990s, significant migrations occurred from the DRC to Uganda, where the security situation was more stable, despite the frequent poaching. In 2020, the movement unexpectedly reversed: a herd exceeding 500 individuals resettled in the Ishasha plain south of Lake Edward. It has since fragmented into multiple groups, indicating that the population is now sustainably re-established. This phenomenon illustrates the importance of maintaining ecological corridors between different sectors and national parks, sometimes located in multiple countries, for long-term species survival.

The savannah elephant population is now estimated at 800 individuals, possibly as high as 1,000, including those north of Lake Edward. Its presence is instrumental in restoring the Ishasha corridor, as it allows the regeneration of the savannah flora. This has a positive impact on the return of ungulates and lions.

The return of the elephants to the Centre Sector testifies to the effectiveness of the Park's measures to eliminate threats from armed groups, poaching and encroachments. The electric fence along the Park's border, in particular, is instrumental to habitat restoration and human–wildlife conflict prevention (see chapter 16). However, there have been several fatal elephant attacks on residents and a few cases of retaliatory poaching.

3.5. Hippopotamus

Seventeen hippopotamus censuses have been conducted since 1959. The population peaked in the mid-1970s, with nearly 30,000 individuals. This is an exceptional number – the world's largest concentration of hippopotamuses, representing 20% of the species globally – owing to effective protection that allowed population growth. The situation contrasts starkly with the 1990s, when the population was decimated. It counted fewer than 1,000 individuals in 2005, a 97% loss over 15 years. Since then, populations have slightly recovered, as numbers fluctuate between 1,000 and 2,000 individuals, depending on diseases (anthrax) and poaching intensity.

In addition to the negative impact on short grasses, the near-disappearance of this mega-herbivore affects fish stocks in Lake Edward, which are also an important protein source for the human population (see chapter 16). The hippopotamus grazes 30 to 50 kg of grass daily, and its excrement feeds plankton and fish. Studies in other African parks (Schoelynck et al., 2019) report a direct correlation between hippopotamus presence and fishing volumes. In Lake Edward, this correlation seems particularly strong, given the exceptionally high numbers of hippopotamuses and fish caught in the 1970s–1980s, which simultaneously collapsed from the 1990s onwards.

Militia members and some corrupt elements of the Armed Forces of the Democratic Republic of the Congo (FARDC) practise hippopotamus poaching. In the early 2000s, poaching was so intense that the price of meat did not exceed 1 dollar per kilo. In 2024, the value of a whole hippopotamus ranges between 500 and 600 dollars, and a kilo of meat fetches around 2 dollars, half that of goat meat. The tusks also fuel the ivory trade. In the early 2000s, prices ranged between 5 and 10 dollars per kilo (value in Goma before resale elsewhere in the country or abroad). Poachers arrested by Park rangers in 2024 mentioned prices between 80 and 100 dollars per kilo, which reflects its greater rarity.

3.6. Lion

The lion (*Panthera leo*) is a difficult species to census. In 1931, Hubert (1947) estimated their number in the Rwindi plain at 250 individuals. Ten years later, it had dropped to around a hundred (Bourlière and Verschuren, 1960). In 1960, detailed observation reports available to Cornet d'Elzius (1996) allowed him to estimate the population south of Lake Edward at 105 to 200 individuals. In the 1970s it was commonly assumed, though not proven by proper censuses, that their numbers had significantly increased due to conservation efforts for the species and its prey. In 1965, tourists had a one in three chance of seeing a lion. Between 1970 and 1990, an observation was practically guaranteed.

In 2006, the species was observed regularly, but during the 2010s lions became almost invisible due to wars, human–

10.19 In the 1970s, the PNVi was home to the largest concentration of hippopotamuses in the world. Over the last 30 years, their number has fallen from 30,000 to less than 1,000. The volume of this species is vital to the fish productivity of Lake Edward.

10.20 Anthrax is a zoonosis caused by a bacterium whose highly resistant spores can survive for many years. At the PNVi, it causes episodes of mass death among the hippopotamuses. Here, a Gorilla Doctors' vet examines a sample taken from a hippo corpse.

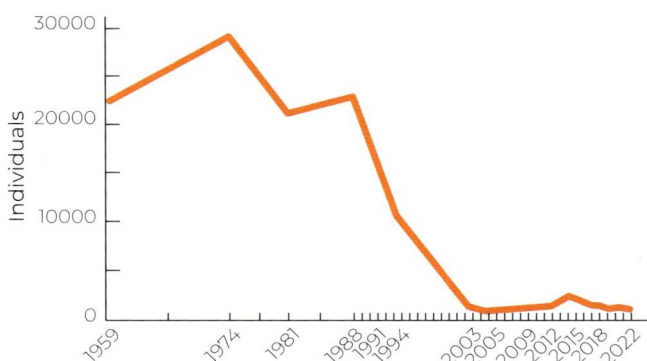

10.21 Evolution of the hippopotamus population.

10.22 Distribution and evolution of the hippopotamus population.

SECTORS	1959	1974	1981	1989	1991	1994	2003	2005	2009	2013	2015	2017	2018	2019	2020	2021	2022
Semliki River	8,811	3,852	2,325	945	1,038	141	34	50	128	117	106	264	203	182	95	52	107
Lake Edward	3,630	9,638	7,769	7,019	6,326	4,011	892	683	403	504	1,204	1,030	742	659	507	577	473
Rwindi River	1,300	1,278	920	2,324	2,121	1,314	78	35	4	0	0	0	0	0	0	0	0
Ishasha River	100	335	462	467	407	400	141	61	500	780	1,096	530	538	529	486	526	535
Rutshuru River	7,340	10,262	7,337	9,121	6,369	4,417	164	58	64	27	0	11	18	33	0	46	23
Marshes	1,175	3,813	2,282	2,949	1,705	566	0	0	39	26	0	8	41	54	111	79	67
TOTAL	22,356	29,178	21,095	22,825	17,966	10,849	1,309	887	1,138	1,454	2,406	1,843	1,542	1,457	1,199	1,280	1,205

wildlife conflicts and habitat degradation. In the PNVi, armed groups targeted prey (topi, kobs and buffalo) and killed lions for trophies. Near the QENP, lions attacked domestic livestock and this led to retaliatory poisonings. Such events may lead to the elimination of entire family clans, as seen in 2018 and 2021, with two poisonings resulting in the deaths of 6 and 11 individuals, including 8 cubs. The reduction in prey numbers due to the spread of invasive plants also affects the QENP populations (more than those in PNVi).

As part of a cross-border project, the Park launched in 2021 a lion restoration programme targeting the threats to their survival. A monitoring and research station was built in Kinyonzo, along the Ishasha River. Daily tracking was conducted using collars, veterinary assistance was available and applied research aimed to minimise habitat degradation by invasive plants. The reintroduction of fire regimes in the Centre Sector also stimulated the reproduction of the ungulates on which they feed.

In 2024, precise numbers of *Panthera leo* in the PNVi are unknown. The species is concentrated in the Ishasha Valley and sightings west of the Rutshuru River are rare, but radio collar data suggests that males frequent the Rwindi plains for short periods. Rangers at Ishango and Kasindi (North Sector) also report vocalisations and footprints, possibly from migratory lions from Uganda.

In 2004, a study on the carrying capacity of the PNVi/QENP transboundary ecosystem estimated the population potential at 905 individuals, provided that sufficient prey biomass is present and human pressures are effectively mitigated (Treves et al., 2009).

10.23   Following the recovery of its prey, the King of the Savannah is gradually recolonising the plains in the Park.

3.7. Warthog and giant forest hog

Between 1958 and 1960, Cornet d'Elzius (1996) estimated the warthog (*Phacochoerus africanus*) population south of Lake Edward to be between 1,732 and 2,700 individuals. In 1970, d'Huart (1971) estimated their population in the same area at 3,874 individuals, while Mertens (1983) estimated it at 1,200 in 1981. Two aerial surveys conducted in 2003 by de Merode (2003) and Kujirakwinja et al. (2006) estimated it at 445 and 694 individuals respectively. In 2010, a new aerial survey by Kujirakwinja et al. (2010) estimated 1,763 individuals. The latest aerial survey (Lamprey, 2023) reported 1,501 individuals.

The precision of aerial surveys is lower for warthogs and giant forest hogs than for more visible species, such as elephants. However, the downward trend shown by these studies confirms the impressions of the field rangers. The population decline in the 2000s is attributable to various factors, including the dwindling of aardvark numbers, whose burrows are regularly occupied by warthogs, and increased human activities in the PNVi, including poaching.

The giant forest hog (*Hylochoerus meinertzhageni*), discovered by scientists in 1904 in a mountain forest in Kenya, is the largest of Africa's wild suids. As one of its few protected strongholds, the PNVi provides an ideal habitat to this species, because it thrives in a mosaic of forested areas, thorny bushes and contiguous savannahs at low altitudes in the Albertine Rift. From 1958 to 1960, Cornet d'Elzius (1996) estimated the population of the entire plain south of Lake Edward to be between 1,200 and 1,500 individuals. In 1974–

10.24   Cross-border collaboration with researchers from the neighbouring Queen Elizabeth National Park led to a joint programme to monitor the lion population. This lioness's radio collar provides information about her activities and movements.

10.25   Despite major fluctuations, the warthog population – a resilient and opportunistic species – has generally held up well against threats to its survival (predators, poaching, epidemics).

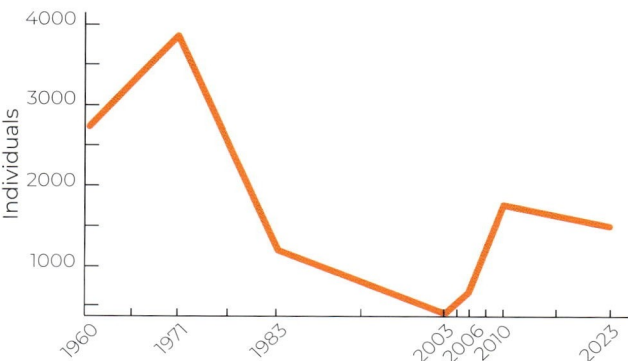

10.26 Evolution of the warthog population.

1975, d'Huart recorded an average population density of 2.62 individuals/km², corresponding with a total population of over 3,000 individuals (d'Huart, 1978). Mertens (1983) estimated it at around 1,500 animals in 1981, and Lamprey (2023), through aerial survey, at only 200.

These significant variations correspond with the substantial, sudden fluctuations observed in wild suids due to epidemics (swine fever), high annual reproduction rates (2 to 6 young per litter), predator population density, poaching pressure and favourable or extreme weather conditions. By way of illustration, Hoier (1952) reported a hunting campaign in 1945–1946 due to the enormous damage caused by suids to crops near the Park. In 18 months, the hunting tally reportedly reached 329 bushpigs, 619 giant forest hogs and 77 warthogs.

10.27 A giant forest hog is surprised by a camera trap on the edge of a pond where he takes his usual mud bath.

3.8. Okapi

Due to its secretive habits, the okapi (*Okapia johnstoni*) was only discovered by scientists in 1901. It was first observed in the Semliki forest, probably near Mundala (Sclater, 1901), and was present on the territory before the creation of the Albert National Park in 1925. No species census has been conducted in the PNVi, but Bourlière and Verschuren (1960) provide a distribution map of the data from the 1950s.

Apart from one unconfirmed sighting in 1988 near the Biangolo River, no observations were reported until 2006, when a survey mission was organised by WWF and the PNVi, supported by the GIC (Gilman International Conservation) Foundation. In eight days, 17 signs were observed between the Makayobo and Lesse rivers. In 2008, another survey conducted by the Park and the Zoological Society of London (ZSL) confirmed the presence of okapi on both sides of the Semliki River. With additional data collected in 2010, the number of individuals was estimated at around 50 to 100 (0.095 okapi/km²), a density comparable to that of the Okapi Wildlife Reserve (Kümpel et al., 2015).

All indications are that a viable population still exists in the PNVi but this needs confirmation from inventories to be conducted north of the Park, including on the right bank of the Semliki River. The security threat posed by the ADF-NALU militias makes this an impossible task in the northern Watalinga area, where the species is also likely to be found.

3.9. Other species

The flagship species mentioned here represent only a fraction of the PNVi's wildlife diversity (see the list of mammals and birds in the annexes). Very few species are regularly monitored, making it hard to quantify their population dynamics over time.

More than 225 mammal species have been observed in the Park, including many rare ones in the Albertine Rift. The Rwenzori duiker (*Cephalophus rubidus*), an endemic species, lives exclusively in this mountain. Camera traps placed in the Rwenzori have recorded several African golden cats (*Caracal aurata*) at a height of over 3,000 m, as well as pangolins, aardvarks, honey badgers and porcupines in the savannahs. The elusive Sitatunga antelope (*Tragelaphus spekii*) was photographed for the first time in 2023, nestled in the reeds at the mouth of the Rwindi River.

The forests harbour an impressive array of rare reptiles and amphibians: Jameson's mamba (*Dendroaspis jamesoni*), Great Lakes viper (*Atheris nitschei*) and Gaboon viper (*Bitis gabonica*), are often observed in the southern forests in the Park, as is the very rare three-horned Rwenzori chameleon (*Trioceros johnstoni*).

Among the more than 760 recorded bird species are some breeding pairs of the iconic shoebill (*Balaeniceps rex*), photographed in 2023 near Kihangiro and in the Lake Edward plains.

4. Savannah biomass evolution

The PNVi has long been renowned for its exceptional, world-record-achieving biomass per unit area. Bourlière and Verschuren (1960) showed that the biomass of ungulates per km² in the savannahs south of Lake Edward (1,250 km²) was four times higher than that of the Serengeti. In 1959, the total weight of the main ungulates was 34,523 tons, compared to 25,567 tons in 1981 and 4,043 tons in 2006.

Some scientists have suggested that the biomass per unit area was abnormally high and caused by the significant

10.28   The spotted hyaena is a ubiquitous predator that feeds on both live prey and carrion.

10.29   Some examples of the many species of snakes in the PNVi (from left to right and from top to bottom): Chifundera's green snake, gaboon viper, rhinoceros viper and Great Lakes bush viper.

10.30 The only species now extinct in the Park, the African wild dog appeared in the 1930s and was exterminated 20 years later. If the density of its prey returns to what it was at that time, reintroducing the species could be envisaged.

number of hippopotamuses, which accounted for three-quarters of the total. They also claimed that the hippopotamuses' presence could harm ecosystems, due to overgrazing and trampling. This suggestion has remained controversial, but is no longer relevant, as the total biomass has dropped by 95% between 1959 and 2024 (including that of hippopotamuses in similar proportions). The low density prevailing for the past 30 years correlates with the degradation of grassland savannahs, colonised by acacias and other shrub formations.

For several decades, poaching was the main and almost sole cause of the decline of large mammals in the PNVi. As with elephant populations, the fluctuations in numbers follow the curve of anti-poaching efforts led by the Park's rangers: flourishing in the 1960s–1970s, declining from the 1980s and inoperative during the war years. Since 2005, the public–private partnership between the Congolese Institute for Nature Conservation (*Institut Congolais pour la Conservation de la Nature* – ICCN) and the Virunga Foundation has, however, allowed the PNVi to regain a foothold and re-engage in the fight against wildlife destruction.

Moreover, since 1994, entire sections of the Park have been converted or degraded by agriculture or logging for charcoal. By the mid-2010s, human encroachment occupied 15% of the Park surface. In 2024, it decreased to 13.5%, or 932 km^2 (see chapter 9). The impact on the Park's ecosystems causes habitat reduction and fragmentation. They also facilitate the spread of invasive species that compete with the native flora favoured by herds, and increase the risk of zoonoses in a region conducive to their development.

After decades of continuous decline, the state of the PNVi's animal populations is concerning but not desperate. No species have disappeared since the Park was created in 1925, except for the wild dog (*Lycaon pictus*), exterminated in the mid-1950s here and elsewhere in Africa. There is every reason to believe that populations can return to their former

10.31   Despite ongoing threats to the integrity of the PNVi, the growing mountain gorilla population symbolises the hope of safeguarding the extraordinary biodiversity it harbours.

levels if sustainable solutions are found to tackle poaching, agricultural encroachment and deforestation. The increased numbers of mountain gorillas over the last 20 years, and the restoration of large savannah fauna since the early 2020s, seem to confirm this cautious optimism.

11.1 Fishing has been practised in Lake Edward since time immemorial. The history of the Park was shaped by trade-offs between using the lake for fishing and protecting the Park's terrestrial ecosystems.

11
Lake Edward

FRÉDÉRIC HENRARD, MÉTHODE BAGURUBUMWE, GRACIEN SIVANZA

The Congolese waters of Lake Edward used to count among the richest in fish worldwide. Illegal fishing is encouraged by armed groups, and the threat of oil exploitation looms. Despite security and political difficulties, the Park works to minimise the impact of fisheries and promote the sustainable exploitation of resources.

1. Ecosystems

Lake Edward, which is located at an altitude of 914 metres, is fed from the north by the Nyamagasani River, flowing down from the Ruwenzori mountains; from the west by the Talya and Duka rivers, descending from the Mitumba mountains; and from the south by the Ishasha, Rutshuru and Rwindi rivers. To the east, other rivers, streaming in from Uganda, also contribute to its water supply. Its area of 2,240 square kilometres is divided between the Democratic Republic of Congo (1,640 square kilometres or 73%) and Uganda (600 square kilometres or 27%). Its maximum depth is 117 metres and its average depth is 30 metres (17 metres in Uganda and 40 metres in the DRC).

Along with some other Rift Valley lakes, Lake Edward is one of the world's richest in fish. Its shallow depth allows

11.2   Until the late 1970s, Lake Edward was home to the largest concentration of hippopotamuses in the world (30,000 individuals).

11.3   The Semliki River originates near Ishango. Since Stanley's time, the lake has been described as one of the sources of the Nile.

surface waters to cool and sink to the bottom ('downwelling'), and the fertiliser from hippo droppings promotes the multiplication of microorganisms that constitute the fishes' diet. The near-disappearance of hippos in the 1990s raised fears of a major decline in fish productivity.

Lake Edward remains relatively untouched and, unlike Lakes Victoria and Tanganyika, has never suffered from the introduction of non-native fish species (Kambere Mulwahali et al., 2015). The fish fauna is similar to Lake George, which is connected to Lake Edward to the northeast by the Kazinga Channel. No fewer than 49 species have been inventoried, including several endemic species. Recent scientific missions indicate that new species may still be discovered, especially in the depths (Borges, 2021). In 2015, the International Union for Conservation of Nature (IUCN) classified 70% of the species as 'of least concern' and identified two vulnerable species (*Haplochromis aeneocolor* and *H. nubilis*), as well as two critically endangered species (*Haplochromis guiarti* and *H. labiatus*).

2. Historical evolution[1]

2.1. Marginal human presence (before 1925)

Studies preceding the creation of the Albert National Park (*Parc National Albert* – PNA) in 1925 are rare. A colonial administration report provides the following insight: 'Over 40 years, according to various direct witnesses, the population of Vitshumbi has dropped from 1,500 to 2,000 inhabitants in 1894 to 92 inhabitants in 1929 and 37 inhabitants in 1934, a reduction of between 96 and 98% of the initial population, due to the sleeping sickness prevailing at Lake Edward in the early 20th century.'[2] (Harroy, 1987) The estimates are based on field observations made by doctors from the Ruzizi-Kivu Hygiene Commission. Fishing was rudimentary and limited to shallow waters: trap fishing (called 'ngana') and net fishing from rafts made of banana trunks. Small plank canoes appeared during the first half of the 20th century.

2.2. New demographic and administrative configuration (1925–1948)

Between 1929 and 1935, Lake Edward was gradually incorporated into the PNA. The pockets of populations established on its shores were expelled as part of an authoritarian environmental policy and control measures against malaria, which caused numerous deaths. At the same time, the lake's economic potential attracted private companies eager to develop industrial fishing. In this context, the creation of the PNA crystallised the opposition from local populations, traditional chiefs and the neighbouring British protectorate –

11.4 Even before the creation of the Park in 1925, fishing was firmly established in Lake Edward. Here, in Kamandi in 1933.

each of whom was, however, prompted by different motivations. The positions taken by colonial authorities on the ground also differed from the ones taken in Brussels within a highly centralised administrative model, and were sometimes contradictory.

A colonial administration report from 1932 mentions 200 people fishing on the lake. In 1934, the Indigenous Labor Administration stated that 'Lake Edward is completely evacuated due to sleeping sickness, which was facilitated by a ban on fishing in the lake, and the populations have been scattered throughout the territory' (Harroy, 1987)[3].

The outbreak of World War II relaxed the control exercised by Brussels. The PNA management took advantage of this relaxation to promote the lake as a food source for the populations in North Kivu, who were suffering from severe protein deficiencies. They also wanted to counter competition from Ugandan fishing and create a more positive attitude towards what later became the PNVi. However, by the end of the war, environmental degradation got worse, with increasing numbers of trees felled to build canoes, uncontrolled movements of people and goods, and an upsurge in poaching and bushfires. Despite a policy of conciliation, the conflicts persisted and continued to feed the anti-colonial propaganda.

2.3. Rise of fishing and the fisheries (1947–1965)

The PNA management sought to establish a compromise between environmental protection and the region's socio-economic realities. Technical and scientific missions validated the development of a fishing policy managed by the colony, in collaboration with local Congolese authorities. In 1947, the 'Van Cools' Commission promoted the rec-

11.5 Traditionally, smoked and dried fish were the main fishery products. Here, in Vitshumbi in 1945. Paved roads leading to urban markets and ice-making have gradually led to the emergence of fresh fish.

B. ACTIVITE EN AFRIQUE

A. PARC NATIONAL ALBERT

Droits indigènes

Le fait essentiel à noter à l'actif du Parc National Albert est le règlement des droits indigènes restés litigieux depuis de nombreuses années. Une commission d'enquête dirigée avec clairvoyance et un grand souci d'équité par M. L. DE WAERSEGGER, Procureur du Roi, a réalisé ses travaux avec la collaboration du Conservateur du Parc National Albert. Les actes de cession ont été passés et les indemnités dues aux indigènes ont été immédiatement liquidées.

Ainsi a pris fin une situation qui entravait considérablement l'exercice du mandat confié à l'Institut.

Moyennant quelques concessions et l'établissement de deux centres de pêche sur le lac Edouard, les indigènes ont cédés tous leurs droits sur les terres englobées dans les limites du Parc National Albert énoncées au décret du 12 novembre 1935 et les arrêtés subséquents du 4 mai 1937 et du 17 mai 1939.

Pêcheries indigènes

Les deux pêcheries, servitude que l'Institut espère voir un jour levée, seront organisées sous forme de coopératives indigènes, sous la direction des autorités territoriales. Situées à Kiavivionge, au Nord du lac Edouard, et à Vitshumbi, au Sud, une enclave a été délimitée à leur intention par les conservateurs. Le cadre de cette tolérance dans les limites du Parc National Albert a été déterminée d'une façon stricte afin de réduire au minimum les incidences fâcheuses qui résultent de cette présence.

Tous les villages de pêcheurs réinstallés sur les rives du lac Edouard et de la Semliki ont été évacués et leurs installations détruites.

Actuellement, seuls des cantonniers séjournent encore dans les villages de Katanda et Bushendo, en Territoire de Rutshuru. A brève échéance, l'entretien des routes traversant le Parc sera assuré par le personnel de l'Institut, avec l'aide matérielle de l'Administration Territoriale. Ainsi toute circulation non contrôlée sera éliminée ou localisée aux seules voies d'accès aux deux pêcheries.

a) Station de Rumangabo

Travaux d'aménagement

L'activité dans ce domaine s'est principalement portée sur l'édification d'habitations en matériaux définitifs pour gardes et travailleurs. Certains aménagements ont été apportés au bâtiment administratif afin de le rendre habitable par le conservateur, en attendant la possibilité de construire une maison à son intention.

11.6 In 1948, the magistrate Léon De Waersegger presided over a commission of enquiry that made recommendations to address the grievances of the indigenous populations. The agreements signed by the Institute of National Parks of Belgian Congo (IPNCB) with the traditional chiefs recognised the right to fish from Vitshumbi and Kyavinyonge. This historic compromise remains the basis for the governance of Lake Edward. Here, an extract from the Annual Report of the IPNCB, 1948.

11.7 Photograph of fishermen at Vitshumbi in 1957. The photo was taken by the former Belgian H.M. King Leopold, who made four long visits to the Park, in 1925, 1933, 1957 and 1959. The thousands of items in his collection constitute exceptional anthropological and naturalist documentation.

ognition of the PNA by traditional chiefs in exchange for granting them fishing rights. Acts of concession were signed, compensations were allocated and the small fishing installations around the lake were destroyed. Two indigenous fishing cooperatives were re-established, with the support of colonial authorities, in the enclaves of Vitshumbi (in the south) and Kyavinyonge (in the north).

In 1948, a Cooperative of Lake Edward Indigenous Fishermen (COPILE) was created – the ancestor of today's Virunga Fisheries Cooperative (COPEVI). From its base in Vitshumbi, it supervised the activities of 250 fishermen under the joint authority of the Provincial Department of Indigenous Affairs and Agriculture (Hunting and Fishing) and the Park Warden, who remained responsible for judicial police functions. Corollary to authorising these two fisheries, allowances were made for the movement of people and goods – with transit rights to Rutshuru, Lubero and Beni – and the use of motorboats on the lake. Fishing and traffic movements remained prohibited elsewhere in the PNA, including in bays and rivers, and internal regulations were imposed on the fisheries to limit environmental risks.

From the very beginning of its existence, the COPILE has had a difficult relationship with the Institute of National Parks of the Belgian Congo (*Institut des Parcs Nationaux du Congo Belge* – IPNCB), which became the Congolese Institute for Nature Conservation (*Institut Congolais pour la Conservation de la Nature* – ICCN) in 1969. The COPILE did not adhere to the agreements, which led the IPNCB to break the agreements and forced the colony governor to arbitrate between the two parties. The tensions between the Park management, the COPILE and the central authority (Kinshasa) persisted over time.

The COPILE was prosperous in its early years, as evidenced by annual production statistics: 2,828 tons in 1950

11.8 Hippopotamuses were everywhere on Lake Edward. Collective memory evokes 'hippo backs like streets of cobblestones' along the banks. Poaching during the war years saw the species almost wiped out.

11.9 Lake Edward was placed under the supervision of the Centre and North Sectors. In 2020, a separate Lake Sector was created to improve the work of the ICCN on waters and in the fisheries. The headquarters of the new sector are set up in Kihangiro.

11.10 The ICCN is mandated to enforce the law on Lake Edward. The rangers collaborate with a wide range of stakeholders, including the army and the police, the judiciary, the fisheries and environment ministries, fishermen's representatives, women's associations and civil society.

and 6,010 tons in 1960 (but only 3,900 tons in 1964). However, an IPNCB study noted that the organisation of fishing in the Congo pales in comparison with Uganda, and estimated that it would be possible to maintain catches at 5,000 tons if sustainable fishing practices were established.[4]

2.4. Years of decline (1965–2019)

The compromise granted by the IPNCB in 1948, which combined customary law and sovereign authority, constitutes the foundation of governance at Lake Edward to this day. It has, however, lost some authority and legitimacy, due to the weakening of State authority and traditional power, and the gradual emergence of new actors. These include fishing committees, local political leaders and various population groups or institutions that settled at Lake Edward without deriving income from fishing, such as traders, churches and schools.

The 1948 agreement was renewed in 1979 and, on this occasion, the cooperative was renamed the COPEVI. The principles remained: traditional chiefs along the lake enjoyed a fishing monopoly in exchange for their commitment to protect the Park. However, they increasingly failed to live up to these renewed commitments and anarchy set in. The COPEVI's mismanagement grew worse, fishing catches decreased and individual fishermen's demands – based on State regulations that had never applied to Lake Edward – created new power dynamics.

In 1984, the COPEVI revised its management model to ensure that financial returns compensated for declining fishing catches. It allowed the transfer of fishing rights to individual shipowners, who became subcontractors. This liberalisation led to a rapid increase of boats and fishermen. Fishing committees were set up and technical administrations were established in the fisheries. Within a few years, all the registration numbers allocated to the COPEVI under the agreement signed with the ICCN were assigned to individual shipowners. The COPEVI's role was limited to selling permits and regulating fishing.

This new configuration did not end the precarious situation of the fishermen hired by individual shipowners to fish for them, as in a feudal system, in exchange for a share of the catches. Apart from denying these fishermen social rights and forming a barrier to the modernisation of the profession, this model also encouraged illegal practices on two levels: the COPEVI earned more money by accrediting an increasing number of canoes – beyond the number of registrations agreed with the ICCN – and private operators who did not receive a registration from the COPEVI turned to armed groups to obtain from them fishing rights in the areas under their control. (Balole Bwami et al., 2008)

This organisational mode profoundly affected the power dynamics among the various actors, which were marked by competition. Population growth, successive regional conflicts starting in 1994 and populism – politicians attracted by the potential of an expanding electorate – further exacerbated tensions. Despite the continued presence of the ICCN during the war years, the lake sub-region gradually spiralled out of control between 2000 and 2015: fishing escaped regulation, authorised fisheries fell into the hands of armed groups, and unauthorised fisheries multiplied.

100 YEARS OF DYNAMICS

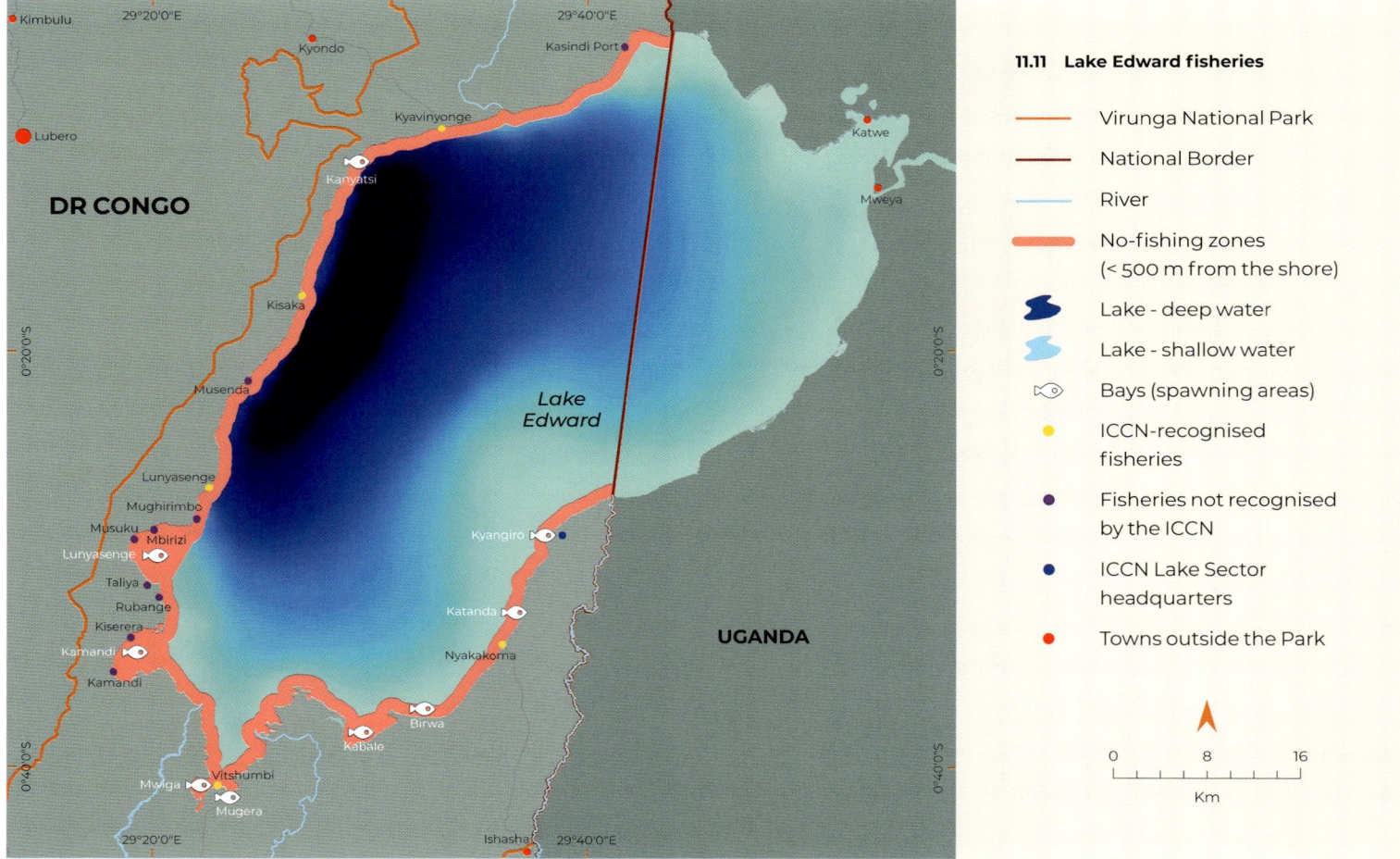

11.11 Lake Edward fisheries

2.5. New governance framework (2019–2024)

In 2019, after a 10-year regulatory vacuum, the ICCN renewed its agreement with the COPEVI for a further 10 years. The objective remains to regulate fishing to benefit local populations while ensuring the protection of Virunga National Park (*Parc National des Virunga* – PNVi). The new agreement introduces several innovations: it recognises two fisheries on the western shore (Kisaka and Kyavinyonge), establishes guiding principles for fishery management (including residency criteria) and confirms the rights of shipowners and individual fishermen. While the ICCN remains the principal State institution, as Lake Edward is part of the PNVi, the new agreement also grants significant roles to other State authorities, including the Ministries of Fisheries, Environment, Health and Education.

The publication of the agreement occurred in a context of political unrest. However, the inclusive approach promoted by the ICCN gradually gained support from stakeholders: technical ministries, the COPEVI, shipowners, fishermen, and women's groups involved in fish processing and sales. Among other results, the ICCN succeeded in creating a database of registered canoes, conducting a census of fishermen, establishing a land-use plan for the fisheries, confirming the State boundary (contested by Uganda), limiting the presence of technical administrations and deploying a participatory policy to handle infractions.

The gradual restoration of State authority was applauded by political leaders and a large segment of the population, but strongly and sometimes violently contested by a minority whose interests were affected: individuals not authorised to settle in the fisheries, armed groups promoting illegal fishing, politicians advocating for the declassification of the PNVi, and various officials susceptible to corruption.

3. Legal framework

Lake Edward, a protected area of national interest managed under Law No. 14/03 of 11 February 2014 on Nature Conservation, is part of the PNVi. As such, the ICCN is responsible for the lake. International commitments made by the DRC, under the UNESCO World Heritage Convention and the Ramsar Convention on Wetlands, reinforce its status as a protected area.

Law No. 14/03 stipulates that fishing is permitted in compliance with conservation objectives. This authorisation is granted as an exception to conservation measures 'in the interest of public health and safety, as well as the food security of populations living near protected areas' (Art. 20). In the PNVi, these provisions are implemented within the framework of the partnership between the ICCN and COPEVI, which is also governed by Articles 8 and 10 of Law No. 15/015 of 25 August 2015, establishing the status of traditional chiefs. This legal and regulatory framework posits that the COPEVI is to carry out fishing activities in Lake Edward with the consent of the ICCN. It does not permit any exception to land ownership rights: no one is authorised to sell or acquire land within the PNVi (including in the fisheries).

Article 4 of Law No. 14/03 establishes the framework for the ICCN cooperation with other State authorities: 'The State and the Province shall adopt and implement appropriate policies, plans, and programs to contribute, among other things, to the economic growth, rural development, poverty reduction, and climate regulation through the natural and biological resources, ecosystems, and natural sites and monuments.' These provisions apply to the services within the fisheries responsible for fishing as well as for health, education and religious practices, among others. On a sovereign level, Article 41 stipulates that the armed forces and the national police may support the ICCN.

It should be noted that Law No. 14/03 applies exclusively to protected areas and no conflicting law can override it. Any previous provisions contrary to this law are repealed by Article 85. Fishing regulations are also applicable, though these are based on older texts, some of which predate 1960.

4. Stakeholders

The ICCN is the principal State authority on Lake Edward, carrying out its mandate in collaboration with other competent authorities, whether sovereign or technical. In 2020, the ICCN created a dedicated sector for governing Lake Edward (Lake Sector). Its territorial jurisdiction includes the lake's surface waters and fisheries. It has 80 rangers, supported by around 50 Navy military personnel (under the ICCN command). Its operational base is located in Kihangiro, on the eastern shore of the lake, equidistant from Vitshumbi and Kyavinyonge.

The COPEVI is the cooperative of traditional chiefs that grew from the COPILE, established in 1948. Its purpose is to catch, process and market fish from Lake Edward. It includes the 11 traditional chiefs and sector chiefs of the areas bordering on the PNVi: the chiefdoms of Baswagha, Batangi and

11.12 The fishermen committees may have several hundred members. They play a major role in changing living and working conditions on Lake Edward. Women's associations organise the processing and sale of fish.

Bamate, and the Bapere sector in Lubero territory; the chiefdoms of Bashu and Watalinga, and the Beni-Mbau and Ruwenzori sectors in Beni territory; the chiefdoms of Bwito and Bwisha in Rutshuru territory; and the Bukumu chiefdom in Nyiragongo territory. The traditional chiefs and sector chiefs are cooperative members of the COPEVI. Territorial administrators may attend meetings in an advisory capacity.

The shipowners hold the fishing licences sold by the COPEVI under the terms of the agreement signed with the ICCN. They typically own the boats and equipment, but hire fishermen to work on the water (up to six fishermen per boat). Fishermen are generally compensated in kind (a portion of the catch). Under the PNVi regulations, neither shipowners nor fishermen own the plots in the fisheries where their houses are built. The fishermen are organised into committees counting up to several hundred members. Over the past 30 years, these committees have played a major role in ending the feudal practices that once governed their daily lives. They perform control, service (in particular input supply) and advocacy functions (for example, for the release of fishermen arrested by the Ugandan army). In 2012, the fishing committees of Vitshumbi and Nyakakoma united within the Committee of Independent Fishermen of Lake Edward (COPEILE), later renamed the Federation of Individual Fishermen's Committees of Lake Edward (FECOPEILE). This federation is the spokesperson of Lake Edward's shipowners and fishermen vis-à-vis the authorities and the public. It played a major role in the fight against oil exploration in 2011–2013.

The women residing in the fisheries have also formed associations. The main purpose of these women's committees is to organise the fish trade. Member contributions also help resolve various social issues, such as illness, accidents and assaults. The number of female committee members is equivalent to that of male association members.

11.13   The fisheries around Lake Edward are becoming small towns. In 2024, the population on the shores of the lake is estimated at 80,000 people (around 10,000 households). Here, an aerial view of Vitshumbi in 2022.

Due to the presence of armed groups, the Armed Forces of the Democratic Republic of the Congo (FARDC – naval and ground forces) are deployed more or less permanently on the water and in the fisheries. These areas also host other State services: national police, including the Ministry of Fisheries, schools and health facilities. Many of these officials do not receive regular salaries and have developed predatory practices towards the inhabitants.

Finally, non-fishing populations have settled in the fisheries since the 1990s: traders, teachers, medical staff, priests and pastors, militia members and the families of these various groups.

5. Set-up of fishing activities

5.1. Regulations

The PNVi management plan divides the Park into three categories: zones of exclusive integral conservation, sensitive protection zones, and integral conservation zones of tourist interest. Additionally, one zone is specific to Lake Edward: a zone for the conservation and sustainable exploitation of resources. The related regulations are defined in the ICCN–COPEVI agreement, which refers to State fishing sector regulations. Specific provisions for Lake Edward include these key points:
- A total of 1,187 boats are authorised. A quota of licences is allocated to each of the five recognised fisheries.
- The registration of shipowners and fishermen provides the means to distinguish between legal and illegal activities (as well as the legitimacy of the residents of the fisheries).

Fishing and related activities are also regulated:
- Hours: Night fishing is prohibited.
- Fishing zones: Fishing is forbidden within 500 metres of the shore, as well as in river mouths and spawning grounds.
- Prohibited fishing practices: Using nets with a mesh size smaller than 4.5 inches, spearfishing (potolo), using a casting net (American-style cast net), tam-tam fishing (kikubo), dragnet fishing (ngurura), fish traps (kitunga), explosives, electric wires, or light for fishing.
- Fraudulent practices: Trading and bartering on the lake (kijeki), salting fish on the lake, unloading at unauthorised locations, allowing the presence of minors in a canoe, and shellfish trading, for example.

5.2. Fisheries

When the PNA was established, the small traditional fisheries along the shores of the lake and neighbouring rivers involved only a few dozen people. The colonial authorities evacuated them at the time, but they were repeatedly re-established. The 1948 agreement between the IPNCB and COPILE recognised two fisheries: Vitshumbi in the south and Kyavinyonge in the north. A third fishery, Nyakakoma, was added in 1965 by the personal decision of President Mobutu, who wanted to grant a favour to Mwami Daniel Ndeze (of the Bwisha chiefdom). Its status

— year 1959
— year 1994
— year 2005
— year 2023

11.14 Evolution of the size of Vitshumbi.

is unique because it falls under the joint authority of the ICCN and the Mwami who, based on the 1965 presidential decision, considers the fishery his private property. As he is the traditional chief of the Bwisha chiefdom, the Mwami is also a member of the COPEVI.

From 1980 to 2010, illegal 'pirate' fisheries proliferated. Some were pseudo-regularised by local authorities and corrupt ICCN agents. Except for Kisaka and Lunyasenge, they often served as strongholds for armed groups, and their survival was precarious due to declining fish catches. In 2019, the new ICCN–COPEVI agreement recognised the Kisaka and Lunyasenge fisheries, raising the number of authorised fisheries to five. This recognition acknowledged the impossibility of restoring the 'ecological corridor' and aimed to end illegal activities on the western coast. Today, the main pirate fisheries are Kasindi port, Katundu, Mosenda, Mbirizi, Musuku, Muhirimbo, Taliha, Kiserera and Kamandi. Most are controlled by local warlords and political leaders seeking votes.

The fisheries on Lake Edward have gradually turned into villages or even small towns. Several factors contribute to this evolution: population explosion, the weakness of the ICCN in the postwar years, the persistent failures of the COPEVI, State interference and political populism. In 2024, the population living on the shores of Lake Edward is estimated at 80,000 people (around 10,000 households),

- year 1959
- year 1989
- year 2006
- year 2023

11.15   Evolution of the size of Kyavinyonge.

with 30,000 in Kyavinyonge, 25,000 in Vitshumbi and 15,000 in Nyakakoma.

5.3. Practices

Fishing on Lake Edward remains rudimentary, despite attempts at semi-industrial development after World War II, mainly by using 'whaler' boats and building landing facilities. These attempts by private operators, and later by the COPEVI, were short-lived.

Fishing has been conducted for decades using canoes and small boats that carry about ten people. The canoes, made of planks, are often motorised. This model has advantages: it provides employment to many people, operations are stable and adaptive, and investment barriers are low (even during conflicts). Conversely, managing fishery resources, particularly regulatory compliance, is greatly complicated.

Two types of fishing are practised on Lake Edward: gillnet fishing and line fishing (or longline fishing), where fish are caught using fry collected in spawning grounds. The boats usually stay on the lake for four to five days, while motorised canoes shuttle to collect the catches and relieve the fishermen.

Five species of fish make up the bulk of the catches: Tilapia (*Oreochromis niloticus eduardianus*), Bagrus (*Bagrus docmak*), Barbel (*Barbus altianalis eduardianus*), Protopterus (*Protopterus aethiopicus aethiopicus*) and

——— non-existing in 1959
——— year 1994
——— year 2006
——— year 2023

11.16 Evolution of the size of Nyakakoma.

11.17 The shipowners own the fishing licences and the boats. Fishermen carry out the fishing work and are paid according to the catch.

11.18 Five species make up the bulk of the catch (mainly bagrus and tilapia). The lake's capacity is between 14,000 and 16,000 tons/year in DRC waters.

11.19 Fishing practices have changed little, despite the arrival of motors and modern inputs. Wooden pirogues make up almost all the boats.

Clarias (*Clarias gariepinus*). Tilapia and Bagrus account for about 90% of the total catch. Clarias has almost disappeared in recent years.

The Ugandan side of the lake and the southeastern part of the Congolese side are the most fish-rich areas due to their shallow depth (they provide 70% of the catches). Fish become scarce towards the west, where the depth exceeds 40 metres. The west coast accounts for 12% of the catches, a share equivalent to that of Congolese fishermen in Ugandan territorial waters. The northern part of the lake represents only 5% of the catches, but motorised canoes allow Kyavinyonge fishermen to operate across the entire lake. The most favourable periods are April–July and September–October, when surface water temperatures are highest (Balole Bwami et al., 2008).

11.20 Clouds of mosquitoes are common on Lake Edward.

11.21 The quality of the fish from Lake Edward is an asset in the battle against competition from imported fish. The industry benefits from the 'Virunga National Park' label, highly prized by consumers.

5.4. Processing and distribution

Fish is sold in various forms: fresh, dried, salted and smoked. Women handle the processing and marketing. Fresh fish represents the majority of sales as it ensures the best remuneration. Salting takes place using traditional methods with rudimentary equipment. Smoking occurs in traditional underground ovens or over open fires.

Fish is consumed within a 50 km radius around the lake. The yields from Nyakakoma and Vitshumbi are destined for the Goma markets, while yields from Kyavinyonge, Lunyasenge and Kisaka are directed towards the markets of Butembo, Kasindi and Beni. Transportation is via motorcycle and truck.

5.5. Revenues

The ICCN estimates the sector's annual revenue at around 45 million dollars. For 2023, statistics report 1,602 tons collected from the recognised fisheries of Vitshumbi, Kyavinyonge, Nyakakoma, Lunyasenge and Kisaka (the five recognised fisheries). Bagrus accounts for 75% of the catches, and Tilapia 20%. These statistics do not include illegal fishing catches, e.g. unrecognised canoes, undersized fish, clandestine landings, or night fishing.

The average price of fish at the landing sites is around 2–3 dollars per piece, depending on species and size. Of this amount, 30% is allocated to expenses, 40% goes to the shipowner and 30% remains for the fishermen (Bene, 2016). The profit margins for fish sold in the city (beyond 5 dollars) are also low due to multiple deductions, such as taxes on the goods, veterinary checks and barriers during transport, and costs such as fuel and ice.

11.22 The fish is consumed within a 50 km radius of the lake. Women are responsible for processing (dried, smoked, fresh) and distributing it to urban markets.

Fish from Lake Edward is less competitive than fish from Uganda, Rwanda and Lake Tanganyika – and frozen Chinese fish, which is imported in great quantities! – due to its price, the variable weight of the catches and the absence of a cold chain. It does, however, have its strengths, in particular its quality and the adaptability of the operators. Lake Edward is also a healthy environment with low exposure to environmental accidents, which ensures the resource's sustainability. The entire sector also benefits from the 'Virunga National Park' label, prized by consumers (Bene, 2016).

6. Threats to the ecosystems

6.1. Fish stock management

There are two authoritative studies regarding the fishery capacities of the Congolese side of Lake Edward: Petit (2006) and Vakily (1989), which establish the Maximum Sustainable Yield (MSY) in a range of 14,000 to 16,000 tons/year. As mentioned earlier, the COPEVI's peak catch was reached in 1960 with 6,010 tons. In 1999, the COPEVI recorded 265 tons taken by licensed ships. In 2023, statistics compiled by the ICCN for the five recognised fisheries (Vitshumbi, Kyavinyonge, Nyakakoma, Lunyasenge and Kisaka) show a catch of 1,602 tons.

Statistics on fishing catches must be treated with caution, as significant biases should be taken into account, including disparities in measurement methods and units, some catches not being counted, clandestine landing points, and so on. Since the 1990s, however, all the studies point to a drastic fall in catches, reflecting the serious management problems that emerged at that time. Lake Edward suffers

11.24   A fisherman working with mosquito nets.

11.25   Ceremony for the destruction of non-compliant equipment.

11.23   In 2021, an ICCN count estimated the number of boats at 1,900. This number remains stable in 2024 despite the deteriorating security conditions caused by the M23.

11.26   Compliance with regulations guarantees the renewal of fish stocks.

11.27 An inspection of dugout canoes by rangers of the Lake Sector. The photo was taken by a drone, which helps to secure deployment in the event of armed groups infiltrating the boats.

from overfishing and fishermen remain poor because their productivity is low. This situation calls for improved governance and regulation, including a reduction of the number of pirogues, compliance with technical standards (protection of spawning grounds and net mesh) and a crackdown on illegal activities (Balole Bwami et al., 2008).

A count of pirogues carried out by the ICCN in 2021 estimated the number of boats at 1,900, whereas the total authorised under the ICCN–COPEVI convention and the specific provisions for the Nyakakoma fishery is 1,187. This number remained stable in 2024, despite the sharp deterioration in security linked to the conflict with the March 23rd Movement (M23).

6.2. Anthropogenic pressures

Pressures from the increase in the fisheries population have an impact on fishery resources and terrestrial ecosystems. The development of fisheries on the west coast has put an end to the movement of wildlife between the PNVi's Centre and North Sectors. The needs of the population generate problematic behaviour, including wood harvesting, small-scale livestock farming, the presence of domestic animals, extensive agriculture and waste production. Finally, despite the efforts of the ICCN, the weakness of the State encourages poaching (of hippos in particular) and trafficking by armed groups.

7. Transboundary dimension

7.1. Institutional cooperation

Cooperation between the DRC and Uganda on Lake Edward is centuries old. It dates back to the time of the Belgian Congo and the British Protectorate of Uganda, when they competed for fisheries and could not agree on anti-poaching measures. Their management models were different: integral conservation in the Congo (which led to the relocation of local populations before re-establishing fisheries at a later stage) and supervision of ancestral fishing activities in Uganda.

These different approaches are at the root of the institutional configurations that still govern the management of the lake today. On the Congolese side, the waters form an integral part of the PNVi and are the responsibility of the ICCN. In Uganda, Lake Edward is not included in the Queen Elizabeth National Park (QENP) but falls under the Depart-

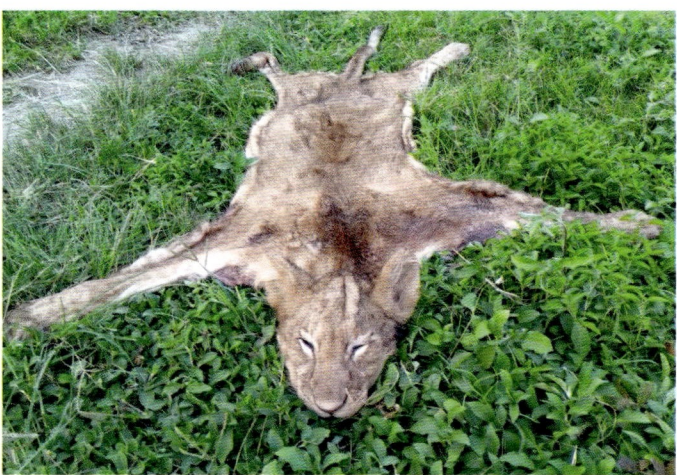

11.28 Fishing presents no threat to the Park, but it does contribute to human pressures. Fishing on the west coast has put an end to the movement of wildlife between the Centre and North Sectors. Here, poaching of a hippopotamus and a lion.

11.29 Lake Edward border limit

The natural displacement of the mouth of the Ishasha River has confused the demarcation of the border between the DRC and Uganda. This has resulted in several armed incidents between the two navies and hundreds of arrests of Congolese fishermen.

- Virunga National Park
- Historical and legal borderline
- Delineation of the border claimed by Uganda due to confusion over a demarcation marker.
- River
- Lake – deep water
- Lake – shallow water
- ICCN-recognised fisheries
- Towns inside the Park

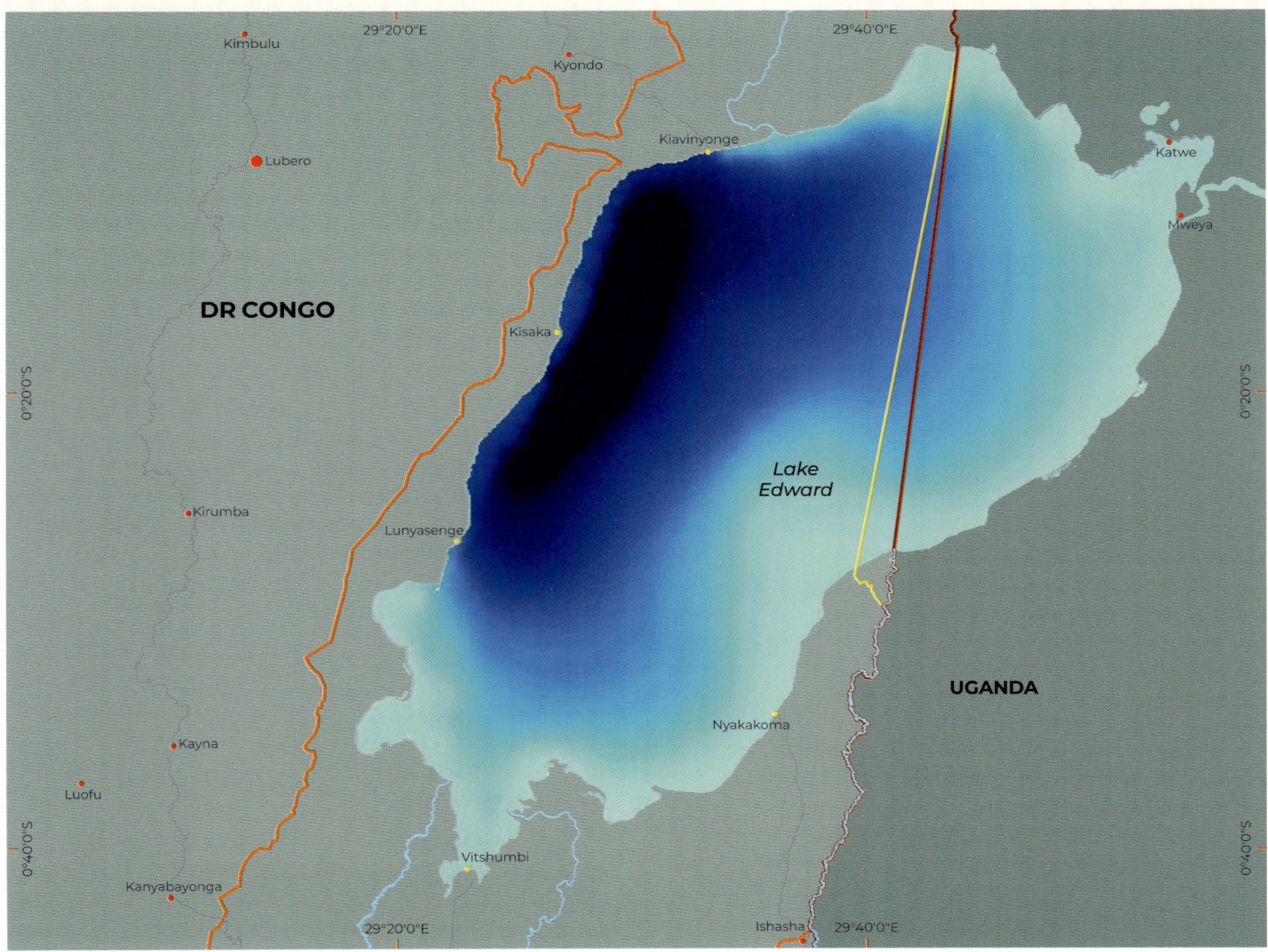

ment of Fisheries Resources of the Ministry of Agriculture, Animal Industries and Fisheries. The role of the Uganda Wildlife Authority (UWA), which is responsible for the terrestrial part of the QENP, is limited to protecting the animals living in the lake. In addition, security aspects are handled by the Uganda People's Defence Force (UPDF) and not by the QENP rangers. On the Ugandan side, fishing on the lake is organised into five territories: Katwe, Rwenshama, Kishenyi, Kazinga and Kayanja. The Department of Fisheries is present in all the fisheries and regulations are strictly enforced.

In 2024, the collaboration between the ICCN and UWA is optimal. Meetings between Park management and on-site coordination are frequent. Consultations are also conducted within the framework of the Greater Virunga Transboundary Collaboration (GVTC, see chapter 13). Operationally, on the lake, each party focuses on its jurisdiction and is careful to avoid any cross-border incidents.

7.2. Demarcation of the lake border

The location of the border on Lake Edward has strained relations between the two countries for about fifteen years – since 2010 – because one of the demarcation points, the mouth of the Ishasha River, had shifted due to the trampling of hippos, which gradually diverted the river's course westwards. Confusion over this landmark (the river mouth) deprived the DRC of a large strip of territory: 5,301.8 hectares of lake area and 697.5 hectares of land. This confusion caused several armed incidents between the two naval forces, including the deaths of 21 military personnel and civilians during waterborne shootouts in 2018. The problem was exacerbated by public mapping platforms like Google Maps, which reproduced the erroneous border.

In 2023, a joint commission from the International Conference on the Great Lakes Region (ICGLR) conducted a field mission to clarify the legal boundary. The commission validated the historical boundary (restoring the DRC's rights) and urged both States to respect it. Recommendations were also made to demarcate the boundary using buoys and to correct the boundary on Google Maps.

7.3. Arrests of Congolese fishermen in Uganda

The waters of Lake Edward are richer in fish in Uganda than in the DRC for two reasons: the water is shallower, and fishing regulations are better enforced. Many Congolese fishermen are tempted – or are forced by the boat owners – to cross the border to increase their income. For a time, confusion over the border exacerbated the

11.30   In 2023, a joint commission of the International Conference on the Great Lakes Region (ICGLR) validated the historic borderline.

11.31 Many Congolese fishermen cross the border to fish in Uganda. Since 2015, the Ugandan army has arrested hundreds of offenders, who were released following protest campaigns initiated by fishermen's committees in the DRC.

problem, as many Congolese fishermen found themselves in Congolese waters that were no longer recognised by Ugandan authorities.

From 2015 onwards, the reactions of the Ugandan army (UPDF, Uganda People's Defence Force) became increasingly violent. Arrests increased and hundreds of fishermen spent months in Ugandan prisons, until they were released following protest campaigns led by fishermen's committees. Hundreds of boats have also been confiscated and several fatal incidents resulting from UPDF gunfire have been documented. This situation will persist until a lasting improvement is made in the security situation and the management shortcomings of the fisheries on the Congolese side are remedied.

8. Stabilisation and sustainable development

Lake Edward lies at the crossroads of conservation and sustainable development issues. The restoration of State authority and the establishment of a governance framework to regulate these issues are *sine qua non* conditions for preserving ecosystems and ensuring the renewal of fishery resources for the benefit of local populations. The ICCN's efforts include the fight against armed groups, the regulation of fishing practices – registration of boats, protection of spawning grounds and checking of inputs – and management of the many population groups living in the fisheries.

The ICCN fulfils its mission from a community perspective. Rangers are deployed in the fisheries and collaboration with the other competent authorities is promoted, including on regulatory issues. The support for the fishing industry within the framework of the Virunga Alliance also helps to promote peaceful relations. It aims to stimulate the capacity of associations and small private entrepreneurs to take initiative by working on the elements structuring the sector: fishing regulations, organisation of the cold chain (thanks to electricity), improvement of transport conditions and facilitation of sales on urban markets. The revival of tourist activities in the Centre Sector (savannah area) is also helping to develop the local economy on the west side of the lake.

1 The historical section up to 1960 draws heavily on the study by Patricia Van Schuylenbergh (2016).
2 African Archives, Hygiene 837, Ruzizi-Kivu Hygiene Commission
3 African Archives, AIMO 163, Indigenous Labor Administration, Rutshuru Annual Reports
4 State Archives: African Archives, AGRI Fund 192, File 76.

Oil exploitation

BANTU LUKAMBO, JOSUÉ MUKURA

Sub-Saharan Africa is a global 'hotspot' for oil exploration. The oil fields in eastern DRC are not part of the 'central basin' that covers the country's centrally located territories, but belong to the Albertine Rift, which extends into Uganda. The supposed oil potential of Virunga National Park (*Parc National des Virunga* – PNVi) is mainly located in the Lake Edward sub-region, which is the subject of much speculation, as the necessary measurements and sampling to evaluate the quantity, quality, accessibility and yield of these deposits have not been carried out (only a few seismic tests have been conducted).

Environmental advocates staunchly oppose oil exploitation in or near protected areas in the DRC, as elsewhere. Their objections are numerous: a massive influx of workers and equipment, the development of permanent infrastructure, such as roads, airports and housing, major ecosystem disruptions, soil and water contamination and increased human pressure, which leads to the prospect of additional agriculture, livestock, deforestation and poaching. In response to these concerns, oil companies promote mitigation measures that, for the most part, fail to reassure local populations about the major and irreversible upheavals induced by future operations. In the case of the PNVi, activists emphasise the critical importance of Lake Edward as a source of fresh water and protein for millions of people. They also point to the increased threat to the habitat of fragile species.

In the early 2010s, the Congolese government granted exploration licences to several oil companies for 'blocks' covering several sub-regions of the PNVi (notably blocks 3, 4 and 5, which included the lake). The prospect of oil exploitation on Lake Edward triggered a large opposition campaign, bringing together lake fishing associations, civil society representatives, local and international NGOs, political leaders and the PNVi's leadership. UNESCO also took a stand by reminding the DRC of its obligations related to the status of the PNVi as a World Heritage Site.

The general mobilisation led the Congolese authorities to revise their plans and, a little later, Total – the company that had acquired the exploration rights – announced it would do the same. However, a new oil exploration company, SOCO, purchased the licence and began conducting seismic studies to quantify the deposits in Lake Edward. Its actions on the ground, carried out with the complicity of local armed groups, were illegal and severely violated human rights, including corruption, threats of violence and torture. Several civilians and PNVi rangers lost their lives during the confrontations. The depiction of SOCO's misconduct in a documentary (*Virunga*) brought the situation to the attention of a wide audience after its release on Netflix. Added to the mobilisation of the local population, the ensuing international outrage forced the company to cease its activities. To date, the government has not authorised the resumption of any exploration campaigns in the PNVi, despite having issued new licences in various regions in 2021.

The threat of oil exploitation in the PNVi could be influenced by major developments taking place in Uganda. The regulatory situation is different because Queen Elizabeth National Park is not listed as a UNESCO World Heritage Site, and the Ugandan authorities seem determined to exploit the country's oil reserves, including those in natural reserves. The exploitable oil reserves in Uganda are estimated at 1.4 billion barrels and the government aims to export 200,000 barrels a day as part of a consortium with Total. The first phase of exploitation focuses on the reserves of Lake Albert (with offshore wells) and Murchison Falls National Park, where drilling has been initiated. In total, 31 extraction zones are planned, with 426 wells and a crude oil processing plant. Transportation will be ensured by a heated underground pipeline (East African Crude Oil Pipeline) connecting the country's oil fields to the Indian Ocean (in Tanzania) over a distance of 1,440 km.

To date, the Ugandan side of Lake Edward is not included in the exploitation projects, but this situation could change. If so, such development would undoubtedly rekindle discussions about the oil potential of Lake Edward in the DRC, and might consequently challenge the integral protected status granted to the PNVi.

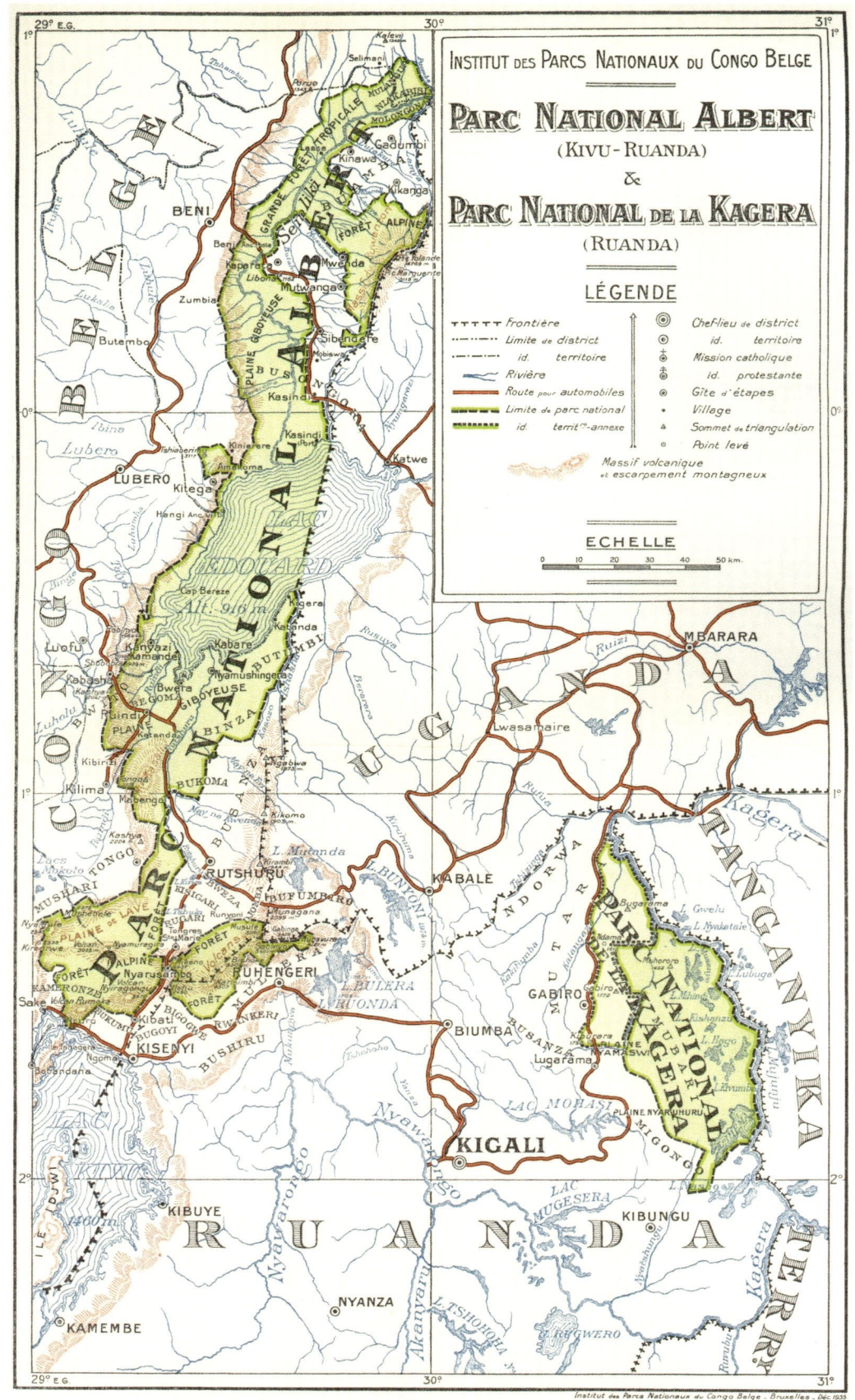

12.1   Since 1934, the Institute of National Parks of Belgian Congo has managed the Albert National Park (PNA) and the Kagera National Park in Rwanda. This 1935 map shows that the PNA included a portion in its extinct volcanoes sector which, after Rwanda's independence, became the Volcanoes National Park.

12
Institution and governance

**JEAN-PIERRE D'HUART, NESTOR BAGURUBUMWE, STANISLAS BAKINAHE,
FRÉDÉRIC HENRARD, JOSÉ KALPERS, ROBIN LAIME, ERASME NGENDE, FILIPPO SARACCO**

The governance of Virunga National Park depends on the solidity of its managing institution and the resources at its disposal. History is rich in lessons on the evolution of the institutional framework. The wisdom and pragmatism of the Park's leaders are among the conditions required for its survival and development.

1. The colonial vision (1925–1960)

The raison d'être of the Albert National Park (*Parc National Albert* – PNA) and the mission of the Institute of National Parks of the Belgian Congo (*Institut des Parcs Nationaux du Congo Belge* – IPNCB) was clearly defined in their founding texts. The decree establishing the Park assigned it 'an exclusively scientific purpose'. As for the responsibility of the IPNCB, this was expressed by King Albert I in these terms: 'Here you have a monument to preserve, a monument nature has built over millennia and which has been given as it has formed to this day, since the early modern age.' In 1933, the future King Leopold III specified that national parks must be 'long-term observatories of natural evolution, as well as places of contemplation and rejuvenation'. In this context, the IPNCB was assigned a triple duty (IPNCB, 1937): complete conservation 'with the most attentive vigilance', scientific exploration for the progress of knowledge, and the opening of certain parts of the parks to controlled tourism.

These philosophical pillars, on which the IPNCB's pre-Independence research and development activities were based, find their origin in the thoughts of Victor Van Straelen, a visionary scientist. As early as 1937, he assigned to the IPNCB a programme of static activities (maintaining the absolute integrity of reserved territories) and dynamic activities (inventory and description of species, observation of ecological phenomena and biological cycles). The vocation of the parks was summarised as follows: 'Absolute reserves will constitute islands of primitive life, surrounded by regions subdued by man. Here, Nature can be studied in its infinite complexity without being further complicated by the disturbing influence of artificial factors. The monitoring of an absolute Nature Reserve will appear as a vast enterprise of experimental ecology' (Van Straelen, 1937). Van Straelen's conceptual considerations have had a lasting influence on the structure of the institution responsible for their implementation and on the legislative framework that establishes the PNVi boundaries (See Appendix 2, Languy, 2005). The IPNCB aimed to 'remove from human interference a natural environment as vast as possible, then study the reactions of this environment left to itself', developing its scientific character with a central focus on the complete protection of nature.

Like the colonial institutional structures, the IPNCB administration was based in Brussels. Its decisions were made in the metropolis, and the management authorities were Belgian or European. The roles assigned to Congolese staff were essential 'technical support functions', including rangers, guides, preparators, taxidermists, workers, road men and porters. The IPNCB, predominantly financed by the Ministry of Colonies, enjoyed legal personality, which gave it great autonomy of action and access to numerous additional funds for its activities and publications.

The administrative body of the IPNCB was the National Parks Commission, composed of a president, a secretary

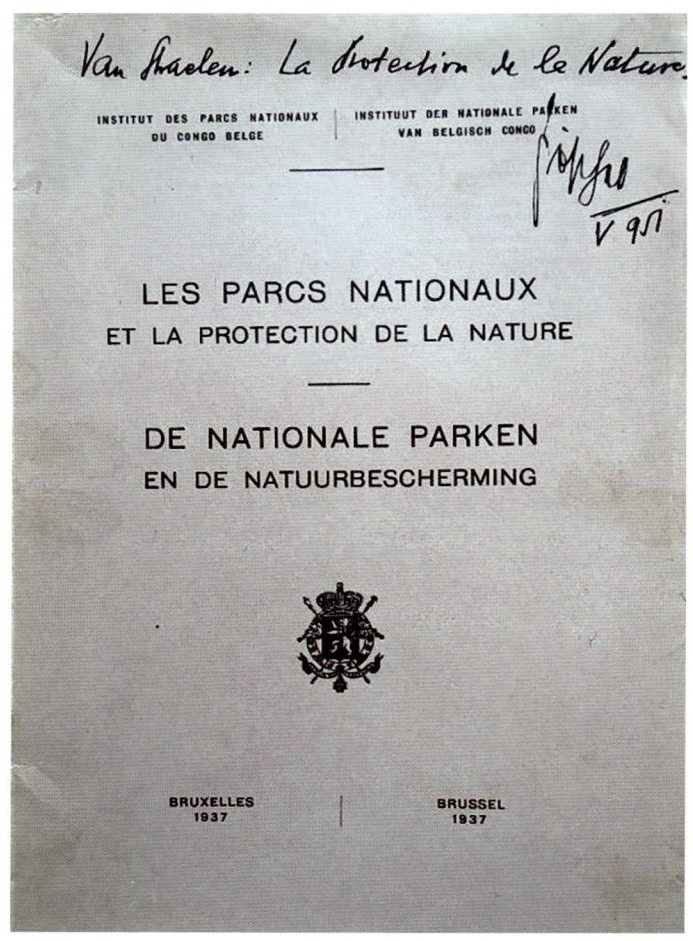

12.2 The vision of the first PNA managers has influenced the policy of nature protection that was implemented by the Institute of National Parks of Belgian Congo as of 1937.

and 24 members appointed by the King. The majority of them came from scientific institutions, one-third from foreign institutions, to reflect the international character of the conservation policy. The executive body was a Management Committee – an offshoot of the commission that delegated its president, secretary and six members, including a representative of the Ministry of Colonies – that met monthly (IPNCB, 1942). Even though most missions and activities occurred at the PNA, the institute maintained this hyper-centralised structure[1] until Independence. The first IPNCB five-year report highlighted the problems related to the distance and slowness of communications between Brussels and the field, which included issues with supply and logistical transport, conflict resolution, staff skills and training.

Initially, the PNA was divided into two Sectors: the South Sector, where the Chief Warden operated first from Rutshuru, then from Rumangabo; and the North Sector, with a Deputy Warden based in Mutsora. The managerial positions were initially held by military officers and later by Belgian scientists. Two more Europeans completed the team: a Works Supervisor and a Visitor Delegate based, from 1936, at the Rwindi camp. From 1934, public interest in the Rwindi–Rutshuru plain attracted increasing numbers of visitors to the PNA (nearly 900 in 1938). By the end of 1939, the African surveillance staff included 28 rangers in the North Sector and 21 rangers and 32 auxiliaries in the South Sector. Despite the Park's distance from the metropolis, the PNA staff managed to implement its programme wonderfully: the delineation of the Park, the establishment of basic structures, surveillance and protection and support for exploration missions.

12.3 The Park's administrative office in Rumangabo, which was also the residence of the Chief Warden, is one of the oldest buildings in the PNVi.

INSTITUTION AND GOVERNANCE

12.4 The PNVi headquarters in Rumangabo is the former residence of the PNA Director. An imposing building dating from 1946, nowadays it houses the Park's operational centre.

12.5 The Operations Centre ('CCOPS') at Rumangabo headquarters oversees the security of the Park, its staff and visitors (including tourists).

12.6 Aerial view of the Rumangabo forest, with the Nyiragongo (left) and Nyamulagira (right) volcanoes in the background. In the foreground, the roofs of the Mikeno lodge pavilions.

12.7 The headquarters of the North Sector of the PNVi in Mutsora.

World War II significantly slowed the development of the PNA, but the institution's scientific vocation remained central. After the war, research activities resumed with renewed vigour. Between 1930 and 1960, as many as 10 major exploration and study missions were sent to the PNA. Between 1945 and 1960, the IPNCB published 298 volumes and booklets totalling 493 studies, 169 of which concerned the PNA alone (Van Schuylenbergh and De Koeijer, 2017).

2. A national institute working with partners (1960–2005)

After Independence, between 1960 and 1967, the parks in the DRC faced significant pressure from poaching and encroachments, which the rangers struggled to contain. The early 1960s also saw a severe deterioration of security, leading to the deaths of several rangers in clashes. Under Dr Jacques Verschuren, mission head and only European remaining at the PNA in 1960–61, the first Congolese park wardens (Mburanumwe, Munyaga, Kajuga, Bakinahe) attempted to organise the staff, whose heroic efforts to defend the Park were notable. The PNA's only resources came from irregular and providential donations from the Frankfurt

12.8 In the difficult and dangerous environment in which the rangers operate, the ICCN and Virunga Foundation pay particular attention to the quality of recruitment, training and oversight.

Zoological Society, the WWF, the 'Foundation for the Promotion of the Study of Congo's National Parks' and a few private donors. This turbulent period was marked by the lack of a central structure at the head of the institution, leaving a demotivated, small, poorly equipped and inadequately trained staff to face too many challenges. The prospect of the Park's utter destruction was hinted at in reports from the field. (Verschuren, 2001)

In 1969, President Mobutu sought the support of the Belgian Cooperation Agency to restore the national parks. Dr Verschuren, responsible for this bilateral cooperation project, was appointed Director of the new National Institute for Nature Conservation (*Institut National de la Conservation de la Nature* – INCN) which would become later, in 1975, the Zairian Institute for Nature Conservation (*Institut Zaïrois pour la Conservation de la Nature* – IZCN). Thanks to the new political, technical and financial support it was

12.9 The rangers continuously patrol the natural habitats, carrying out many tasks: surveillance, people and infrastructures protection, ecological monitoring, law enforcement, etc.

12.10 The pylons erected at strategic locations enable the operation of a telecommunications network covering the entire Park.

granted, it established itself as a strong institution. In 1973, the General Directorate centralised all administrative and financial management services in Kinshasa, along with an Environmental Directorate, while the technical and scientific management was entrusted to a technical-scientific Directorate based in Goma. 1978 saw a radical change: the IZCN was detached from the services of the Presidency, a new ordinance law created a Board of Directors and a Management Committee, and the IZCN was placed under the supervision of the Ministries of Environment and Portfolio (INCN/IZCN, 1973–1977). During the 1980s, with the creation of new national parks and the availability of a regular budget, the IZCN staff was extended and a growing number of technical agents were sent for training at the Garoua Wildlife School in Cameroon.

By the late 1980s, a new paradigm emerged in the conservation sector: protected areas were no longer seen as zones to be kept free from human interference – except notably for tourism, which had become a fully fledged economic sector – and their management teams needed to consider the social dimension of their environment. In 1987, the European Union's 'Kivu Program' provided its support to the PNVi, marking the beginning of the EU's structural support for nature conservation in Zaire and introducing the concept of 'value chains' to enhance the natural resources of the Park.

In 1991, the World Bank commissioned a review of the IZCN's structure and management in preparation for supporting the institute. The recommendations included strengthening environmental education, increasing collaboration with neighbouring communities, scrutiny of the budgets allocated for research and tourism, strengthening internal organisational relations, the creation of Regional Directorates, the creation of a Directorate for Projects and Planning, the revision of staff status, and the adoption of a revenue-sharing key, between the site, local communities and the General Directorate (Mcpherson, 1991). The study concluded that the institute lacked the necessary financial resources to fulfil its mission, was heavily dependent on external donors, and would need to improve its management to secure contributions. Following nationwide unrest in 1991, several donors, including the World Bank, suspended their aid to the conservation sector and the study's recommendations were never implemented. However, discussions with several partners who stood by the IZCN resulted in the founding of two Regional Directorates, in North and South Kivu, and a revenue-sharing system ensuring that operational costs were covered.

In 1997, the Regional Directorates became Provincial Directorates. The country's recurrent instability continued

12.11 Construction of a bridge over the Rutshuru River at Nyamushengero, on the site of the old ferry, linking the Rwindi plains to the Lulimbi area.

to affect the institute – now known as the Congolese Institute for Nature Conservation (*Institut Congolais pour la Conservation de la Nature* – ICCN) – and the management of all parks. Several major partners withdrew, the government could no longer fund the institute's regular budget, and staff salaries were paid rarely and haphazardly. This situation of neglect further increased the ICCN's dependency on external donors.

During the 1990s, the very existence of the PNVi was threatened. In 1994, nearly 2 million people fled the Rwandan genocide and ensuing conflicts over a period of days. On 15 July alone, 500,000 people arrived in Goma, to be joined by 300,000 more in the following days. Water, firewood and food resources, essential for the refugees' survival, were available in the PNVi's South Sector. Three emergency camps were quickly set up on the Park borders at Kibumba, Mugunga and Katale. By late 1994, the camp population was estimated at 720,000 (Delvingt, 1994). The camps remained in place for two years, until new conflicts in the region forced the refugees to disperse. The impact on the Park of these large human populations was devastating, causing deforestation, bamboo cutting, poaching, wandering livestock, waste dumping (including medical waste), disorder and insecurity (Languy & de Merode, 2006).

Between November 1996 and 2002, successive rebellious uprisings severed contact between Kinshasa and the eastern part of the country, and between the General Directorate and the PNVi. In 2000, the rebel movement Congolese Rally for Democracy–Goma (RCD–Goma) took power in parts of eastern DRC. It created an 'ICCN Coordination' in Goma, assuming the prerogatives of the General Directorate and overseeing the management of Kahuzi-Biega National Park and most of the South Sector of the PNVi. The Liberation Movement (RCD-ML) controlled a territory that included the northern part of the PNVi and entrusted what had been the responsibility of the ICCN to its Chief of the Agriculture Department. As a result, the Park and its staff came under the control of two rebel movements supported by Rwanda and Uganda.

From the beginning of the conflict, the Park's equipment and vehicles dwindled due to looting, requisitions and destruction. Disarmed, the rangers left their patrol posts and regrouped in the stations. Between 1996 and 2005, more than a hundred rangers lost their lives due to their commitment to protecting the Park. Left without clear directives, equipment and pay, some deserted. Supported by several NGOs (PICG, SZF, WCS, WWF), the South Sector of the PNVi continued to operate despite the immense difficulties posed by the conflict. Apart from occasional support from the Virunga Environmental Project (PEVi–Kacheche) and the Zoological Society of London (ZSL), the Centre and North Sectors were left to their own devices and suffered from poaching, deforestation and invasions, including in the fisheries around Lake Edward.

The ICCN staff faced a dilemma of allegiance: they wanted to maintain contact with the General Directorate and their colleagues in other protected areas, but they also had to comply with the local political authority. The fracture with Kinshasa created problematic situations, as the RCD–Goma ICCN Coordination managed the staff without consulting the ICCN General Directorate in Kinshasa, which held the employees' records. This situation caused confusion at the station and Provincial Directorate levels, as well as among the partners supporting the ICCN. In 2006, some 150 agents, who had been appointed during the war, had not been officially confirmed by the General Directorate.

During the latter part of the war years (2001–2004), the ICCN received vital support from the UNESCO/United Nations Foundation project in support of World Heritage Sites. UNESCO dispatched a 'diplomatic mission' urging the three concerned governments (DRC, Uganda and Rwanda) to respect their commitments under the World Heritage Convention and to communicate to the military forces occupying the area their hierarchy's desire to respect the Park and its staff. The ICCN's partners supported this approach and formed a Site Coordination Committee ('CoCoSi'). UNESCO paid bonuses to the rangers and other partners pooled their resources to cover the managers' bonuses. Despite the poor security situation and the degraded political context, a minimum level of support was provided that contributed to the PNVi's survival during the war.

12.12 Drilling of a well for the ranger post in Ishasha.

Institutional structure

Founded in 1925, the PNVi falls under the jurisdiction of the Congolese Institute for Nature Conservation (*Institut Congolais pour la Conservation de la Nature* – ICCN), an institution of the DRC. The Virunga Foundation (VF) is a British charitable organisation with a mission to contribute to the protection of the Park and the sustainable development of neighbouring communities.

In 2015, the ICCN and the VF renewed their cooperation agreement – a public–private partnership (PPP) established to run until 2040. On the ground, ICCN agents and VF employees work under a unified management.

The Virunga Belgium Fund is a non-profit organisation (ASBL) based in Belgium that focuses on raising awareness and funds. The Virunga Production CIC (community interest company), based in Great Britain, manages the VF's audiovisual rights.

Several commercial legal entities support the implementation of activities. Their goal is to contribute to the wellbeing of neighbouring communities and ensure the financial autonomy of the Park through revenue generation. These are private companies with a social purpose.

Virunga Energies SAU (formerly Virunga SARL) manages the production, distribution and sale of electricity. Virunga Development SARL oversees the management of industrial parks. Grameen Virunga supervises financial loans to entrepreneurs who are clients of Virunga Energies SAU. The first two are 100%, and the third 67%, owned by Virunga Energies SAU (with the remainder held by the Grameen Trust).

SICOVIR SARL (Société Industrielle et Commerciale des Virunga) is a soap and edible palm oil factory based in Mutwanga. Virunga Enzymes SARL markets an enzyme extracted from papaya latex. Virunga Chocolat SARL, also established in Mutwanga, produces the only chocolate in the country that is entirely 'made in Congo'. The capital of these three companies is shared between the Virunga Foundation and local and international entrepreneurs. Virunga Origins SARL, owned by the Virunga Foundation, facilitates the distribution and marketing of products in the DRC, Europe and the USA.

The management of tourism in the Park, entrusted to the VF under the PPP with the ICCN, does not require the founding of a commercial enterprise as the exploitation of protected areas is governed by the ICCN's statutes at the national level.

Virunga SRL is based in Belgium and acts as an investment fund between the VF and the commercial entities established in the DRC. This legal arrangement allows for the benefits of the double taxation agreement between Belgium and the DRC. As a result, all entities within the Virunga Alliance pay taxes exclusively in the DRC.

The administrators of the Virunga Alliance subsidiaries serve their mandates voluntarily. The statutes and financial statements of each entity are public.

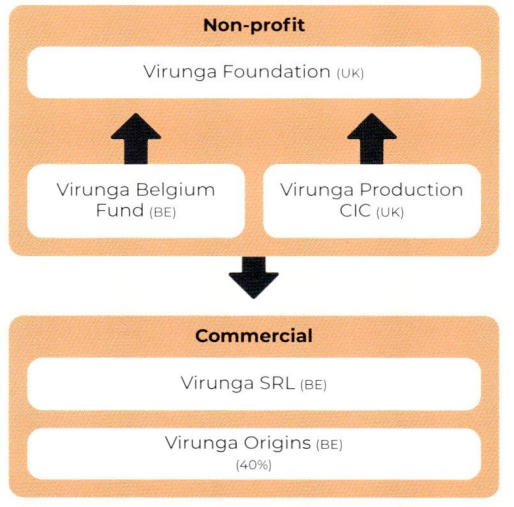
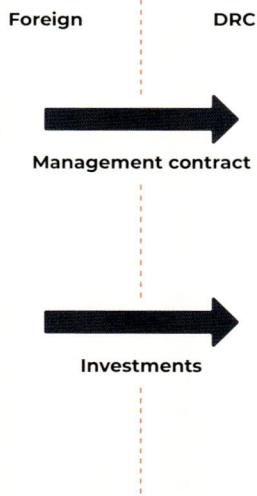
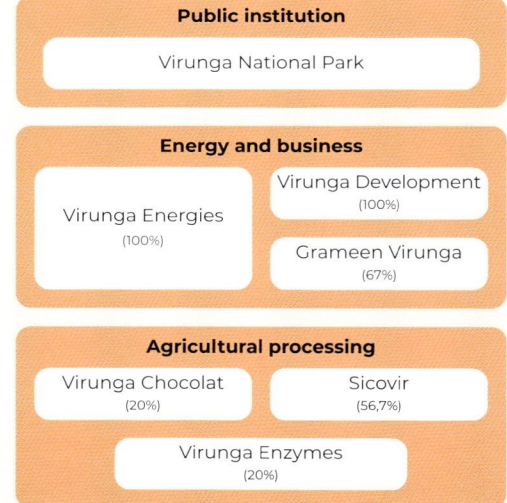

Operational structure

The PNVi's organisational chart makes a distinction between the programme and the support departments. The former implements activities related to the PNVi's missions: protecting the Park – primarily fulfilled by the ICCN staff – and ensuring the sustainable exploitation of natural resources for the benefit of neighbouring populations (the Virunga Alliance). The latter encompasses the administrative and logistical services that enable the achievement of programmatic goals.

The PNVi uses digital technologies to enhance its operational efficiency. An integrated enterprise resource planning system (ERP) and a geographic information system (GIS) simplify administrative processes, allow data integration and analysis, and stimulate innovation. The Park is often asked to share its management tools with other protected areas. These collaborations require the development of open architecture systems with customised integrations that each protected area can adapt to its specific operational context.

The PNVi and Virunga Energies SAU independently ensure all logistical support for their activities. This approach poses a colossal challenge: vast areas must be covered, the state of the roads is poor and the security situation is dire – attacks often occur at the sites or during transport. The supply, infrastructure, land transport and aviation departments provide an on-the-ground presence, often in extreme conditions, by implementing the latest technologies. Drones, in particular, greatly contribute to operations.

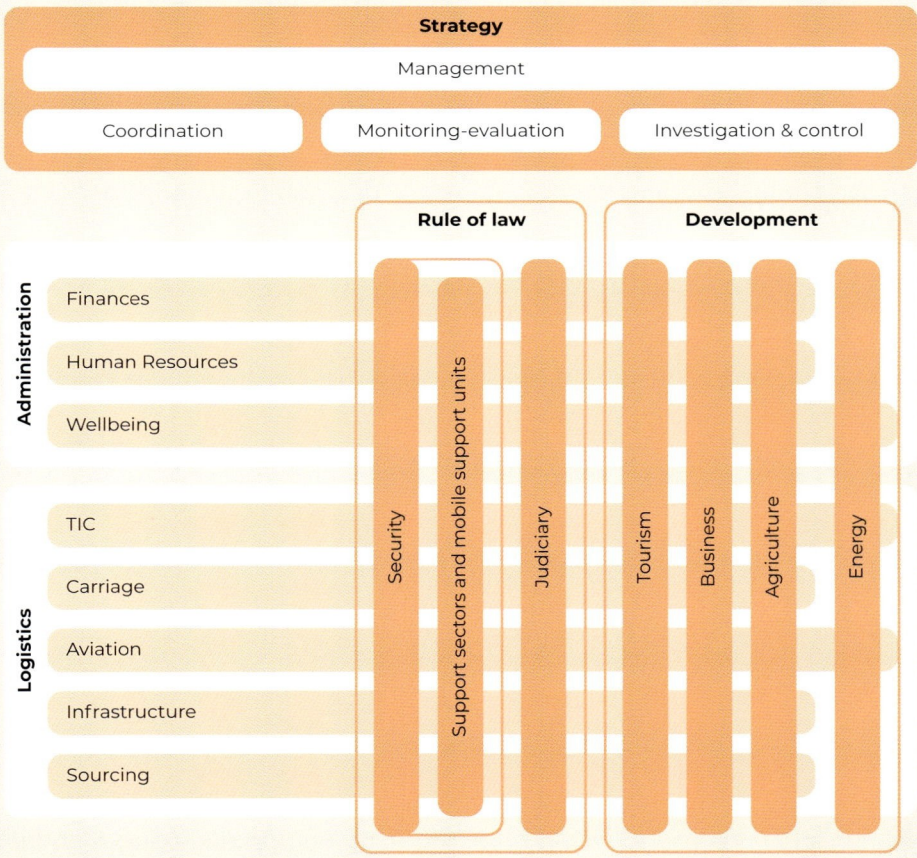

3. Institutional review towards the public–private partnership (2005–2025)[2]

With the return of relative calm to the eastern part of the country, in 2006 a new institutional review of the ICCN was undertaken with the support of the European Union. This review assessed the strengths and weaknesses of the institute with a view to guiding its restructuring and setting the priorities for intervention by external partners (AGRECO–EU, 2006). The final report outlined the areas that determine an organisation's institutional capacity, namely: (1) the rules of the game (the external environment), including the status and positioning of the ICCN; (2) the roles of and relationships between the various actors, starting with the coherence of the institute's missions; (3) the internal organisation, as well as the material and financial resources; and (4) the human resources and their management. The review also highlighted the significant disparity in the support provided to protected areas within the national network and the prioritisation of certain themes in the National Biodiversity Conservation Strategy, a key strategic document of the ICCN.

The recommendations from the institutional review were implemented in part, depending on the interest shown by the ICCN and donors and the available funding. As a logical follow-up, the EU financed a Program to Support the Reform of the ICCN (PARICCN), implemented from 2009 to 2012. The PNVi was chosen as a pilot site for biometric registration and redeployment of staff: 141 rangers were transferred (with financial support to the protected areas that received them), 97 staff members were retired, and the contracts of 77 unfit agents were not renewed, though all received financial compensation. At the same time, the programme supported the appointment of 50 new agents to rejuvenate the workforce, reducing the average age from 47 in 2009 to 38 in 2012.

In 2005, one of the ICCN's partners, the Africa Conservation Fund-UK – later renamed first WildlifeDirect and then Virunga Foundation (VF) in 2011 – proposed to the General Directorate that it take over the management and development of the PNVi, including its staff and finances. The two institutions developed a public–private partnership (PPP), formalised with several management contracts, whose terms were adjusted after joint evaluations. These contracts 'reaffirm their intention to ensure the conservation of the PNVi and its sustainable development in the interest of the local, national and international community, as well as to contribute to the strengthening of the ICCN's capacities at the national level'. The first management contract for the PNVi was signed between the ICCN and ACF-UK in November 2005 and was valid for five years. It was renewed for 10 years in 2011 and 25 years in 2015 (until 2040).

12.13   Pilots and technicians are trained in a range of operational applications based on aerial surveillance by plane, light aircrafts or drones.

12.14 The PPP has contributed to professionalising the management of the PNVi in terms of organisation, logistics and human relations.

12.15 Numerous information and consultation meetings are necessary to make the Virunga Alliance a reality.

The PPP between the ICCN and Virunga Foundation shook up the conservation landscape in the DRC with its innovative managerial approach. In the context of violence and insecurity in the PNVi, the agreement introduced a new dimension to protected area management: the development of the Park and its periphery was seen as an economic lever that should help to restore peace and improve the wellbeing of the surrounding communities. The PNVi managers relied on the new PPP to implement a societal approach to conservation – called the 'Virunga Alliance' – which became an integral part of the Park's conservation efforts (see chapter 17). This new socio-economic approach involved gaining the support of local communities and authorities for a sustainable development strategy in four sectors: environmentally responsible tourism, energy provision by means of hydroelectric production, agricultural transformation and the promotion of entrepreneurship.

Like other protected areas in the national network, the Park also developed a Management and Development Plan (*Plan d'Aménagement et de Gestion* – PAG) in line with the ICCN's standard model and the National Biodiversity Conservation Strategy. Each iteration of the PNVi's Management and Development Plan was discussed with stakeholders in the Park's periphery. This approach of consultation with neighbouring populations has resulted in, among other things, the creation of the Lake Sector in 2021, covering Lake Edward and the fisheries established along its shores.

4. Adaptability in a continuously changing environment

The successive visions developed over the last 100 years by PNVi managers, who were all mandated to safeguard the same territory, have varied considerably.

12.16 The Park Director with female staff at a Women's Day celebration in Rumangabo.

12.17 The Park rangers team at the Goma marathon.

INSTITUTION AND GOVERNANCE

12.18 Specialist departments support the implementation of law enforcement, nature protection and development programmes. The hangar is to house the Park's chocolate factory.

12.19 Some construction sites are very isolated. The logistics involved are complex and require meticulous planning.

12.20 The construction undertaken in the Park provides work and income for many locals. Here, a column of day labourers heads for a section of the Park boundary to be fenced off.

12.21 Working conditions in the field are tough and require resourcefulness and determination.

100 YEARS OF DYNAMICS

12.22 Recruited based on the same selection criteria as men, female rangers successfully carry out the same missions.

Widely divergent, even diametrically opposing, approaches were implemented in the course of the century. The colonial administration prioritised separating human activities from natural evolutionary cycles by prohibiting any intervention in their dynamics. In this logic, the complete protection of fauna and flora justified displacing small resident communities within the Park, even though their way of life was compatible with their natural environment. By contrast, a century later, the ICCN–VF partnership cannot envision a future for the Park without closely involving its neighbouring communities, thanks to the socio-economic benefits of the Virunga Alliance.

The contemporary context cannot be compared to that in which Belgian colonists operated a century ago. Demographics, social, political and economic issues, security conditions, and even the composition of wildlife and flora have significantly evolved. The fact that the philosophy and priorities of the institution responsible for the protection of the Park, as well as its governance and management methods, have adapted to this ever-changing environment is both logical and necessary. As this adaptation facilitates a combination of World Heritage preservation, on the one hand, and sustainable development and peace for neighbouring communities, on the other, the PNVi will earn the respect of current and future generations in the DRC and beyond its borders.

1. The structure, development and actions of the pioneers of the institution are detailed in chapter 2 by historian Patricia Van Schuylenbergh.
2. The first PPP in DRC, for Garamba National Park, was conceived by African Parks and the ICCN in 2004 and signed in September 2005. The PPP between the ICCN and Virunga Foundation also takes on a role as an actor in a green economy, in addition to conservation and stabilisation assignments. The combination of these three functions is deemed essential in a conflict region.

Budget and financing

The operational cost of the Park for 2023, borne by the VF, amounted to 22.6 million dollars. This includes salary payments, operations, new infrastructure construction and development programmes, excluding electricity.

The European Union is the primary donor to the VF, providing nearly 75% of its revenue. Its support covers all programmes: Park operations, tourism, agriculture and entrepreneurship. The United States Agency for International Development (USAID) is the second-largest institutional donor.

In 2024, private foundations contributed 10% of total funding. The list includes, among others: Howard G. Buffett Foundation, The World We Want, The Schmidt Family Foundation, Wellspring, Packard, Re:wild, Packard Foundation, Last Chance for Animals and IUCN N. Funds raised from the public represent about 6% of the budget. Salaries of approximately 700 government employees (rangers and administrative staff) are complemented by the Congolese state.

The revenues of the Park, from tourism and agricultural processing, represent about 3% of its income. Electricity sales do not represent a revenue source yet, as the loans negotiated by Virunga Energies are to be repaid first. The situation has significantly evolved since 2016–2018, when the revenues were more substantial – about 20% of total income – thanks to high levels of tourism activity. The deterioration of security, the Ebola and Covid-19 epidemics and the eruption of the Nyiragongo have severely impacted this growth.

The Virunga Foundation and Virunga Energies SAU fulfil all their tax obligations in the DRC and pay no taxes abroad. Their contribution to the State budget in 2023 was about 6 million dollars, including a contribution to the funding of other protected areas in the country.

Human resources

At the end of 2024, the PNVi is the largest employer in North Kivu Province. In addition to ICCN rangers, it employs civilians to carry out the programmes of the Virunga Alliance (tourism, energy, agriculture, entrepreneurship) and to perform support functions. The profiles are varied, including electrical engineers, agronomists, tourist reception agents, financial managers and logisticians.

Daily workers provide occasional support for manual tasks, such as the construction of hydroelectric power plants or fence maintenance. They work in alternating 22-day shifts, following local labour laws. Thousands of people benefit from this system every year.

Union representation was set up within Virunga Energies and the VF in 2023. For ICCN rangers – who are State agents with a sovereign mandate – an ad hoc consultation mechanism is in place.

Following national legislation, positions occupied by expatriates are limited to functions that cannot be filled on the local job market. This approach motivates continuous efforts to strengthen the organisation's capacities, including supervision, training, scholarships and internships.

PNVi staff are always paid at the beginning of the month. This reality is not taken for granted in DRC, where civil servants and private company employees may have to go without income for long periods. Staff also receive an annual bonus, equal to one month's salary, and medical insurance for themselves and their dependents. A 'welfare' department ensures medical support in the Park's clinics, coordinates evacuations, improves working conditions and provides psychological assistance in case of severe trauma.

A sewing workshop allows the widows of deceased rangers to engage in income-generating activities. Their products are sold in local markets and upscale boutiques in Europe and the USA. The social programme also covers the school fees of orphans under 18.

12.23 Evolution of staff numbers at the PNVi (1956–2024).

YEAR	IPNCB/ICCN RANGERS	CIVILIAN STAFF
1956	385	• 6 European managers • 262 artisans and manual labourers
1960	240	• 115 manual labourers
1975	314	• 14 administrative managers • 194 full-time equivalent daily workers
1986	542	
1991	429	
2002	460	
2006	689	
2022	764	• 483 Virunga Foundation staff • 266 Virunga Energies staff • 546 full-time equivalent daily workers • Dependants: 106 widows and 270 orphans
2024	760 (including 31 women)	• 506 Virunga Foundation staff • 296 Virunga Energies staff • 977 full-time equivalent daily workers • Dependants: 113 widows, including 39 hired, and 245 orphans

Sources: IPNCB, 1956, 1961; IZCN, 1975; d'Huart, 1987, 2003; McPherson, 1991; ICCN, 2006; Virunga Foundation, 2024.

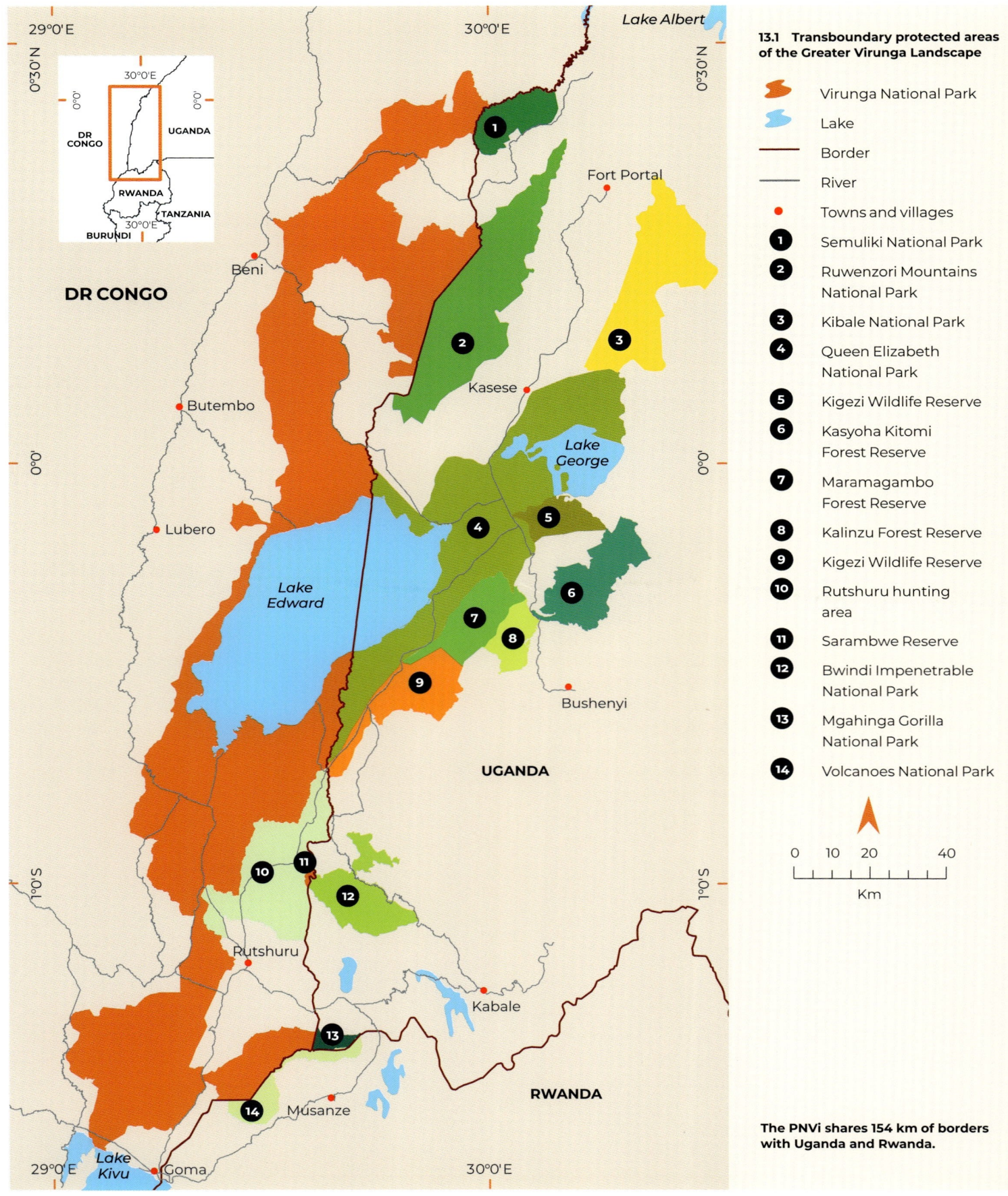

13
Transboundary dimension

JEAN-PIERRE D'HUART, MÉTHODE BAGURUBUMWE, ANNETTE LANJOUW, RODRIGUE MUGARUKA, MUSTAFA NSUBUGA, LAURA PARKER

Virunga National Park shares its borders with Uganda and Rwanda. Transboundary collaboration is essential to protect the biodiversity of contiguous protected areas within the Greater Virunga Landscape.

Virunga National Park (*Parc National des Virunga* – PNVi) shares 154 km of borders with Uganda and Rwanda. Fifteen contiguous protected areas (PA), stretching from the northern shore of Lake Kivu to the southern shore of Lake Albert, form the backbone of what is referred to as the 'Greater Virunga Landscape', which includes six national parks: five in Uganda (Mgahinga Gorilla, Bwindi Impenetrable, Queen Elizabeth, Ruwenzori Mountains and Semuliki) and one in Rwanda (Volcanoes National Park). In Uganda, these parks are contiguous with other PA, such as wildlife and forest reserves. This assemblage covers a significant portion of the Albertine Rift, the western branch of the East African Rift.

1. Reasons for a cross-border approach

1.1. Exceptional ecosystems spanning international borders

The Greater Virunga Landscape consists of a rare assortment of forest habitats, savannahs, mountains, volcanoes, lakes and other wetlands that extend across borders. It is inhabited by a dynamic, constantly growing human population. The region has known massive population displacements caused by civil instability, but also an economic collapse forcing local populations to rely on the land for food and shelter. Their standard of living has deteriorated since the mid-1990s.

1.2. Unique unbounded wildlife

The landscape is home to exceptional species, many of which are endemic and of great national and international interest. Mountain gorillas, in particular, only inhabit two forest blocks: the Virungas and Bwindi. The population is divided between about one thousand gorillas in the Virunga massif (with one-third in PNVi) and 600 in Bwindi (Virunga Foundation, 2021; Bwindi Impenetrable Forest NP, 2022). The high human density around these forest blocks makes any expansion of the gorillas' habitat highly uncertain as it would require relocation of local communities to allow the reforestation and expansion of the PA[1]. The mountain gorilla is a flagship species in the three countries, not only because of its rarity and the fascination it exerts on humans but also because of the enormous economic potential it represents through tourism. For these reasons, the mountain gorilla has become a very tangible symbol of the need for coordinated management by the three countries. Their numerous other shared and valuable resources include the fish production in Lake Edward, the hydrological functions of the mountain forests, the climbing of the Ruwenzori and dormant volcanoes, and wildlife tourism on either side of the Ishasha and Semliki rivers.

From a wildlife conservation perspective, it has been observed that during noticeable disturbances in one park, large mammals take refuge in droves in the contiguous park. Although these 'trips abroad' may cause temporary problems

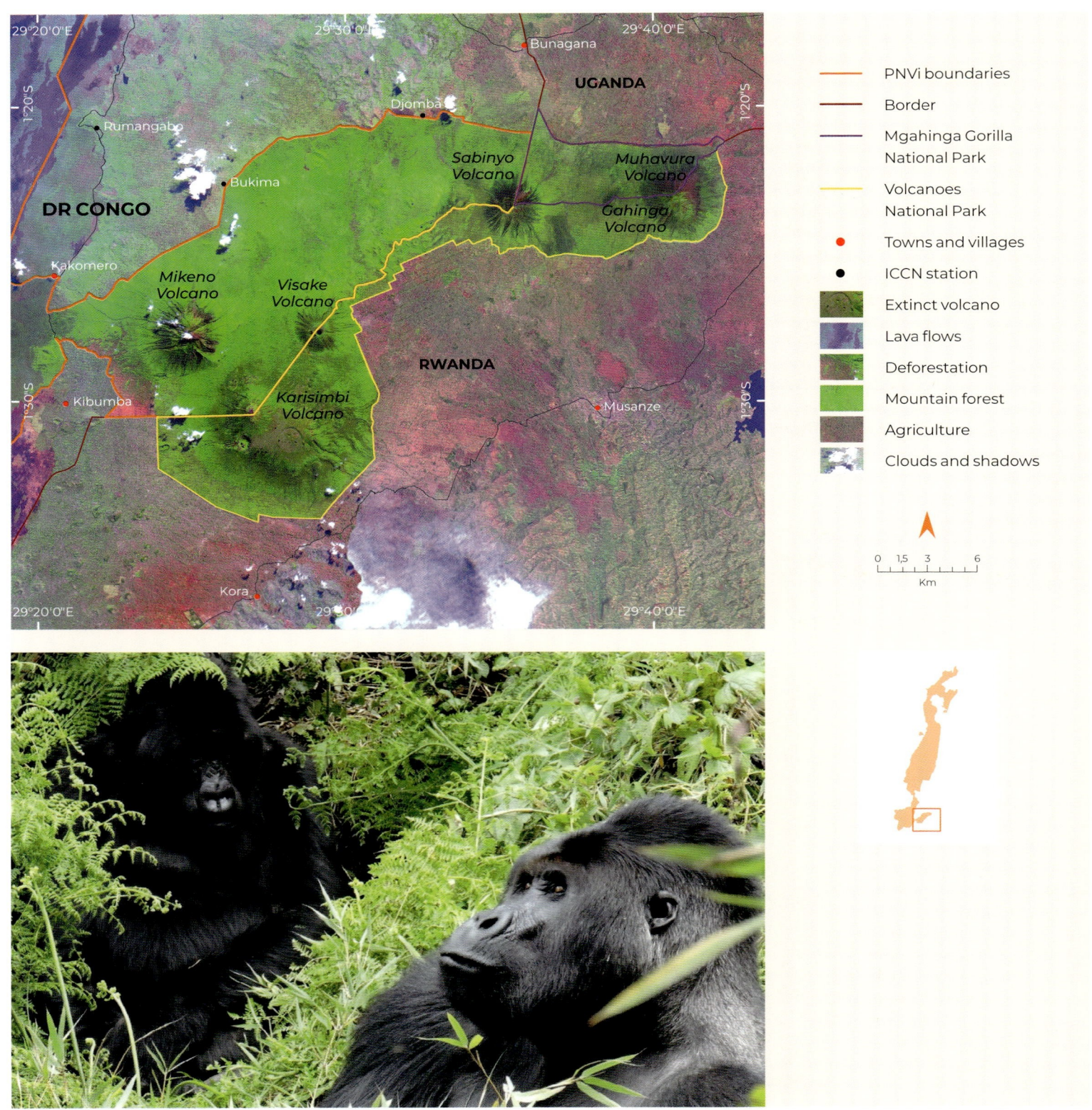

13.2 The Mikeno sector of the PNVi is the Congolese section of the Virunga massif, shared with Rwanda and Uganda where it is protected by the Volcanoes National Park and the Mgahinga Gorilla National Park, respectively. Safeguarding the world's only population of mountain gorillas – the symbolic and fragile emblem of Virunga National Park – depends on good coordination between the managers of the neighbouring parks.

13.3 In the 2010s, insecurity due to encroachment and poaching forced the elephants of the PNVi to cross the Ishasha River and take refuge in the Queen Elizabeth National Park. Since August 2020, almost 600 elephants have returned en masse to repopulate the PNVi savannahs.

13.4 The population density in the areas surrounding the volcanoes is one of the highest in Africa. Access to the protected areas is made all the easier by the fact that the national parks have no buffer zones between their boundaries and the neighbouring communities.

due to the excess biomass of ungulates and ensuing habitat and crop destruction, the benefit to wildlife of having a natural extension serving as a refuge, shelter, food reserve or overflow area, depending on the case, is clear.

1.3. Demographic pressure

A major threat to these forest blocks is encroachment (or even invasions) by local populations. The population density around these forests is one of the highest in Africa, exceeding 400 individuals/km², while the average population density in the DRC is 42 people per km² (World Bank, 2021). As 90% of the population practises subsistence farming, many people enter the PA to supplement their food needs or extract marketable resources (timber, charcoal, etc.). Access to resources in the PA is all the easier because there are no real buffer zones between the national parks and neighbouring communities.

1.4. Regional political events

Conflicts have caused massive population displacements, especially after the 1994 genocide in Rwanda, during which two million people fled the country and dispersed into neighbouring countries. The Virunga volcanoes region was in the middle of these regional conflicts that heightened threats to this ecosystem. Conservation plans initially focused on supporting the authorities governing the PA to allow them to continue their conservation activities. However, faced with a whole host of problems, NGOs and donors had to adopt a 'reactive' approach, adapting to evolving situations and intervening only when security

13.5 From left to right, the Sabinyo, Gahinga and Muhavura volcanoes, as seen from the Rwandan side.

conditions allowed it and funds were available (Thorsell, 1991). Notably, the influx of refugees to the edge of the PNVi led to the destruction of the site's biodiversity, to the extent that UNESCO included the property on its List of World Heritage Sites in Danger.

1.5. Natural resources and conflicts

The link between natural resources and conflicts has garnered international attention for several decades. Specialists from various disciplines have argued that the scarcity of natural resources, unequal access to resource benefits and general environmental degradation may lead to economic, political and social tensions, ultimately resulting in violent conflicts. Despite the criticism that empirical evidence has not proven any causal links (rapid population growth > environmental degradation > violence), many researchers, multilateral institutions and governments see environmental cooperation as a major opportunity to avoid conflicts, improve population wellbeing and create opportunities for lasting peace.

The cross-border dynamics required to seize this opportunity may necessitate partners to jointly establish certain basic conditions: trust, converging interests, interdependencies, shared gains, and creating rules, procedures and institutions to foster a peaceful atmosphere. The process of cross-border conservation collaboration incorporates these elements. Regular meetings on matters of national interest, such as PA management or biodiversity protection, can help optimise a climate of cooperation (Refisch & Jenson, 2016).

2. Towards cross-border collaboration

Cross-border natural resource management may be defined as 'any cross-border cooperation process that facilitates or enhances natural resource management for the benefit of the parties in the region concerned' (Biodiversity Support Programme, 1999). Since this complex of PA contains shared ecosystems and resources, it would be unthinkable to manage the Park while neglecting the fact that it belongs to a larger international ensemble. Though the need for cross-border collaboration to manage these PA was recognised long ago, this collaboration only materialised in the 1990s.

At that time, operational mechanisms for a regional ecosystem approach were conceived and gradually implemented. Until then, PA were conserved and managed as per tradition, on the national level. Each country's portion of the ecosystem was considered subject only to that country's sovereign right, with little regard to the neighbouring country's vision or what was happening in the region's PA.

13.6 During trilateral meetings, the managers of the contiguous national parks work together on transboundary strategic plans.

13.7 Specific collaboration between the PNVi and the Queen Elizabeth National Park involves monitoring the lion population, which occasionally crosses the border.

Initially, the conservationists' collaboration efforts, with support from NGOs such as the Wildlife Conservation Society (WCS) and the International Gorilla Conservation Programme (IGCP[2]), focused on the 'heart of Virunga' before expanding, in 2003, to all the contiguous PA of the PNVi, in what is known as the Greater Virunga Landscape. This approach prioritises on-the-ground collaboration, with links to higher political levels forged only when this cooperation proves effective and begins to yield tangible results.

This does not mean there was no high-level involvement in the cross-border process. As early as 2001, the Executive Directors of the PA authorities in Rwanda (Rwandan Office of Tourism and National Parks – ORTPN[3]), Democratic Republic of Congo (Congolese Institute for Nature Conservation – ICCN) and Uganda (Uganda Wildlife Authority – UWA) jointly defined the initial management objectives of cross-border collaboration. Three years later, the general objectives of this collaboration in the central Albertine Rift were established on a much larger scale, as they linked conservation with development goals. In 2004, these were defined as follows:

- Cooperative conservation of biodiversity and other transboundary natural and cultural values;
- Promotion of integrated land-use planning and management to reduce threats to PA;
- A shared vision of cross-border collaboration;
- Trust, understanding and cooperation among wildlife authorities, NGOs, communities, users and other stakeholders to achieve sustainable conservation, thus contributing to peace;
- Sharing regional resources, skills, experience and best practices to ensure effective biodiversity and cultural resources management;
- Increasing conservation benefits and, at regional level, awareness-raising and sharing of these benefits and conservation values among stakeholders;
- Strengthening cooperation in research, monitoring and information management programmes;
- Ensuring that biodiversity conservation in the region contributes to poverty reduction.

13.8 Aerial counts enable the managers of neighbouring parks to monitor changes in the populations of large savannah mammals.

The donor community provided significant resources, facilitating the establishment of formal international collaboration. Thus the Greater Virunga Landscape became part of a strategic planning process for the Albertine Rift that brought together many NGOs and PA management authorities operating in this ecoregion.

In October 2005, the ministers overseeing the three national agencies signed the Goma Tripartite Declaration[4] on transboundary collaborative management of the central Albertine Rift PA area network. This declaration recognised the importance of developing a Transboundary Strategic Plan, officially recognising it when finalised and endorsing it in an official document. A cross-border collaboration[5] treaty signed in Kampala in 2015 aimed for collaborative management of the PA network, hoping to contribute to biodiversity conservation, tourism development and poverty reduction. In 2024, this treaty was still awaiting ratification by each of the three parliaments.

The first Transboundary Strategic Plan was officially adopted in May 2006, and in 2007 an Executive Secretariat, the Greater Virunga Transboundary Collaboration (GVTC) was created and established in Kigali to formalise and operationalise this collaboration. Its roadmap, the Transboundary Strategic Plan (Plan Stratégique Transfrontalier – PST), was developed in a highly participative manner and has been updated since then for five-year periods. The PST outlines priorities for collaboration focusing on sharing experiences and expertise to develop tourism, promote scientific research, train staff, pursue ecological monitoring, raise awareness among the local population and reduce pressure on natural resources.

3. Effectiveness and achievements

Administrators, institutional managers, technicians and NGOs meet regularly to discuss shared management issues, review the priorities of the Transboundary Strategic Plan and attempt to implement them better. The availability of financial resources and/or the sociopolitical and security contexts of each country do not allow the principles and recommendations of cross-border collaboration to be applied with the same intensity. Despite the commendable efforts of the Greater Virunga Transboundary Collaboration, the more pragmatic, less rigid priorities of the national plans tend to take precedence over those of the PST. Moreover, the expected outcomes of the various meetings are rarely translated into tangible and sustainable achievements on the ground (d'Huart and Brugière, 2013).

Nevertheless, there are many examples of effective collaboration between neighbouring partners, including:
- Total censuses of gorillas coordinated by the three countries;
- A protocol for tourist visits to gorillas in the three countries;
- Coordinated aerial censuses between PNVi and Queen Elizabeth NP;
- Mixed or coordinated surveillance patrols along shared borders to ensure the protection and integrity of the parks;
- The development of joint strategies for ecosystem restoration in the Ishasha Valley, including a lion population recovery strategy and an invasive plants management protocol;

13.9 Joint surveillance patrols are regularly organised on both sides of the borders. Here, preparation for operations with the rangers of Queen Elizabeth National Park (Uganda) and Volcanoes National Park (Rwanda).

13.10 Following cross-border negotiations, the invasion of the Karuruma region (North Sector of PNVi) by Hima pastoralists from Uganda and their cattle ended with their voluntary return in April 2006, with logistical assistance from the ICCN and its partners.

- An agreement between managers of the PNVi and Mgahinga Gorilla NP to prevent crop depredation with an electric fence;
- Facilitation by the Volcanoes National Park of the release of PNVi rangers on patrol who mistakenly crossed the border;
- Facilitation by UWA of the return and reception of 350 Ugandan shepherd families who, with their 5,000 cattle, had settled in the northern savannahs of PNVi;
- Channels for swift informal communication between rangers to report emergencies.

Transboundary collaboration is a process rather than a goal in itself. Officially designating a transboundary PA – in the future perhaps a vast Peace Park? – will not engender true collaboration, but working together, communicating, coordinating activities, developing joint plans and conducting joint or coordinated activities will. This process aims to establish a collaborative framework, involve partners from the three countries and ensure that achieved results are perceived as genuinely shared victories. The basic condition being, of course, the restoration of lasting peace.

1 However, such a project aiming to extend the Volcanoes National Park is being prepared in Rwanda.
2 IGCP is a regional programme set up in 1991 by a coalition of three NGOs: the African Wildlife Foundation (AWF), now replaced by Conservation International (CI), Fauna and Flora International (FFI) and the World Wildlife Fund (WWF). See: https://igcp.org/library/
3 Nowadays called Rwanda Development Board.
4 http://www.tbpa.net/docs/treaties_MOUs/AlbertineRiftTripartiteDeclaration-English.pdf
5 https://greatervirunga.org/the-treaty/

CHALLENGES AND PERSPECTIVES
---

14 — **Social and environmental justice** 237

15 — **Security and peace** 243

16 — **Boundaries and respect of limits** 255

17 — **The Virunga Alliance**
Introduction 269
Tourism 273
Energy 282
Entrepreneurship 295
Agriculture 301
Impact 311

14.1   How residents and visitors from all over the world view the Park is determined by the conditions in which they live.

14

Social and environmental justice

EPHREM BALOLE, JÉRÔME GABRIEL, FRÉDÉRIC HENRARD

Faced with demographic pressures, conflicts and extreme poverty, how can a Park of invaluable biological value be preserved? How should environmental and social justice be promoted while simultaneously enhancing the use of resources to benefit local populations? The future of Virunga National Park is at the crossroads of these challenges.

1. An evolving context

When the Albert National Park was created in 1925, Belgian Congo had a population of about 10 million inhabitants (de Saint Moulin, 1987). The mountainous Kivu, particularly along the Albertine Rift, had the highest population density in the country, yet this was still relatively low (Muzinga, 2001). To preserve the exceptional biodiversity in this sub-region, 800,000 hectares of territories, including lava plains, arable lands, forests, mountains, rivers and a lake, were dedicated to full conservation. This decision entailed – and continues to entail – an opportunity cost for the populations, some of whom had to leave their homes.

One hundred years later, the population of North Kivu has increased exponentially. Over 6 million people now live around Virunga National Park (*Parc National des Virunga* – PNVi), many of whom are settled in urban centres. Goma and Butembo each have over one million inhabitants, Beni has 500,000 and Kiwanja, Lubero and Oicha each have between 50,000 and 100,000 inhabitants. These crowds live less than a day's walk from the Park's borders, and the pressure on the land has now reached its maximum. Agricultural lands are often overexploited and eroded, while the parklands have become the most fertile in the region.

A significant portion of the population – primarily those living in extreme poverty – claims the right to exploit the Park's natural resources to meet their vital needs. This anthropogenic pressure poses a direct threat to the PNVi

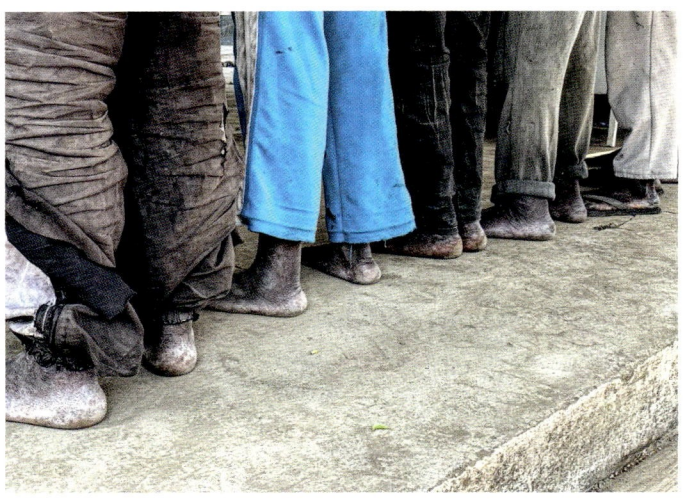

14.2 Illegal fishermen in Lake Edward appear in court.

14.3 There have been numerous refugee camps on the outskirts of the Park since the genocide in Rwanda in 1994. The second M23 conflict (since 2022) has also resulted in massive population displacements.

ecosystems, the disappearance of which would cause irreparable harm to future generations.

In this context, the equation is enormously complex: how to preserve a natural park of global value in a human context with enormous pressures from poverty, violence, demography and weak State authority? These are the issues affecting environmental and social justice at the PNVi.

2. Opportunity cost for the local populations

The intrinsic value of the PNVi is priceless (Languy & de Merode, 2006). No quantified economic estimate can take the Outstanding Universal Values (OUVs) of the UNESCO World Heritage Convention into account (see the UNESCO section in chapter 7). These heritage values, particularly significant at the PNVi, include the Ishango archaeological site, various flagship and endemic species, and exceptional landscapes.

By recognising the exceptional heritage value of the Park, the international community implicitly encourages the necessary sacrifices for its conservation. This recognition also motivates the significant funding from international donors, in solidarity with the host country, to support the protection of the PNVi and the improvement of the living conditions of the surrounding populations.

The 'opportunity cost' is the expression of the income local populations would derive from alternative uses of the Park were it not designated as a full protection zone. A simplified – and therefore necessarily reductive – calculation allows us to quantify this foregone income.

The loss of income is mainly due to the non-exploitation of the lands for agriculture, as fishing in Lake Edward, which covers 20.7% of the PNVi territory, is already permitted (see chapter 11). After subtracting snowy peaks, mountainous lands, lava fields and uncultivated lands, the arable area of the Park represents about 65% of its surface, or around 500,000 hectares. This area would suffer the destruction of wildlife, flora and ecosystems if the Park's protection was not ensured. The annual average yield of the region's agricultural lands (sold and self-consumed production) equals 2,000 dollars/ha/year. Based on these two parameters, the annual opportunity cost of the PNVi can be estimated at 1 billion dollars annually (i.e. the total arable land not exploited, multiplied by the average yield per hectare). Ending social and environmental injustice at the PNVi requires creating economic alternatives for the surrounding populations with a value equal to, or greater than, this opportunity cost.

3. A political environment that exacerbates violence and injustice

For three decades, the PNVi has been the epicentre of the cycles of war in eastern DRC. The populations of North Kivu are constantly subjected to violence and displacement, and their livelihoods pilfered. People have repeatedly lost their savings, been forced to rebuild their homes and restart their agricultural, livestock or commercial activities from scratch. This permanent instability keeps them in a state of extreme vulnerability.

SOCIAL AND ENVIRONMENTAL JUSTICE

14.4 The 'tshukudus' transport goods despite the poor state of the roads. They are much appreciated by the local population for having supplied the city of Goma during the M23 siege in 2013.

The wars result from the weakness of the rule of law, which is also felt during periods of calm. Even when a fragile peace prevails, social injustice, corruption and the poor quality of basic public services (security, roads, health and education) perpetuate the cycle of poverty.

These deficiencies, in turn, hinder development programmes or even prevent them from being carried out by the Congolese state and international partners. Often, these programmes are isolated interventions, or limited to providing humanitarian aid to alleviate suffering.

4. Valorisation of ecosystem services

An ecosystem service is an asset or a service that humans can derive from ecosystems, directly or indirectly, to ensure their wellbeing. The valorisation and transformation of natural resources are carried out individually (survival logic) or collectively (investment to provide a public service). In figurative terms, an ecosystem service is a gift from nature to humanity to ensure life on Earth.

Two prerequisites are essential for valuing the ecosystem services of Virunga National Park: the restoration of the rule of law and good governance. The first involves

14.5 The charcoal production (makala) in the Park is organised by armed groups. Makala is essential for boiling water (and preventing cholera), cooking food and heating at higher altitudes.

14.6 Dwellings generally consist of four walls and a tin roof. Electricity is only available in localities connected to the Virunga Energies network.

imposing State authority, restoring peace and security, and establishing rigorous and fair judicial procedures. The second involves the equitable distribution of national wealth, without which the vast disparities between rich and poor will persist, forcing the latter to survive at the expense of natural resources. In other words, the PNVi's future will not be assured unless the Park's protection efforts are supported by a State capable of fulfilling its sovereign missions, and the populations can envision a decent, peaceful future.

Establishing social and environmental justice – which implies changing political and economic power dynamics – inevitably creates many winners and fewer, but sometimes powerful, losers. The former are the ones who benefit directly and indirectly from new sustainable and shared development opportunities. They start businesses, albeit often very small ones, or grow industries that generate economic activities by taking advantage of the investment context. Along with the rest of the population, they enjoy collective benefits, such as street lighting, access to water, and improved public services in education, health, security and justice. The losers are those who see the exceptional privileges they derive from plundering the PNVi – poaching, agriculture, charcoal production, illegal fishing, etc. – taken away from them. While they also benefit from the new collective advantages, they primarily seek to preserve their unduly acquired personal gains.

5. The Virunga Alliance for addressing injustice

The purpose of the Virunga Alliance, conceived in the specific context of North Kivu, is to valorise three ecosystem services of the Park: tourism, water and agriculture.

The beauty and biological diversity of the PNVi dazzle the world, making it an exceptional tourist attraction. The tourism sector creates jobs, serves as a calling card for the country and generates a lot of multiplier effects. Similarly, forest preservation secures the rain cycle that guarantees water supply. The waterways have the potential for energy creation, in the form of hydroelectricity, that can transform the region's economic fabric. Finally, the agriculture on the PNVi's periphery feeds the population, but provides little income to farmers. The transformation of agricultural products, on the other hand, creates added value that enhances food security.

Thanks to the Virunga Alliance programmes, the PNVi can create significantly more wealth than the opportunity cost of its preservation. A first study (Balole, 2018) estimates the PNVi's economic potential at 3 billion dollars (1990 parameters) on the assumption that the conditions for sustainable natural resource exploitation are implemented. A second study (Cambridge Econometrics) quantifies the impact on GDP of the Virunga Alliance programmes at 329 million dollars by 2030 and 1 billion dollars by 2047. It also estimates that the PNVi value chains will create over 107,000 jobs by 2030. These studies, and the empirical results collected by the PNVi teams, demonstrate the direct and indirect driving effects of the Virunga Alliance, which may structure a new economic fabric in North Kivu.

SOCIAL AND ENVIRONMENTAL JUSTICE

14.7 Farming provides a livelihood for around half the population of North Kivu. Farming practices are often extensive and not very productive.

The creation of the PNVi and the subsequent population growth have caused a sense of injustice to pervade the Park's surrounding communities. This sentiment persists among many who ask: 'What does this park bring us?' The changes initiated by the Virunga Alliance provide an answer to these questions, by demonstrating that the benefits of conservation outweigh alternative uses, especially extensive agriculture. An increasing number of decision-makers and inhabitants of North Kivu have realised that the PNVi has become the engine of the region's economic and social growth. The Virunga Alliance programmes are critical to addressing the social and environmental injustice that still strongly affects the populations surrounding the Park.

14.8 Access to drinking water is a daily concern for hundreds of thousands of people in both urban and rural areas.

15.1 Park installation in Niamitwitwi (Centre Sector).

15 Security and peace

FRÉDÉRIC HENRARD, LUCIEN MUNYANTWARI, ÉRASME NGENDE

Virunga National Park faces multiple armed groups that threaten its integrity, the lives of its personnel and of the surrounding populations. Reforming and strengthening the Park's security system warrants law enforcement in a complex and dangerous context.

1. Presence of armed groups

Virunga National Park (*Parc National des Virunga* – PNVi) region has been the scene of a low-intensity conflict since the mid-1990s, following the genocide of the Tutsis in Rwanda and the ensuing regional destabilisation. The militias in North Kivu number between 1,500 and 6,000 members, depending on the periods of conflict. The militias combat the Armed Forces of the DRC (FARDC) while also fighting one another. Occasionally, forces from neighbouring countries join them in battles on Congolese territory.

The militias conduct various illegal and criminal activities in the PNVi: charcoal trade, illegal fishing, illegal agriculture, poaching, ivory trafficking, kidnappings, extortion and racketeering. They also trigger land conflicts by encouraging invasions, pressuring local populations and taxing their

15.2 Members of an armed group in training observed by the Park's aviation department. One person shoots at the plane when he is spotted.

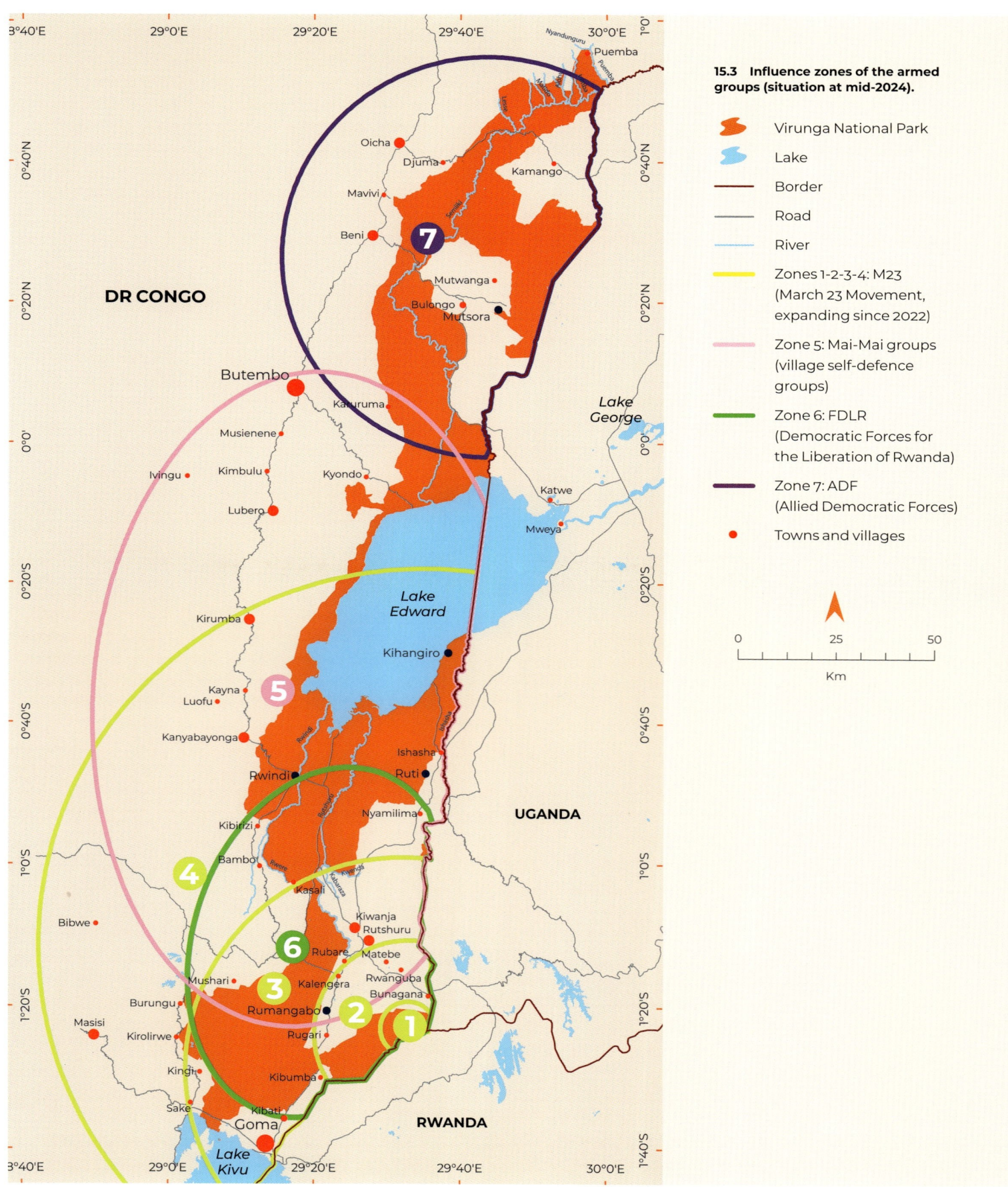

15.3 Influence zones of the armed groups (situation at mid-2024).

income. The PNVi monitoring and evaluation department estimates the turnover from illegal activities at 170 million dollars annually.

The conflict between the March 23 Movement (M23) and FARDC, combined with a coalition of local self-defence groups, is strengthening the 'historical' militias. The M23 consists of ex-rebels from the CNDP (National Congress for the Defence of the People), a rebel administration established in 2006–2009 in Kivu that set itself up as a defender of the Tutsi community. The Rwandan army, deployed on Congolese territory, supports its offensive, which adds an inter-States dimension to the conflict. The group attacked in 2012–2013 and 2022–2024 (conflict still ongoing at the time of writing), conquering large portions of territory in Rutshuru and Masisi territories and taking control of Goma. The first attacks were carried out from the militias' historical bases near the Rwandan and Ugandan borders, at the heart of the PNVi, in the mountain gorilla sector. Arms trafficking and related criminality driven by this conflict generate deep uncertainty regarding the prospects for the long-term pacification of the region, especially as self-defence groups ('wazalendos') often assimilate with local militias. When the political conditions are met, a comprehensive Disarmament, Demobilisation and Reintegration (DDR) programme will be needed to accompany and facilitate the combatants' return to civilian life.

The deployment of rangers on the PNVi territory is conditional on the intensity of the ongoing conflicts. Excluding the M23 conflict, their deployment covers about 70% of the PNVi surface, except the northern extremities controlled by the Ugandan ADF-NALU militias and the southern region of Masisi, an area of lesser ecological value.

In the South Sector, besides the M23 group, the PNVi is also a camping ground for the FDLR (Democratic Forces for the Liberation of Rwanda), descendants of the perpetrators of the Rwandan genocide (Hutus). A coalition of small militias with shifting allegiances also strives to control portions of territory and/or groups of people. The city of Goma, nestled between Lake Kivu, the PNVi and Rwanda, is an additional security challenge for the rangers. The city is experiencing a demographic explosion and is home to many displaced people, which pushes the city to expand into the Masisi region and onto the volcano slopes. Agricultural encroachments and charcoal trafficking to Goma are the main threats to the South Sector.

Around the Centre Sector, the Mai-Mai – village self-defence groups that first emerged during the 1990s – have been seeking to establish themselves on the shores of Lake Edward. Their agricultural influence has receded since the early 2020s thanks to increased control by the rangers. The groups now exert their influence through sometimes violent incursions into the PNVi, including poaching, illegal fishing, and lending support to agricultural encroachments.

Parts of the North Sector are stable, but the security situation can be volatile, depending on the sub-regions. The 'Grand Nord' suffers extreme violence from the ADF-NALU group originating from Uganda with radical Islamist leanings, which commits countless civilian massacres. Since 2022, the threat posed by this group has been contained thanks to joint actions by the FARDC and the Ugandan army, the UPDF (Uganda People's Defence Force). The group conducts incursions near Mount Ruwenzori and attempts to redeploy in Uganda, where it commits terrorist acts.

2. Law enforcement

The rangers are mandated to protect the PNVi by patrolling, observing and detecting violations that cause harm to the protected area. At times, they must face militias to regain control of certain areas. For their safety, the use of force and lethal means (firearms) is necessary in the context of the violence perpetrated by these militia around the PNVi and its periphery.

The PNVi rangers arrest several thousand people annually. Most are released after an – often cordial – check or, in the case of a minor offence, an awareness-raising session.

In accordance with Congolese law, detainees are referred to a civil or military prosecutor – depending on their presumed affiliation with an armed group – after a report has been drafted to establish the facts and offences. From this

15.4 Arrest of a poacher. A report about each arrest is written before the person is handed over to the judicial authorities.

CHALLENGES AND PERSPECTIVES

15.5 Destruction of an illegal charcoal kiln. The operation is dangerous because the trafficking is organised by armed groups.

15.6 Court files 2022–2024

	2022	2023	2024 (May)
DEFENDANTS	721	582	151
JUDGED	180	125	48
CONDEMNED	162	114	43
ACQUITTED	18	11	5
ONGOING CASES	–	53	80
WITHOUT FOLLOW UP	541	404	23

point in the procedure, the enforcement becomes the responsibility of the judicial authorities (prosecutor and magistrate). If any illicit products are seized, they are usually destroyed or donated to charities.

As the Congolese courts have limited human and logistical resources, they release some defendants on the condition that they pay a compromise fine. This practice, though legal, can fuel corruption. The most serious cases are brought to trial. Major offences include, in descending order: illegal agriculture, illegal fishing, charcoal production, poaching, wildlife trafficking, unauthorised works (including the destruction of the Park's electric fence), criminal association, illicit possession of arms and/or ammunition and participation in an armed group.

A law firm specialising in environmental and penal law ensures that the offences are followed up and the judicial process implemented. This is organised in two stages: first at the prosecutor's office for the investigations, then in court for the rulings. Trials are sometimes held in 'field hearings' in villages, for proximity and educational purposes. In jurisdictions bordering the Park, the litigants brought to the judicial authorities by PNVi rangers represent up to 80% of investigated cases.

15.7 Mobile court organised in the town of Rutshuru (2022). The scheme alleviates logistical constraints, reduces the backlog of court cases, and promotes awareness among judges and the general public.

3. Legal framework

The PNVi rangers are agents of the Congolese Institute for Nature Conservation (*Institut Congolais pour la Conservation de la Nature* – ICCN). Their mission, prerogatives and status are specified in several legislative and regulatory instruments, in particular:
- The Law on fundamental principles of environmental protection (Law No. 11/009 of 09/07/2011);
- The Law on nature conservation (Law No. 14/003 of 11/02/2014);
- The Decree establishing the Corps responsible for securing national parks and related reserves (Decree No. 15/012 of 15/06/2015);
- The Decree setting the statutes of a public establishment named the 'Congolese Institute for Nature Conservation' (Decree No. 10/15 of 10/04/2010);
- The Law to regulate hunting (Law No. 82-002 of 28/05/1982).

Interventions by the rangers are governed by International Human Rights Law, not International Humanitarian Law (relating to the Law of War), as identified by the International Committee of the Red Cross (ICRC), the authority on legal analysis of armed conflicts. They are guided also by the principles of legality, proportionality, necessity and precaution. In this context, the use of force is permitted in the following circumstances:
- in self-defence or to defend others against an imminent threat of death or serious injury; or
- to prevent a serious offence that is endangering human lives; or
- to arrest a person posing a risk to the lives of others and resisting the authority of the rangers, or to prevent the person's escape; and
- only when less extreme measures are insufficient to achieve said objectives.

In other words, the rangers intervene to maintain law and order and enforce the law against attacks on property and individuals committed on the PNVi territory and, within certain limits, in its immediate vicinity (e.g. for seizures or pursuit rights).

ICCN rangers collaborate with other sovereign institutions, mainly the FARDC and the Congolese National Police (PNC). FARDC operations intent on pursuing war objectives within the Park do not involve the ICCN. Where rangers are deployed, interventions are planned jointly, with the ICCN ensuring primary command. Outside the Park, interventions by the rangers are limited to passive protection of tourist sites, hydroelectric plants and agricultural or indus-

15.8 More than 230 rangers have lost their lives in the course of their duties over the last 20 years. The majority of these deaths were the result of attacks by armed groups. Here, burial of a ranger (2020).

15.9 The military Governor of North Kivu visiting the Park's headquarters in Rumangabo, and a planning meeting with the army and the police.

15.10　Construction of a Forward Operating Base (FOB). FOBs are better protected and have replaced patrol posts, as the latter increased the risk of fatal attacks on rangers.

15.11　Concealment exercise in the savannah.

trial projects – all activities carried out within the Virunga Alliance context – and transporting people and goods.

The Virunga Foundation supports the ICCN by providing training, equipment and supervision. It also pays bonuses to supplement State-paid salaries. This collaboration does not imply any delegation of public authority, which remains the exclusive prerogative of the ICCN.

4. Institutional reform

The Virunga Foundation and the ICCN have invested heavily in reforming the security system in the PNVi. This reform was launched in 2009 with financial support from the European Union. The objective was to rid the PNVi rangers, numbering 1,030 at the time, of the many elements illegally recruited by the rebel administration of the RCD (Congolese Rally for Democracy). Problems included insubordination and non-payment of wages for several years, which in turn resulted in extortion and corruption. Prior to 2009, the PNVi hierarchy, itself involved in mafia networks, actively contributed to the illegal exploitation of natural resources.

Between 2008 and 2010, a new management was appointed and given an ambitious reform mandate. Personnel illegally recruited during the civil war were dismissed, and a code of conduct was established. Judicial investigations were initiated against rangers suspected of corruption, leading to the conviction of seven senior officers, including the former Director and two of the three sector chiefs. Honest rangers were installed in senior positions, and a new command framework was set up.

In 2009, a public–private partnership (PPP) was established between the Virunga Foundation (then called the Africa Conservation Fund) and the ICCN. This gave a new impetus to the ongoing institutional reform.

Between 2010 and 2012, various technical and financial measures intended to increase control, discipline, efficiency and motivation among the rangers were implemented. Older staff were retired, reassigned to non-critical functions or transferred to other sites. The remaining rangers were registered as State agents with the ICCN (a process named 'mechanisation'). Salaries were to be paid via bank transfer ('bancarisation') and a financial reserve was established to guarantee salary payments for three months. All positions received job descriptions, and a performance evaluation system was established, particularly for promotions. Command principles and methods were restructured.

SECURITY AND PEACE

5. Personnel, selection, recruitment and training

As of mid-2024, the PNVi employed 760 rangers in service (up from 480 in 2016), including 31 women. Over the past decade, more than 100 rangers lost their lives in the line of duty, the majority due to attacks by armed groups.

To effectively combat poaching and militias, a minimum of 700 rangers, and ideally 1,000, are needed to maintain a stable force. Accounting for attrition, due to retirement, death, illness, resignations or dismissals, a minimum recruitment of 80 rangers every two years is required to maintain staffing levels. Six recruitment cycles have been conducted at the PNVi since 2010.

Recruitment calls are published in the North Kivu Province and neighbouring provinces. Candidates must be Congolese nationals, aged between 18 and 25, hold a D6 (baccalaureate) diploma, and have no criminal record nor affiliations with armed groups. Thousands of applications flood in for each cycle, and applications by female candidates are encouraged. The pre-selection lasts one day and involves physical tests and interviews to assess candidates' motivation. Successful candidates subsequently undergo a four-day selection process including medical exams, additional physical tests and cognitive aptitude assessments. Recruitment reserves may be established for future calls.

Candidates that pass this process then undergo basic training for 16 to 24 weeks, depending on group size. Training is provided by national and international instructors, including ICRC representatives, at the PNVi training centre in Ishango. Training modules cover legal frameworks, nature conservation and weapon use, and include a wide range of simulations. Special attention is paid to human rights, rules of engagement and the handling of detainees, minors and women, as well as to sexual violence. Based on the skills demonstrated during this phase of basic training, some rangers may receive additional eight-week training to join the mobile support units (UMA) that handle high-risk missions. Beyond the basic training, these rangers receive small group refresher training sessions intended to develop the leadership skills required from senior and intermediate officers.

6. Command and control

The ICCN's legal principles are complex to implement in the volatile and dangerous Park environment. Rangers often face armed adversaries whose violent actions disregard any rules. Moreover, their uniforms resemble the ones worn by the armed forces, though their respective missions and rules of engagement are different. The ICCN's rules of engage-

15.12 The Ishango training centre hosts the new recruits and the refresher courses for those already serving as rangers.

15.13 Rangers' parade at the Park's training centre in Ishango.

15.14 Rangers on the move in the rain.

CHALLENGES AND PERSPECTIVES

15.15   The canine unit can detect people, explosives and ivory.

15.16   Operations are monitored from the command centre at the Park's headquarters in Rumangabo.

15.17   The Park has several surveillance aircrafts. It is home to the only pilot training school in the DRC.

ment are central to training and supervision and require a thorough knowledge of national and international legal frameworks.

A procedural manual (Standard Operating Procedures) translates these principles into practical instructions, mandatory during field interventions.

Rangers' actions are based on the intelligence cycle: interactions with local communities, information collection, analysis, action planning and evaluation. Community support is crucial for anticipating hostile actions and preventing confrontations. Human intelligence is complemented by a sophisticated detection system that includes aerial surveillance (small planes like 'Bat Hawks' and drones).

The security command is based at the PNVi headquarters in Rumangabo. A control centre oversees six operational centres serving four sectors and two UMA. Their interventions are decentralised but tightly controlled: detection of illegal activities, decision-making, intervention and incident closure, in a digital tracking system. This controlled subsidiarity boosts effectiveness by combining local initiative with hierarchical visibility. Only non-routine large-scale operations are covered by a specific operation order.

VHF radios and trackers on personnel and vehicles, supported by an autonomous communication network across the Park, provide the means to track and trace all personnel. In case of danger, significant logistical means, including planes, boats and land vehicles, facilitate the rapid deployment of reinforcements and experienced advisors.

7. Discipline and sanctions

All personnel, including the rangers, must adhere to a code of conduct, committing to ethics and values that complement legal obligations. PNVi rangers are accountable for their actions. Any incident causing injury or death to a third party, or potentially having contributed to either, will be reported to the competent judicial authorities. Judicial decisions always take precedence over any disciplinary measures the institution may take as a precaution or sanction.

The Internal Control Department can investigate, or be tasked with investigating, potential fraud. An Investigation Unit comprising six experienced lawyers investigates allegations made by internal or external sources, or at the hierarchy's request. This unit works on a confidential basis and reports directly to the PNVi Director.

Two disciplinary councils are in place: one for ICCN and Virunga Foundation personnel and another for Virunga Energies – the company implementing the Virunga Alliance's Energy programme – personnel. The councils can impose sanctions ranging from warnings to dismissal for gross misconduct, and may be combined with pay deductions of varying amounts. For ICCN personnel, the ultimate dismissal decision rests with the ICCN General Directorate, following a provisional suspension decided by the PNVi management. Serious cases are referred to judicial authorities and may involve legal action.

8. Community-based approach

Hierarchy and staff at the PNVi continuously interact with traditional authorities, elected officials, private companies, civil society representatives, and environmental and human rights NGOs. 'Community rangers', rangers trained in dialogue with local communities, help to manage expectations and address grievances. A toll-free number displayed in villages allows residents to report any misconduct by personnel.

The PNVi rangers contribute to the safety of the civilian population. They organise, for instance, daily protected convoys for vehicles travelling the national road through the Park, drastically reducing attacks by militias seeking to kidnap and ransom travellers. Between 2018 and 2020, the rangers also played a crucial role in combating the Ebola virus by organising health checks at strategic points within the Park.

9. Non-belligerent status

Occasionally, over the past 30 years, parts of the Park and its surroundings have been occupied by militias with political claims. FDLR, ADF and M23 are the most significant, best organised and most violent armed groups. The areas where they operate within the Park are considered war zones, where the ICCN cedes control to the FARDC.

A particular case involved the M23 group from 2012–2013 and 2022–2024. Having been residual between 2013 and

15.18 Victory for the Park team in the Virunga football provincial competition.

CHALLENGES AND PERSPECTIVES

15.19 Poster of the toll-free number distributed in local villages to collect information on problematic behaviour by the Park's agents.

15.20 Convoy of civilian vehicles on Route Nationale 2, which crosses the Park (Centre Sector). The number of attacks has decreased drastically since the system was set up.

2022, the group has grown steadily with support from neighbouring countries, moving out of the Mikeno forest to control vast areas (up to 10,000 km²) encircling Goma. Heavily backed by the Rwandan Defence Force, who are also present on Congolese territory, it provides semi-administration over the territories it controls, in close proximity to the Park.

Such situations are anticipated in the Nature Conservation Law (Law No. 14/003 of 02/11/2014): 'personnel assigned to the surveillance of protected areas are apolitical and benefit from a non-belligerent status in peacetime or armed conflict' (art.42) and 'any protected area enjoys necessary neutrality and special protection against actions violating their integrity and compromising basic conservation principles in peacetime and armed conflict' (art.44). See chapter 6 for additional details on how these principles were put into practice.

In the context of the war waged by M23, these provisions allow the ICCN to maintain activities deemed essential for nature protection, even in enemy-occupied areas, such as monitoring of the mountain gorilla population. The ICCN's non-belligerent status also enables Virunga Energies to con-

15.21 Community mobilisation for the construction of the FOB in Mutsora. The rangers collaborate with the army to support rapid deployments in the event of an alert about the presence of ADF in the villages.

SECURITY AND PEACE

15.22   Temperature checks on travellers to combat Ebola (2019). A similar system was in place for the Covid-19 epidemic (2021).

tinue providing hydroelectric production essential for the survival of the population. These measures are executed in strict accordance with the directives from the highest political and military authorities.

16.1 The demarcation of the PNVi boundaries is a political, economic and environmental issue. The Park covers over 13% of the province of North Kivu, which has a population of over six million.

16

Boundaries and respect of limits

MÉTHODE BAGURUBUMWE, JEAN-PIERRE D'HUART, FRÉDÉRIC HENRARD,
LÉONARD K. MUBALAMA, LUCIEN MUNYANTWARI

Demographic pressure and conflicts threaten the integrity of the Park. The drawing of its boundaries is the result of historic conciliations with local communities. However, tensions remain. The participatory demarcation methodology brings together the population and the authorities to strengthen local ownership.

The population density in North Kivu is increasing due to demographic evolution and conflict-related displacement. In the periphery of Virunga National Park (*Parc National des Virunga* – PNVi), population density varies between 6 and 600 inhabitants per square kilometre, depending on the sub-regions, with an average of about 300 inhabitants. This growing human concentration poses a serious threat to the integrity of the PNVi, as it drives many people to invade its territory.

Armed groups contribute to this threat by exploiting natural resources and encouraging encroachments from which they generate income. The involvement of certain politicians and community leaders also exacerbates the situation. They manipulate local communities – who are often illiterate or poorly informed about legal issues – using various means, including electoral promises, incendiary speeches, disinformation campaigns or financial rewards, to encourage them to break nature protection laws. The consequences are disastrous: destruction of natural habitats, animosity towards the PNVi representatives (sometimes leading to violent and deadly attacks) and tensions between communities contributing to security instability and undermining the region's economic development (Decaro and Debeve, 2017). The communities living near the PNVi are, as a result, forced to choose between protecting their environment and ensuring survival in an unstable political and security context.

1. Legislative framework

The boundaries of the PNVi reflect the political, social and environmental changes that have occurred over decades. Since the creation of the Albert National Park (*Parc National Albert* – PNA) in 1925, they have evolved with the combined objective of meeting nature protection requirements and serving the socio-economic interests of the region (Vikanza, 2018).

The 21 April 1925 decree establishing the PNA was a global milestone: the designated area became the first national park in Africa. It preserved about 20,000 hectares around the extinct Mikeno, Karisimbi and Visoke volcanoes, intending to protect mountain gorillas. The initial decree did not specify the exact boundaries of the Park, leaving this task to the Governor General, who fulfilled it gradually.

The decree of 18 August 1927 significantly extended the PNA to the territory of Rwanda-Urundi, resulting

in the future Volcanoes National Park (now in Rwanda). This extension highlights the continuous – and ongoing – attention to transboundary conservation in the Great Lakes region.

The decree of 9 July 1929 marked a major turning point. It granted the PNA a legal civil personality and significantly increased its surface area, now covering about 200,000 hectares. For the first time, clear boundaries were set, dividing the Park into sectors with annexed territories serving as buffer zones, foreshadowing a holistic approach to protected area management.

The decree of 6 November 1934 allowed the PNA to manage other national parks in the Belgian Congo and the trust territories. This gave rise to the Institute of National Parks of Belgian Congo and Ruanda-Urundi (IPNCB) that was, after Independence, to become the Congolese Institute for Nature Conservation (*Institut Congolais pour la Conservation de la Nature* – ICCN).

The decree of 12 November 1935 extended the Park boundaries to include all the Belgian waters of Lake Edward, the southern part of the Semliki plain and the Ruwenzori and Tshiaberimu massifs, adding 450,000 hectares.

The royal decrees of 1937 and 1939 made some minor adjustments, preparing the ground for the royal decree of 15 May 1950, which radically modified the boundaries to reflect the arbitrations made by the Commission for Inquiry and Conciliation with the neighbouring populations (see below). This decree was the last major revision of the Park boundaries.

16.2 Since the early years of the Park, the delineation of its boundaries is marked by boundary stones and signs.

16.3 In the gorilla sector, lava stone walls were built with the help of local farmers to prevent damages to crops and mark the Park boundary.

16.4 The Park expansions were decided in Brussels based on field reports sent in by local managers. Here, the royal decree of 1937, which made a technical adjustment to the boundaries.

The Park boundaries have been established by legislative acts dating back to the colonial period and have not been modified by any of the successive Congolese governments (Languy, 2005). To date, the total surface area of the PNVi is 784,368 hectares, representing 13.19% of North Kivu Province.

In the DRC, the declassification of part, or all, of a protected area is a government responsibility operating under the authority of the President of the Republic (law 14/03 of 11 February 2014, article 35). The procedure requires a decree from the Prime Minister, which can be subject to prior consultations with national representation and civil society to legitimise the process.

2. Relations with local communities

Since its creation in 1925, the PNA has been defined in regulatory texts as a 'zone of integral protection', excluding any human presence within its boundaries and implying the expulsion of populations settled on its territory. These expulsions marked the beginning of conflicts still plaguing the PNVi today (Nzanbandora, 2003).

The gradual extension of the boundaries caused tensions by encroaching on lands that had been sparsely populated – a few hundred inhabitants at most – but used for farming. In particular, the 1935 decree multiplied disputes in the Beni and Lubero territories, where local leaders and traditional chiefs opposed the Park's expansion.

In response to these growing tensions, the colonial power established a Commission for Inquiry and Conciliation (ordinance n°10/Agri of 5 January 1947). It was tasked

CHALLENGES AND PERSPECTIVES

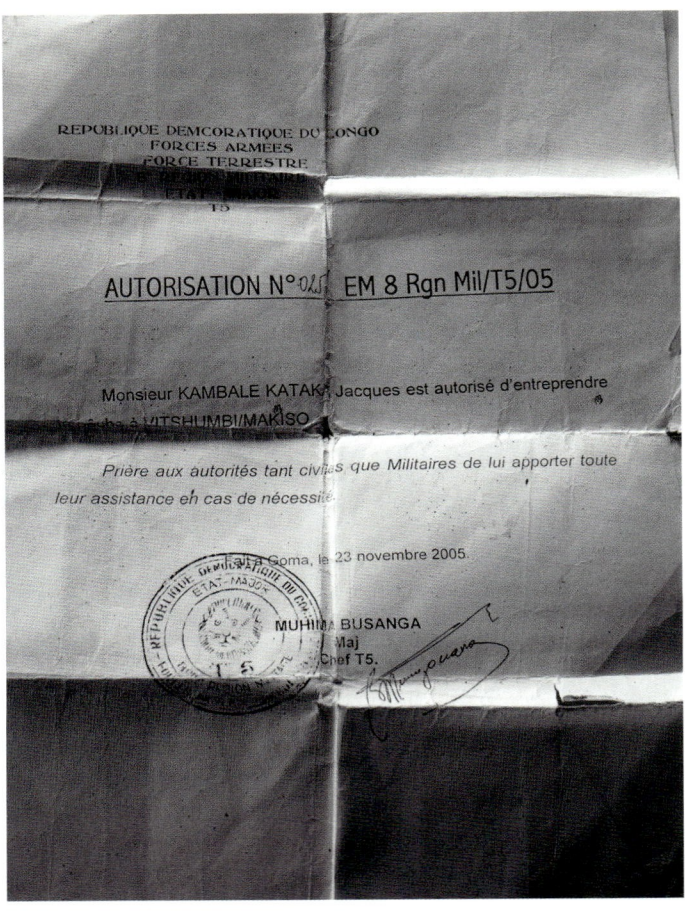

16.5 The 1990s were characterised by political instability and weakened State authority, including that of the ICCN. Here, an illegal permit to fish on Lake Edward.

with investigating the needs of indigenous populations to provide a definitive solution to land and territorial conflicts, by reconciling the interests of local communities with conservation imperatives. Its first objective was to determine the subsistence needs and traditions of the neighbouring populations, using field surveys. The second objective was to define regulatory accommodation arrangements to minimise the negative impact of human activities on conservation. Finally, the commission had to propose boundary modifications to address the population's grievances and recommend expropriations, where these were essential for biodiversity preservation.

Consultations with local leaders and traditional chiefs led to consensual proposals guiding the boundary revision, enshrined in the royal decree of 15 May 1950. They also validated the recognition of the Lake Edward fisheries (see chapter 11) and approved tolerances valid to date, such as the collection of deadwood, access to water and passage rights.

The Zairian and then Congolese governments did not modify any of the PNA boundaries after Independence in 1960. They continued the protection efforts by establishing the ICCN, recruiting rangers and specialised personnel, supporting research programmes and promoting tourism. During the Zairian era, security strategies were implemented to deter illegal activities and, if necessary, take repressive measures.

16.6 From 2005, the partnership between the ICCN and Virunga Foundation strengthened the Park's management capacities. Law enforcement stabilised encroachments. Here, arrest of a farmer using a tractor for illegal farming (North Sector).

The 1990s were characterised by political instability and weakening state authority, including that of the ICCN. In 1994, the massive influx of Rwandan refugees and the emergence of armed groups marked the beginning of a period of destruction of the PNVi. The destabilisation of eastern DRC also encouraged the resurgence of conflicts with some population groups regarding the PNVi boundaries.

Since 2005, the partnership between the ICCN and the Virunga Foundation has strengthened the management capacity of the PNVi (see chapter 12). It has helped to stabilise and gradually reduce invasions, which now affect 13% of the PNVi's surface (see chapter 9).

3. Conflict management and prevention

Despite notable improvements between 2010 and 2024, land disputes and human–wildlife conflicts in the PNVi have persisted. Tensions are fuelled by these factors:
- The boundaries of the PNVi were modified by eight legislative texts between 1925 and 1950. This has, sometimes intentionally, caused confusion, exacerbated by divergent interpretations.
- The disappearance of numerous boundary markers installed between the 1930s and 1960s has fuelled confusion. Their disappearance made it hard for residents to understand the boundaries.
- Unofficial agreements by some corrupt ICCN representatives – because they remained unpaid during conflict periods – have fuelled disputes.
- Demographic pressure and the growing need for fertile land for agriculture and livestock push communities to encroach on the Park's lands.
- Armed groups profit financially from invasions, and some politicians use them for electoral purposes.

Contemporary protected area management integrates respect for human rights. The ICCN Grievance Management Mechanism guide (guide sur les Mécanismes de Gestion des Plaintes – MGP) promotes participatory governance to resolve conflicts with local communities. This approach includes mediation, arbitration and the creation of local conflict management committees. It also applies to boundary disputes.

4. Participatory demarcation

Since the 1990s, many people have crossed the PNVi boundaries to settle or work there, often voluntarily, but sometimes involuntarily. This situation has led to the expression of two boundaries: the 'ICCN boundary', known and recognised by the ICCN and based on legal texts; and the 'population boundary', recognised by residents based on the past or alleged location of old markers.

Confusion between these definitions prompted the PNVi management to develop a participatory demarcation methodology (Languy, Hugel and Buliard, 2011). Its objective was to establish legal boundaries in an impartial and well-argued manner and ensure their recognition by political and administrative authorities, customary authorities and local populations. This recognition by all parties helps to resolve old conflicts and prevent new disputes.

Several principles must be respected to ensure transparency, fairness and legality:
1. The PNVi status: The PNVi is an asset of national and global value. Participatory demarcation is not mandated to redefine boundaries specified in the Official Journal, the 1935 Decree and the 1950 Decree. Any other interpretation lacks a legal basis.
2. Right to information: Local communities have the right to know the boundaries to plan their activities, especially farming. Transparency is essential to avoid misunderstandings and conflicts.
3. Boundary recognition: The physical demarcation of boundaries must be accepted by all stakeholders. This involves the active participation of the population during marker installation.
4. Official registration: Demarcated boundaries must be recorded using geographic coordinates and documentation detailing the analysis used for their identification.
5. Neighbouring communities: The ICCN has to endeavour to support communities that respect the PNVi and, as much as possible, help them find alternative livelihoods to replace unsustainable exploitation of natural resources.

The participatory demarcation process involves three steps:
1. The first step is to establish and document the exact position of legal PNVi boundaries through legal text analysis and field surveys, using cartographic tools. This step is conducted both remotely and on-site for maximum accuracy. The results are compiled and presented to the ICCN for validation. This step facilitates the building of foundations for clear, well-documented comprehension of the legal boundaries.

16.7 An example of modernising boundary delineation: descriptive markers are transposed into GPS bearings for precise mapping. This exercise helps eliminate misunderstandings about the actual or supposed course of the boundary.

PARAGRAPH	S140	S141	S142	S143	S144
Legislative texts Compilation (unofficial translation)	The Kamokanda stream to its source at the foot of Mount Tsahi	A line joining this source to the summits of Mount Tshahi and Mount Bitingu	From this mountain, a straight line leads to the source of the Kalagala river, near Mount Rwanguba	This river to the path from Mabenga to Tongo. The trail runs along the foot of the Kasali mountains	This trail to its junction with the Butaku river
On-site aspect Commentary on the legal text			The Kalagala river is not permanent	The path was replaced later on with a carriageway	The path was replaced later on with a carriageway
Demarcation Signs PV Photos	no S140_B055	no	yes P037 – P038 PVS1/8/05 S142_A340	yes P038 – P040 PVS1/8/06 S143_B123 S143_B127	yes P040 – P049 PVS2/03/06 S144_A995 S144_B030 S144_A011
Modern formulation Starting point (Lat/long)	01°00'53"S 29°14'15"E	01°02'40"S 29°17'24"E	01°04'25"S 29°17'38"E	01°04'30"S 29°17'49"E	01°04'31"S 29°19'24"E
Intermediary points	Geographical coordinates of signs and GPS routes in certain sectors				
Point of arrival (Lat/long)	01°02'40"S 29°17'24"E	01°04'25"S 29°17'38"E	01°04'30"S 29°17'49"E	01°04'31"S 29°19'24"E	01°11'32"S 29°17'11"E
Length Nature	8,359 m Brook	3,244 m Straight line	1,003 m Straight line	3,098 m River	14,672 m Road

2. The second step consists of explaining the survey conclusions to the political and traditional authorities and the local populations, including residents. This consultation is designed to develop a common understanding regarding the exact location of the boundaries. This stage often takes a long time and may be accompanied by public debate that can be virulent.
3. The third step concerns boundary demarcation. This consists of signs and blocks installed at the agreed locations. The signing of minutes attests to the general

16.8 Participatory demarcation involves a wide range of participants: political and customary authorities, civil society, organised groups and individual locals. The aim is to reach a common understanding of the boundaries of the Park.

16.9 The public debates accompanying participatory demarcation can be virulent. They are sometimes exploited by individuals or pressure groups who benefit from perpetuating the Park's encroachments.

BOUNDARIES AND RESPECT OF LIMITS

16.10　New bollards are built where the old ones used to be. In insecure areas, they are sturdy enough to prevent opponents from demolishing them.

16.11　The erection of the new signs generally marks a time of social and political appeasement. Central figures: Chantal Shalukoma, PNVi Deputy Director in 2021, and Jean-Baptiste Ndeze, Customary Chief (Mwami) of Rutshuru and Vice-Minister of Customary Affairs (2024).

recognition of these signs and their exact location. This formal stage generally marks a time of social and political calm.

The participatory demarcation process is laborious and may last several months or even years. Progress depends on numerous external factors, such as the security of the concerned areas, stakeholder engagement and political support. The interests of community leaders may also influence the debates. Since the programme was launched in 2001, 1,165 kilometres of the PNVi boundaries have been demarcated (65%). This percentage is higher in areas unaffected by conflicts.

5. Construction of electric fences

After participatory demarcation, it can be useful to materialise the boundary by installing a fence in addition to the markers. Fences help to end illegal cultivation and reforest previously invaded areas. They also cut off armed groups from their bases in the PNVi and optimise the deployment of the rangers, who are no longer scattered over long distances, which leaves them vulnerable to attack by armed groups. Allowing residents to maintain the fences, and earn a small income from their work, also promotes good relations and collaboration at the local level.

Fences are often requested by the population, especially farmers, to prevent crop destruction by wild animals and attacks on people. The significant decrease in insecurity, particularly kidnappings, in localities near the fences also drives requests from residents, civil society and political representatives. Conversely, individuals who profit from

16.12　Recognition of the PNVi boundary is a prerequisite to protect the area. Here, protected edges in the North and Centre Sectors.

CHALLENGES AND PERSPECTIVES

16.13 The fences put an end to illegal cultivation, weaken armed groups, and protect crops and people from wild animals. They may be simple or robust, depending on the wildlife they are designed to contain.

trafficking and agricultural invasions oppose their construction, sometimes violently.

Fences may vary in type, from simple to robust, depending on which wildlife they are designed to contain. They may also include a detection system, if required, for security reasons. Construction projects involve several hundred workers to clear the path over dozens of kilometres, bring in materials and equipment, and set up installations. The high cost of the works limits the possibility of installing fences along the entire demarcated boundary.

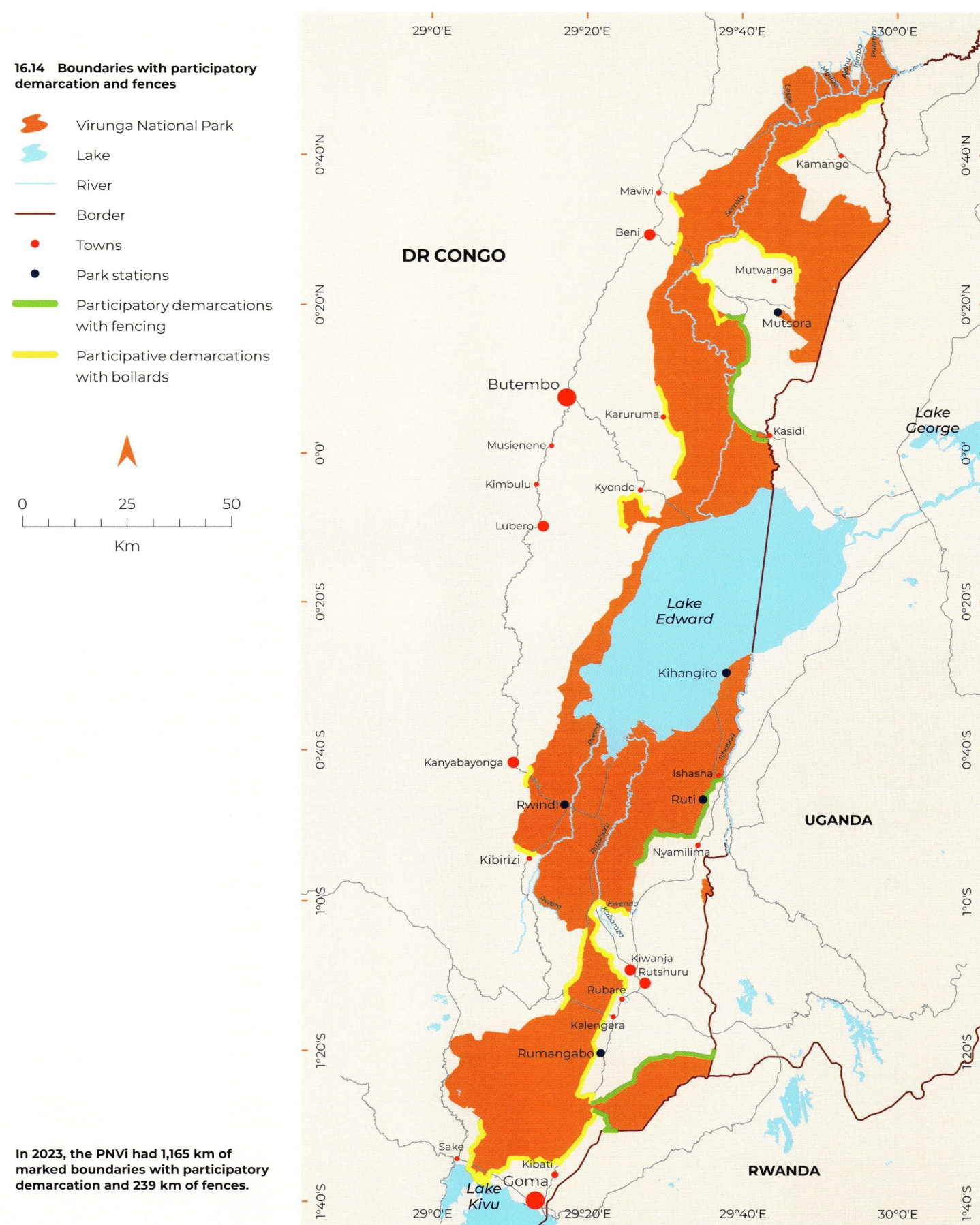

16.14 Boundaries with participatory demarcation and fences

In 2023, the PNVi had 1,165 km of marked boundaries with participatory demarcation and 239 km of fences.

CHALLENGES AND PERSPECTIVES

In 2023, the PNVi had 150 km of fences in the South Sector (including 61 km around the gorilla sub-sector), 41 km in the Centre Sector and 48 km in the North Sector. Reconstructing fences in the South Sector, which were destroyed during the M23 conflict that began in 2022 and remains ongoing, will be a post-conflict priority.

16.15   Building the fences requires several hundreds of workers. Maintenance is carried out by residents, who earn a modest income from their service.

The Rutshuru hunting area

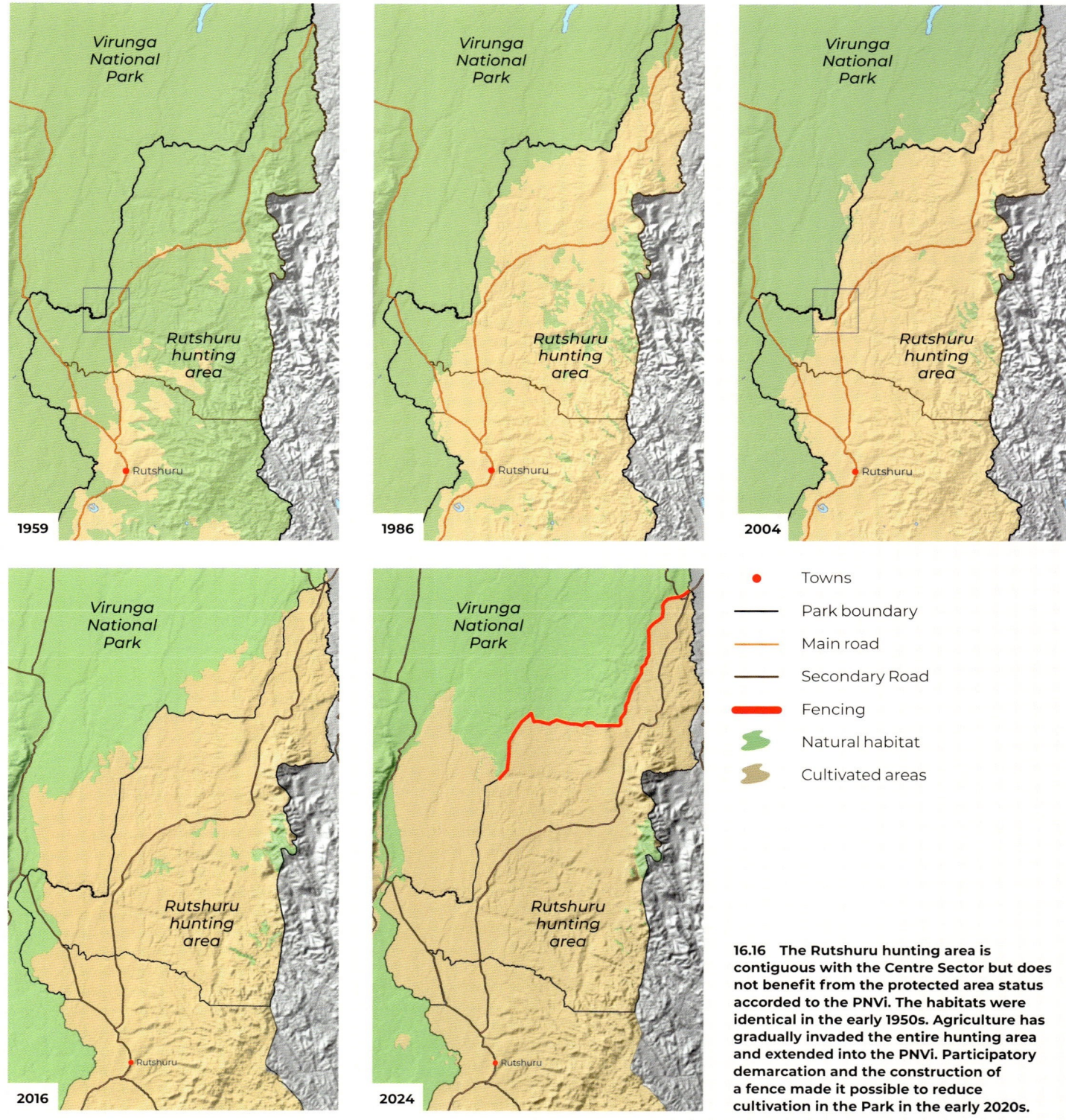

16.16 The Rutshuru hunting area is contiguous with the Centre Sector but does not benefit from the protected area status accorded to the PNVi. The habitats were identical in the early 1950s. Agriculture has gradually invaded the entire hunting area and extended into the PNVi. Participatory demarcation and the construction of a fence made it possible to reduce cultivation in the Park in the early 2020s.

Human–wildlife conflicts

The International Union for Conservation of Nature (IUCN) defines human–wildlife conflicts as struggles arising when the presence or behaviour of wild animals constitutes a real or perceived direct and recurring threat to human interests or needs, causing disagreements between groups of people and negative impacts on people or wildlife.

These conflicts are increasingly frequent, severe and widespread due to population growth, agricultural expansion, infrastructure development, climate change and other habitat loss factors. They can occur wherever human and wildlife habitats overlap.

Such conflicts force managers of protected areas to find solutions to protect residents, strengthen trust in the Park's protection and prevent retaliation against wildlife. Measures include the construction of barriers, such as fences, grills, walls and trenches, implementing monitoring and early warning systems and promoting deterrents and repellents. Managers also recognise the need to improve local living conditions and to allow residents, as far as possible, to benefit from the conservation efforts. Of course, these measures require a clear understanding of protected area boundaries.

Within the PNVi, the risk of incidents is increasing due to the restoration of large fauna in several of the Park's sub-regions and the absence of buffer zones on the periphery. Gorillas, elephants, lions, leopards, buffaloes, bush pigs and baboons can provoke the anger of farmers by devouring crops, attacking livestock or even injuring or killing people. On the shores of Lake Edward, hippopotamuses charge canoes and crocodiles attack fishermen in shallow water.

Over the past ten years, about thirty fatal incidents have been documented. Beyond the tragedies that these represent for the families, managing these incidents is complex due to legislative ambiguities. Neither law 14/03 of 11 February 2014 on nature conservation, nor other specialised laws, address the issue. Faced with this legal void, common law should apply, notably the Congolese Civil Code (Book III), which deals with the responsibilities of animal owners. However, according to the doctrine, wild animals are not concerned as it is impossible to control them. These legal uncertainties compel the PNVi management to prevent incidents as much as possible and, whenever an incident does occur, to show empathy and solidarity. In such cases, the assistance pro-

16.17 The return of elephants in the Centre Sector in the early 2020s saw a resurgence in crop destruction and attacks on people. Here, an ICCN deployment in the fields, near the Park where an elephant was reported.

vided to victims, or their dependents, is granted as consolation rather than compensation.

In the spirit of the Virunga Alliance, concerted management of human–wildlife conflicts involves creating synergies between human development and nature conservation. Gradually, these synergies will materialise the United Nations' 2050 Vision for Biodiversity: 'a world where humanity lives in harmony with nature and where wildlife and other living species are protected.'

16.18 Letter of complaint about elephant incursions in 1959. Conflicts are on the increase because the human population is growing.

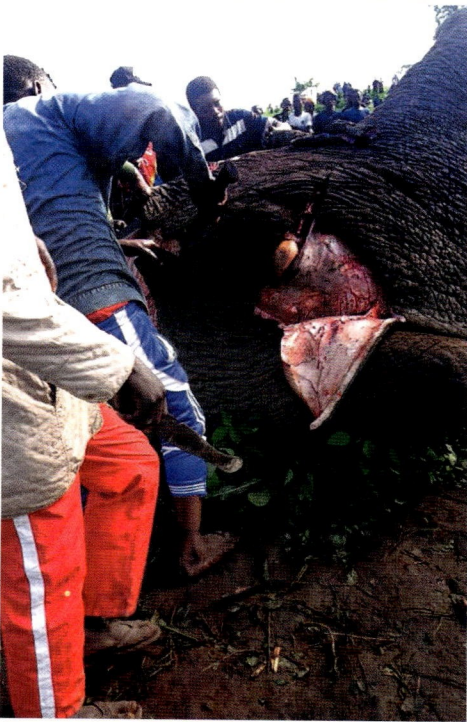

16.19 Elephant killed by the population after an attack on farmers.

17.1 Aerial view of the canopy in the Mikeno sector.

17

The Virunga Alliance
Introduction

EMMANUEL DE MERODE

The future of Virunga National Park must be built with and for the people of North Kivu. Guided by this fundamental principle, the Virunga Alliance aims to turn the Park into an instrument of prosperity and peace. Its vision is based on three pillars: tourism, energy and entrepreneurship, and agriculture.

Virunga National Park (*Parc National des Virunga* – PNVi) was thriving in the late 1980s, but almost disappeared during the years of war. The collapse of the state, assaults by armed groups and the presence of millions of refugees within its territory severely disrupted its ecosystems. Twenty years on, its recovery is the result of immense efforts to return the Park to a golden age many can still recall.

Against a backdrop of poverty and violence in North Kivu, protecting this UNESCO World Heritage Site is not straightforward: how can we ask the PNVi's neighbours, among the poorest populations on Earth, who have suffered unprecedented violence for 30 years, to ensure the preserva-

17.2 A woman begs a ranger to protect the farmers in an area occupied by an armed group (South Sector).

CHALLENGES AND PERSPECTIVES

17.3   Aerial view of the city of Butembo.

17.4 The Virunga Alliance brings together public authorities, private sector and civil society. Exchanges and dialogue promote ownership of the objectives.

tion of this exceptional protected area? The daily struggle for survival excludes considerations of heritage conservation: all that matters is cultivating a plot of land, cutting down trees to produce charcoal, or poaching to obtain some meat. However sublime it may be, the PNVi seems like a glaring social and environmental injustice to them.

The Virunga Alliance aspires to resolve this antagonism. If the Park is to have a future, it must be hand in hand with and for the people of North Kivu. The PNVi is brimming with natural resources waiting to be sustainably harnessed: these must be mobilised without delay to benefit the surrounding populations. Such an ambition cannot, of course, be implemented solely by the will of a public institution: it requires the support of authorities, the participation of the private sector and the involvement of civil society. Together, they can protect the Park's natural resources while at the same time putting them at the service of development and peace[1].

The Virunga Alliance also aims to secure the necessary funding to protect the PNVi. Ensuring the operation of the protected area – starting with the regular payment of ranger salaries – incurs significant costs, which the Congolese state is, as yet, unable to cover. According to the management contract between the Congolese Institute for Nature Conservation (*Institut Congolais pour la Conservation de la Nature – ICCN*) and the Virunga Foundation, the financial revenues from the Virunga Alliance allow the PNVi to continue its mission and build up its capacity.

To achieve this vision, the Virunga Alliance pursues three objectives: protecting the Park, reducing poverty and contributing to peace. Its development programmes, designed for the benefit of the surrounding communities, are structured around three pillars: tourism, energy and entrepreneurship, and agriculture. The educational aspect, on hold during the war years, has also been relaunched, to promote Park protection and sustainable development among the population.

The ambition is great, but the challenges match the stakes: to make Virunga National Park a driver of peace and prosperity in North Kivu and beyond.

1. Objectives

Protect: Removing the Park from the World Heritage Sites in Danger List

The Virunga Alliance aims to safeguard, protect and rehabilitate the Park.

Even during the war years, even when they received no salary, the ICCN rangers never abandoned their mission to protect the PNVi. Thanks to their commitment and bravery, the wildlife and flora are being restored. Though still fragile, the ecosystems show remarkable resilience: once shielded from human interference, they can recover quickly with minimal support.

In addition to combating poaching, the preservation of the Park primarily involves protecting its habitats. Illegal occupations cover approximately 14% of its surface. Providing alternative livelihoods and stimulating economic activity around the Park are essential policies to reduce these occupations.

Develop: Creating jobs and sustainable economic activity

The Virunga Alliance is pursuing an agenda of economic and social transformation.

Conditions must be established to create jobs and increase the population's income. The ultimate goal is to generate 1 billion dollars in annual economic activity – a figure equivalent to the PNVi's opportunity cost[2] – and to create 100,000 jobs. Such an ambition is necessary to tangibly compensate the surrounding populations who bear the burden of conservation.

The Park is currently the largest employer in North Kivu but, equally importantly, it drives a new green economy at the provincial level. The new jobs benefit people who previously struggled to meet their basic needs. Knowing that one person with a regular income supports an average of eight people (the size of a household), the beneficiaries number in the tens, or even hundreds, of thousands. The support lent by the Virunga Alliance to public services also greatly contributes to the collective wellbeing.

Pacify: Restoring the rule of law and offering alternatives to armed groups

The Virunga Alliance contributes to stabilisation efforts by creating a sustainable and law-abiding economy.

The motivations for joining an armed group are complex: protection against threats; access to income, food and alcohol; political indoctrination or forced recruitment. Likewise, leaving an armed group is not easy: defectors may be ostracised by their community, threatened by former comrades or pursued by the army and the police. In this context, Disarmament, Demobilisation and Reintegration (DDR) programmes have often failed. The main reason is the lack of sustainable economic opportunities for demobilised individuals, who, in the absence of alternatives for themselves and their families, return to combat and perpetuate the cycle of violence.

Without specifically targeting any individual militia members – to avoid creating a sense of discrimination among other population categories – the Virunga Alliance strives to deprive armed groups of their labour pool. It creates conditions that give the militia members a choice: either they continue to behave as predators or they lay down their arms in return for a better life. By creating an environment that benefits the entire community, the Virunga Alliance ensures that professional opportunities allow for the gradual reintegration of the militia members. Meanwhile, the fight against natural resource trafficking deprives the armed groups of their financial means, and the presence of rangers in communities deters them from committing their misdeeds.

2. Three pillars of action

Each pillar pursues specific objectives that contribute to the development of the PNVi and its surroundings.

Tourism is the Virunga Alliance's showcase. In addition to generating income, it raises visitors' awareness of the region's challenges and resources. Potential investors gain a positive experience from it, leading them to consider new projects in the area. It also contributes to the population's sense of pride.

Energy production and distribution are key to the development of this region, which has never been electrified. The Virunga Alliance aims to produce 105 megawatts from the Park's rivers. In 2024, four power plants are already operational. When construction is complete, there will be eight in total. Besides the provision of electricity to households and public infrastructure, the main objectives of PNVi's energy production are to stimulate economic activity, create jobs and increase incomes. A training and credit access programme supports local entrepreneurs who do not have access to commercial bank loans.

The vast majority of the population relies on agriculture and fishing. The region is fertile, but its potential is underexploited. The Virunga Alliance aims to invigorate the agricultural sector by developing value chains of production, processing and distribution. The renovation of access roads, essential for improving crop transport, is also on the agenda.

3. A participatory approach

The Virunga Alliance cannot succeed solely by the will of the leadership teams of the ICCN and Virunga National Park staff. It requires the participation of all the vital forces in North Kivu: political decision-makers, sovereign authorities, the private sector, civil society and the general public. The Virunga Alliance, launched in 2013, is regularly debated in public workshops, expert meetings and media discussions. These exchanges offer the opportunity to air grievances, offer proposals and revise common objectives.

---

1. It should be noted that the link between environmental protection and human development has long been a concern of the PNVi. Patricia Van Schuylenbergh (2015) recalls the positions expressed by former Park Directors: 'Victor Van Straelen, the first co-administrator of the Albert National Park and founder of the Institute of National Parks of Belgian Congo (IPNCB), was the first to publicly denounce the disruption to the natural balance caused by the colonial era's impact on soil fertility and agricultural practices, and to demonstrate the usefulness of national parks for the survival of future generations. Under his influence, Jean-Paul Harroy, curator of the Albert National Park and future President of the International Union for Conservation of Nature (IUCN), published *Afrique, terre qui meurt* (Africa, a dying land) at the end of 1944. (...) *The media coverage of his commitments in some fifteen books and more than 200 articles, as well as his lectures and statements on radio and television, gradually converged on his main battle horse: the axiom of development, population and environmental protection. Following in the footsteps of his friend René Dumont, with his warnings and predictions he will ensure that the voice of conservationists is heard more regularly on a global scale.'
2. See also the calculations developed in chapter 14: Social and environmental justice.

Tourism

JULIE WILLIAMS, VIANNEY HARAKANDI, FRÉDÉRIC HENRARD, PATIENT LIGOLI

Virunga National Park ranks among the most prestigious tourist destinations in the world. Its opening to visitors has seen good times and setbacks. In addition to the economic benefits, tourism is a business card that promotes a positive message about the region.

1. History of tourism[1]

In 1925, the Institute of National Parks of Belgian Congo and Ruanda-Urundi (IPNCB) assigned protection and research objectives to the Albert National Park (*Parc National Albert* – PNA). Tourism began to develop after the 1933 London Conference, which encouraged countries to open their protected areas to a cautious form of tourism, modelled after the English and American parks, which also served as recreational spaces for the general public. An initial programme was launched in collaboration with the colony's official tourism organisations. Tourism was tolerated for the financial windfall it brought, while also feeding the colonial propaganda that aimed to raise public awareness in the metropole about nature conservation in Africa.

Before World War II, visitors to Virunga National Park (*Parc National des Virunga* – PNVi) were rare: primarily wealthy Europeans and Americans stopping by with cameras

17.5 The Kibumba lodge, built on the rim of an ancient crater at the foot of Mount Mikeno, welcomes gorilla visitors.

during motorised tours between Cairo and Cape Town. After the war, tourism promotion intensified: brochures and postcards were published in Belgium, Congo and neighbouring British colonies. Conferences and film screenings were organised in the metropolis and abroad.

The 1950s saw increasing enthusiasm for nature tourism, including hunting. This was still orchestrated by the Tourism Office of Belgian Congo and Ruanda-Urundi, which reported 745 visitors in 1939, 2,200 in 1952 and 6,434 in 1960.

Notable visitors included Prince Leopold of Belgium, the future King Leopold III, who made four extended stays in 1925, 1933, 1957 and 1959. During these expeditions, he collected thousands of items constituting anthropological and naturalist documentation of exceptional value.

As is still the case today, visitors to the PNVi had to pay a daily permit fee and were accompanied by staff. The first areas that were opened to visitors included the Nyamulagira volcano, Mount Ruwenzori and the Rwindi plain, where observing large mammals was particularly popular. The commercial success of the savannah sector justified the construction of a hotel in Rwindi, which opened in 1946 and was inspired by South Africa's Kruger Park. Later constructions showcased local craftsmanship, with thatched-roof huts inspired by Ugandan lodges (similar to contemporary lodges in Virunga National Park).

Tourism continued after the PNA was renamed PNVi in 1959, following Congolese Independence. The scientific reticence of the early years was swept aside and research and commercial exploitation of the protected area were now pursued simultaneously. Significant investments in infrastructure were made by the state, as well as by private operators. A tourism boom was reached in the 1970s with the

17.6 The Rwindi hotel, in the savannah sector, was accessible by road in half a day from Goma (photo: 1948).

17.7 Tourist brochure in Dutch published by the IPNCB in 1948. Translation: 'The Albert National Park is a public asset created for the benefit of all. Help us promote its objectives. Help us protect nature.'

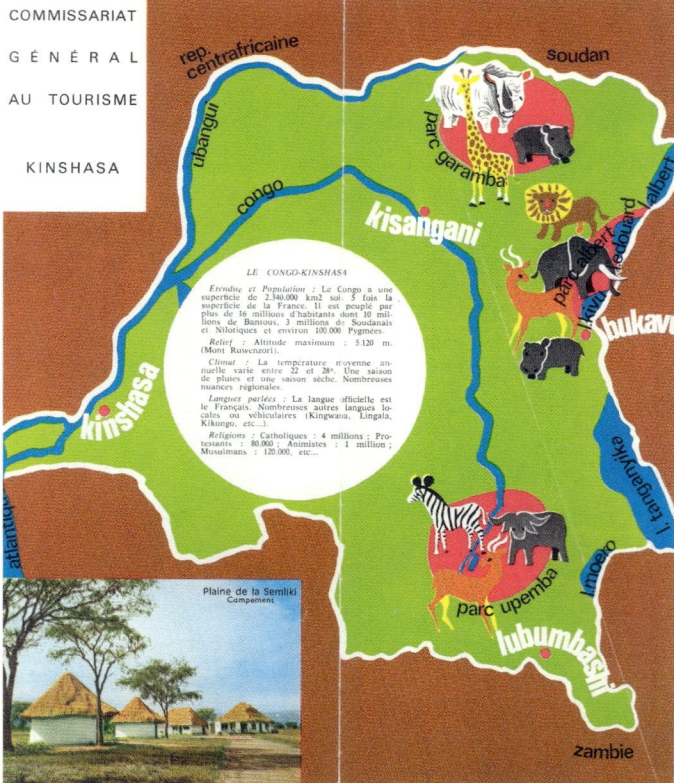

17.8 Tourist map of protected areas in Zaire.

17.9 Postcard of the Mutwanga hotel (1950s).

emergence of many Congolese tour operators, two local airlines, and the construction of new hotels in Rwindi and Mutwanga. Backpackers from all over the world appeared in the villages, to stock up before boarding the trucks that would carry them across the protected areas in East Africa.

Visits to the PNVi were part of an integrated circuit with Kahuzi-Biega National Park, where visitors could observe the gorillas, which were not yet accessible in the Mikeno sector. In Virunga, activities focused on savannah observations – starting from the Rwindi hotel, accessible by road in just half a day from Goma – and sport fishing in Lake Edward. Less frequented but still accessible were the May Ya Moto hot springs, the two volcanoes and Mount Ruwenzori. In the mid-1980s, the habituation of chimpanzees in Tongo was completed successfully, followed in 1992 by the habituation of mountain gorillas, thanks to the European Union's Kivu Program.

The weakening of state authority, the mass arrival of Rwandan refugees and the wars of the 1990s threatened the very survival of the PNVi and, by extension, its tourist activity. Two events left a lasting impression and ended all visits to the South Sector: the deadly attack on tourists near Mabenga in 1995, and the looting of the Rwindi hotel in 1996. In the North Sector, ascents of the Ruwenzori had to be suspended due to the hostility of an armed group opposed to the Kinshasa government (the 'Kasindians'). The Mutwanga hotel met a similar fate to that of the Rwindi hotel.

Despite this dangerous context, a few intrepid visitors sought support from tour operators and some of the rangers – often left without any income – who offered their services individually. Tourism activities therefore continued unofficially during periods of calm, and some income from tourism was maintained (notably the habituation of great apes). Between 1998 and 2006, the Congolese Rally for Democracy (RCD) – a Congolese rebel group collaborating with Rwanda – revived visits to the volcanoes and gorillas. The RCD gave its activities a veneer of legitimacy by paying dividends to the local Park director – who was not part of the Congolese Institute for Nature Conservation (*Institut Congolais pour la Conservation de la Nature* – ICCN) – and carrying out some community projects following the 'revenue-sharing model' that prevails in Rwanda.

The appointment of a new management team at the PNVi in 2008 marked the reassertion of control over tourism activities by the ICCN. The rampant privatisation (by businessmen) of the conflict years came to a halt, which inevita-

17.10 The dilapidated swimming pool of the Rwindi hotel after the looting in 1996.

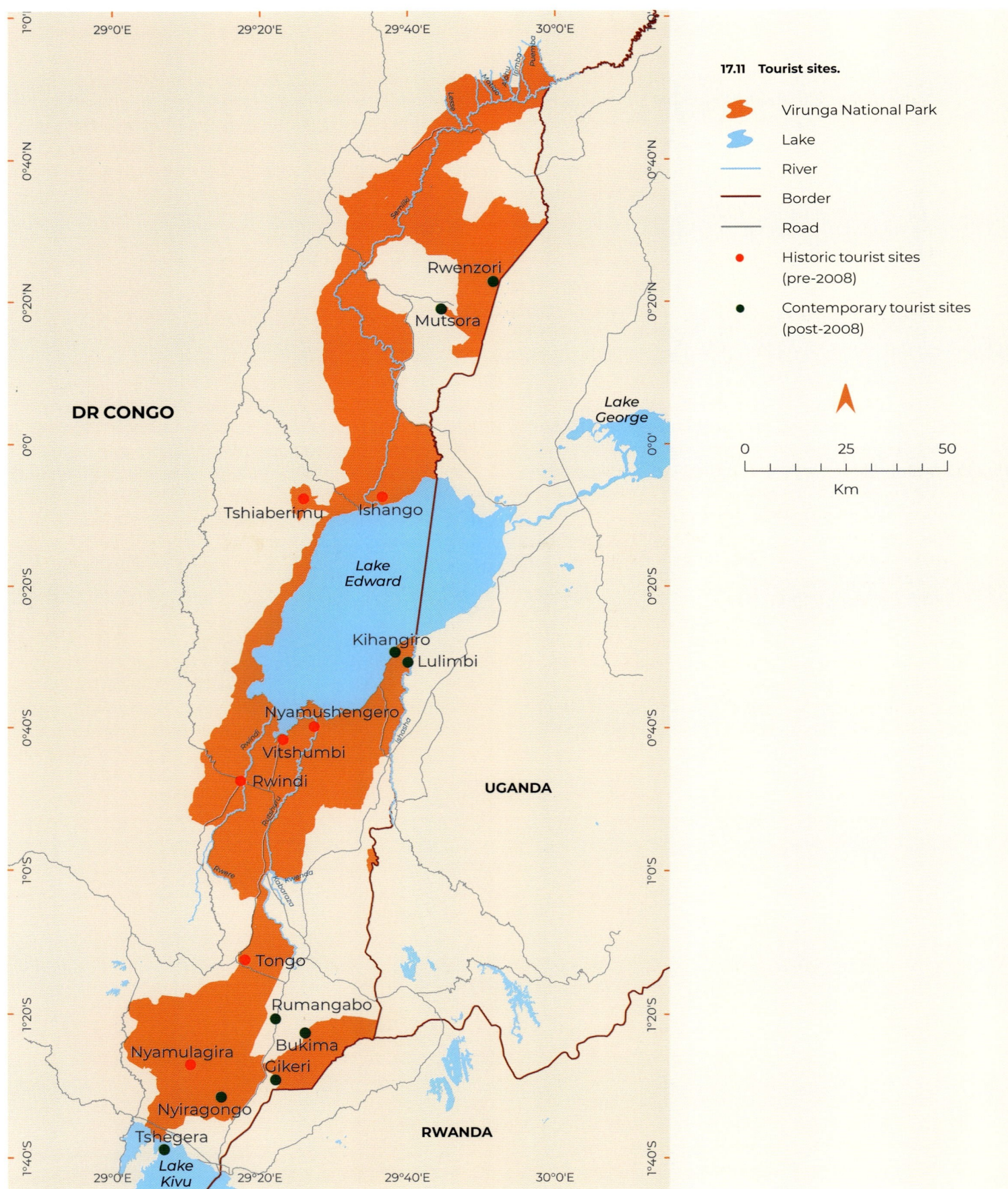

17.11 Tourist sites.

bly caused tensions with certain tour operators and rangers. ICCN visitor permits were reinstated, and the operational framework was revised, to account for the still volatile security context. The Park organised secure transportation, hosted its guests in Park facilities and ensured visitor protection with rangers trained as guides. The return of the ICCN, which is now collaborating with the Virunga Foundation, helped to relaunch its tourism activities, which after 10 years of effort reached a new peak.

2. Recent tourist activity

The tourism revival did not start from scratch, as volcano ascents and gorilla visits had been maintained during the war years. The resurgence also benefited from a spillover effect, as international tourists in Rwanda were seeking lower-priced options. Initially, visitors to the Park were content with minimal comfort: tented nights and close accompaniment by rangers, staying close to nature. These new 'made in Virunga' stays acquired the charm and reputation that would define them: authenticity. The first destinations in the revival years were the volcanoes, the Mikeno gorillas and the Tongo chimpanzees.

For a decade, significant investments were made in infrastructure and hospitality quality. The ICCN rangers and a hundred civilian employees received continuous training, from top chefs, among others. Some even completed internships abroad. In 2009, the Nyiragongo chalets, carried up to the summit by porters, welcomed their first visitors. The Lulimbi tented camp, in the savannah, was established in 2011. The construction of the Rumangabo lodge – located at the PNVi's headquarters, much to the delight of tourists, who enjoyed soaking up the operational atmosphere – began in 2011 and was completed in 2014 (after the first conflict involving the March 23 Movement – M23). In 2014 and 2015, the Bukima tented camps followed, located in the gorilla sector and Tshegera Island on Lake Kivu, which a judge returned to the PNVi in 2014 after illegal occupation by a private owner. In 2016, improved security in the North Sector allowed the revival of Ruwenzori ascents from Mutsora (in limited numbers, with a maximum of a few dozen annually). The tents at the new Gikeri lodge, near Kibumba, welcomed their first visitors in 2017 after two years of habituating nearby gorilla families. The growing number of visitors justified the development of high-end tourism, to complement the range of existing accommodation. In this context, the Bukima tented camp, renamed 'Ngila', was transformed into a luxury facility. In 2022, the camp was destroyed during renewed clashes with M23 before it could welcome its first visitors. The renovation of

17.12   The Mikeno lodge, completed in 2014, is located at the Park headquarters in Rumangabo.

17.13 It takes a day to climb the volcanoes. Travellers spend the night in chalets at the summit. The view of the molten lava and the city of Goma is breathtaking.

the savannah camp in the Ishasha Valley, situated in the Centre Sector, where elephants returned in 2020, was completed in early 2024.

Visitor numbers grew significantly in the mid-2010s: 400 visitors in 2014, 2,176 in 2015, 3,671 in 2016 and 4,813 in 2017. Most were American or European, but a gradual diversification was noted with visitors from Asia (Japan, China, Korea), South America (Argentina, Chile) and Africa (Maghreb, Kenya, South Africa). On the TripAdvisor site, 91% of visitors awarded Virunga National Park a maximum score. Among numerous press articles, a critique in *The Telegraph* summarised the spirit of the time: 'Virunga National Park is one of the most fascinating destinations I have visited. Intense, diverse, and incredibly engaging. Tourism can help a lot, and those who can should go there. It's life, real life, that you'll find there.'

A series of tragic events abruptly slowed this success: a deadly attack on a convoy and the kidnapping of two tourists in 2018, the Ebola epidemic in 2019 and the Covid-19 pandemic in 2020–2021, which brought global tourism to a halt (and posed a significant risk to mountain gorillas, who are highly sensitive to human viruses). Visitor numbers fell to 2,012 in 2018, 1,701 in 2019 and 1,290 in 2020. The resumption of the M23 conflict forced the suspension of operations in November 2021.

The sole exception was Tshegera Island, off the coast of Goma, which continued to welcome numerous visitors who enjoyed walking, having barbecues or kayaking. The destination also hosted schools for educational stays and cultural festivals. Visitor numbers hovered around 4,000 a year.

17.14 Visits to the habituated gorillas are limited to one hour so as not to disturb their way of life. Trackers guide tourists to their last position in the forest.

17.15   A Congolese tourist observes lions in the Centre Sector in 1964. The Lulimbi camp is now a savannah tourist attraction.

3. The PNVi tourism specificities

The wonders of the Park certainly have the power to attract enthusiasts from around the world. The context of North Kivu is, however, challenging for stays that meet international standards in the sector: rampant insecurity, logistical issues (particularly transportation), health risks, among others. To overcome the many daily challenges, the teams at the Department of Tourism must be especially professional, committed and creative. Promoting the PNVi also requires the support of influential tour operators to attract customers who are keen to make a positive impact with their stay in a unique destination.

The message conveyed by the PNVi to its guests is powerful: a park of stunning beauty, with unmatched natural riches, fighting for its survival in a sea of poverty and violence. Their stay does not hide this reality and their interactions with the staff contribute to the visitors' immersion. The hospitality in their accommodation is unpretentious but comfortable, rangers act as their guides, and they can easily interact with the local population. Combined with memorable tourist experiences, such as encounters with gorillas and elephants, or viewings of the lava lake at night, this approach lends an unparalleled sense of authenticity to a stay at the Park. After their visit, tourists often wish to continue supporting the PNVi through donations, advocacy, projects or maintaining contact over many years.

The success of tourism in the 2010s turned the PNVi into the flagship tourist destination in the DRC. An agreement between the Park and the Directorate-General of

17.16   Margherita Peak is the third highest mountain in Africa. The vegetation is spectacular, particularly the giant ferns, several times the size of a human.

Migration (DGM) contributed to this success by creating a mechanism that allows visitors to submit their visa applications to the PNVi, which charges itself with obtaining their residence permit from the DGM. This system has been highly successful and is gradually being extended to other protected areas in the country. Some collaborations were carried out in 2021 and 2023 with the Kahuzi-Biega Park (South Kivu) and the Garamba Park (Haut-Uele) to revive the major tourist circuits that previously existed until the late 1980s. Contacts are also maintained with Queen Elizabeth Park to facilitate cross-border stays in both the DRC and Uganda.

Promotion of domestic tourism is ongoing: initiatives such as reduced rates to match local purchasing power, promotional campaigns, contests with free stays, and visits to schools and associations. Despite the efforts made, however, the attendance of the Congolese public remains modest. Generally speaking, apart from certain groups committed to environmental protection, the general public shows limited interest in 'nature' tourism. This situation might evolve, as the Covid-19 pandemic showed in 2020–2021 when the closure of borders pushed the urban middle class to take an interest in nearby destinations, and Tshegera Island became a must-see for residents of Goma and passing visitors. The

17.17   Tshegera Island, located in Lake Kivu, is shaped by the crater of an ancient volcano. The island is a popular destination for the residents of Goma.

boom in domestic tourism after Congolese Independence also reminds us that public interest – families visiting the Rwindi hotel to observe savannah mammals – could be revived when the security situation allows.

4. Impact

Tourism at the PNVi employs around a hundred people during prosperous periods (including managers, reception staff, drivers and logisticians), as well as offering numerous indirect jobs: gorilla trackers (often former poachers, numbering up to 120), porters, suppliers, transporters, as well as local tour operators (about thirty in Goma alone).

In 2017–2018, revenue from tourism at the PNVi amounted to 5 million dollars. Financial returns for the Congolese state included support for other protected areas (851,000 dollars), visa fees (nearly 400,000 dollars) and VAT (267,000 dollars). Following the management contract between the Virunga Foundation and the ICCN, 30% of the revenue from tourist permits was used to fund community projects (e.g. public lighting and free electricity for schools and hospitals).

Tourism and environmental protection go hand in hand, with visitors being made aware of the fragility of ecosystems. Beyond this environmental showcase, tourist stays also act as a catalyst for a multi-sectoral development dynamic. A visit to the PNVi often changes the perspective of political and economic decision-makers: they become aware of the challenges faced and sometimes wish to engage in discussions about investment projects that will promote development. In this way, tourism becomes a calling card that spreads a positive message about the region's challenges and the determination of its inhabitants to undertake development projects.

Tourism also brings about profound changes in host communities. The presence of rangers helps secure villages and roads, while access to new jobs, both skilled and unskilled, and increased tourist spending improve the living conditions of hundreds of people. There are many stories of young people with basic education diplomas, intelligent, motivated and armed with an unwavering smile, climbing the ranks through training: a firewood collector may become a porter, then a waiter, a kitchen assistant and, one day, a head chef for VIP visitors.

The impact of tourism is both significant and immediate: its protection becomes imperative as the wellbeing of the entire community depends on it. Problematic behaviours (notably tree cutting and poaching) are reported and awareness activities are enthusiastically received. Each year, the tourist lodges host hundreds of children who discover the Park's fauna and flora, interact with the rangers and are educated about sustainable development issues.

Finally, one benefit cannot be quantified: the pride tourism instils in the staff responsible for protecting the PNVi. The wonder and gratitude visitors have expressed are powerful encouragements, motivating the rangers to continue their work. Empathy for the widows and orphans of those who have died in the line of duty also strengthens the sense of brotherhood within the teams.

[1] The section up to 1960 is based on the publications by Patricia Van Schuylenbergh: 'Virunga, star des medias: les tribulations du plus ancien parc naturel d'Afrique' (Van Schuylenbergh, 2015) and 'Virunga: archives et collections d'un parc national d'exception' (Van Schuylenbergh & De Koeijer, 2017).

CHALLENGES AND PERSPECTIVES

Energy

JÉRÔME GABRIEL, EPHREM BALOLE, JOSUÉ DUHA, FRÉDÉRIC HENRARD

Virunga National Park provides clean, reliable and low-cost electricity to the population of North Kivu. The activities are implemented by Virunga Energies, a dedicated company 100% owned by the Park. In continuous development, the programme transforms the lives of thousands of businesses and households.

1. Ten years of work

The Energy programme was launched in 2009 with the installation of the Mutwanga micro-hydroelectric plant. Its construction spanned five years, with a 1.8 million dollar investment from tourism and a grant from the European Union. The plant generates 300 kW of power thanks to its flow rate of 2.3 cubic metres per second and drop height of 18 metres. It is named after the village where the energy is distributed, near the North Sector's headquarters (Mutsora) of Virunga National Park (*Parc National des Virunga* – PNVi).

The arrival of electricity in the villages of Mutwanga and Mutsora was unprecedented in rural North Kivu. In addition to public lighting, domestic connections and improved hospital services, an unexpected result emerged: villagers began to harvest flying termites using traps equipped with red lights, generating a new income source.

The Virunga Energies teams learned the electricity trade at the Mutwanga I plant. With this expertise, they could undertake the next step: constructing a large-scale hydroelectric plant in Matebe, in the Rutshuru territory, near the PNVi's South Sector.

17.18 Virunga Energies is implementing the Energy programme as part of a partnership between the Institute for Nature Conservation in Congo (ICCN) and Virunga Foundation.

THE VIRUNGA ALLIANCE

17.19   The construction of the Mutwanga mini power station in 2009 marked the launch of the programme. Here, the first employee, who is still in service.

17.21   The Matebe hydroplant was built under bombardment during the M23 conflict in 2013–2015. Here, the construction of the canal and the penstock.

17.20   The villagers harvest flying termites using traps fitted with red lights. This provides them with a new income.

17.22   Part of the water from the Rutshuru River is diverted to feed the power station's turbines. The environmental impact is minimal because no dam is required.

Hydroelectricity

MICHEL VERLEYEN

Why is the area around the Park conducive to hydroelectric power generation?

The outskirts of the PNVi benefit from copious rainfall due to the mountains and dense forests, which feed powerful rivers. Their flow rate allows for the production of hydroelectric power.

How are the production sites selected?

The analysis of river courses and the identification of sites with significant elevation differences are first done on a map. The sites must be located on the periphery of the PNVi because human activities within its territory are prohibited. After the cartographic research, an aerial survey can be organised. These flights last several hours because it is necessary to identify the most suitable routes and locations for the future construction site. Next, an on-site exploration is required to confirm the aerial observations. This often takes several days due to difficult terrain. Ground observations can confirm the elevation difference and measure the river's flow rate. This process is repeated several times to assess the variations in water flow throughout the seasons. Finally, all data is sent to an engineering office to confirm the hydroelectric potential of the site.

How is hydroelectric power produced?

The PNVi power plants are built using the 'run-of-the-river' system. This method takes advantage of the natural course of rivers without constructing a dam upstream (which significantly minimises the ecological impact). The principles are simple: water falls from a high point, accumulating kinetic energy (resulting from speed), and this energy is converted into electricity using a turbine and an alternator. The set-up requires four components:

1. A portion of the river water is diverted at a point with a significant elevation difference. The diversion is carried out using a water intake structure.
2. The water is channelled into a load chamber via a canal. A sedimentation basin slows the water and filters out sediments.
3. Once it is ready, the water is injected into the penstock (made of long cast-iron pipes). In the penstock, the water accumulates energy as it descends the slope.
4. At the end of its descent, the water rapidly spins a turbine (at several hundred revolutions per minute). The turbine transmits mechanical energy to the alternator (a large block of steel and copper) that produces the electricity. The water can then return to the natural course of the river.

The simplified theoretical equation for energy conversion into hydroelectricity is expressed as follows: power (in kW) = water flow rate (in m^3/s) × gravity × drop height (in m) × liquid density (in kg/dm^3). The amount of energy produced depends on the river's flow rate and drop height.

What are the characteristics of hydroelectric power?

Hydroelectric power is considered the cheapest form of green energy. It produces no CO_2, it is stable (as long as the river's flow rate is regular) and the cost of construction and operation is relatively low. The facilities may also last for several decades if properly maintained. It is therefore essential to train competent technicians who can ensure the longevity of the installations.

How did the PNVi develop its construction capabilities?

A strategy of internalising capabilities was implemented, as external operators refused to work in North Kivu. A few international experts gradually trained Virunga Energies' employees and managed the construction projects in parallel. Multiple levels of training were provided: theoretical training, on-site learning, and internships for executives in major companies in Belgium and France. Local teams gradually took on responsibilities and now have the skills to manage the projects autonomously.

This epic construction took place amid regular bombings during the March 23 Movement (M23) occupation from 2013 to 2015. The President of the Republic inaugurated the new plant on 16 December 2015. With a flow rate of 18 cubic metres per second and a drop height of 85 metres, it produces 13.2 MW of electricity – 44 times more than the Mutwanga I plant. The project required a 20 million dollar investment and the labour of thousands of people. Visitors

17.23   Laying power lines in Rutshuru territory and towards Goma requires skilled personnel, which include a significant number of women.

17.24   The construction of the Luviro power station began in 2016. Here, the construction of the canal and sedimentation basin.

17.25   The worksite at Luviro posed many challenges: isolation in the forest, torrential rain, insecurity and the Ebola epidemic.

Legal framework and finances

EPHREM BALOLE, JÉRÔME GABRIEL

After a monopoly of five decades for the Société Nationale d'Electricité (SNEL), on 17 June 2014, the Congolese government carried out a far-reaching reform of the electricity sector by adopting Law 14/011. The new legislation liberalises all components of the sector: production, transmission, distribution, commercialisation, importation and exportation. The new governance framework is implemented by several bodies: COPIREP (Steering Committee for the Reform of Public Enterprises), ARE (Electricity Sector Regulatory Authority) and ANSER (National Agency for Energy Services in Rural and Peri-urban Areas). Regarding hydroelectric power, the central government's jurisdiction is limited to the Congo River, transboundary watercourses and rivers crossing provinces. Provincial jurisdictions cover watercourses within the same province.

Virunga Energies has been, and remains, a pioneer in implementing sector reform. At the start of its activities, a regulatory framework for the sector was non-existent, certainly at the provincial level. The development of the company has led to the creation of several normative instruments: technical analysis of files, production and distribution concessions, operating contracts (including pricing), land and tax provisions, and competition among operators. The development of Virunga Energies has therefore served as a spur to develop the governance framework applicable to all operators.

The liberalisation of the sector greatly improves the population's access to various energy sources. However, the historic operator continues to hinder innovations and excessive taxation is discouraging investors – even 'social' ones like Virunga Energies – who therefore tend to focus on lucrative urban market areas. Virunga Energies is actively contributing to discussions to address these challenges.

Virunga Energies' projects require significant investments, funded with a combination of grants and loans. The company finances its activities through public funding sources and private investors: the European Union, USAID, Belgian Development Cooperation, the World Bank, the Howard G. Buffett Foundation, The Schmidt Family Foundation, The World We Want and British International Investment (BII). The vision, trust and courage shown by these partners – few financial actors dare to invest in North Kivu – are key to the programme's success. Testifying to the company's solidity, Virunga Energies is the first company in eastern DRC to be granted a loan from a foreign investment bank (BII).

In 2023, Virunga Energies' budget amounted to 21.7 million dollars. Operating expenses (including debt interest) totalled 7.2 million dollars, and investment expenses (mainly for the construction of power plants and networks) amounted to 14.5 million dollars. The cumulative amount of investments since the company's creation (2013) exceeds 150 million dollars, and the main loan of 19.6 million dollars runs until 2030. In accordance with the contract between the ICCN and the Virunga Foundation – of which Virunga Energies is a subsidiary – all of the company's infrastructure and equipment will be handed over to the Congolese state when the management contract ends in 2040.

admire the stunning Matebe Business Center that sits adjacent to the plant.

Just months after the construction of the plant was complete, the first families in the Rutshuru territory received electricity. The towns of Kiwanja and Rutshuru and the localities along the national road towards Goma (RN2) were progressively connected between 2016 and 2018. The rural economy gradually transformed with the arrival of numerous mills and agricultural factories.

As the network reached the outskirts of Goma, construction teams began work on the next plant. In the northeast of the Centre Sector, in Lubero territory, the Luviro River, with a flow rate of 7 cubic metres per second and a drop height of 235 metres, offers a production capacity of 14.6 MW. The construction site had to be set up in the forest before the works could commence, which required the rehabilitation of 80 km of road as well as building an airstrip on a mountain. The construction, which begun in late 2016, faced numerous challenges: the isolation of the forest, heavy rains, security threats from armed groups and an outbreak of Ebola. The cost of the plant, initially estimated at 20 million dollars, increased by an additional 10 million dollars. This overrun led the company to raise funds in the form of debt (9 million dollars). The Luviro plant was inaugurated in October 2020.

The construction of the Luviro plant network, which had to cross 60 km of forest before reaching inhabited areas, began in 2017. The network now serves the towns of

17.26 The Luviro power station supplies electricity to the Lubero territory and the outskirts of the town of Butembo.

17.27 A high-voltage line is needed to carry large quantities of electricity to the city of Goma, where consumption is growing exponentially.

CHALLENGES AND PERSPECTIVES

17.29 The second power station at Mutwanga is fed by water collected at the foot of Mount Ruwenzori. It is channelled to the turbine via the DRC's only aqueduct.

Kimbulu, Lubero and Musienene (near Butembo). The first businesses and households were connected in December 2020. As in the Rutshuru territory, progress was slow due to the low purchasing power in rural areas. Nevertheless, the arrival of electricity did boost the local economy as it facilitated the creation of an industrial park in Musienene.

In 2018, the Matebe plant network was extended to Goma. Between 2019 and 2020, two-thirds of the city – within the concession area granted to Virunga Energies in the poorest neighbourhoods – was gradually covered. Anticipating increased consumption, Virunga Energies began constructing a new high-voltage line from the Matebe plant. It was commissioned in September 2022, just before the start of new hostilities between M23 and the Congolese army. The increased distribution capacity is complemented by substations transporting greater amounts of electricity over longer distances. The project is expected to be completed in 2025.

At the northern end of the Park, between 2018 and 2020, the Mutwanga I plant, which had served as a test for the entire Energy programme, was replaced by the Mutwanga II plant. The new plant generates 1.4 MW of electricity with a flow rate of 0.8 cubic metres per second and a drop height of 198 metres. Despite its modest size, the project was challenging as the water intake had to be constructed in a mountain torrent. The system required building an aqueduct – the only one of its kind in the DRC – and placing pipes along the mountainside. The beauty of the site and the structures make this a particularly photogenic plant.

The construction of the Rwanguba plant – also located on the Rutshuru River and adjacent to the Matebe plant – began in 2022. With a flow rate of 13 cubic metres per second and a drop height of 195 metres, it complements the Matebe plant to supply the city of Goma, where consumption is increasing exponentially. Work on each of the 14 MW tur-

17.28 Because of the difficult terrain in Mutwanga, the pipes had to be laid on mountainsides by workers trained in mountaineering.

17.30 The Rwanguba power station, completed in 2024, required the construction of the longest penstock in Africa (576 pipes – each weighing 10 tons – over 4.5 km).

bines is planned in two phases. The first phase was completed during the conflict with M23, which forced teams to work in isolation for several months and to evacuate the site during bombings. The hydroplant was declared operational at the end of 2024 after 2.5 years of hard work, under exceptionally difficult conditions, while phase 2 is being prepared.

2. A transformative impact

By the end of 2024, Virunga Energies will operate four hydroelectric plants (Mutwanga, Matebe, Luviro, Rwanguba) and a small solar farm (Nyamilima), producing 45 MW, of which 30 MW is allocated to Rutshuru territory and Goma. The energy is 100% green and the plants prevent the release of 100,000 tons of CO_2 annually.

Distribution is provided by several networks totalling hundreds of kilometres[1]:
- the Mutwanga Network (from the Mutwanga plant): 21 km of low-voltage, 6 km of medium-voltage and 5 distribution zones.
- the Rutshuru Network (powered by the Matebe and Rwanguba plants): 179 km of low-voltage, 95 km of medium-voltage and 67 distribution zones.
- the Goma Network (powered by the Matebe and Rwanguba plants): 289.7 km of low-voltage, 37.5 km of medium-voltage and 42 distribution zones.
- the Lubero Network (powered by the Luviro plant): 71.2 km of low-voltage, 67.5 km of medium-voltage and 25 distribution zones.
- a high-voltage line: 45 km long, between Goma and the Matebe and Rwanguba plants.

By the end of 2024, Virunga Energies will have nearly 35,000 customers, with a yearly growth rate of 4,000 to 6,000 new subscribers. All connections are made using smart meters that allow consumption to be measured and regulated remotely. A prepayment policy is in place: consumers purchase electricity credit to be used when they wish. Different tariffs, approved by regulatory authorities, apply to households and businesses. A system called 'mini dealers' allows a customer to connect their neighbours for a very low price, to pool costs and reduce the risk of fires, which are common with illegal connections.

Virunga Energies also supports several essential public services:
- 3 water pumping stations in Goma benefit from preferential rates, to ensure water supply to poor neighbourhoods.
- 78 healthcare facilities, including 18 in rural areas, receive electricity for free.
- 49 public utility infrastructures (hospitals, schools, courthouses) also benefit from free electricity.
- 3,334 public lighting lamps serve a population of 1.3 million people.

This performance requires a solid corporate structure. Virunga Energies is vertically integrated, covering electricity production, transmission, distribution and marketing. Given the difficult environment in North Kivu, the company operates under direct management, with occasional recourse to outside expertise. In addition to part-time workers, it has 280 employees (including 39 women and 7 expatriates), organised in three departments: power plant construction, network construction and operations. The

17.31 The Rwanguba plant complements the Matebe plant to supply the city of Goma. Here, a resistance test of the factory housing the turbines.

CHALLENGES AND PERSPECTIVES

17.32 Prepayments allow consumers to buy electricity credit whenever they want.

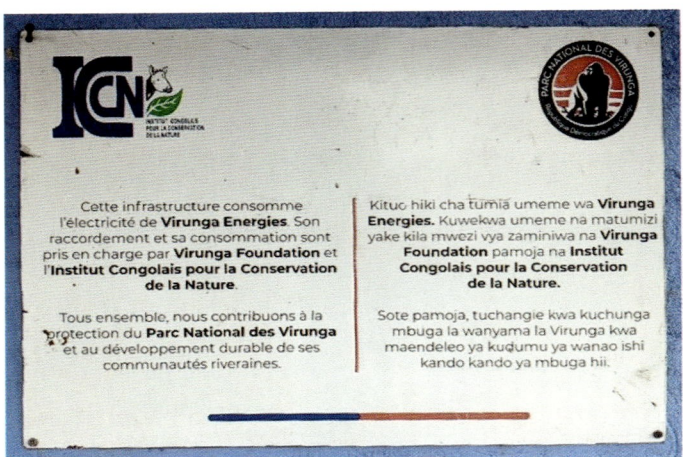

17.33 Virunga Energies is a company with a social purpose. In addition to its reasonable rates for businesses and private individuals, its electricity is supplied free of charge to many hospitals, schools, courts, etc.

17.34 Public lighting serves a catchment area of 1.3 million people.

company has all the civil engineering equipment required to fulfil its mission.

The construction of a power station and its network requires hiring many skilled and unskilled workers. Their numbers vary depending on the project phase, from a minimum of 100 to sometimes more than 1,000 people working in 8-hour shifts. After the construction phase, operations require a smaller workforce (a few dozen employees and specialised technicians).

3. Challenges and complexity

From an engineering perspective, the construction of the Matebe plant was the most complex project, due to the rocky and marshy terrain. At Luviro, logistics made the work daunting: 200 tons of materials had to be brought to the site, including two 40-ton alternators from Mombasa. Transport required building 80 km of roads with sufficiently wide turns to allow convoys to pass under heavy rain. Armed group attacks, an Ebola outbreak and the presence of snakes further complicated the situation. At Rwanguba, the challenge was the length of the penstock (the longest in Africa): 4.5 km constructed with 576 pipes, each 8 x 2 metres and weighing 10 tons. At Mutwanga, on the steep slopes of the Ruwenzori, the challenge was to suspend 2 km of pipes along the mountainside to bring water to the plant's canal. The complexity of the work required a former paratrooper training workers in mountaineering.

Security is an ongoing challenge at construction sites and during operations. The Matebe and Rwanguba plants were built during the M23 occupations of the Rutshuru territory (a decade apart). Construction teams were evacuated numerous times as shells were fired at the installations. The Luviro sites were also attacked several times by local armed groups. In May 2021, the Nyiragongo eruption damaged several kilometres of high-voltage lines, requiring dangerous repairs on hot lava. The site was also targeted during the conflict with M23: explosives were placed on pylons, and bombings repeatedly cut the power lines, forcing repair teams to negotiate to avoid getting caught in the crossfire. Over the years, insecurity has claimed the lives of around twenty workers and guards responsible for protecting the construction sites and logistical convoys.

The selection of personnel and continuous training are essential for the success of construction projects and operations. The first employees were often recruited from local farmers. They had no qualifications in electricity and did not

17.35 The eruption of Nyiragongo in May 2021 damaged the high-voltage line and the water distribution network in Goma. Repair work was carried out on the hot lava.

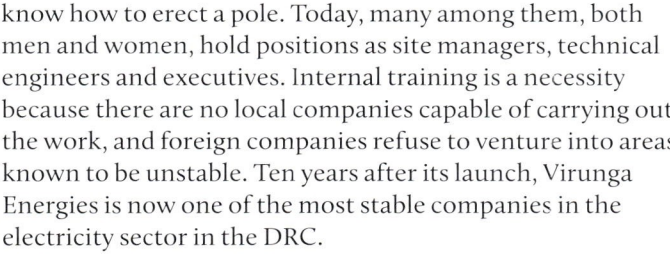

know how to erect a pole. Today, many among them, both men and women, hold positions as site managers, technical engineers and executives. Internal training is a necessity because there are no local companies capable of carrying out the work, and foreign companies refuse to venture into areas known to be unstable. Ten years after its launch, Virunga Energies is now one of the most stable companies in the electricity sector in the DRC.

4. Outlook

The goal remains to generate at least 105 MW of renewable energy on the outskirts of the PNVi. Phase 2 of the Rwanguba power plant (for an additional 14 MW) is the next major project. Other hydroelectric plants will be constructed on a case-by-case basis, depending on available funding, and where rivers have sufficient flow and elevation. Virunga Energies is also planning to install solar farms in regions where the conditions for hydroelectric production are not present.

17.36 In-house training is necessary because subcontracting is impossible. Here, training engineers at ORES in Belgium.

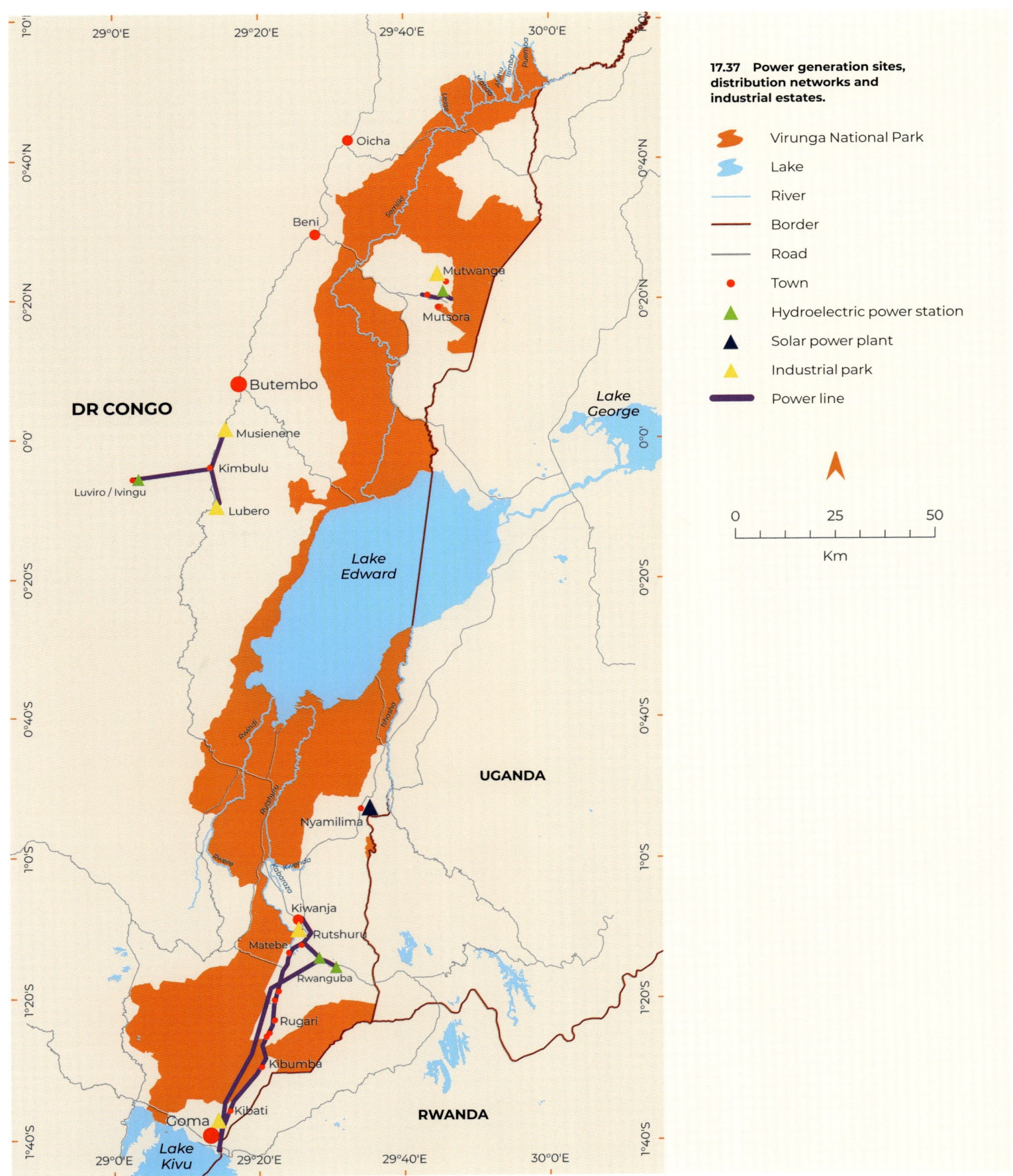

17.37 Power generation sites, distribution networks and industrial estates.

The interconnection of networks is yet to become a reality in North Kivu: every operator distributes 'their' electricity on 'their' network. Pooling capacities is, however, essential to ensure resilience during peak consumption periods. This is particularly true in Goma, where the need for interconnection is significant: three Congolese operators are active there, and the Rwandan and Ugandan networks can also supply electricity across the border. Besides the technical aspects of harmonising different voltages, the interconnection of intra-DRC and cross-border networks requires a precise regulatory framework that the sector's regulatory authorities have yet to establish.

Virunga Energies is a pioneer in the DRC, with a mission of sustainable development benefiting the PNVi and surrounding populations. It shares its unique wealth of experience with other national parks wishing to undertake similar projects. In North Kivu, the company also supports humanitarian projects, such as UNICEF's 2023–2024 efforts to supply water to refugee camps.

17.38   Engineer Michel Verleyen with H.E. President Joseph Kabila Kabange at the inauguration of the Matebe power station on 16 December 2015.

17.39   The interconnection of networks will provide greater resilience during consumption peaks. Cross-border interconnections will contribute to regional economic integration.

1   The network consists of three types of lines: high voltage, medium voltage and low voltage. High-voltage lines transport large quantities of electricity over long distances without incurring losses. Medium-voltage lines form the backbone of the network in the distribution regions. Low-voltage lines supply residential or industrial areas within a 600 m radius. An average of 150 connections are provided in rural areas and 500 in urban areas.

Hydroelectricity, Bitcoins and artificial intelligence

JÉRÔME GABRIEL

Bringing power plant equipment online requires simulating significant consumption to test its resistance under normal operating conditions. The traditional solution is to install a load bank – equivalent to a large electrical resistor – that dissipates energy as heat. This is a costly (several hundred thousand dollars) and technically complex solution. Moreover, it has to be maintained for as long as the electricity consumption of the new plant does not reach a sufficiently high and stable level.

For the commissioning of the Luviro plant in 2020, an alternative solution was considered: replacing the load bank with computers that also consume a lot of energy. This set-up allows the testing of the installations and has the additional benefit of generating revenue. Six months later, the first Bitcoins were being 'mined' by Virunga Energies.

From a technical perspective, the solution is optimal: the power consumption of the computers prevents consumption fluctuations that could damage the equipment (when a mill connected to the grid stops operating, for instance). Financially, the Bitcoin revenues – produced with zero CO_2 emissions thanks to the plant's green energy – allow for early repayment of loans negotiated for the construction, without having to wait until the network is completed. A further benefit is that, in a logic of circular development, the computer-generated heat can be reused to accelerate cocoa drying, for instance. Four years after the first trial at Luviro, the Bitcoin-producing computers account for 7 MW of consumption. They will be phased out as and when local consumption gradually absorbs all the power generated by the plants.

This solution has caught the interest of specialist media and those working in the sector, because it could accelerate the construction of new plants in the DRC. Whether for Bitcoin computers or artificial intelligence – a field expected to see significant developments in the future – this set-up ensures a rapid return on investment that limits the financial risks during the first years of operation of the new facilities.

17.40 The production of Bitcoins protects the power stations' equipment and generates income to repay the loans.

Entrepreneurship

VIKTOR WEINAND, AUDACE HAMULI, FRÉDÉRIC HENRARD

Job creation is driven by small- and medium-sized enterprises. The Park assists them with a unique system of access to credit based on electricity consumption, develops industrial zones and provides training to entrepreneurs.

Starting a business in North Kivu is not easy: violent attacks undermine the ability to undertake projects, poverty pushes young people to join armed groups, corruption erodes the rule of law, and the lack of basic infrastructure (roads, energy, and banking systems to name but a few) hinders business growth.

The Energy programme aims to provide businesses with electricity – to stimulate economic growth and create jobs – but experience shows that the potential of the programme to help SMEs grow is limited by their lack of access to credit. Borrowing programmes are available in urban centres but on prohibitive terms: interest rates exceed 40% per year, repayment periods rarely extend beyond a year, and the borrower must pledge property worth at least 20,000 dollars. In response, the Entrepreneurship programme's primary goal is to offer a credit package that meets the repayment capacity of entrepreneurs living near Virunga National Park (*Parc National des Virunga* – PNVi).

The development of the SME sector is also hampered by the lack of land on which to set up their businesses. The land needs to be financially accessible, close to main roads, connected to electricity and water, and safe from thieves and

17.41 The Entrepreneurship programme supports several hundred SMEs. Here, a welding workshop.

CHALLENGES AND PERSPECTIVES

17.42 Bakery.

17.43 Production of bottled water.

17.44 Carpentry.

17.45 Poultry house.

even armed groups. These requirements represent an impossible equation for most SMEs. The second goal of the Entrepreneurship programme is to address this land issue.

As SMEs develop, their lack of management capabilities often presents a third bottleneck. Business leaders make mistakes that can sometimes, despite their hard work, prove fatal to their businesses. The Entrepreneurship programme therefore also aims to provide them with management support.

These three workstreams contribute to the goals of the Virunga Alliance: they create added economic value, reduce dependency on imports (especially food) and stimulate job creation.

1. Electricity credits

The PNVi's lending formula is unprecedented: the loan amount is repaid through electricity purchases, the cost of which is increased by a percentage corresponding to the borrower's repayment capacity. To be eligible, they must be connected to the Virunga Energies electricity grid and present a consumption history of at least six months. They must also be in good standing administratively (which is not always the case in North Kivu) and present a land ownership title or lease contract for at least five years.

The entrepreneur's electricity consumption and business plan are analysed. The analysis determines the percentage markup on the kilowatt-hour (kWh) price for loan repayment. An Investment Committee reviews each case before

17.46 Cutting lava paving stones. They are a durable and inexpensive alternative to bitumen and concrete for the streets of Goma.

deciding whether to grant a loan. In most cases, the projected electricity consumption allows for the loan to be repaid over four years.

For example:
- An SME pays 0.24 dollars per kWh for electricity to Virunga Energies (the rate negotiated with the Regulatory Authority);
- The entrepreneur is granted a 1,000 dollar loan by Virunga Development;
- The electricity price charged to the SME is increased by 20%, amounting to 0.048 dollars per kWh (which is still lower than the price of a generator, approximately 0.6 dollars per kWh);
- Based on the SME's estimated consumption (according to their business plan), the SME repays the borrowed capital (1,217.40 dollars) over four years.

The system reduces the burden on the borrower by:
- Matching repayment capacity with electricity consumption, an indicator of the company's economic activity;
- Considering the seasonality of commercial activity (an essential factor in rural areas);
- Eliminating fixed repayment deadlines, as the borrower repays when they purchase electricity.

The system also reduces the risk for the lender by:
- Assessing the borrower's risk profile, based on their current and projected electricity consumption;
- Continuously and objectively analysing their repayment capacity;
- Its ability to cut off the electricity supply in the event of default.

In simple terms, the system is flexible for the borrower, who can repay a higher amount when their activity peaks and a lower amount when it slows down. It is also secure for the lender, who holds the borrower captive through the electricity supply.

Portfolio value

There are two categories of loans: microcredits ranging from 300 to 15,000 dollars and SME loans exceeding 15,000 dollars. The portfolio reached nearly 5 million dollars in February 2024.

17.47 Loans portfolio (February 2024).
The 'Virunga' loans refer to industrial projects supported by PNVi: chocolate factory, oil press, biscuit factory, etc.

	MAJOR LOANS	MICRO-CREDITS	VIRUNGA	TOTAL
Number of loans	11	781	10	802
Capital investments ($)	746,370	1,472,091	2,729,246	4,947,707
Average amount of the loans ($)	67,852	1,885	305,925	6,169

2. Partnerships

As a non-governmental organisation (NGO), the Virunga Foundation is not authorised to engage in banking activities. The credit programme is implemented with Equity BCDC, which has a strong presence in North Kivu and has been a pioneer in the microcredit sector since 1984. The Virunga Foundation provides the capital for the loans, analyses the files and shares its opinion on the granting of loans. It is up to Equity BCDC to validate the credit, after verification, and finalise the loan contract with the borrower. This partnership between a banking institution, an NGO and a nature park is unprecedented. It ensures the solidity of investments, in compliance with banking regulations, for the benefit of SMEs neighbouring the PNVi.

An evolution is underway to make the granting and management of loans more autonomous, under the direct responsibility of the Virunga Foundation. A new partnership with Grameen Trust, the bank founded in 1989 by Professor Muhammad Yunus, the 2006 Nobel Peace Prize laureate, should facilitate the professionalisation of the management of the programme.

3. Industrial parks

Minimum logistical conditions must be met to allow the SMEs to develop: access to electricity, proximity to major roads (despite their poor condition) and access to water. The predatory attitude of tax services adds to these material challenges.

The five industrial parks of the PNVi address these difficulties (see the maps of hydroelectric plants and industrial parks in the previous chapter). Located on the outskirts of

17.48   Flour mill.

17.49   Aerial view of Goma industrial park.

17.50   Industrial parks development (June 2024).

INDUSTRIAL PARK	SURFACE	PROGRESS
Mutwanga (North)	4 ha	Completed 10 operational SMEs
Goma (South)	6 ha	Completed 23 operational SMEs
Rutshuru (South-East)	26 ha	Potential for 50 SMEs Suspended because of the M23 conflict
Lubero (West)	16 ha	Potential for 35 SMEs 10 operational SMEs
Musienene (West)	200 ha	Potential for 120+ SMEs 5 operational SMEs

the Park, they offer access to electricity and water, shared security for the facilities and legal assistance. The grouping of businesses also discourages questionable tax inspections as entrepreneurs come forth with collective protests. It is possible to rent a 100 m² plot, with or without a warehouse, for 75 and 100 dollars per month, respectively.

Most SMEs established in the industrial parks are active in the food sector, including flour (wheat and corn), bakery, biscuit production, cooking oil, baby food, cocoa (chocolate), egg production and chia seeds. Diversification is underway, including water treatment, metallurgy, waste recycling, volcanic stone paving, paint manufacturing and natural fertiliser production.

The Musienene zone was granted 'Special Economic Zone' status by the Congolese government. Entrepreneurs who establish themselves there are exempt from import and profit taxes for five years.

4. Training

Congolese higher education has some shortcomings. Traineeship opportunities are sorely lacking. Local companies are few and far between and gaining experience abroad is not an option, as visas are hard to obtain. The resulting management errors hamper the growth of SMEs and sometimes lead to their failure.

In partnership with local training centres, the Entrepreneurship programme provides training in basic management, finance and accounting, as well as land and tax law. Coaching (mentorship) for business plan development and loan application preparation is also provided. Nearly 500 entrepreneurs have benefited from this support between 2019 and 2024.

17.51   Training for entrepreneurs.

17.52 Several hundred thousand people practise subsistence farming in the immediate vicinity of the Park.

Agriculture

BASTIEN ALARD, MERDI KAMBALE BARAKA, FRÉDÉRIC HENRARD

The Park promotes agricultural production, transformation and distribution. In fields and factories, traceability combines environmental protection, access to a decent income and the fight against illegal trafficking. With support from the private sector, 'made in Virunga' products are set to conquer the markets.

North Kivu has enormous agricultural potential: the region benefits from a favourable climate, fertile soils enriched by volcanic eruptions, consistent rainfall, a varied farming history and a young, entrepreneurial workforce.

Despite these favourable conditions, the situation is bleak. Over half of North Kivu's population engages in subsistence farming (often extensive), using outdated techniques and depleted seed strains. Before the arrival of Virunga Energies, agricultural processing was almost non-existent, so raw materials were being exported to neighbouring countries and re-imported as processed products, at prohibitive costs. Poor road conditions, extortion of farmers by armed groups and population displacements due to conflicts also disrupt agricultural activities, which has resulted in food insecurity affecting 71% of the population (according to data from the United Nations).

This situation has a direct impact on Virunga National Park (*Parc National des Virunga* – PNVi) itself, as its immediate periphery is being used as farmland by hundreds of thousands of people. Forced to survive, they often have no choice but to encroach on the Park to expand their crops (see the encroachments map in chapter 9). These encroachments are encouraged by powerful landowners and armed groups, who use small farmers as a front, only to subsequently extort them.

1. Targeted objectives

The PNVi has neither the means nor the ambition to modernise the entire agricultural sector of North Kivu. However, given its predominant role in the economy of the province and the fact that uncontrolled agricultural development poses a serious threat to the Park's ecosystems, the Virunga Alliance aims to develop value chains of production, processing and distribution across the agricultural sector.

Its interventions focus on sectors that can generate structural changes and spur private sector investment. Whether implemented by the Virunga Alliance or by third parties aligning with its initiatives, these efforts aim to increase incomes and stimulate job creation in the surrounding communities. The Agriculture programme is implemented in rural areas that do not benefit from the other Virunga Alliance interventions (Tourism, Energy, Entrepreneurship). Working with cooperatives and associations, the programme reaches tens of thousands of direct and indirect beneficiaries, often overlooked by the development programmes in North Kivu, as they live far from urban centres, in areas where armed groups hold significant influence.

The activities were launched in 2017 and are a long-term commitment, as interventions in the agricultural sector require time and perseverance before they can yield results.

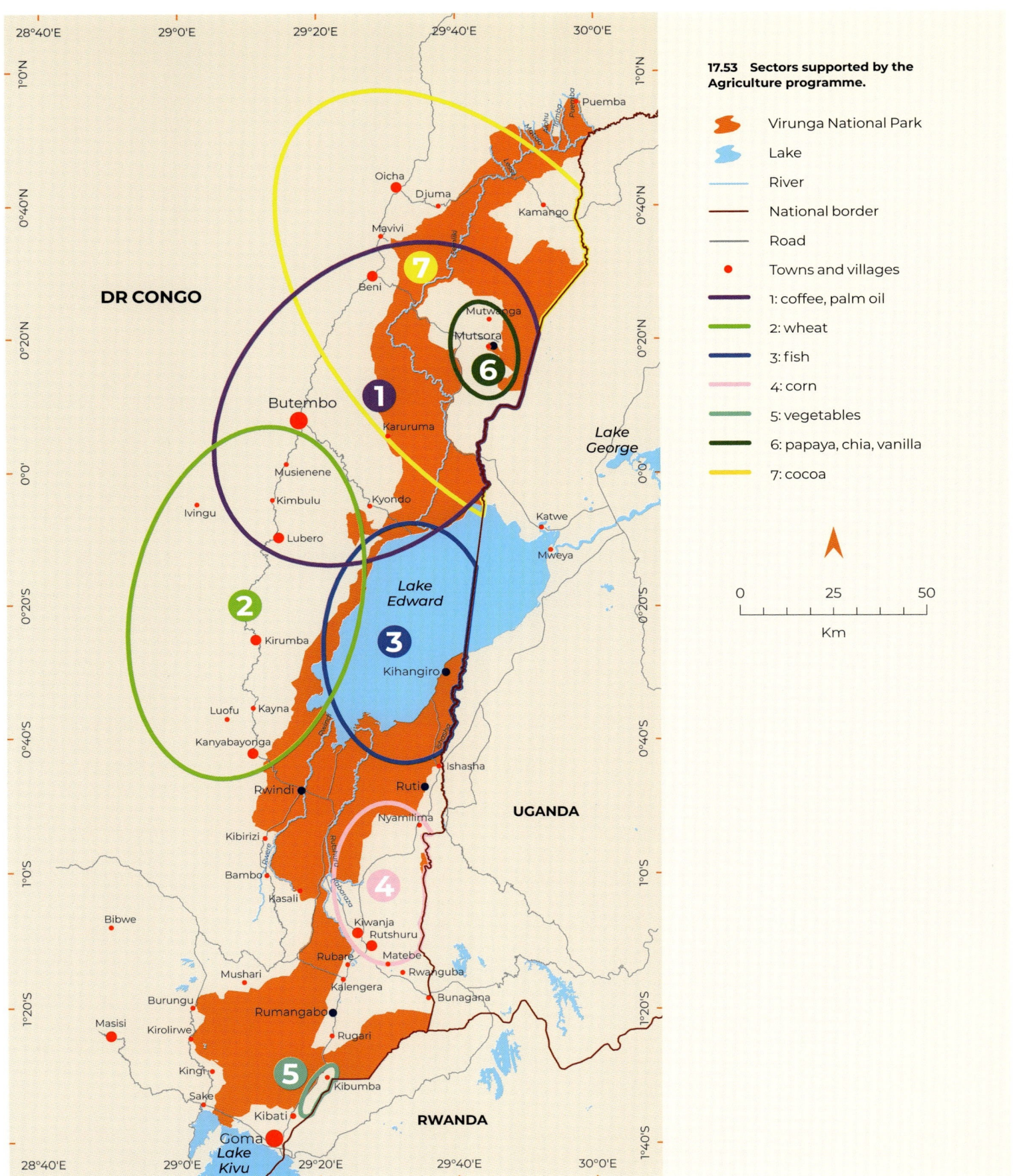

17.53 Sectors supported by the Agriculture programme.

2. Agricultural value chains

Efforts are made to enhance the three links constituting agricultural value chains: production, processing and distribution. Their integration, and collaborations with the private sector, avoid the pitfalls of traditional rural development projects. The latter focus predominantly on production, sometimes also on marketing, without considering the profitability of the entire chain. Beyond the initial phase, which requires subsidised investments, this approach ensures the long-term sustainability of the interventions implemented by the Agriculture programme.

Production is generally low as soils are depleted, seeds have lost their quality, and planting and harvesting techniques have become outdated. Significant efforts are devoted to renewing inputs (which requires extensive nurseries), teaching new techniques, and building storage infrastructure. Alternating crops are promoted to ensure year-round production and reduce the risks of a single harvest.

Processing adds value to agricultural products. Facilitated by the production of hydroelectricity, processing generates a new type of non-land-based employment. The processing units are specific to each sector: flour mills and biscuit factories for wheat, oil mills and soap factories for palm oil, corn mills, coffee processing and roasting, and industrial chocolate production, among others. For the most part, partner cooperatives supply the raw materials, and the machines run on Virunga Energies' green energy.

Market access is essential to ensure the viability of the sector. Poor road conditions and nitpicking – sometimes predatory – controls by state authorities complicate the functioning of supply chains and compliance with commercial commitments. The distribution areas include local, national and international markets (first Europe, then the United States). For example, soaps from the PNVi are sold in eastern Congo, chocolate can be bought in supermarkets in Kinshasa, and coffee is available online and in speciality shops in Europe. Virunga Origins, a dedicated distribution company, carries out this work. A study is underway to facilitate access to Kinshasa, a city heavily dependent on imports to feed its population, by creating a green logistics corridor on the Congo River.

3. Green, fair and non-violent agriculture

Providing a decent income to farmers living on the PNVi's periphery is not just a matter of ethics: it is a necessity to ensure the Park's protection. Improving living conditions drastically reduces the risk of illegal crop cultivation and keeps farmers from joining armed groups to feed their families. The system supporting this approach is product traceability, from field to final customers, to attain three requirements:

- **Environmental Protection:** by geolocating each farmer, the PNVi ensures that agricultural products do not contribute to deforestation (either inside or outside the Park) and that practices are sustainable and environmentally friendly. The 'Organic' certification mechanism makes it possible to verify the farmers' compliance with these commitments.
- **Access to a Decent Income:** Traceability guarantees that each producer is paid directly for their products and that no unscrupulous intermediaries capture the added value. Combined with Fair Trade and Rainforest Alliance certifications, it enables the distributor to negotiate better prices with international customers who want to ensure that their contracts contribute transparently to the development of the region.
- **Combating Trafficking and Conflicts:** Agricultural production sometimes finances armed groups. Traceability through cooperatives and processing units ensures that financial flows are legal and benefit producers and the Congolese state, without fuelling trafficking, corruption and violence.

17.54   Product traceability is beneficial for the entire population because it ensures environmental protection and decent incomes, and supports the fight against trafficking.

17.55 Palm oil nursery.

17.56 Harvesting palm oil nuts before processing.

17.57 Manufacturing of 'blue bar' soap for washing.

4. Value chains on the PNVi outskirts

The outskirts of the PNVi are fertile, and the farms – sometimes artisanal, sometimes industrial until the war years – are numerous. As resources are limited, a selection is made based on their importance (the number of farm workers), proximity to the Park (to limit encroachments), technicality and processing potential. International experts and the Congolese government's technical services are involved in this process. The following description does not cover all activities but illustrates the adopted approach.

4.1. Palm oil

Palm oil played a major economic role until the 1980s. Tens of thousands of farmers relied on it, and this locally produced oil was used for cooking. The sector gradually became moribund: palm trees aged, processing plants disappeared and imports from Indonesia and Malaysia replaced local consumption.

In July 2024, nearly 200,000 palm trees grown in nurseries were distributed to about 2,000 farmers. They must adhere to a strict rule: the seedlings are meant to replace old palm trees, and no forest can be cut down to create new fields. The farmers also receive training to grow their plants and harvest the nuts. The production is ensured by Sicovir. Its soap factory is located at the heart of the sector, in Mutwanga, where the company has installed the first industrial press in North Kivu – soon to be followed by three more – and produces 800 tons of soap each month: blue bars for laundry and soap for personal hygiene. It employs approximately one hundred workers, and a refinery to start producing cooking oil again is planned for 2025.

4.2. Cocoa

The commercialisation of cocoa beans is profitable, but it fuels the conflict that has plagued the Beni region for a decade. The Allied Democratic Forces (ADF) armed group seeks to seize the beans – massacring the farmers who harvest them – and sells them to clandestine networks. The term 'blood cocoa' is therefore commonly used, in analogy with 'blood diamonds'. This situation has prompted the PNVi to invest in the sector, in an attempt to address this root cause of the conflict.

The PNVi collaborates with cooperatives established in areas targeted by ADF massacres. Activities include building fermentation centres to increase the value of the beans (with a bonus for high quality) and ensuring traceability. Efforts also focus on improving drying techniques. Over 50,000 tons were sold to the PNVi's chocolate factory in Mutwanga, or to international buyers, in 2023. Three thousand farmers benefited from this initiative.

THE VIRUNGA ALLIANCE

17.60 Producing 'made in DRC' chocolate at the Mutwanga chocolate factory.

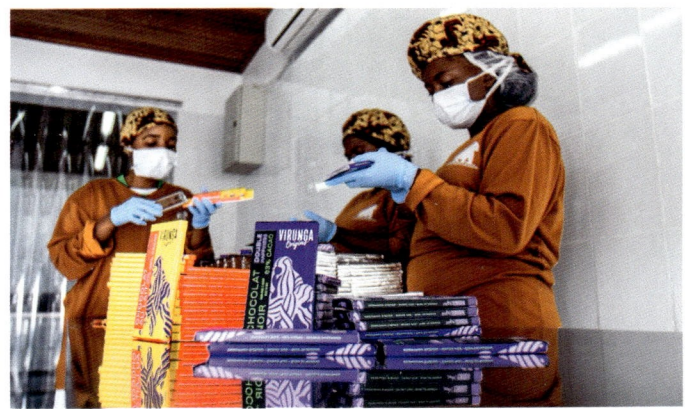

17.58 Drying and sale of cocoa beans.

17.61 The packaging evokes the imagery of the Park.

17.59 Virunga chocolate advert. Translation: 'Taste for yourself, it's good quality, 100% local and 100% Congolese.'

4.3. Corn

Corn cultivation is growing in importance due to its high yield and because dietary habits are changing, as corn is mixed with cassava to enhance the flour's nutritional quality. Initially, harvests were sent from the Rutshuru territory to Uganda and Rwanda for processing into flour. Volumes decreased significantly due to degenerated seeds, poor agricultural practices (hand-shelling) and diseases.

The project employs 2,000 farmers, who receive advice from agronomists working with the cooperatives. Interventions focus on renewing seeds (in collaboration with two local entrepreneurs) and producing flour, using the 160 mills connected to the Virunga Energies network that benefit from a loan from the Entrepreneurship programme. The revival of the sector has yielded spectacular results: all of the flour is sold in local markets, and the World Food Programme – which previously distributed humanitarian aid

17.62 Small-scale mechanisation for corn processing.

17.63 Production of corn flour (electric mill).

with imported flour – also sources from the region. Unfortunately, all activities have been halted since 2022, as the epicentre of the M23 conflict is in the Rutshuru territory. They will, however, resume after the conflict ends.

4.4. Coffee

Coffee is an ancient crop in North Kivu, which has also declined for various reasons: ageing trees, diseases (tracheomycosis), loss of know-how, fraud and corruption, and marketing problems (due to poor road conditions and conflicts). In recent years, global market trends – rising demand and redistribution of producing regions due to climate change – have created newly favourable conditions. The PNVi's Agriculture programme is capitalising on this new dynamic in the sector.

The work is carried out with two cooperatives federating more than 6,500 producers (20% of whom are women) over a production area of 2,500 hectares. Similar to the approach with cocoa, interventions focus on improving yields and maintaining stable quality through a series of measures: replacing old trees, training in harvesting techniques, constructing washing stations and storage facilities to preserve quality, and setting up laboratories to analyse beans (an important element of commercialisation). Financial management support is also provided to manage the complex commercialisation process, which may, depending on the situation, lead to significant gains or debts. The marketing aspect is ensured through certifications (Organic, Fair Trade, Rainforest Alliance) and promotion at international trade fairs. Within five years, coffee production has increased from 4 to 31 containers, exported to 12 international buyers.

17.64 Drying coffee beans.

17.65 Coffee products consumed in the DRC.

4.5. Wheat

The Lubero territory used to be the wheat granary of the DRC, with flourishing crops allowing significant industrial processing. Since the 1990s, however, the sector has come to a complete halt: seeds are no longer available and the old mills have stopped operating. The economic fabric of the territory has been severely impoverished.

In 2021, the PNVi set itself the challenge of reviving the sector. The task is monumental and requires a phased approach. In 2024, activities are concentrated in 12 villages where 2,000 small producers collectively cultivate 900 hectares of agricultural land. In 2023, planting 317 tons of seeds – in collaboration with state technical authorities working to improve seed quality – yielded 320,000 tons. Spreading best practices and mechanising the harvesting process, a practice almost unheard of in Kivu, will further improve this initial result. Downstream, the construction of a mill, a bakery and a biscuit factory will create the necessary outlets to ensure the viability of the sector. Consumption will be entirely covered by local markets, which currently have to make do with low-quality imported products.

4.6. Other crops

Besides the major value chains mentioned above, the PNVi supports other crops sectors that employ a smaller number of beneficiaries (a few hundred): papaya, chia seeds, vegetables, vanilla (a struggling sector experiencing a revival), honey (which is highly successful in the DRC), as well as aromatic and medicinal plants. The same approach is applied: improving production, promoting processing and accessing markets.

For details on the fish sector in Lake Edward, see chapter 11.

17.66 Harvesting and small-scale mechanisation for wheat processing.

17.67 Farmers in front of a field and bags of chia.

CHALLENGES AND PERSPECTIVES

17.68 Harvesting potatoes.

17.69 Vanilla farmers sleep in their fields at night to prevent theft.

17.70 Honey potted by the widows of PNVi rangers.

5. Partnerships

The Agriculture programme works with 32 cooperatives and producer groups totalling 12,000 members[1]. This approach helps to structure production, teach new techniques, share risks, stabilise quality and share information about problems, such as threats posed by armed groups.

The involvement of the private sector is essential to ensure the sustainability of the interventions. However, due to insecurity, local and international investors are reluctant to support or initiate industrial projects in North Kivu. For this reason, the PNVi has no choice but to establish its own processing units and manage product commercialisation in collaboration with the few entrepreneurs who believe in the region's potential.

Since 2012, five companies have been set up, with the Virunga Foundation as a capital shareholder:
- Virunga Enzymes SARL: founded in 2012 and based in Mutwanga, the company markets an enzyme extracted from papaya latex. Its activities create a market for 15,000 small latex producers, all receiving technical and financial support. The raw material is processed in Beni and Mutwanga before being sold to international companies in the pharmaceutical and food industries. The Ruwenzori region offers excellent soil and an ideal microclimate, making the DRC the leading producer of this enzyme.
- Sicovir SARL (Société Industrielle et Commerciale des Virunga): This company, founded in 2014 and based in Mutwanga, produces soap from palm oil. The produc-

17.71   Virunga Enzymes SARL markets an enzyme extracted from papaya latex.

17.72   Sicovir SARL manufactures soap and soon also cooking oil.

tion of table oil is under study. Details of its activities are provided above.
– Virunga Development SARL: founded in 2016 and based in Goma, the company manages loans to entrepreneurs and industrial parks (see previous chapter). It invests in two bakeries (in Butembo and Goma), a mill (in Lubero) and a biscuit factory (also in Lubero) that will be operational at the beginning of 2025. These four units will drive the wheat sector by consuming nearly 50 tons daily. Approximately one hundred people will find employment there.
– Virunga Chocolat SARL: this company, founded in 2019 and based in Mutwanga, produces the only chocolate made entirely in Congo, from bean to bar. Its products are popular with the general public in the DRC and Europe thanks to the quality – under the supervision of renowned chocolatier Dominique Persoons – and the positive image that they convey.
– Virunga Origins SRL: founded in 2021 and based in Belgium, the company organises the distribution and international marketing of 'made in Virunga' products. Priority is given to the European market and online sales, before exploring the American market.

Other than Virunga Origins, all companies are registered in and pay taxes in the DRC. They are governed by commercial law yet pursue a social purpose, as their profits must be reinvested locally to benefit neighbouring communities. In addition to their commercial results, they hope to stimulate similar investments by other operators.

Collaboration with the private sector provides access to expertise in specialised fields, such as palm oil refining, cocoa butter production or spray-drying papaya latex. International companies such as Puratos, Natix, Maselis, Malongo and Rombouts contribute to these efforts. Similarly, to ensure the distribution, partnerships have been set up with major names like Kin Marché, Colex, Colruyt and Bio-Planet.

If partners wish, the PNVi logo – the famous gorilla in the orange circle – is made available to them to boost sales by leveraging the name and reputation of the Park. A similar system also exists at the local level, where products stamped with the Park label, such as fish from Lake Edward, enjoy a favourable reputation.

6. Measuring the impact

Empirical observations suggest that the results achieved by the Agriculture programme in the vicinity of the PNVi are substantial. The Mutwanga region, for instance, which has been targeted for multiple interventions, is experiencing an economic boom: people from outside the area are flocking there to find employment, living standards have improved (notably thanks to the hospital now being powered by electricity), houses are in better condition and conflicts with the PNVi are non-existent.

Aside from these immediate observations, specialists acknowledge the challenges of evaluating the impact of agricultural development programmes. This is a complex task as there are many factors of success (or failure) and any effects of interventions will be felt over the long term. Among other measures, defining a 'living income' indicator, against which the purchase price of agricultural products can be measured, is gradually becoming the sector standard.

It is reasonable to assume that the Agriculture programme has a structuring effect in the regions where it is deployed because it combines two key dimensions: 1) in addition to the gradual end to monocultures, integrated work across all sectors is generating stable and sustainable incomes for farmers; and 2) increased production volumes and higher purchase prices, due to certifications, generate additional income. The benefits are felt at a household level and at a community level, as a result of bonuses paid by certain international buyers (50 dollars per ton of certified cocoa beans, for instance, which helps to renovate water points, agricultural feeder roads or schools).

It should be noted that the results achieved in export-oriented sectors – cocoa and coffee, but also vanilla and papaya – partially depend on global market fluctuations. Coffee and cocoa, in particular, have benefited from a favourable global context. Conversely, factors specific to North Kivu, such as its unfavourable taxation on investments and ongoing insecurity, severely undermine the results.

A symbolic outcome must also be mentioned: around 15 widows of the PNVi rangers are employed in agricultural processing, and their number is growing. Their presence serves as a reminder that the Agriculture programme remains closely linked to the existence, survival and future of the Park.

---

[1] This total does not include the fishing associations of Lake Edward, which have about 10,000 members, many of whom are women who play a predominant role in the processing and marketing of fish.

Impact

EPHREM BALOLE, FRÉDÉRIC HENRARD, MARIJKE VERPOORTEN

The Virunga Alliance pursues an agenda of economic and social transformation by leveraging the Park's natural resources. Initial studies demonstrate positive results in the fight against poverty, the reduction in violence, and the ownership of the approach by local communities.

When the Albert National Park was created in 1925, an integral conservation model prevailed. In the 1980s, participatory management of protected areas, also known as 'community conservation', became the preferred mode. The Virunga Alliance is developing a conservation–development nexus paradigm that goes even further: a green economy in which nature contributes to the population's wellbeing. Environmental protection is central to a comprehensive vision for society and communal living.

In this context, the impact of the Virunga Alliance should be measured on several levels: social life, economic growth, the quality of public services, governance and conflict dynamics, which complement the traditional measures to preserve protected areas. Virunga National Park (*Parc National des Virunga* – PNVi) is focusing on these aspects with the support of several scientific institutions, including the University of Antwerp (Belgium), the University of Cambridge (Great Britain) and the French National Institute for Agriculture, Food and Environment (INRAE, France).

17.73 Measuring impact also covers the socio-economic aspects.

CHALLENGES AND PERSPECTIVES

17.74   Job creation and economic growth are key to tackling development and stabilisation challenges.

17.75   Among other indicators, socio-economic growth is measured by the increase in land prices.

1. Business and job creation

An evaluation conducted by the PNVi in 2022 estimates that the Virunga Alliance has created 12,000 direct, indirect and induced jobs (without measuring the impact on income growth). In addition to the 2,500 direct jobs in the PNVi and its affiliated entities (notably Virunga Energies), 6,000 indirect jobs have been identified in small- and medium-sized enterprises (SMEs) connected to the Virunga Energies network or supported by the Entrepreneurship and Agriculture programmes. The induced jobs include 3,500 additional positions with suppliers or subcontractors of the preceding categories. Jobs within public administrations are not included.

By the end of 2023, 1,614 micro, small- and medium-sized enterprises were connected to the Virunga Energies network. 8% of them existed before 2016, the year of the first connections, and 13% of households used their subscriptions to start income-generating activities. Most SMEs are active in agricultural processing: cassava, corn or rice mills, oil presses, livestock feed, chick incubators, cold storage, fruit juice production, and others. A few years after the arrival of electricity, a second wave of SMEs developed, mostly in urban areas, including restaurants and bars, water purification (bottled water), bakeries, soap-making, tailoring, carpentry, mechanics, welding, stone cutting and administrative services (phone recharges and public secretarial services). Most SMEs (95%) source and sell their products in North Kivu, maximising local economic value. Their growth allows consumers to find local products that partially substitute imported goods (mainly staple foods).

SMEs that receive an electricity loan under the Entrepreneurship programme create an average of 5 full-time jobs and 4.8 temporary jobs (for varying periods). The average age of employees is 25, and 80% stem from the immediate vicinity of the PNVi. Most jobs are unskilled (manual labour), with 20% filled by university graduates. Women make up 15% of the workforce.

In 2022, the M23 conflict severely disrupted this growth dynamic, causing massive population displacement in the Rutshuru territory and cutting off all supply routes. Electricity consumption in the area dropped from 2 MW to 400 kW, and most of the 554 SMEs connected to the electric grid, which had generated 40% of the new jobs, were closed or relocated to Goma.

2. Multiplier effects

A study commissioned by the European Union in 2020 from the data analysis and economic modelling firm Cambridge Econometrics measured the macroeconomic impact of the Virunga Alliance programmes. The analysis considered a combination of two scenarios: (1) the 2015–2025 period, during which economic activities are affected by conflicts; and (2) the 2026–2030 period, during which 'normal' economic growth has become possible thanks to a peaceful political-security context.

The study drew several conclusions (as of 2020):
– Agriculture will have the greatest impact on GDP by 2030, preceding other sectors such as fishing and retail.
– The number of jobs created by the Virunga Alliance could reach 72,000 in 2025 and exceed 100,000 in 2028.
– The Virunga Alliance programmes generate 81 million dollars in GDP (2020) and the goal of 1 billion dollars driven by the green economy of the Virunga Alliance can be achieved by 2050.

17.76   The arrival of electricity has brought about profound economic and social changes.

17.77   The use of electric cookers to replace charcoal is changing eating habits.

17.78   Electricity is an essential input for the water pumps on which over a million people in Goma depend.

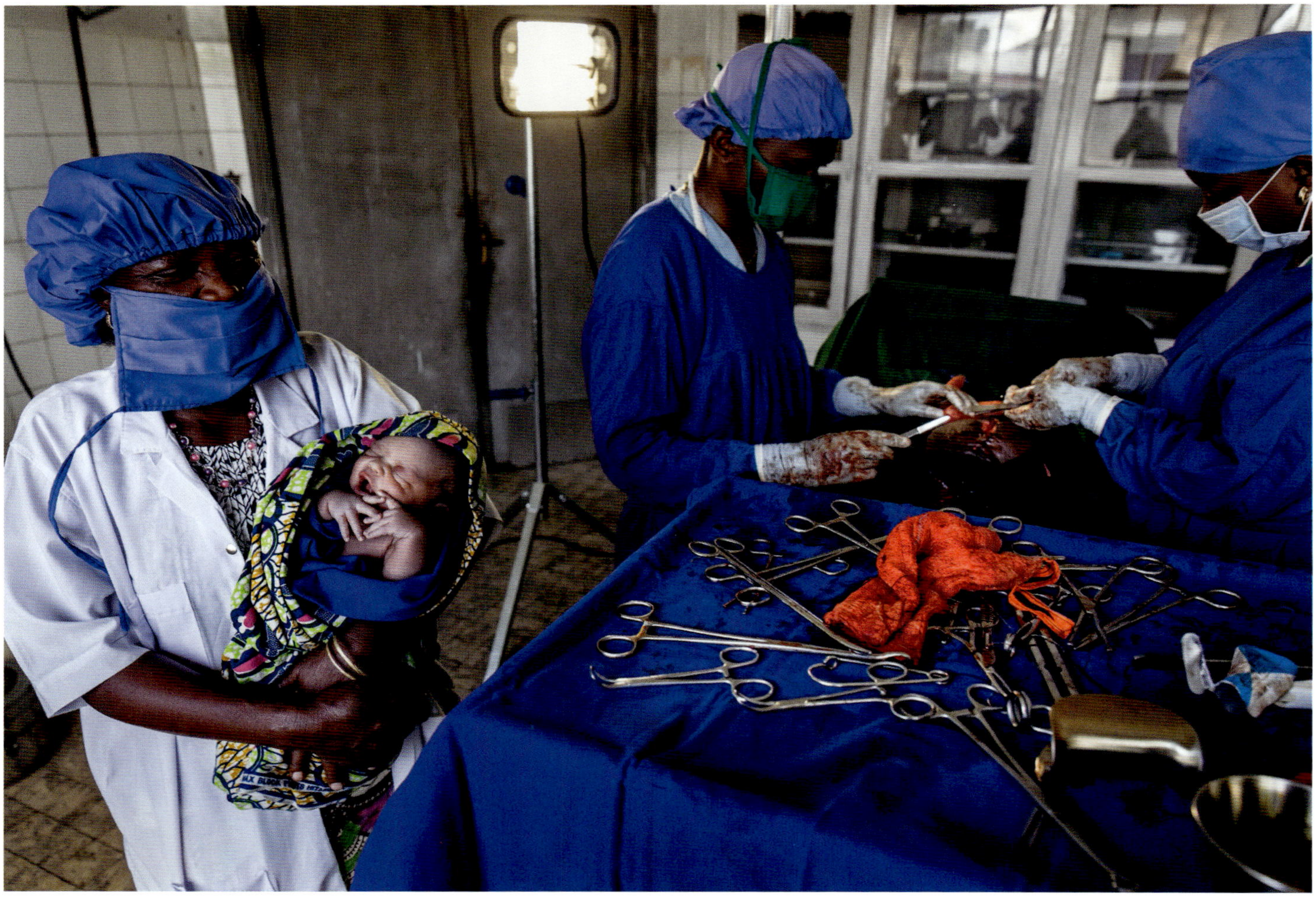

CHALLENGES AND PERSPECTIVES

17.79 Thanks to electricity, hospitals can offer 24/7 assistance and store medicines.

17.80 Access to IT tools for the most disadvantaged depends on cheap energy. Here, training at the Don Bosco Institute in Goma.

– The contributions of the Virunga Alliance to state revenues will reach 60 million dollars in 2025 and 100 million dollars in 2030.

3. Basic services and social life

Improving public services has a significant impact on the population's wellbeing. Daily life is transformed in multiple areas. As a result of the electrification of pumping stations on Lake Kivu, water is now accessible to 400,000 people in poor neighbourhoods and displaced persons camps in Goma. The construction and maintenance of a gravity-fed network (without active driving force) near the mountain gorilla sector make the Park's spring water accessible to about 100,000 people. The 2,578 public lighting lamps installed in urban centres benefit a population exceeding one million. All report a beneficial impact on crime levels (women especially), the opening hours of small businesses and social life in general. The health sector is making a significant qualitative leap: medicines are stored in refrigerators, air conditioning relieves patients and emergency services can work continuously. Even prison employees – who benefit from a free electricity supply, as do schools, medical centres, police stations and courts in rural areas – report improved living and working conditions.

4. Impact on armed conflicts

Between 2009 and 2022, the ACLED (Armed Conflict Location and Event Data) database of the New York University, which compiles acts of violence in eastern DRC, recorded more than 8,800 incidents in North Kivu. About 4,000 were confrontations between armed groups, 3,500 concerned violence against civilians and 1,200 were popular protests. During the same period, the University of Antwerp analysed the level of violence near the hydroelectric power plant sites (Stoop and Verpoorten, 2024). The availability of 60,000 temporary jobs corresponded to a 93% reduction in incidents in the affected sub-regions. In areas where armed groups had a strong presence, increased fighting with the army was observed as sites and transportation required securing, which confirmed that government interventions should be combined with socio-economic interventions to ensure safe conditions. The positive impact faded after 18 months, which confirmed that at some point socioeconomic development programmes and the restoration of state authority must take over to ensure long-term reductions in violence.

Another study conducted by the PNVi in 2019–2021 demonstrates the positive impact of economic activity on the influence of armed groups. The study focused on a sample of 909 SMEs connected to the Virunga Energies network, representing 3,240 jobs, mainly in the Rutshuru territory. Business owners were asked, with anonymity guaranteed, whether some employees had previously been members of armed groups. Of these entrepreneurs, 58% answered no, 17% said they were unaware, and 25% reported having such profiles in their workforce. The responses put the total number of ex-members of armed groups at 11–12% of the workforce (350–400 people). The responses also indicate that former combatants have found jobs in other businesses or started their own. Only one testimony reported an individual who had returned to his former violent activities. A preventive dimension is also shown through the employees' profiles: 50% of employees were initially unemployed, and 20% were students – economically less integrated groups representing a recruitment target for armed groups. This study confirms that stimulating the SME fabric helps reduce violence by integrating militia members into the legal economy and diminishing young men's interest in joining their ranks.

5. Governance and tax revenues

The Congolese tax system is complex. National legislation establishes direct and indirect taxation, implemented by three financial agencies: the General Directorate of Taxes (DGI), the General Directorate of Customs and Excise (DGDA) and the General Directorate of Administrative, State, and Participation Revenues (DGRAD). Each year,

17.81   Studies show the positive impact of economic activity on the stranglehold of armed groups. Here, civilian protection convoy and PNVi participation in the National Day parade (2009).

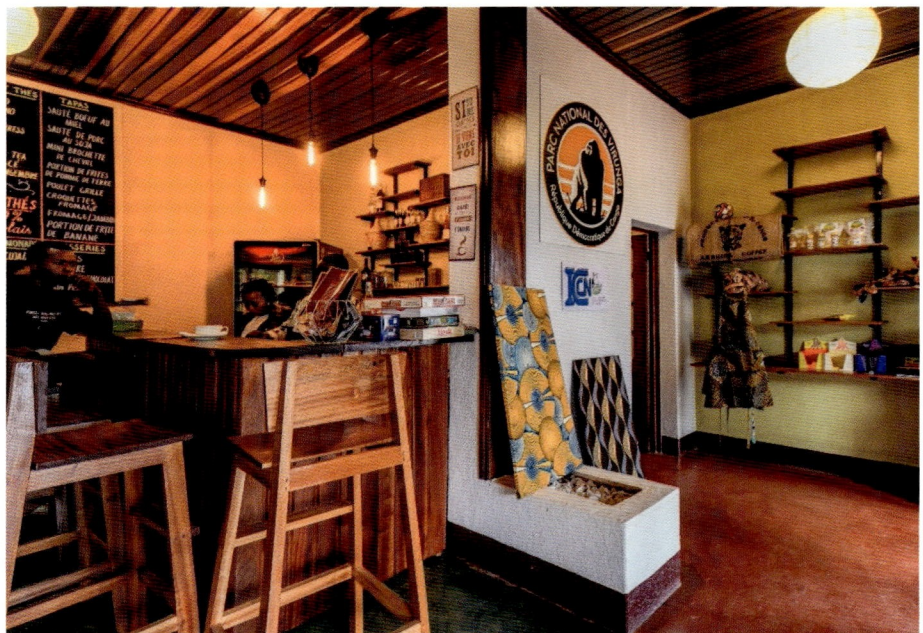

17.82 *Espace Virunga* in Beni promotes local 'made in Virunga' products and provides a meeting place for youth movements, local associations and artists.

a Public Finance Law (LOFIP) sets the taxes and duties levied by the various ministries. In addition to the central government's tax authority, decentralisation laws allow decentralised entities (provinces and chiefdoms/sectors) to collect taxes. Finally, numerous inter-ministerial decrees mandate agencies, funds, institutes, banks and state services to collect taxes.

This prolific regulation fuels corruption. It encourages state actors to track or even provoke infractions so that they can impose fines and transactional penalties. This situation can be a nightmare for economic operators, who are subject to harassment or even physical threats. In addition to the difficult security situation, these tax excesses heavily undermine the private sector investment capacity.

The entities forming the Virunga Alliance (the PNVi, Virunga Energies, agricultural companies, etc.) have a policy of paying legally established taxes, asserting their rights in compliance with administrative procedures and not engaging in dubious 'arrangements'. Since cash payments expose entities to abuse, all payments are made through banks. This rigour can, however, provoke retaliation or lead to legal conflicts.

In 2023, the Virunga Alliance's direct contribution to the state budget was around 6 million dollars. This does not include the contributions of the hundreds of businesses whose activities are made possible by its programmes. The tax revenues generated by these companies certainly amount to several tens of millions of dollars per year.

6. Public and political ownership

The Virunga Alliance positions the PNVi as a credible, resilient, long-term actor, the only entity in North Kivu capable of managing a sizeable economic development programme. This strong position has it (majority) supporters and (minority) opponents.

A second scientific study conducted in 2019–2021 by the University of Antwerp looked at the attitudes of the people living near the PNVi (Lunanga and Maombi, 2024). Here, 55% of respondents stated that they had a positive or very positive opinion of the PNVi's actions, 35% expressed no opinion and 10% felt the impact was negative. The last category of respondents generally includes people who benefit directly or indirectly from illegally exploiting natural resources. The positive majority opinion of the PNVi and its programmes is the opposite of the (negative) opinion of other state actors. The people interviewed said that in the event of a security crisis, they had more confidence in the PNVi rangers – perceived as belonging to an institution keen to provide solutions – and indicated they would seek shelter with them.

The attitude of political players is ambivalent: some decision-makers resolutely support the PNVi's initiatives and encourage the population to adopt a sustainable, law-abiding development approach; others tend towards populism and defend their own, often illegal, interests. There are also cases of jealous local authorities, who temporarily fuel rhetoric hostile to the PNVi, in the hope of initiating interac-

17.83 Organising workshops about the Park encourages dialogue and enhances ownership.

tions that could lead to the launch of development programmes in the sub-region concerned, and then claiming credit for the establishment of these programmes. Such political wait-and-see attitudes do not exist at the national level, where the highest political authorities support the objectives of the Virunga Alliance.

CONCLUSION

18 — One hundred years of effort and pride   321

Appendix

     Appendix 1   Acronyms   326

     Appendix 2   Statement of limits   327

     Appendix 3   List of senior managers   330

     Appendix 4   List of mammals   331

     Appendix 5   List of birds   335

     Appendix 6   Authors' biographies   341

     Appendix 7   Bibliography   345

Acknowledgements   351

Photo credits   352

18.1 Thoughts and reflections from a legendary animal.

18

One hundred years of effort and pride

EMMANUEL DE MERODE, MÉTHODE BAGURUBUMWE, EPHREM BALOLE, JEAN-PIERRE D'HUART, FRÉDÉRIC HENRARD, MARC LANGUY

It may seem illusory to draw conclusions from the fact that an atypical national park, whose chaotic history could well have ended in its destruction on multiple occasions, has survived for a hundred years. Yet that was exactly what, 20 years ago, the editors of *Parc National des Virunga: Survie du premier parc d'Afrique* (Virunga National Park: Survival of Africa's first park) attempted to do (Languy & de Merode, 2006). The book inspired some clear reflections.

The authors saw the rebuilding of Virunga National Park (*Parc National des Virunga* – PNVi) after the wars as the most urgent concern. They felt that priority should be given to restoring the PNVi boundaries by fighting on three fronts: ending illegal land sales, preventing agricultural encroachment and resolving the refugee problem. An additional endeavour was to ensure respect for the law by improving cooperation with the courts and reducing the presence of the military. Three conditions were identified for the long-term survival of the PNVi: an end to random funding, the availability of the PNVi's resources and improved management, particularly of human resources. The authors concluded that these crucial measures required decision-makers to make difficult decisions, revealing their willingness to safeguard this priceless Congolese and world heritage.

Where do we stand now, 20 years on? Have the lessons learned and the prospects for the future changed in any way? Yes…and no.

Lessons learned from the past

Passion and boldness
The decision to create an institution specifically to manage a nature reserve is a testament to the boldness and passion of several visionary individuals. The 'national park' was a new concept in Africa in 1925, and its promoters faced fierce opposition. Admittedly, the objectives set out a hundred years ago – to put nature 'under a glass dome' to protect it from human activity and study its natural components – are unsuited to the reality in today's Congo. At the time, the role of humans was not part of the equation, and the management method was subject to a great deal of trial and error. Still, this approach has resulted in numerous exploration missions that have generated vast scientific knowledge about biodiversity, ecological processes and habitat dynamics. As Van Schuylenbergh and de Koeijer (2017) point out, these missions made a major contribution to the international reputation of the PNVi and the institutions responsible for its management.

Support from the authorities
Each political phase following Independence has profoundly influenced the operations of the Congolese Institute for Nature Conservation (*Institut Congolais pour la Conservation de la Nature* – ICCN) and the national parks in Zaire/Congo. After the difficult post-Independence decade, a recovery occurred in the 1970s and 1980s. The appropriation of nature conservation at the presidential level, supported by NGOs and international funding, ensured progress. Under the leadership of Jacques Verschuren and then Samy Mankoto, the ICCN was restructured, new parks were created, a large number of national managers emerged, and the institution was present in international forums. All of which boosted the success of the PNVi. Yet even though national legislation and international agreements did offer protection, the political, judicial and administrative support required for the law to be applied correctly remained inadequate. A lack of understanding of the issues at stake, the favouring of personal interests and plain corruption have even, at times, harmed the PNVi.

CONCLUSION

18.2   Like the survival of the park, the future of the Rwenzori snows depends on people's willingness to rise to the challenges we face today.

Openness to partnerships

The PNVi has always attracted the attention of international partners, who included it among their strategic priorities. As one of the 'stars' of the global network of protected areas, the PNVi attracts interest from governmental cooperation agencies, private foundations and NGOs. Thanks to their support, the PNVi can launch monitoring and research programmes, recruit and train staff, purchase equipment and rebuild infrastructure. Tourist safari promotion and the habituation of the gorillas have also been decisive in establishing the first embryo of self-financing. Whether modest or considerable, this financial and technical support has made a more or less lasting contribution to the institution's efficiency.

Resilience in the face of conflict

The succession of wars following the events of 1994 in Rwanda had a profound impact on the ICCN and the PNVi. Some earlier achievements were wiped out, but the war periods also brought a wealth of learning experiences. Efforts to raise the awareness of political forces and military authorities of the need to protect the Park were often crowned with success, thanks to the atypical initiatives of various institutions (the European Union, UNESCO, the United Nations Foundation and GTZ, among others) supporting the ICCN and organised diplomatic lobbying for Congolese protected areas. At the same time, NGOs rallied around the PNVi's management to help respond to the most urgent needs. The respect commanded by its consistently claimed and implemented strict political neutrality got the PNVi through the war years.

Resistance to human pressures

Demographic pressure and the need for arable land make the PNVi's mission to protect particularly delicate. Poverty and a lack of socio-economic opportunities are the root causes of a threat that runs through the history of the PNVi from its origins to the present day and – we must assume – into the future. The Park leaders have implemented various community conservation initiatives in response to this situation, including environmental education, consultation and joint boundary demarcations. These initiatives have proved random in space and time and were rarely sustainable. Having learned from these experiences, the Virunga Alliance has set itself the ambition of achieving long-term structural impact.

Reorientation of the management strategy

Adaptability and sustainability

The political, security and socio-economic contexts require constant adaptation of the management plan and the Virunga Alliance in the field. In conjunction with financial autonomy, this flexible attitude has enhanced the institute's professionalism and promoted the region's economic development. Adaptability to a complex environment has proven to be a key booster of long-term success for the PNVi.

Public–private partnership

Despite some criticism, PNVi leaders have made courageous decisions to adapt to the context in which they operated. Eighty years after the creation of the Park, the year 2005 marked a profound turning point, when the ICCN and the Virunga Foundation entered into a public–private partnership. Its objectives and method were decidedly innovative in the field of nature conservation, and some pedagogical skills were – and still are – required to explain that this is the management model best suited to the PNVi's contemporary challenges. This pioneering arrangement has since been replicated and benefits many protected areas in the DRC and across Africa.

Ecosystem valuation

The launch of the Virunga Alliance in 2013 facilitated the mobilisation of a broad coalition of local stakeholders who favour preserving the Park. By engaging in activities belonging to various socio-economic sectors, the PNVi departs drastically from traditional modes of managing protected areas. To ensure its survival, it seeks to improve the wellbeing of the surrounding communities and ultimately contribute to the return of peace. Twelve years on, the achievements of the Virunga Alliance demonstrate how the PNVi has, despite significant challenges, managed to preserve the integrity of its boundaries and to become a major economic player at the regional level. Despite this rapid progress, it must be noted that insecurity and poverty remain widespread, and the numerical projections of demographic growth and deforestation remain alarming (Christensen & Arsanjani, 2020).

Education and ownership

The protection of the Park and the valuation of its ecosystem services create a link between ecological and economic values. For instance: forest conservation → rainfall patterns → river flow → hydroelectric production. Or: the preservation of hippos → the presence of microorganisms in Lake Edward → fish abundance → fishing potential. Admittedly, nature conservation is not always a top priority for a developing country, but demonstrating the tangible link between environmental protection and economic development is the way to contribute to the PNVi's preservation objectives.

Looking to the future

At the time of this assessment, thoughts inevitably turn to the many rangers and staff members whose unjust deaths testify to their courage and dedication over the past century to protect the Park and ensure its future.

Managing a protected area on the scale of the PNVi is no mean task. In the context of North Kivu, it can even be described as a mission impossible. How do you consolidate the resurgence of ecosystems that remain fragile despite the successes achieved? How do you align such interventions with the presence of armed groups and ongoing attacks? How do you ensure law enforcement despite weaknesses in the rule of law? How do you resist aspirations for oil and mining exploitation? How do you anticipate changes and tensions resulting from climate change? How do you further develop the Virunga Alliance to meet the expectations of the surrounding populations? The responsibilities of the PNVi's guardians are immense and complex.

Answering these questions will require more than the ICCN–Virunga Foundation partnership. Several *sine qua non* conditions must be met to lay the foundations for lasting success. Like their predecessors in 2006, the editors of this book complement the recommendations made earlier with the following new ones:

- The PNVi will not survive without political stability and the strict application of democratic principles in the DRC and across the wider region, essential for security and peace.
- The future of the PNVi can only be assured by raising the awareness of authorities and local populations, thereby strengthening their ownership of sustainable development and the Virunga Alliance.
- To ensure the sustainability of management and investment, the PNVi's resources must be consolidated, a greater contribution must be made from the state budget, and partners must continue to be mobilised.

After 100 years of existence, notwithstanding all its ups and downs, the PNVi is still alive, vibrant and going strong. Its rebirth certainly is a source of pride, but the threats that continue to beset it are cause for serious concern.

The achievements of the last 20 years, in the face of an incredibly challenging context, warrant cautious optimism. The political context and security situation allowing, the extraordinary successes of the past provide hope for a bright future for the PNVi and the local communities.

Appendix

Appendix 1
Acronyms

ACF-UK	Africa Conservation Fund – United Kingdom
ADFLC	Alliance of Democratic Forces for the Liberation of Congo-Zaire
ALIR	Army for the Liberation of Rwanda
AWF	African Wildlife Foundation
BBC	British Broadcasting Corporation
bp	Before present
CAMPFIRE	Communal Areas Management Programme For Indigenous Resources
CARPE	Central African Regional Program for the Environment
CITES	Convention on International Trade in Endangered Species of Flora and Fauna
COPEVI	Virunga Fisheries Cooperative
COPILE	Cooperative of Lake Edward Indigenous Fishermen
CRSN	Natural Sciences Research Centre (Lwiro)
DFGF(E)	Dian Fossey Gorilla Fund (Europe)
DFGF(I)	Dian Fossey Gorilla Fund (International)
DGD	Directorate-General for Development Cooperation and Humanitarian Aid (Belgium)
DGM/DSR	Directorate-General of Migration/Directorate Security and Intelligence
DRC	Democratic Republic of Congo
EU	European Union
FAO	Food and Agriculture Organization of the United Nations
FARDC	Armed Forces of the Democratic Republic of Congo
FAZ	Zairian Armed Forces
FDLR	Democratic Forces for the Liberation of Rwanda
FFI	Fauna and Flora International
FFPS	Fauna and Flora Preservation Society (now FFI)
FFRSA	Foundation for Promoting Scientific Research in Africa
FOB	Forward Operating Base
FZS	Frankfurt Zoological Society
GD	General Director
GIC	Gilman International Conservation Foundation
GIS	Geographic Information System
GIZ	German Society for International Cooperation
GM	General Management
GPS	Global Positioning System
GVO	Goma Volcano Observatory
GVTC	Greater Virunga Transboundary Collaboration
ICCN	Congolese Institute for Nature Conservation
ICDP	Integrated Conservation and Development Program
IEC	Independent Election Commission
IGCP	International Gorilla Conservation Programme
IIED	International Institute for Environment and Development
IJZBC	Institute of Zoological and Botanical Gardens of Congo
IMF	International Monetary Fund
INCN	National Institute for the Conservation of Nature
INEAC	National Institute for Agronomic Study of the Belgian Congo
IPNCB	Institute for the National Parks in Belgian Congo
IRCC	International Red Cross Committee
IRSAC	Institute for Scientific Research in Central Africa
IRSNB	Royal Belgian Institute of Natural Sciences
ITFC	Institute for Tropical Forest Conservation
IUCN	International Union for Conservation of Nature
IZCN	Zairian Institute for Nature Conservation
LEM	Law Enforcement Monitoring
LRA	Lord Resistance Army
Ltd	Limited company
LWF	Lutheran World Federation
MBG	Meise Botanic Garden
MECNEF	Ministry of Environment, Conservation of Nature, Water and Forests
MGVP	Mountain Gorilla Veterinary Project
MIKE	Monitoring the Illegal Killing of Elephants
MIST	Management Information System (UWA)
MONUC	UN Mission in the DRC
MSF	Doctors Without Borders
NGO	Non-governmental organisation
NTFPS	Non-timber forest products
NYZS	New York Zoological Society (later WCS)
OCC	Operational Command Centre
OCHA	Office for the Coordination of Humanitarian Affairs
ORTPN	Rwandan Office for Tourism and National Parks
OWR	Okapi Wildlife Reserve
PA	Protected area
PAG	Development and Management Plan
PARCID	Project to Support the Strengthening of Institutional Capacities of the General Management of the ICCN
PDG	President and General Manager
PEVi	Virunga Environmental Programme (WWF)
PNG	Garamba National Park
PNKB	Kahuzi-Biega National Park
PNS	Salonga National Park
PNVi	Virunga National Park
pp	Patrol post
PPP	Public–private partnerships
PRSP	Poverty Reduction Strategy Paper
QENP	Queen Elizabeth National Park
QEPA	Queen Elizabeth Protected Area
RBM	Ranger-based monitoring
RCD-Goma	Rally for Congolese Democracy (Goma)
RCD-K/LM	Rally for Congolese Democracy (Kisangani/Liberation Movement)
RCD-N	Rally for Congolese Democracy (National)
RPF	Rwandan Patriotic Front
SMEs	Small- and medium-sized enterprises
SMLLC	Single-member limited company
SOMIKIVU	Kivu Mining Society
SPOT	Satellite for observation of Earth
SYGIAP/DOPA	Digital Observatory for Protected Areas
TSP	Transboundary Strategic Plan
UCL	UCLouvain
UN	United Nations
UNDP	United Nations Development Programme
UNEP	United Nations Environment Programme
UNESCO	United Nations Educational, Scientific and Cultural Organization
UNF	United Nations Foundation
UNHCR	United Nations High Commissioner for Refugees
USAID	U.S. Agency for International Development
USD	United States Dollars
UWA	Uganda Wildlife Authority
VF	Virunga Foundation
WCS	Wildlife Conservation Society
WWF	World Wide Fund for Nature
ZSL	Zoological Society of Londo

Appendix 2
Statement of limits

The following text is taken from a royal decree for which no official translation exists

S001 D'un point partant de la rive Nord du lac Kivu et du bord Est de la coulée de lave du volcan Rumoka;

S002 Ensuite le bord oriental de la coulée de lave jusqu'au pied occidental de la colline Nyamutsibu;

S003 De là une droite jusqu'au pied occidental de la colline Nyabusa;

S004 A partir de ce point, une droite joignant la borne1 située à 300 mètres à l'Ouest du gîte de Rusayo, sur le chemin Rusayo-Sake;

S005 De cette borne, une droite joignant la borne2 située sur la pente méridionale du mont Mbati;

S006 De cette borne, une droite joignant la borne3 de Kisagara, près de Rusayo, sur le chemin Rusayo-Kibati;

S007 De ce point, le chemin Rusayo-Kibati jusqu'au carrefour (borne4) du sentier allant au village Mutaho;

S008 De ce point, une ligne joignant le pied Nord-Ouest de la colline Bubunugu (ou Mutaho) et contournant le pied de cette colline par le Nord, pour rejoindre le sommet le plus septentrional de la colline Bitunguru (arbre isolé);

S009 De ce point, une ligne passant par le pied méridional des monts Katandali et Kanyambuzi, puis par le col qui sépare ce dernier mont du mont Mudjoga pour atteindre la tête du ravin Kavumu, au pied Sud du mont Kavumu;

S010 Ce ravin jusqu'à son embouchure dans la clairière (borne 5) de Kavumu;

S011 Le bord méridional de cette clairière marqué par une piste aboutissant à la route carrossable Ngoma-Rutshuru à 1 km. 400 du village de Kibati (borne 6);

S012 A partir de ce point, le bord occidental de la route carrossable Ngoma-Rutshuru jusqu'au carrefour du chemin Rugari-Kanzenze-Nyamlagira-Mushari;

S013 A partir de ce point, le bord septentrional du chemin Rugari-Kanzenze-Mushari jusqu'à une borne située à environ 4 km à l'Ouest du carrefour de Rugari;

S014 De cette borne, une ligne joignant la borne située à 2 km à l'Est du pied de la colline Nyasheke-Nord;

S015 Ensuite le pied oriental de la colline Kurushari et une borne située sur le sentier Rutshuru-Tongo, à 4 km. à l'Ouest de son point de jonction avec la route carrossable Rutshuru-Ngoma;

S016 De cette borne, une droite joignant le confluent des rivières Rutshuru et Rugera;

S017 A partir de ce confluent, le bord supérieur oriental (côté rive droite) du ravin de la rivière Rutshuru, jusqu'au parallèle du confluent de la rivière Kabarasa avec la May-Na-Kwenda;

S018 Ce parallèle jusqu'à la May-Na-Kwenda;

S019 La rive Sud de la May-Na-Kwenda jusqu'à l'intersection du sentier Rutshuru-Kalimbo-Kabare;

S020 Ce sentier jusqu'à la rivière Ngesho;

S021 Le bord supérieur méridional du ravin de cette rivière, vers l'amont, jusqu'au marais Nyamborokota;

S022 Le bord de ce marais, par le Sud et l'Est, jusqu'à l'embouchure de la rivière Tshabaganda;

S023 Le bord supérieur méridional du ravin de cette rivière jusqu'au confluent de la rivière Kakoma;

S024 Le bord supérieur méridional du ravin de la Kakoma jusqu'à sa source;

S025 Le parallèle de cette source jusqu'à sa rencontre avec la rivière Kasozo;

S026 Le bord supérieur oriental du ravin de la Kasozo jusqu'à son embouchure dans la rivière Ishasha;

S027 L'Ishasha (frontière de la Colonie) jusqu'à son embouchure dans le lac Edouard;

S028 La frontière de la Colonie, à travers les eaux du lac Edouard, jusqu'à l'embouchure de la rivière Lubilia dans le lac Edouard;

S029 La Lubilia jusqu'à son point d'intersection avec la route carrossable de Beni à Kasindi;

S030 Le bord occidental de cette route jusqu'à l'ancien sentier reliant le village de Mutwanga au mont Libona, sentier coupant les têtes des rivières Butowa et Mahimbi;

S031 Ce sentier vers l'Ouest jusqu'à son intersection avec la route carrossable de Beni à Kasindi;

S032 Le bord méridional de cette route jusqu'à un point situé à un kilomètre à vol d'oiseau de son intersection avec la rivière Semliki;

S033 De ce point, vers le Nord, une ligne parallèle à la rive droite de la Semliki et distante de celle-ci de 1 kilomètre à vol d'oiseau jusqu'à son point de rencontre avec la rivière Musenene ou Lusilube;

S034 La rive gauche de cette rivière jusqu'à son point d'intersection avec le parallèle du confluent des rivières Modidi et Biangolo;

S035 Ce parallèle jusqu'à ce confluent;

S036 La rive gauche de la rivière Biangolo jusqu'à une borne (altitude approximative 1.700 m)

S037 La projection verticale sur le terrain de la polygonale reliant les points de rencontre de la courbe de niveau de cette borne avec les contreforts avancés du massif du Ruwenzori et ce jusqu'à la rivière Talya;

S038 La rive gauche de cette rivière jusqu'à son confluent avec la rivière Buliba;

S039 La rivière Talya, vers l'aval, jusqu'à son confluent avec la rivière Bongeya;

S040 Le méridien de ce confluent jusqu'au pied de la colline Bulima;

S041 Le pied méridional des collines Bulima et Ulese, jusqu'à l'extrémité Sud-Ouest de cette dernière;

S042 Le parallèle de cette extrémité jusqu'à son point d'intersection avec la piste caravanière de Mutwanga à Kasindi;

S043 Cette piste jusqu'à une borne située entre le village de Kimene et l'ancien gîte de Mutwanga;

S044 De cette borne une droite de125 m de longueur, parallèle au village de Kimene;

S045 De l'extrémité de cette droite une perpendiculaire jusqu'à son point d'intersection avec le ravin situé à50 m au Sud du signal géodésique de Mutwanga;

S046 Ce ravin jusqu'à sa rencontre avec la piste caravanière Mutwanga à Kasindi;

S047 Cette piste vers le Sud, jusqu'à son point d'intersection avec le ruisseau Cokoye;

S048 Ce ruisseau jusqu'au méridien de la source du ruisseau May Ya Moto;

S049 Ce méridien jusqu'à cette source;

S050 Une droite joignant cette source à celle de la rivière Mboa;

S051 Le parallèle de la source de la Mboa jusqu'à sa rencontre avec la rivière Buliba.

S052 La rive droite de cette rivière jusqu'à sa source;

S053 Une droite joignant cette source au sommet du mont Buliki;

S054 Une droite joignant ce sommet à la source du ruisseau Kamesonge;

S055 La rive droite de ce ruisseau jusqu'à son embouchure dans la rivière Lume;

S056 La rive gauche de la rivière Lume jusqu'à une borne (altitude approximative 2.000 m)

S057 Puis vers l'Ouest la projection verticale sur le terrain de la polygonale reliant les points de rencontre de la courbe de niveau de cette borne avec les contreforts avancés du massif du Ruwenzori, et ce jusqu'au point de rencontre avec le méridien de la source la plus septentrionale de la rivière Ulubu.

S058 Ce méridien,vers le Sud, jusqu'à cette source ;

S059 Une droite joignant cette source à la source la plus méridionale de cette même rivière;

S060 De cette source, une droite joignant la source de la rivière Tako, affluent de la Lubilia (frontière de la Colonie);

S061 La frontière de la Colonie vers le Nord jusqu'à son point d'intersection avec la rivière Rusege Sud (confluent de la Lamya et de la Rusege Sud);

S062 La rive droite de cette rivière Rusege Sud, vers l'amont, jusqu'à sa source;

S063 Une droite joignant cette source au col situé entre les monts Kirindera et Turwarubere;

S064 Le parallèle passant par ce col jusqu'au point où il rencontre la rivière Ruanoli;

S065 La rive droite de cette rivière, vers l'aval, jusqu'à son point d'intersection avec le sentier qui relie le village Bogemba au mont Teye;

S066 Ce sentier jusqu'au sommet du mont Teye;

S067 La crête qui se détache, vers l'Ouest, du mont Teye jusqu'à son extrémité;

S068 La droite joignant cette extrémité au point de la rive gauche de la rivière Kombo le plus rapproché de cette extrémité;

S069 La rive gauche de cette rivière jusqu'à son point de rencontre avec une borne (altitude approximative 1.500 m)

S070 Puis vers le Sud-Ouest la projection verticale sur le terrain de la polygonale reliant les points de rencontre de la courbe de niveau de cette borne avec les contreforts avancés du massif du Ruwenzori et ce jusqu'à la rivière Djalele ou Musanonde;

S071 La rive droite de cette rivière, vers l'aval, jusqu'à son point d'intersection avec le prolongement d'une droite joignant le confluent de la Mavea ou Lamya et de la Molingo au point où le sentier Katuka-Pakioma-Botshula coupe la rivière Djobulo;

S072	Cette droite jusqu'au confluent de la Mavea ou Lamya et de la Molingo;
S073	La rive gauche de la rivière Mavea ou Lamya, vers l'aval, jusqu'à un point situé à un kilomètre en aval de son point d'intersection avec la piste caravanière Kapamba-Kinawa;
S074	De ce point, une ligne parallèle à la piste caravanière passant par les villages de Kapamba, Kinawa, Alundja, Kapera, Zoa et distante de cette piste de 1 kilomètre, vers l'Ouest, à vol d'oiseau jusqu'à une borne située à un kilomètre à vol d'oiseau au Nord du village de Djenda (Kasimoto);
S075	Le parallèle passant par cette borne jusqu'au point où il rencontre la rivière Lamya (frontière de la Colonie);
S076	La rive gauche de la Lamya jusqu'à son embouchure dans la Semliki;
S077	La Semliki jusqu'à l'embouchure de la rivière Puemba;
S078	La rive gauche de cette rivière, vers l'amont, jusqu'à son confluent avec la Nyaduguru;
S079	De ce point, une droite jusqu'à la source de la rivière Malibotu;
S080	La rive gauche de cette rivière jusqu'à son confluent avec la rivière Irimba;
S081	La rive gauche de cette rivière jusqu'à son intersection avec le parallèle passant par le confluent des rivières Batonga et Paru (Pulu) (ce dernier étant un cours d'eau temporaire);
S082	Ce parallèle jusqu'à ce confluent;
S083	De ce point une droite jusqu'à la borne sise à la tête du vallon Nyamangose, en bordure de la piste «Tshabi Semliki, chefferie Watalinga»;
S084	De ce point, le lit creusé par les eaux de ruissellement jusqu'au pied du vallon Nyamangose (borne);
S085	Le parallèle passant par la borne sise au pied du vallon Nyamangose jusqu'à son intersection avec la rivière Maginda (borne);
S086	La rive droite de la Maginda vers l'amont jusqu'à son inter-section avec le sentier marqué par le point d'altitude 923 et longeant le pied de l'escarpement de Kamariba.
S087	Ce sentier vers l'Ouest jusqu'au carrefour situé près de la rivière Matido;
S088	A partir de ce carrefour, l'ancienne piste caravanière d'Irumu et Boga à Vieux-Beni, piste de 1925-1926 passant successivement par le village actuel de Selemani (Boga) et par les anciens emplacements des villages de Bopo, Kibondo, Alimaci, Adonga, Gamala, Gamalendu, Mutshanga, Baruti, Kartushi, Lupanzula, Molemba, Amici, Kitihire, Kalumendo, jusqu'à son intersection avec la rivière Djuma;
S089	La rive droite de cette rivière, vers l'amont, jusqu'à son point d'intersection avec le méridien qui passe par le point où la rivière Malulu quitte le pied oriental de l'escarpement;
S090	Ce méridien jusqu'à ce point d'intersection de la rivière Malulu et du pied de l'escarpement;
S091	De ce point, vers le Sud, le pied oriental de l'escarpement jusqu'à un point près du mont Luka, à 2 kilomètres au Nord de l'ancien lazaret où sentier longeant le pied de l'escarpement et venant de Zumbia (gîte) pénètre dans l'escarpement;
S092	Ce sentier, passant par l'ancien lazaret de Beni, par Zumbia (gîte), par Kitero, entre les monts Misebere et Tahamogota, par Kasolenge et Tschamohoma (Kadiadia) jusqu'à son point de rencontre avec la rivière Lusia;
S093	La rive droite de cette rivière vers l'aval jusqu'à son point d'intersection avec le prolongement d'une droite joignant les sommets des monts Katshe et Katundu;
S094	De ce point, une ligne passant par les sommets des monts Katundu, Katshe, Mokondene, Daboma, Kavega, Kasiakake, Itobola et Kebo;
S095	Du sommet du mont Kebo, une droite jusqu'au point où la rivière Kinyamiga est coupée par cette droite joignant les sommets des monts Kebo et Walengiro;
S096	La rive droite de la rivière Kinyamiga vers l'aval jusqu'à son intersection avec la piste caravanière passant au mont Buselio;
S097	Cette piste vers le Sud jusqu'à son point d'intersection avec le prolongement d'une droite joignant les sommets des monts Bikingi et Buselio;
S098	De ce point, une ligne passant par les sommets des monts Buselio, Bikingi, Busoga, Manyoni, Tshanzu et Birimu;
S099	Du sommet du mont Birimu jusqu'au point de la rivière Tambwe le plus rapproché de ce mont;
S100	De ce point, la rive gauche de la rivière Tambwe, vers l'amont, jusqu'à l'embouchure du ruisseau Tshabolere;
S101	La rive gauche de ce ruisseau jusqu'à sa source;
S102	Une droite joignant cette source à celle du ruisseau Kakoko, affluent de droite de la Nyamoisa;
S103	De cette source (au mont Kalumba), la rive droite du ruisseau Kakoko jusqu'au point où il est coupé par le sentier Kinierere à Kasembe (Nkuku);
S104	Ce sentier jusqu'au point où il coupe la crête du mont Kitolu;
S105	Cette crête jusqu'à la tête du ravin Karuasa se détachant de l'éperon Kitolu du mont Mandimba;
S106	De cette tête, une droite joignant le point où la piste caravanière de Gitse à Kinierere rencontre le ruisseau Lutimbi, à l'Ouest du village de Kinierere;
S107	Cette piste Kinierere-Gitse, par la crête Musimba et le mont Kerongo jusqu'au point le plus rapproché de la source du ruisseau Bolekerere;
S108	Une droite joignant ce point à cette source;
S109	La rive gauche de ce ruisseau jusqu'à son confluent avec la rivière Kalibira;
S110	La rive gauche de cette rivière à son confluent avec la rivière Talya;
S111	La rive gauche de cette rivière, vers l'amont, jusqu'au point où elle est franchie par le sentier Kitega-Gitse;
S112	Cette piste vers le Sud jusqu'au point où elle rencontre le prolongement d'une droite joignant les sommets des monts Beasa et Katendere;
S113	De ce point, la ligne de crête jalonnée par les monts Katendere, Beasa, Kanei, Niamonindu et Niondo;
S114	Une ligne passant par le sommet du mont Nguli et joignant la source du ruisseau Logese;
S115	La rive droite de ce ruisseau jusqu'à son embouchure dans la rivière Tshondo;
S116	La rive droite de cette rivière, vers l'aval jusqu'à son point d'intersection avec une droite joignant les sommets des monts Musenzeru et Niarusunzu;
S117	Cette droite jusqu'au mont Musenzeru;
S118	De ce mont, une droite jusqu'au mont Kasiiro;
S119	De ce mont, une droite joignant le sommet de la colline Musoti, le village de Nguli restant en dehors du Parc;
S120	De ce sommet, une droite joignant le point où le sentier Kitega-Nguli coupe l'éperon Kateka-Bakole du mont Niondo;
S121	De ce point, une ligne passant par les sommets des monts Kasanga, Busega, Katembo, Loarama, Mapombo, Garara, Bekoha, Kanyiro (un des petits sommets du mont Ikanga), Liassa, Luterero, Bokara, Kabiniri (Kaliniro), Metseka, Kiongoto, Kasanga, Mubiriri et Kalero;
S122	Du sommet de ce mont la crête du mont Kalero jusqu'à son extrémité Sud;
S123	De cette extrémité une ligne joignant les sommets des monts Bukweri, Lunde ou Nyamoninde, Kahungu;
S124	La croupe méridionale, dénommée Bolambo, du mont Kahungu;
S125	Une ligne joignant ce point, dénommé «Bolambo», au confluent de la rivière Butega et de la Talya;
S126	Une ligne joignant ce mont au sommet du mont Mushenge;
S127	De ce sommet une ligne joignant le mont Kalingio, le point Mbulamasi du mont Mushanga, le point Kaboha du mont Kitetsa, le point Kasoso du mont Kilambo;
S128	Ensuite de ce point une droite joignant le mont Ndwale;
S129	Ensuite la crête jalonnée par les monts Ndwale, Kigende, Kaboha (dénommé erronément Kiboha), Kitobo, Shobobia, Lutare, Hahie, Mchembya.
S130	Ensuite une droite joignant ce mont à l'extrémité Nord du mont Lutepa et laissant à l'Est le mont Miegenie;
S131	La chaîne des monts Lutepa-Nyabuki;
S132	Une droite joignant ce mont au sommet des monts Lubwe, Berama, Kasongolere, puis la crête Kasongolelo, Boswekwa, Kierere et Kashwa;
S133	Une ligne joignant ce mont aux monts Kisololwe, Kiniamuyaga, Miholo;
S134	La crête des monts Miholo, Hangira, Kibiru;
S135	Ensuite une ligne suivant la crête jalonnée par les monts Katwa, Matofu, Musima et prolongée jusqu'au ravin Buhula;
S136	A partir de ce point, le bord Sud du ravin Buhula jusqu'à sa rencontre avec la rivière Kibirizi;
S137	Cette rivière jusqu'au bord occidental du ravin de la Ruindi;
S138	La rive gauche de la Ruindi, en amont jusqu'au confluent de la rivière Rwehe;
S139	Le thalweg de cette rivière jusqu'à son confluent avec le ruis-seau Kamokanda, en laissant en dehors du Parc la mine de fer du mont Kakorwe, située sur la rive droite de la Rwehe;
S140	Le ruisseau Kamokanda jusqu'à sa source au pied du mont Tshahi;
S141	Une ligne joignant cette source au sommet des monts Tshahi et Bitingu;
S142	De ce mont une droite joignant la source de la rivière Kalagala, située près du mont Rwanguba;
S143	Cette rivière jusqu'au sentier de Mabenga à Tongo, sentier longeant le pied des monts Kasali;
S144	Ce sentier jusqu'à son point d'intersection avec la rivière Butaku;
S145	De ce point une droite au pied occidental du mont Rugomba;
S146	Le méridien de ce point, jusqu'à sa rencontre avec le parallèle passant par l'extrémité Sud de la colline Butambira;
S147	Ce parallèle jusqu'à sa rencontre avec la piste de Tongo à Tshumba;
S148	La piste de Tongo à Tshumba, dans la plaine de lave, jusqu'à son intersection (carrefour de Mariage) avec le sentier Rugari-Kansenze (Nyamlagira)-Mushari;
S149	Ensuite une droite joignant ce carrefour au sommet du mont Mushebele;
S150	Puis la crête Mushebele-Katunda jusqu'au sentier Tshumba-Ngesho-Gandjo;
S151	Ce sentier jusqu'à la limite Est du bloc des concessions de Ngesho;

S152 Ensuite une ligne contournant à l'Est, au Sud et à l'Ouest les concessions du Comité National du Kivu, 26, 71b et 71a jusqu'à l'intersection avec le sentier Tshumba-Katumo;

S153 Ensuite ce sentier vers l'Ouest jusqu'à la limite orientale de la concession Katumo 79e;

S154 De ce point une droite vers le sommet du mont Kishusha;

S155 Ensuite la limite orientale du marais sis au pied du mont Kishusha;

S156 De là un alignement vers une borne située sur le promontoire occidental du mont Kamatombe;

S157 De ce point un alignement vers une borne placée au sommet du ravin M'Bili;

S158 De cette borne un alignement vers la borne se trouvant sur l'ancien sentier Ngandjo-Kingi, excluant des limites du Parc National Albert les collines Shange et Modeya;

S159 Ensuite cette piste jusqu'à son point le plus proche de la source de la rivière Bulemo;

S160 De ce point une droite jusqu'à cette source;

S161 Ensuite cette rivière en aval jusqu'au bord du marais de la Nyamuragira;

S162 Le marais jusqu'à l'angle Nord-Ouest de la concession forestière Marchal à Mugando;

S163 Les limites Nord et Est de cette concession jusqu'à son angle Sud-Est;

S164 Ensuite une droite en direction du Sud-Est rejoignant le bord occidental de la coulée de lave de 1938 du Nyamuragira;

S165 Ensuite le bord occidental de cette coulée de lave jusqu'à son intersection avec la parallèle passant par l'endroit où elle se divise en deux bras;

S166 Ensuite ce parallèle jusqu'à l'endroit précité;

S167 Ensuite le bord occidental de la branche orientale de la coulée de 1938 jusqu'au lac Kivu.

S168 Ensuite la rive Nord du lac Kivu vers l'Est, jusqu'au bord Est de la coulée de lave du volcan Rumoka;

S169 De plus, l'île Tshegera sera dans son entièreté comprise dans le Parc National Albert; par contre, les terres habitées et cultivées des collines de Nzuru, Mihonga et Kabazana seront exclues du Parc; à cet effet, la limite actuelle de ces terres sera abornée définitivement.

Secteur Mikeno

S170 A partir de la frontière du Ruanda-Urundi du point où elle est coupée par une droite reliant le sommet de la colline Bugeshi-Mukuru au sommet du mont Arama;

S171 Cette droite jusqu'au sommet du mont Arama;

S172 De ce point, une droite jusqu'au col séparant ce mont du mont Hehu;

S173 Cette droite jusqu'au sommet du mont Hehu;

S174 De ce point une droite jusqu'au ravin Kabagwetu (plaque Parc National Albert);

S175 Ensuite une droite joignant l'abreuvoir de Kikeri, le marais mais non l'abreuvoir restant inclus dans le Parc;

S176 Ensuite un alignement en direction du sommet du mont Mashaye jusqu'à sa rencontre avec le ravin Kanyamagufa (borne);

S177 Ensuite ce ravin jusqu'à sa rencontre avec la route carrossable Ngoma-Rutshuru (borne);

S178 Ensuite le bord oriental de cette route carrossable jusqu'au ravin Masisi (borne);

S179 Ce ravin jusqu'à son origine, au flanc Ouest de la colline Kasenyi;

S180 Ensuite une piste allant au col qui sépare les monts Bushandjogoro et Rwanguba (borne);

S181 De ce point une droite joignant le ravin Mugari au point où il est coupé par la piste caravanière du Rugari au Kibumba;

S182 Ensuite cette piste jusqu'à sa rencontre avec le ravin Kifurura;

S183 Ce ravin jusqu'à l'abreuvoir situé à 1 km. en amont;

S184 De cet abreuvoir une droite joignant le sommet de la colline Nyamariri;

S185 De ce point une droite jusqu'à l'abreuvoir du ravin Kizenga;

S186 Ensuite une droite jusqu'au sommet de la colline Kizenga (rive droite du ravin);

S187 Puis le sentier Kizenga-Katwa jusqu'au point où il rencontre la concession de Kikeri de la Mission de Tongres-Sainte-Marie;

S188 Ensuite les limites méridionale et orientale de cette concession jusqu'à son angle Nord-Est;

S189 De cet angle, une droite joignant le sommet de la colline Kabazogeye;

S190 Ensuite un alignement en direction du sommet du mont Gashole (alignement qui traverse les ravins Kasasa et Margarure) jusqu'à l'endroit où il est recoupé par un autre alignement partant du sommet de la colline la plus orientale du groupe de Bukima et tangent au bord oriental de la mare Kinyamutukura;

S191 Ensuite cet alignement jusqu'au sommet de la colline la plus orientale du groupe de Bukima;

S192 De ce sommet une ligne joignant les sommets des monts Nyangurube, Nyakiriba et Gugo;

S193 De ce point, une droite jusqu'au pied occidental de la colline Kizunga;

S194 Ensuite une ligne longeant le pied occidental de la crête Tshananke (le sommet de la crête à la courbe de 2.100 m.) jusqu'au point où elle rencontre le ravin Rutabagwe;

S195 Ce ravin jusqu'à l'étang Nyandizima;

S196 Le bord méridional de cet étang jusqu'à la tête du ravin Rukunga;

S197 Ce ravin jusqu'à son point d'intersection avec la droite joignant le sommet le plus septentrional du mont Runyoni au mont Tshanzu;

S198 Cette droite à partir de ce point d'intersection jusqu'au sommet du mont Tshanzu;

S199 Ensuite une droite joignant les sommets des monts Rurindzargwe et Mugongoyindzovu;

S200 Ensuite le parallèle de ce dernier sommet jusqu'à son point de rencontre avec la frontière belgo-anglaise.

Appendix 3
List of senior managers

List of Directors, Assistant Directors, Administrator Wardens, Principal Wardens, Senior Wardens and Wardens. For the sake of brevity, this list does not include the many other executives (Assistant, Technical or Scientific Wardens, Station Managers and Visit Delegates) who supported these roles. The years correspond to the approximate time when they joined the institution. Some of these senior managers held various positions over many years of service.

Sources: Nestor & Méthode Bagurubumwe, personal communication; Stanislas Bakinahe, personal communication; INCN/IZCN (1973–1977); Samy Mankoto, personal communication; Norbert Mushenzi, personal communication; Patricia Van Schuylenbergh (2006); Jacques Verschuren (2001).

1928	HEMELEERS René
1931	DERSCHEID Jean-Marie
1933	HACKARS Henri-Martin
	de WITTE Gaston-François
1935	HARROY Jean-Paul
1937	HOIER Rasmus
	HUBERT Ernest
1945	VAN COOLS Georges
	HAEZAERT Julien
1953	RITS A. E.
1954	KINT Octave
	GILLIARD Albert
	de WILDE d'ESTMAEL Jacques
1956	DE SAEGER Henri
	DONIS Camille
1958	CORNET d'ELZIUS Claude
	MICHA Marc
1960	MBULA Bonaventure
	MBURANUMWE Anicet
1961	BAHIZI Marcel
1962	KANYERE Théodore
	MUNYAGA Basile
1964	RENZAHO Jean
1966	BAKINAHE Stanislas
1967	DIMOLOYELE Marcel
1969	BIGOHE Déogratias
1970	KAJUGA Déogratias
1971	MUSHENZI Norbert
	LUKWESA MATWE Makata
1972	MWANA NGONDI Floribert
1973	TATALA TATIKA Anselme
1974	BILALI Elias
	IYHEMOPO Nathanaël
1975	MAKABUZA Joseph
1981	BATECHI Faustin
1982	KUNIEKI Toko
1983	MBULA Déogratias
1986	CHIFURURA Isaac
1987	LUHUNU Sébastien
1990	VUNDA Nestor
	KAKULE Pierre
1991	WATHAUT Alexandre
	MUHINDO Laurent
	LULENGO Simon
1995	KABUNDA Marc
	MUJINYA Irénée
	MASHAGIRO Honoré

PPP ICCN–Virunga Foundation:
Directors and Assistant Directors

2008	de MERODE Emmanuel
2008	MUSHENZI Norbert
2009	ATAMATO Gédéon
2015	MBURANUMWE Innocent
2018	SHALUKOMA Chantal
2022	MUGARUKA Rodrigue

Appendix 4
List of mammals

Nomenclature and English names according to Wilson & Reeder (2005), Mammal Diversity Database (2022) and, for the primates, de Jong & Butynski (2023). French names according to Lynx Nature Books (2023).
List compiled by Marc Languy and Andy Plumptre (2006 edition), completed and updated by Jean-Pierre d'Huart (2025 edition).

* Due to recent taxonomic reviews of Primates, Carnivores and Artiodactyla, subspecies are only mentioned for these three orders.

ORDER/family	Genus/species/subspecies*	French name	English name
TUBULIDENTATA			
Orycteropodidae	*Orycteropus afer*	Oryctérope	Aardvark
HYRACOIDEA			
Procaviidae	*Dendrohyrax arboreus*	Daman des arbres	Southern Tree Hyrax
PROBOSCIDEA			
Elephantidae	*Loxodonta africana*	Eléphant de savane	African Bush Elephant
Elephantidae	*Loxodonta cyclotis*	Eléphant de forêt	African Forest Elephant
PRIMATES			
Lorisidae	*Perodicticus ibeanus ibeanus*	Potto est-africain	Eastern Potto
Galagidae	*Galagoides demidovii*	Galago de Demidoff	Demidoff's Dwarf Galago
Galagidae	*Galagoides thomasi*	Galago de Thomas	Thomas's Dwarf Galago
Galagidae	*Galago matschiei*	Galago de Matschie	Spectacled Lesser Galago
Galagidae	*Galago senegalensis senegalensis*	Galago du Sénégal	Senegal Lesser Galago
Galagidae	*Otolemur crassicaudatus monteiri*	Galago à queue touffue	Silver Galago
Cercopithecidae	*Cercopithecus ascanius schmidti*	Cercopithèque ascagne	Red-tailed Monkey
Cercopithecidae	*Cercopithecus denti*	Cercopithèque de Dent	Dent's Monkey
Cercopithecidae	*Cercopithecus hamlyni*	Cercopithèque de Hamlyn	Owl-faced Monkey
Cercopithecidae	*Cercopithecus mitis kandti*	Cercopithèque à diadème (Singe doré)	Golden Monkey
Cercopithecidae	*Cercopithecus mitis stuhlmanni*	Cercopithèque à diadème (Singe bleu)	Blue Monkey
Cercopithecidae	*Cercopithecus mitis doggetti*	Cercopithèque à diadème (Singe argenté)	Silver Monkey
Cercopithecidae	*Cercopithecus neglectus*	Cercopithèque de De Brazza	De Brazza's Monkey
Cercopithecidae	*Chlorocebus tantalus budgetti*	Vervet tantale	Budgett's Tantalus
Cercopithecidae	*Allochrocebus lhoesti*	Cercopithèque de L'Hoest	L'Hoest's Monkey
Cercopithecidae	*Papio anubis*	Babouin anubis	Olive Baboon
Cercopithecidae	*Colobus angolensis ruwenzorii*	Colobe d'Angola	Angola Colobus
Cercopithecidae	*Colobus guereza occidentalis*	Colobe guéréza	Western Guereza
Cercopithecidae	*Piliocolobus semlikiensis*	Colobe de la Semliki	Red Colobus
Cercopithecidae	*Lophocebus albigena johnstoni*	Lophocèbe à joues grises	Grey-cheeked Mangabey
Cercopithecidae	*Cercocebus agilis*	Mangabey agile	Agile Mangabey
Hominidae	*Gorilla beringei beringei*	Gorille de montagne	Mountain Gorilla
Hominidae	*Gorilla beringei graueri*	Gorille des plaines de l'Est	Eastern Lowland Gorilla
Hominidae	*Pan troglodytes schweinfurthii*	Chimpanzé oriental	Eastern Chimpanzee
AFROSORICIDA			
Tenrecidae	*Micropotamogale ruwenzorii*	Micropotamogale du Rwenzori	Rwenzori Otter-shrew
Chrysochloridae	*Chrysochloris stuhlmanni*	Taupe-dorée de Stuhlmann	Stuhlmann's Golden Mole
MACROSCELIDEA			
Macroscelididae	*Rhynchocyon cirnei*	Sengi de Cirne	Checkered Sengi
LAGOMORPHA			
Leporidae	*Lepus victoriae*	Lièvre des savanes	African Savanna Hare
ERINACEOMORPHA			
Erinaceidae	*Atelerix albiventris*	Hérisson à ventre blanc	Four-toed Hedgehog
SORICIOMORPHA			
Soricidae	*Crocidura hirta*	Crocidure roussâtre	Lesser Red White-toothed Shrew
Soricidae	*Crocidura jacksoni*	Crocidure de Jackson	Jackson's White-toothed Shrew
Soricidae	*Crocidura lanosa*	Crocidure laineuse	Kivu Long-haired White-toothed Shrew
Soricidae	*Crocidura maurisca*	Crocidure d'Entebbe	Gracile White-toothed Shrew
Soricidae	*Crocidura montis*	Crocidure de montagne	Montane White-toothed Shrew
Soricidae	*Crocidura nanilla*	Crocidure pygmée	Savanna Dwarf White-toothed Shrew
Soricidae	*Crocidura nigrofusca*	Crocidure brun-noir	African Black White-toothed Shrew
Soricidae	*Crocidura niobe*	Crocidure niobé	Niobe's White-toothed Shrew
Soricidae	*Crocidura olivieri*	Crocidure d'Olivier	African Giant White-toothed Shrew
Soricidae	*Crocidura tarella*	Crocidure de Rutshuru	Tarella White-toothed Shrew
Soricidae	*Crocidura turba*	Crocidure turbulente	Turbo White-toothed Shrew

Family	Species	French name	English name
Soricidae	*Paracrocidura maxima*	Crocidure à tête large	Greater Large-headed Shrew
Soricidae	*Ruwenzorisorex suncoides*	Pachyure du Rwenzori	Rwenzori Shrew
Soricidae	*Scutisorex somereni*	Pachyure de Someren	Armored Hero Shrew
Soricidae	*Suncus megalurus*	Pachyure grimpeuse	Climbing Shrew
Soricidae	*Sylvisorex granti*	Pachyure de Grant	Grant's Forest Shrew
Soricidae	*Sylvisorex lunaris*	Pachyure de la lune	Moon Forest Shrew
Soricidae	*Sylvisorex vulcanorum*	Pachyure des volcans	Volcano Forest Shrew
Soricidae	*Myosorex babaulti*	Musaraigne de Babault	Babault's Mouse Shrew
Soricidae	*Myosorex blarina*	Musaraigne du Rwenzori	Montane Mouse Shrew

CHIROPTERA

Family	Species	French name	English name
Pteropodidae	*Eidolon helvum*	Roussette paillée d'Afrique	African Straw-coloured Fruit Bat
Pteropodidae	*Epomophorus labiatus*	Epomophore labiaire	Little Epauletted Fruit Bat
Pteropodidae	*Epomophorus wahlbergi*	Epomophore de Wahlberg	Wahlberg's Epauletted Fruit Bat
Pteropodidae	*Epomops franqueti*	Epomophore de Franquet	Franquet's Epauletted Fruit Bat
Pteropodidae	*Hypsignathus monstrosus*	Hypsignathe monstrueux	Hammer-headed Fruit Bat
Pteropodidae	*Lissonycteris angolensis*	Lissonyctère d'Angola	Angolan Soft-furred Fruit Bat
Pteropodidae	*Myonycteris torquata*	Myonyctère à collier	Little Collared Fruit Bat
Pteropodidae	*Rousettus aegyptiacus*	Roussette d'Egypte	Egyptian Rousette
Pteropodidae	*Stenonycteris lanosus*	Roussette à poils longs	Long-haired Fruit Bat
Rhinolophidae	*Rhinolophus alcyone*	Rhinolophe alcyone	Halcyon Horseshoe Bat
Rhinolophidae	*Rhinolophus clivosus*	Rhinolophe de Cretzschmar	Geoffroy's Horseshoe Bat
Rhinolophidae	*Rhinolophus eloquens*	Rhinolophe éloquent	Eloquent Horseshoe Bat
Rhinolophidae	*Rhinolophus fumigatus*	Rhinolophe de Rüppell	Rüppell's Horseshoe Bat
Rhinolophidae	*Rhinolophus landeri*	Rhinolophe de Lander	Lander's Horseshoe Bat
Rhinolophidae	*Rhinolophus ruwenzorii*	Rhinolophe du Rwenzori	Ruwenzori Horseshoe Bat
Hipposideridae	*Hipposideros caffer*	Phyllorine de Cafrerie	Sundevall's Leaf-nosed Bat
Hipposideridae	*Doryrhina cyclops*	Phyllorhine cyclope	Cyclops Leaf-nosed Bat
Megadermatidae	*Lavia frons*	Mégaderme à ailes orangées	Yellow-winged False-Vampire
Emballonuridae	*Taphozous mauritianus*	Taphien de Maurice	Mauritian Tomb Bat
Nycteridae	*Nycteris arge*	Nyctère de Bates	Bates's Slit-faced Bat
Nycteridae	*Nycteris grandis*	Grand Nyctère	Large Slit-faced Bat
Nycteridae	*Nycteris hispida*	Nyctère hérissé	Hairy Slit-faced Bat
Nycteridae	*Nycteris macrotis*	Nyctère de Dobson	Large-eared Slit-faced Bat
Nycteridae	*Nycteris nana*	Nyctère nain	Dwarf Slit-faced Bat
Nycteridae	*Nycteris thebaica*	Nyctère de Thébaïde	Egyptian Slit-faced Bat
Molossidae	*Mops ansorgei*	Tadaride d'Ansorge	Ansorge's Free-tailed Bat
Molossidae	*Mops bemmeleni*	Tadaride de van Bemmelen	Gland-tailed Free-tailed Bat
Molossidae	*Mops pumilus*	Petite Tadaride	Little Free-tailed Bat
Molossidae	*Mops brachypterus*	Tadaride à ailes courtes	Short-winged Free-tailed Bat
Molossidae	*Mops midas*	Tadaride midas	Mida's Free-tailed Bat
Molossidae	*Mops nanulus*	Tadaride naine	Dwarf Free-tailed Bat
Molossidae	*Tadarida fulminans*	Tadaride de Thomas	Malagasy Free-tailed Bat
Verspertilionidae	*Scotophilus nigrita*	Scotophile de Schreber	Schreber's Yellow Bat
Verspertilionidae	*Pipistrellus nanulus*	Pipistrelle minuscule	Tiny Pipistrelle
Verspertilionidae	*Vansonia rueppellii*	Pipistrelle de Rüppell	Rüppell's Bat
Verspertilionidae	*Glauconycteris argentata*	Glauconyctère argenté	Common Butterfly Bat
Verspertilionidae	*Glauconycteris poensis*	Glauconyctère d'Abo	Abo Butterfly Bat
Verspertilionidae	*Glauconycteris variegata*	Glauconyctère réticulé	Variegated Butterfly Bat
Verspertilionidae	*Nycticeinops crassulus*	Vespère à grosse tête	Broad-headed Serotine
Verspertilionidae	*Mimetillus moloneyi*	Mimétille de Moloney	Moloney's Mimic Bat
Verspertilionidae	*Pseudoromicia tenuipinnis*	Vespère à ailes blanches	White-winged Serotine
Verspertilionidae	*Myotis bocagii*	Murin de Du Bocage	Bocage's Myotis
Verspertilionidae	*Myotis tricolor*	Murin tricolore	Temminck's Myotis
Verspertilionidae	*Myotis welwitschii*	Murin de Welwitsch	Welwitsch's Myotis
Verspertilionidae	*Miniopterus inflatus*	Minioptère à couronne	Greater Long-fingered Bat

PHOLIDOTA

Family	Species	French name	English name
Manidae	*Phataginus tricuspis*	Petit Pangolin	Common African Pangolin
Manidae	*Phataginus tetradactyla*	Pangolin à longue queue	Long-tailed Pangolin
Manidae	*Smutsia gigantea*	Pangolin géant	Giant Pangolin

CARNIVORA

Family	Species	French name	English name
Felidae	*Felis lybica*	Chat ganté	African Wild Cat
Felidae	*Leptailurus serval lipostictus*	Serval	Serval
Felidae	*Caracal aurata aurata*	Chat doré	Golden Cat
Felidae	*Panthera leo leo*	Lion	Lion
Felidae	*Panthera pardus pardus*	Léopard	Leopard
Viverridae	*Civettictis civetta congica*	Civette d'Afrique	Civet
Viverridae	*Genetta servalina bettoni*	Genette servaline	Servaline Genet
Viverridae	*Genetta genetta dongolana*	Genette commune	Common Genet
Viverridae	*Genetta maculata stuhlmanni*	Genette à grandes taches	Rusty-spotted Genet
Viverridae	*Genetta victoriae*	Genette géante	Giant Genet
Nandinidae	*Nandinia binotata*	Nandinie	Palm Civet
Herpestidae	*Atilax paludinosus*	Mangouste des marais	Marsh Mongoose
Herpestidae	*Bdeogale nigripes*	Mangouste à pattes noires	Black-footed Mongoose
Herpestidae	*Crossarchus alexandri*	Mangouste d'Alexander	Alexander's Cusimanse
Herpestidae	*Herpestes sanguineus*	Mangouste svelte	Common Slender Mongoose
Herpestidae	*Herpestes ichneumon*	Mangouste d'Egypte	Egyptian Mongoose

Herpestidae	*Ichneumia albicauda ibeanus*	Mangouste à queue blanche	White-tailed Mongoose
Herpestidae	*Mungos mungo*	Mangouste rayée	Banded Mongoose
Hyaenidae	*Crocuta crocuta*	Hyène tachetée	Spotted Hyena
Canidae	*Lupulella adustus*	Chacal rayé	Side-striped Jackal
Canidae	*Lycaon pictus* (†)	Lycaon (†)	African Wild Dog (†)
Mustelidae	*Aonyx capensis*	Loutre à joues blanches	African Clawless Otter
Mustelidae	*Hydrictis maculicollis*	Loutre à cou tacheté	Spotted-necked Otter
Mustelidae	*Mellivora capensis*	Ratel	Honey Badger
Mustelidae	*Ictonyx striatus*	Zorille commune	Zorilla
Mustelidae	*Poecilogale albinucha*	Zorille à nuque blanche	African Striped Weasel
ARTIODACTYLA			
Suidae	*Hylochoerus meinertzhageni meinertzhageni*	Hylochère	Giant Forest Hog
Suidae	*Phacochoerus africanus massaicus*	Phacochère commun	Common Warthog
Suidae	*Potamochoerus larvatus hassama*	Potamochère du Cap	Bushpig
Hippopotamidae	*Hippopotamus amphibius*	Hippopotame commun	Common Hippopotamus
Tragulidae	*Hyemoschus aquaticus*	Chevrotain aquatique	Water Chevrotain
Giraffidae	*Okapia johnstoni*	Okapi	Okapi
Bovidae	*Damaliscus lunatus jimela*	Topi	Topi
Bovidae	*Nesotragus batesi*	Antilope naine	Dwarf Antelope
Bovidae	*Syncerus caffer caffer*	Buffle d'Afrique	Cape Buffalo
Bovidae	*Syncerus caffer nanus*	Buffle de forêt	Forest Buffalo
Bovidae	*Syncerus caffer mathewsi*	Buffle de montagne	Virunga/Mountain Buffalo
Bovidae	*Tragelaphus eurycerus eurycerus*	Bongo	Bongo
Bovidae	*Tragelaphus scriptus bor*	Antilope harnachée	Bushbuck
Bovidae	*Tragelaphus spekii spekii*	Sitatunga	Sitatunga
Bovidae	*Cephalophus nigrifrons kivuensis*	Céphalophe à front noir du Kivu	Kivu Black-fronted Duiker
Bovidae	*Cephalophus nigrifrons nigrifrons*	Céphalophe à front noir commun	Black-fronted Duiker
Bovidae	*Cephalophus silvicultor curticeps*	Céphalophe à dos jaune	Yellow-backed Duiker
Bovidae	*Cephalophus dorsalis castaneus*	Céphalophe à dorsale	Bay Duiker
Bovidae	*Cephalophus leucogaster arrhenii*	Céphalophe à ventre blanc	Uele White-bellied Duiker
Bovidae	*Cephalophus rubidus*	Céphalophe du Rwenzori	Rwenzori Red Duiker
Bovidae	*Philantomba monticola aequatorialis*	Céphalophe bleu	Blue Duiker
Bovidae	*Cephalophus weynsi*	Céphalophe de Weyns	Weyns's Duiker
Bovidae	*Sylvicapra grimmia campbelliae*	Céphalophe de Grimm	Bush Duiker
Bovidae	*Kobus ellipsiprymnus defassa*	Cobe à croissant	Waterbuck
Bovidae	*Kobus kob thomasi*	Cobe de Buffon	Uganda Kob
Bovidae	*Redunca redunca bohor*	Rédunca commun	Reedbuck
RODENTIA			
Sciuridae	*Euxerus erythropus*	Ecureuil de Geoffroy	Striped Ground Squirrel
Sciuridae	*Funisciurus carruthersi*	Ecureuil de Carruthers	Carruther's Mountain Squirrel
Sciuridae	*Funisciurus pyrropus*	Ecureuil de Cuvier	Fire-footed Rope Squirrel
Sciuridae	*Heliosciurus gambianus*	Ecureuil de Gambie	Gambian Sun squirrel
Sciuridae	*Heliosciurus ruwenzorii*	Ecureuil du Rwenzori	Ruwenzori Sun Squirrel
Sciuridae	*Heliosciurus rufobrachium*	Ecureuil de Waterhouse	Red-legged Sun Squirrel
Sciuridae	*Paraxerus alexandri*	Ecureuil d'Alexander	Alexander's Bush Squirrel
Sciuridae	*Paraxerus boehmi*	Ecureuil de Boehm	Boehm's Bush Squirrel
Sciuridae	*Protoxerus stangeri*	Ecureuil de Stanger	Forest Giant Squirrel
Gliridae	*Graphiurus murinus*	Loir murin	Forest African Dormouse
Spalacidae	*Tachyoryctes splendens*	Rat-taupe est-africain	African Root Rat
Nesomyidae	*Cricetomys emini*	Cricétome d'Emin	Forest Giant Pouched Rat
Nesomyidae	*Cricetomys kivuensis*	Cricétome du Kivu	Kivu Giant Pouched Rat
Nesomyidae	*Delanymys brooksi*	Delanymys palustre	Delany's Swamp Mouse
Nesomyidae	*Dendromus insignis*	Dendromus des montagnes	Montane African Climbing Mouse
Nesomyidae	*Dendromus melanotis*	Dendromus gris	Gray African Climbing Mouse
Nesomyidae	*Dendromus messorius*	Dendromus des bananiers	Banana African Climbing Mouse
Nesomyidae	*Dendromus mystacalis*	Dendromus de Heuglin	Chestnut African Climbing Mouse
Nesomyidae	*Dendromus nyasae*	Dendromus du Kivu	Kivu African Climbing Mouse
Muridae	*Deomys ferrugineus*	Déomys roux	Congo Forest Rat
Muridae	*Lophuromys luteogaster*	Rat hérissé à ventre fauve	Buff-bellied Brush-furred Rat
Muridae	*Lophuromys medicaudatus*	Rat hérissé à longue queue	Western Rift Brush-furred Rat
Muridae	*Lophuromys rahmi*	Rat hérissé de Rahm	Rahm's Brush-furred Rat
Muridae	*Lophuromys ansorgei*	Rat hérissé d'Ansorge	Ansorge's Brush-furred Rat
Muridae	*Lophuromys woosnami*	Rat hérissé de Woosnam	Woosnam's Brush-furred Rat
Muridae	*Gerbilliscus kempii*	Gerbille de Kemp	Northern Savanna Gerbil
Muridae	*Aethomys kaiseri*	Aethomys de Kaiser	Kaiser's Rock Rat
Muridae	*Arvicanthis niloticus*	Rat roussard du Nil	African Grass Rat
Muridae	*Colomys goslingi*	Rat de Gosling	East African Wading Rat
Muridae	*Dasymys incomtus*	Dasymys d'Afrique	African Shaggy Rat
Muridae	*Dasymys montanus*	Dasymys de montagne	Ruwenzori Shaggy Rat
Muridae	*Dasymys rwandae*	Dasymys du Rwanda	Rwandan Shaggy Rat
Muridae	*Grammomys dolichurus*	Grammomys du Cap	Woodland Thicket Rat
Muridae	*Grammomys dryas*	Grammomys du Rwenzori	Albertine Rift Thicket Rat
Muridae	*Grammomys kuru*	Grammomys du Congo	Eastern Rainforest Thicket Rat
Muridae	*Hybomys lunaris*	Hybomys du Rwenzori	Moon Mountains Striped Mouse
Muridae	*Hybomys univittatus*	Hybomys de Peters	Peters's Striped Mouse
Muridae	*Hylomyscus denniae*	Hylomysque du Rwenzori	Montane Wood Mouse
Muridae	*Hylomyscus stella*	Hylomysque stella	Stella Wood Mouse

Muridae	*Lemniscomys macculus*	Rat rayé d'Ouganda	Buffoon Striped Grass Mouse
Muridae	*Lemniscomys striatus*	Rat rayé d'Afrique	Typical Striped Grass Mouse
Muridae	*Malacomys longipes*	Malacomys du Gabon	Common Swamp Rat
Muridae	*Mastomys erythroleucus*	Mastomys roux-blanc	Reddish-white Multimammate Mouse
Muridae	*Mastomys natalensis*	Mastomys du Natal	Natal Multimammate Mouse
Muridae	*Mus bufo*	Souris crapaud	Toad Mouse
Muridae	*Mus musculoides*	Souris de Temminck	West African Pygmy Mouse
Muridae	*Mus triton*	Souris triton	Grey-bellied Mouse
Muridae	*Mylomys dybowskii*	Mylomys de Dybowski	Dybowski's Three-toed Grass Rat
Muridae	*Oenomys hypoxanthus*	Oenomys à museau roux	Common Rufous-nosed Rat
Muridae	*Pelomys fallax*	Pélomys du Mozambique	East African Groove-toothed Swamp Rat
Muridae	*Praomys degraaffi*	Praomys de De Graaff	De Graaff's Soft-furred Mouse
Muridae	*Praomys jacksoni*	Praomys de Jackson	Jackson's Soft-furred Mouse
Muridae	*Congomys verschureni*	Congomys de Verschuren	Verschuren's Swamp Mouse
Muridae	*Rattus rattus*	Rat noir	Roof Rat
Muridae	*Stochomys longicaudatus*	Rat fléché	Target Rat
Muridae	*Thamnomys kempi*	Thamnomys de Kemp	Kemp's Thicket Rat
Muridae	*Thamnomys major*	Thamnomys de Hatt	Hatt's Thicket Rat
Muridae	*Thamnomys venustus*	Thamnomys de Thomas	Thomas's Thicket Rat
Muridae	*Zelotomys hildegardeae*	Zelotomys de Hildegarde	Hildegarde's Broad-headed Mouse
Muridae	*Otomys denti*	Otomys de Dent	Dent's Vlei Rat
Muridae	*Otomys dartmouthi*	Otomys de Dartmouth	Rwenzori Vlei Rat
Muridae	*Otomys tropicalis*	Otomys tropical	East African Vlei Rat
Anomaluridae	*Anomalurus beecrofti*	Anomalure de Beecroft	Beecroft's Anomalure
Anomaluridae	*Anomalurus derbianus*	Anomalure de Derby	Lord Derby's Anomalure
Anomaluridae	*Anomalurus pusillus*	Anomalure pygmée	Lesser Anomalure
Anomaluridae	*Idiurus macrotis*	Anomalure à longues oreilles	Long-eared Pigmy Anomalure
Anomaluridae	*Idiurus zenkeri*	Anomalure de Zenker	Zenker's Pygmy Anomalure
Hystricidae	*Atherurus africanus*	Athérure africain	African Brush-tailed Porcupine
Hystricidae	*Hystrix africaeaustralis*	Porc-épic du Cap	Cape Porcupine
Thryonomyidae	*Thryonomys gregorianus*	Petit aulacode	Lesser Cane Rat
Thryonomyidae	*Thryonomys swinderianus*	Grand aulacode	Greater Cane Rat

Species very probably present, based on their distribution and habitat

Procaviidae	*Heterohyrax brucei*	Daman de Bruce	Bush Hyrax
Soricidae	*Crocidura attila*	Crocidure d'Attila	Hun White-toothed Shrew
Soricidae	*Crocidura crenata*	Crocidure sauteuse	Long-footed White-toothed Shrew
Soricidae	*Crocidura dolichura*	Crocidure à longue queue	Long-tailed White-toothed Shrew
Soricidae	*Crocidura fuscomurina*	Crocidure de Heuglin	Bicolored African White-toothed Shrew
Soricidae	*Crocidura hildegardeae*	Crocidure de Hildegarde	Hildegarde's White-toothed Shrew
Soricidae	*Crocidura kivuana*	Crocidure du Kivu	Kivu White-toothed Shrew
Soricidae	*Crocidura littoralis*	Crocidure des rives	Naked-tailed White-toothed Shrew
Soricidae	*Crocidura luna*	Crocidure séléné	Moonshine White-toothed Shrew
Soricidae	*Crocidura roosevelti*	Crocidure de Roosevelt	Roosevelt's White-toothed Shrew
Soricidae	*Sylvisorex johnstoni*	Pachyure de Johnston	Johnston's Forest Shrew
Pteropodidae	*Scotonycteris bergmansi*	Scotonyctère de Bergmans	Bergmans's Fruit Bat
Hipposeridae	*Macronycteris gigas*	Phyllorhine géante	Giant Leaf-nosed Bat
Hipposeridae	*Hipposeridos ruber*	Phyllorhine de Noack	Noack's Leaf-nosed Bat
Molossidae	*Mops condylurus*	Tadaride d'Angola	Angolan Free-tailed Bat
Verspertilionidae	*Scotophilus nux*	Scotophile noisette	Nut-coloured Yellow Bat
Verspertilionidae	*Glauconycteris gleni*	Glauconyctère de Glen	Glen's Butterfly bat
Vespertilionidae	*Kerivoula lanosa*	Kérivoule laineuse	Lesser Woolly Bat
Vespertilionidae	*Kerivoula smithii*	Kérivoule de Smith	Smith's Woolly Bat
Herpestidae	*Xenogale naso*	Mangouste à long nez	Long-nosed Mongoose
Muridae	*Hylomyscus aeta*	Hylomysque de Thomas	Beaded Wood Mouse
Muridae	*Hylomyscus parvus*	Petit Hylomysque	Lesser Wood Mouse
Muridae	*Mus minutoides*	Souris naine	Sub-Saharan Pigmy Mouse
Muridae	*Mus sorella*	Souris de Thomas	Thomas's Mouse
Muridae	*Pelomys hopkinsi*	Pélomys de Hopkins	Hopkins's Groove-toothed Swamp Rat
Muridae	*Pelomys minor*	Pélomys nain	Least Groove-toothed Swamp Rat

Species possibly present, but at the edge of their range

Leporidae	*Lepus capensis*	Lièvre du Cap	Cape Hare
Pteropodidae	*Epomophorus minor*	Epomophore nain	Minor Epauletted Fruit Bat
Molossidae	*Mops aloysiisabaudiae*	Tadaride du Duc des Abruzzes	Duke of Abruzzi's Free-tailed Bat
Molossidae	*Mops thersites*	Tadaride railleuse	Railer Free-tailed Bat
Rhinolophidae	*Rhinolophus hilli*	Rhinolophe de Hill	Hill's Horseshoe Bat
Bovidae	*Oreotragus oreotragus*	Oréotrague	Klipspringer
Suidae	*Potamochoerus porcus*	Potamochère roux	Red River Hog
Sciuridae	*Funisciurus anerythrus*	Ecureuil de Thomas	Thomas's Rope Squirrel
Muridae	*Lophuromys dudui*	Rat hérissé de Dudu	Dudu's Brush-furred Rat
Muridae	*Aethomys hindei*	Aethomys de Hinde	Hinde's Rock Rat
Muridae	*Praomys misonnei*	Praomys de Misonne	Misonne's Soft-furred Mouse
Hystricidae	*Hystrix cristata*	Porc-épic à crête	Crested Porcupine

Appendix 5
List of birds

List compiled by Marc Languy in July 2024, adapted and updated from Plumptre & al, 2007, with contributions by Melihat Veysal, Julie Williams and Augustin Rwimo Shengeri.
The nomenclature follows the International Ornithological Congress World Bird List, v. 14.1 (Gill et al., 2024).

Families/Species (EN)	Genus	Species
ANATIDAE		
Fulvous Whistling Duck	*Dendrocygna*	*bicolor*
White-faced Whistling Duck	*Dendrocygna*	*viduata*
White-backed Duck	*Thalassornis*	*leuconotus*
Spur-winged Goose	*Plectropterus*	*gambensis*
Knob-billed Duck	*Sarkidiornis*	*melanotos*
Egyptian Goose	*Alopochen*	*aegyptiaca*
African Pygmy Goose	*Nettapus*	*auritus*
Northern Shoveler	*Spatula*	*clypeata*
Blue-billed Teal	*Spatula*	*hottentota*
Garganey	*Spatula*	*querquedula*
Northern Pintail	*Anas*	*acuta*
Cape Teal	*Anas*	*capensis*
Eurasian Teal	*Anas*	*crecca*
Red-billed Teal	*Anas*	*erythrorhyncha*
African Black Duck	*Anas*	*sparsa*
Yellow-billed Duck	*Anas*	*undulata*
Southern Pochard	*Netta*	*erythrophthalma*
Maccoa Duck	*Oxyura*	*maccoa*
NUMIDIDAE		
Black Guineafowl	*Agelastes*	*niger*
Helmeted Guineafowl	*Numida*	*meleagris*
Western Crested Guineafowl	*Guttera*	*verreauxi*
Plumed Guineafowl	*Guttera*	*plumifera*
ODONTOPHORIDAE		
Nahan's Partridge	*Ptilopachus*	*nahani*
PHASIANIDAE		
Red-winged Francolin	*Scleroptila*	*levaillantii*
Blue Quail	*Synoicus*	*adansonii*
Common Quail	*Coturnix*	*coturnix*
Harlequin Quail	*Coturnix*	*delegorguei*
Red-necked Spurfowl	*Pternistis*	*afer*
Heuglin's Spurfowl	*Pternistis*	*icterorhynchus*
Handsome Spurfowl	*Pternistis*	*nobilis*
Scaly Spurfowl	*Pternistis*	*squamatus*
CAPRIMULGIDAE		
Bates's Nightjar	*Caprimulgus*	*batesi*
European Nightjar	*Caprimulgus*	*europaeus*
Square-tailed Nightjar	*Caprimulgus*	*fossii*
Swamp Nightjar	*Caprimulgus*	*natalensis*
Fiery-necked Nightjar	*Caprimulgus*	*pectoralis*
Montane Nightjar	*Caprimulgus*	*poliocephalus*
Freckled Nightjar	*Caprimulgus*	*tristigma*
Pennant-winged Nightjar	*Caprimulgus*	*vexillarius*
APODIDAE		
Scarce Swift	*Schoutedenapus*	*myoptilus*
Mottled Spinetail	*Telacanthura*	*ussheri*
Sabine's Spinetail	*Rhaphidura*	*sabini*
African Palm Swift	*Cypsiurus*	*parvus*
Mottled Swift	*Tachymarptis*	*aequatorialis*
Alpine Swift	*Tachymarptis*	*melba*
Common Swift	*Apus*	*apus*
Pallid Swift	*Apus*	*pallidus*
African Black Swift	*Apus*	*barbatus*
Little Swift	*Apus*	*affinis*
White-rumped Swift	*Apus*	*caffer*
Horus Swift	*Apus*	*horus*

Families/Species (EN)	Genus	Species
MUSOPHAGIDAE		
Great Blue Turaco	*Corythaeola*	*cristata*
Eastern Grey Plantain Eater	*Crinifer*	*zonurus*
Rwenzori Turaco	*Gallirex*	*johnstoni*
Ross's Turaco	*Tauraco*	*rossae*
Black-billed Turaco	*Tauraco*	*schuettii*
OTIDIDAE		
Black-bellied Bustard	*Lissotis*	*melanogaster*
CUCULIDAE		
Black Coucal	*Centropus*	*grillii*
Black-throated Coucal	*Centropus*	*leucogaster*
Blue-headed Coucal	*Centropus*	*monachus*
White-browed Coucal	*Centropus*	*superciliosus*
Blue Malkoha	*Ceuthmochares*	*aereus*
Jacobin Cuckoo	*Clamator*	*jacobinus*
Levaillant's Cuckoo	*Clamator*	*levaillantii*
Diederik Cuckoo	*Chrysococcyx*	*caprius*
African Emerald Cuckoo	*Chrysococcyx*	*cupreus*
Yellow-throated Cuckoo	*Chrysococcyx*	*flavigularis*
Klaas's Cuckoo	*Chrysococcyx*	*klaas*
Dusky Long-tailed Cuckoo	*Cercococcyx*	*mechowi*
Barred Long-tailed Cuckoo	*Cercococcyx*	*montanus*
Olive Long-tailed Cuckoo	*Cercococcyx*	*olivinus*
Common Cuckoo	*Cuculus*	*canorus*
Black Cuckoo	*Cuculus*	*clamosus*
African Cuckoo	*Cuculus*	*gularis*
Madagascar Cuckoo	*Cuculus*	*rochii*
Red-chested Cuckoo	*Cuculus*	*solitarius*
COLUMBIDAE		
Lemon Dove	*Columba*	*larvata*
African Olive Pigeon	*Columba*	*arquatrix*
Speckled Pigeon	*Columba*	*guinea*
Western Bronze-naped Pigeon	*Columba*	*iriditorques*
Afep Pigeon	*Columba*	*unicincta*
Ring-necked Dove	*Streptopelia*	*capicola*
Mourning Collared Dove	*Streptopelia*	*decipiens*
Dusky Turtle Dove	*Streptopelia*	*lugens*
Red-eyed Dove	*Streptopelia*	*semitorquata*
Laughing Dove	*Spilopelia*	*senegalensis*
Blue-spotted Wood Dove	*Turtur*	*afer*
Blue-headed Wood Dove	*Turtur*	*brehmeri*
Emerald-spotted Wood Dove	*Turtur*	*chalcospilos*
Tambourine Dove	*Turtur*	*tympanistria*
African Green Pigeon	*Treron*	*calvus*
Namaqua Dove	*Oena*	*capensis*
HELIORNITHIDAE		
African Finfoot	*Podica*	*senegalensis*
SAROTHRURIDAE		
Buff-spotted Flufftail	*Sarothrura*	*elegans*
White-spotted Flufftail	*Sarothrura*	*pulchra*
RALLIDAE		
African Crake	*Crecopsis*	*egregia*
Corn Crake	*Crex*	*crex*
Lesser Moorhen	*Paragallinula*	*angulata*
Common Moorhen	*Gallinula*	*chloropus*
Red-knobbed Coot	*Fulica*	*cristata*

Common name	Genus	Species
Allen's Gallinule	Porphyrio	alleni
African Swamphen	Porphyrio	madagascariensis
Black Crake	Zapornia	flavirostra
GRUIDAE		
Grey Crowned Crane	Balearica	regulorum
PODICIPEDIDAE		
Great Crested Grebe	Podiceps	cristatus
Little Grebe	Tachybaptus	ruficollis
PHOENICOPTERIDAE		
Greater Flamingo	Phoenicopterus	roseus
Lesser Flamingo	Phoeniconaias	minor
TURNICIDAE		
Black-rumped Buttonquail	Turnix	nanus
Common Buttonquail	Turnix	sylvaticus
BURHINIDAE		
Water Thick-knee	Burhinus	vermiculatus
RECURVIROSTRIDAE		
Black-winged Stilt	Himantopus	himantopus
Pied Avocet	Recurvirostra	avosetta
CHARADRIIDAE		
Grey Plover	Pluvialis	squatarola
Little Ringed Plover	Charadrius	dubius
Common Ringed Plover	Charadrius	hiaticula
Three-banded Plover	Charadrius	tricollaris
White-crowned Lapwing	Vanellus	albiceps
Crowned Lapwing	Vanellus	coronatus
Long-toed Lapwing	Vanellus	crassirostris
Senegal Lapwing	Vanellus	lugubris
African Wattled Lapwing	Vanellus	senegallus
Spur-winged Lapwing	Vanellus	spinosus
Brown-chested Lapwing	Vanellus	superciliosus
Caspian Plover	Anarhynchus	asiaticus
White-fronted Plover	Anarhynchus	marginatus
Tibetan Sand Plover	Anarhynchus	atrifrons
Kittlitz's Plover	Anarhynchus	pecuarius
ROSTRATULIDAE		
Greater Painted-snipe	Rostratula	benghalensis
JACANIDAE		
Lesser Jacana	Microparra	capensis
African Jacana	Actophilornis	africanus
SCOLOPACIDAE		
Eurasian Curlew	Numenius	arquata
Eurasian Whimbrel	Numenius	phaeopus
Black-tailed Godwit	Limosa	limosa
Common Snipe	Gallinago	gallinago
Great Snipe	Gallinago	media
African Snipe	Gallinago	nigripennis
Common Sandpiper	Actitis	hypoleucos
Spotted Redshank	Tringa	erythropus
Wood Sandpiper	Tringa	glareola
Common Greenshank	Tringa	nebularia
Green Sandpiper	Tringa	ochropus
Marsh Sandpiper	Tringa	stagnatilis
Common Redshank	Tringa	totanus
Ruddy Turnstone	Arenaria	interpres
Curlew Sandpiper	Calidris	ferruginea
Little Stint	Calidris	minuta
Temminck's Stint	Calidris	temminckii
Ruff	Calidris	pugnax
GLAREOLIDAE		
Bronze-winged Courser	Rhinoptilus	chalcopterus
Temminck's Courser	Cursorius	temminckii
Black-winged Pratincole	Glareola	nordmanni
Rock Pratincole	Glareola	nuchalis
Collared Pratincole	Glareola	pratincola
LARIDAE		
African Skimmer	Rynchops	flavirostris
Little Tern	Sternula	albifrons
Gull-billed Tern	Gelochelidon	nilotica
Whiskered Tern	Chlidonias	hybridus
White-winged Tern	Chlidonias	leucopterus
Grey-headed Gull	Chroicocephalus	cirrocephalus
Black-headed Gull	Chroicocephalus	ridibundus
Lesser Black-backed Gull	Larus	fuscus
CICONIIDAE		
African Openbill	Anastomus	lamelligerus
Marabou Stork	Leptoptilos	crumeniferus
Yellow-billed Stork	Mycteria	ibis
Saddle-billed Stork	Ephippiorhynchus	senegalensis
Abdim's Stork	Ciconia	abdimii
White Stork	Ciconia	ciconia
African Woolly-necked Stork	Ciconia	microscelis
ANHINGIDAE		
African Darter	Anhinga	rufa
PHALACROCORACIDAE		
Reed Cormorant	Microcarbo	africanus
Great Cormorant	Phalacrocorax	carbo
THRESKIORNITHIDAE		
Sacred Ibis	Threskiornis	aethiopica
Hadada Ibis	Bostrychia	hagedash
Glossy Ibis	Plegadis	falcinellus
African Spoonbill	Platalea	alba
Eurasian Spoonbill	Platalea	leucorodia
ARDEIDAE		
Dwarf Bittern	Ixobrychus	sturmii
Little Bittern	Ixobrychus	minutus
Black-crowned Night Heron	Nycticorax	nycticorax
Black Heron	Egretta	ardesiaca
Little Egret	Egretta	garzetta
White-backed Night Heron	Calherodius	leuconotus
Green-backed Heron	Butorides	striata
Madagascar Squacco Heron	Ardeola	idae
Squacco Heron	Ardeola	ralloides
Western Cattle Egret	Bubulcus	ibis
Grey Heron	Ardea	cinerea
Goliath Heron	Ardea	goliath
Black-headed Heron	Ardea	melanocephala
Purple Heron	Ardea	purpurea
Great Egret	Ardea	alba
Yellow-billed Egret	Ardea	brachyrhyncha
SCOPIDAE		
Hamerkop	Scopus	umbretta
BALAENICIPITIDAE		
Shoebill	Balaeniceps	rex
PELECANIDAE		
Great White Pelican	Pelecanus	onocrotalus
Pink-backed Pelican	Pelecanus	rufescens
PANDIONIDAE		
Osprey	Pandion	haliaetus
ACCIPITRIDAE		
Black-winged Kite	Elanus	caeruleus
African Harrier Hawk	Polyboroides	typus
Palm-nut Vulture	Gypohierax	angolensis
European Honey Buzzard	Pernis	apivorus
African Cuckoo Hawk	Aviceda	cuculoides
Hooded Vulture	Necrosyrtes	monachus
White-backed Vulture	Gyps	africanus
Rüppell's Vulture	Gyps	rueppelli
White-headed Vulture	Trigonoceps	occipitalis
Lappet-faced Vulture	Torgos	tracheliotos
Western Banded Snake Eagle	Circaetus	cinerascens
Brown Snake Eagle	Circaetus	cinereus
Black-chested Snake Eagle	Circaetus	pectoralis
Congo Serpent Eagle	Dryotriorchis	spectabilis
Bateleur	Terathopius	ecaudatus
Bat Hawk	Macheiramphus	alcinus

Common Name	Genus	Species
Crowned Eagle	*Stephanoaetus*	*coronatus*
Martial Eagle	*Polemaetus*	*bellicosus*
Long-crested Eagle	*Lophaetus*	*occipitalis*
Wahlberg's Eagle	*Hieraaetus*	*wahlbergi*
Booted Eagle	*Hieraaetus*	*pennatus*
African Hawk Eagle	*Aquila*	*spilogaster*
Cassin's Hawk Eagle	*Aquila*	*africana*
Tawny Eagle	*Aquila*	*rapax*
Lizard Buzzard	*Kaupifalco*	*monogrammicus*
Gabar Goshawk	*Micronisus*	*gabar*
Long-tailed Hawk	*Urotriorchis*	*macrourus*
Chestnut-flanked Sparrowhawk	*Accipiter*	*castanilius*
Black Sparrowhawk	*Accipiter*	*melanoleucus*
Little Sparrowhawk	*Accipiter*	*minullus*
Ovambo Sparrowhawk	*Accipiter*	*ovampensis*
Rufous-breasted Sparrowhawk	*Accipiter*	*rufiventris*
Red-chested Goshawk	*Accipiter*	*toussenelii*
Western Marsh Harrier	*Circus*	*aeruginosus*
Pallid Harrier	*Circus*	*macrourus*
Montagu's Harrier	*Circus*	*pygargus*
African Marsh Harrier	*Circus*	*ranivorus*
Black Kite	*Milvus*	*migrans*
Yellow-billed Kite	*Milvus*	*aegyptius*
African Fish Eagle	*Haliaeetus*	*vocifer*
Augur Buzzard	*Buteo*	*augur*
Common Buzzard	*Buteo*	*buteo*
Mountain Buzzard	*Buteo*	*oreophilus*

TYTONIDAE
Western Barn Owl	*Tyto*	*alba*
African Grass Owl	*Tyto*	*capensis*

STRIGIDAE
African Barred Owlet	*Glaucidium*	*capense*
Red-chested Owlet	*Glaucidium*	*tephronotum*
African Scops Owl	*Otus*	*senegalensis*
Long-eared Owl	*Asio*	*otus*
Spotted Eagle Owl	*Bubo*	*africanus*
Verreaux's Eagle Owl	*Ketupa*	*lactea*
Fraser's Eagle Owl	*Ketupa*	*poensis*
African Wood Owl	*Strix*	*woodfordii*

COLIIDAE
Speckled Mousebird	*Colius*	*striatus*
Blue-naped Mousebird	*Urocolius*	*macrourus*

TROGONIDAE
Narina Trogon	*Apaloderma*	*narina*
Bar-tailed Trogon	*Apaloderma*	*vittatum*

UPUPIDAE
Eurasian Hoopoe	*Upupa*	*epops*
African Hoopoe	*Upupa*	*africana*

PHOENICULIDAE
White-headed Wood Hoopoe	*Phoeniculus*	*bollei*
Forest Wood Hoopoe	*Phoeniculus*	*castaneiceps*
Green Wood Hoopoe	*Phoeniculus*	*purpureus*
Common Scimitarbill	*Rhinopomastus*	*cyanomelas*

BUCEROTIDAE
Congo Pied Hornbill	*Tockus*	*fasciatus*
Crowned Hornbill	*Lophoceros*	*alboterminatus*
Red-billed Dwarf Hornbill	*Lophoceros*	*camurus*
White-thighed Hornbill	*Bycanistes*	*albotibialis*
Piping Hornbill	*Bycanistes*	*fistulator*
Black-and-White-Casqued Hornbill	*Bycanistes*	*subcylindricus*
Black-casqued Hornbill	*Ceratogymna*	*atrata*
Eastern Dwarf Hornbill	*Horizocerus*	*granti*
Eastern Long-tailed Hornbill	*Horizocerus*	*cassini*

CORACIIDAE
Lilac-breasted Roller	*Coracias*	*caudatus*
European Roller	*Coracias*	*garrulus*
Broad-billed Roller	*Eurystomus*	*glaucurus*
Blue-throated Roller	*Eurystomus*	*gularis*

ALCEDINIDAE
Chocolate-backed Kingfisher	*Halcyon*	*badia*
Striped Kingfisher	*Halcyon*	*chelicuti*
Grey-headed Kingfisher	*Halcyon*	*leucocephala*
Blue-breasted Kingfisher	*Halcyon*	*malimbica*
Woodland Kingfisher	*Halcyon*	*senegalensis*
African Dwarf Kingfisher	*Ispidina*	*lecontei*
African Pygmy Kingfisher	*Ispidina*	*picta*
Malachite Kingfisher	*Corythornis*	*cristatus*
Shining-blue Kingfisher	*Alcedo*	*quadribrachys*
Giant Kingfisher	*Megaceryle*	*maxima*
Pied Kingfisher	*Ceryle*	*rudis*

MEROPIDAE
White-throated Bee-eater	*Merops*	*albicollis*
European Bee-eater	*Merops*	*apiaster*
Red-throated Bee-eater	*Merops*	*bulocki*
Black Bee-eater	*Merops*	*gularis*
Blue-headed Bee-eater	*Merops*	*muelleri*
Southern Carmine Bee-eater	*Merops*	*nubicoides*
Cinnamon-chested Bee-eater	*Merops*	*oreobates*
Blue-cheeked Bee-eater	*Merops*	*persicus*
Little Bee-eater	*Merops*	*pusillus*
Olive Bee-eater	*Merops*	*superciliosus*
Blue-breasted Bee-eater	*Merops*	*variegatus*

LYBIIDAE
Yellow-billed Barbet	*Trachyphonus*	*purpuratus*
Grey-throated Barbet	*Gymnobucco*	*bonapartei*
Sladen's Barbet	*Gymnobucco*	*sladeni*
Red-rumped Tinkerbird	*Pogoniulus*	*atroflavus*
Yellow-rumped Tinkerbird	*Pogoniulus*	*bilineatus*
Yellow-fronted Tinkerbird	*Pogoniulus*	*chrysoconus*
Western Tinkerbird	*Pogoniulus*	*coryphaeus*
Speckled Tinkerbird	*Pogoniulus*	*scolopaceus*
Yellow-throated Tinkerbird	*Pogoniulus*	*subsulphureus*
Yellow-spotted Barbet	*Buccanodon*	*duchaillui*
Hairy-breasted Barbet	*Tricholaema*	*hirsuta*
Spot-flanked Barbet	*Tricholaema*	*lacrymosa*
White-headed Barbet	*Lybius*	*leucocephalus*
Double-toothed Barbet	*Pogonornis*	*bidentatus*

INDICATORIDAE
Cassin's Honeybird	*Prodotiscus*	*insignis*
Brown-backed Honeybird	*Prodotiscus*	*regulus*
Zenker's Honeyguide	*Melignomon*	*zenkeri*
Least Honeyguide	*Indicator*	*exilis*
Greater Honeyguide	*Indicator*	*indicator*
Spotted Honeyguide	*Indicator*	*maculatus*
Lesser Honeyguide	*Indicator*	*minor*
Willcock's Honeyguide	*Indicator*	*willcocksi*
Dwarf Honeyguide	*Indicator*	*pumilio*
Scaly-throated Honeyguide	*Indicator*	*variegatus*
Lyre-tailed Honeyguide	*Melichneutes*	*robustus*

PICIDAE
Red-throated Wryneck	*Jynx*	*ruficollis*
Brown-eared Woodpecker	*Pardipicus*	*caroli*
Buff-spotted Woodpecker	*Pardipicus*	*nivosus*
Nubian Woodpecker	*Campethera*	*nubica*
Fine-banded Woodpecker	*Campethera*	*taeniolaema*
Little Spotted Woodpecker	*Campethera*	*cailliautii*
Yellow-crested Woodpecker	*Chloropicus*	*xantholophus*
Bearded Woodpecker	*Chloropicus*	*namaquus*
Cardinal Woodpecker	*Dendropicos*	*fuscescens*
Gabon Woodpecker	*Dendropicos*	*gabonensis*
Speckle-breasted Woodpecker	*Dendropicos*	*poecilolaemus*
Elliot's Woodpecker	*Dendropicos*	*elliotii*
African Grey Woodpecker	*Dendropicos*	*goertae*
Olive Woodpecker	*Dendropicos*	*griseocephalus*

FALCONIDAE
Grey Kestrel	*Falco*	*ardosiaceus*
Lanner Falcon	*Falco*	*biarmicus*
Red-necked Falcon	*Falco*	*chicquera*
African Hobby	*Falco*	*cuvierii*
Lesser Kestrel	*Falco*	*naumanni*
Peregrine Falcon	*Falco*	*peregrinus*

Common Name	Genus	Species
Eurasian Hobby	Falco	subbuteo
Common Kestrel	Falco	tinnunculus
PSITTACIDAE		
Grey Parrot	Psittacus	erithacus
Red-fronted Parrot	Poicephalus	gulielmi
Meyer's Parrot	Poicephalus	meyeri
Brown-necked Parrot	Poicephalus	fuscicollis
Red-headed Lovebird	Agapornis	pullarius
Black-collared Lovebird	Agapornis	swindernianus
CALYPTOMENIDAE		
African Broadbill	Smithornis	capensis
Rufous-sided Broadbill	Smithornis	rufolateralis
Grey-headed Broadbill	Smithornis	sharpei
PITTIDAE		
African Pitta	Pitta	angolensis
Green-breasted Pitta	Pitta	reichenowi
PLATYSTEIRIDAE		
Rwenzori Batis	Batis	diops
Ituri Batis	Batis	ituriensis
Eastern Black-headed Batis	Batis	minor
Chinspot Batis	Batis	molitor
Jameson's Wattle-eye	Platysteira	jamesoni
Chestnut Wattle-eye	Platysteira	castanea
Yellow-bellied Wattle-eye	Platysteira	concreta
Brown-throated Wattle-eye	Platysteira	cyanea
MALACONOTIDAE		
Pink-footed Puffback	Dryoscopus	angolensis
Northern Puffback	Dryoscopus	gambensis
Red-eyed Puffback	Dryoscopus	senegalensis
Black-headed Gonolek	Laniarius	erythrogaster
Papyrus Gonolek	Laniarius	mufumbiri
Tropical Boubou	Laniarius	major
Lowland Sooty Boubou	Laniarius	leucorhynchus
Willard's Sooty Boubou	Laniarius	willardi
Lühder's Bush-Shrike	Laniarius	luehderi
Albertine Sooty Boubou	Laniarius	holomelas
Bocage's Bush-Shrike	Chlorophoneus	bocagei
Fiery-breasted Bush-Shrike	Malaconotus	cruentus
Doherty's Bush-Shrike	Telophorus	dohertyi
Lagden's Bush-Shrike	Malaconotus	lagdeni
Many-coloured Bush-Shrike	Chlorophoneus	multicolor
Gorgeous Bush-Shrike	Telophorus	viridis
Orange-breasted Bush-Shrike	Chlorophoneus	sulfureopectus
Brubru	Nilaus	afer
Brown-crowned Tchagra	Tchagra	australis
Marsh Tchagra	Bocagia	minuta
Black-crowned Tchagra	Tchagra	senegalus
VANGIDAE		
Black-and-white Shrike Flycatcher	Bias	musicus
African Shrike Flycatcher	Megabyas	flammulatus
Yellow-crested Helmet Shrike	Prionops	alberti
Rufous-bellied Helmet Shrike	Prionops	rufiventris
CAMPEPHAGIDAE		
Black Cuckooshrike	Campephaga	flava
Petit's Cuckooshrike	Campephaga	petiti
Red-shouldered Cuckooshrike	Campephaga	phoenicea
Blue Cuckooshrike	Cyanograucalus	azureus
Grey Cuckooshrike	Ceblepyris	caesius
Grauer's Cuckooshrike	Ceblepyris	graueri
ORIOLIDAE		
African Golden Oriole	Oriolus	auratus
Black-headed Oriole	Oriolus	larvatus
Black-winged Oriole	Oriolus	nigripennis
Eurasian Golden Oriole	Oriolus	oriolus
Mountain Oriole	Oriolus	percivali
DICRURIDAE		
Fork-tailed Drongo	Dicrurus	adsimilis
Velvet-mantled Drongo	Dicrurus	modestus
MONARCHIDAE		
Red-bellied Paradise Flycatcher	Terpsiphone	rufiventer
African Paradise Flycatcher	Terpsiphone	viridis
Blue-headed Crested Flycatcher	Trochocercus	nitens
LANIIDAE		
Northern Fiscal	Lanius	humeralis
Red-backed Shrike	Lanius	collurio
Isabelline Shrike	Lanius	isabellinus
Grey-backed Fiscal	Lanius	excubitoroides
Mackinnon's Shrike	Lanius	mackinnoni
Lesser Grey Shrike	Lanius	minor
CORVIDAE		
White-necked Raven	Corvus	albicollis
Pied Crow	Corvus	albus
STENOSTIRIDAE		
White-tailed Blue Flycatcher	Elminia	albicauda
African Blue Flycatcher	Elminia	longicauda
White-bellied Crested Flycatcher	Elminia	albiventris
White-tailed Crested Flycatcher	Elminia	albonotata
Dusky Crested Flycatcher	Elminia	nigromitrata
PARIDAE		
Stripe-breasted Tit	Melaniparus	fasciiventer
Dusky Tit	Melaniparus	funereus
White-winged Black Tit	Melaniparus	leucomelas
NICATORIDAE		
Western Nicator	Nicator	chloris
Yellow-throated Nicator	Nicator	vireo
ALAUDIDAE		
Rufous-naped Lark	Mirafra	africana
White-tailed Lark	Mirafra	albicauda
Flappet Lark	Mirafra	rufocinnamomea
Red-capped Lark	Calandrella	cinerea
PYCNONOTIDAE		
Slender-billed Greenbul	Stelgidillas	gracilirostris
Yellow-eyed Bristlebill	Bleda	ugandae
Red-tailed Bristlebill	Bleda	syndactylus
Yellow-throated Leaflove	Atimastillas	flavicollis
Spotted Greenbul	Ixonotus	guttatus
White-tailed Greenbul	Thescelocichla	leucopleura
Joyful Greenbul	Chlorocichla	laetissima
Simple Greenbul	Chlorocichla	simplex
Honeyguide Greenbul	Baeopogon	indicator
Kakamega Greenbul	Arizelocichla	kakamegae
Olive-breasted Greenbul	Arizelocichla	kikuyuensis
Red-tailed Greenbul	Criniger	calurus
Eastern Bearded Greenbul	Criniger	chloronotus
Cameroon Sombre Greenbul	Eurillas	curvirostris
Little Grey Greenbul	Eurillas	gracilis
Yellow-whiskered Greenbul	Eurillas	latirostris
Little Greenbul	Eurillas	virens
White-throated Greenbul	Phyllastrephus	albigularis
Toro Olive Greenbul	Phyllastrephus	hypochloris
Cabanis's Greenbul	Phyllastrephus	cabanisi
Yellow-streaked Greenbul	Phyllastrephus	flavostriatus
Icterine Greenbul	Phyllastrephus	icterinus
Red-tailed Leaflove	Phyllastrephus	scandens
Dark-capped Bulbul	Pycnonotus	tricolor
HIRUNDINIDAE		
White-headed Saw-wing	Psalidoprocne	albiceps
Square-tailed Saw-wing	Psalidoprocne	nitens
Black Saw-wing	Psalidoprocne	pristoptera
Grey-rumped Swallow	Pseudhirundo	griseopyga
Banded Martin	Neophedina	cincta
Brown-throated Martin	Riparia	paludicola
Sand Martin	Riparia	riparia
Rock Martin	Ptyonoprogne	fuligula
Ethiopian Swallow	Hirundo	aethiopica
Angola Swallow	Hirundo	angolensis
Barn Swallow	Hirundo	rustica
Wire-tailed Swallow	Hirundo	smithii
Western House Martin	Delichon	urbicum

Common Name	Genus	Species
Lesser Striped Swallow	Cecropis	abyssinica
Red-rumped Swallow	Cecropis	daurica
Red-breasted Swallow	Cecropis	semirufa
Mosque Swallow	Cecropis	senegalensis
MACROSPHENIDAE		
Moustached Grass Warbler	Melocichla	mentalis
Grey Longbill	Macrosphenus	concolor
Yellow Longbill	Macrosphenus	flavicans
Northern Crombec	Sylvietta	brachyura
Red-faced Crombec	Sylvietta	whytii
Lemon-bellied Crombec	Sylvietta	denti
White-browed Crombec	Sylvietta	leucophrys
Green Crombec	Sylvietta	virens
ERYTHROCERCIDAE		
Chestnut-capped Flycatcher	Erythrocercus	mccallii
HYLIIDAE		
Green Hylia	Hylia	prasina
PHYLLOSCOPIDAE		
Red-faced Woodland Warbler	Phylloscopus	laetus
Willow Warbler	Phylloscopus	trochilus
Brown Woodland Warbler	Phylloscopus	umbrovirens
ACROCEPHALIDAE		
Grauer's Warbler	Graueria	vittata
Great Reed Warbler	Acrocephalus	arundinaceus
Lesser Swamp Warbler	Acrocephalus	gracilirostris
Greater Swamp Warbler	Acrocephalus	rufescens
Sedge Warbler	Acrocephalus	schoenobaenus
Common Reed Warbler	Acrocephalus	scirpaceus
African Yellow Warbler	Iduna	natalensis
Mountain Yellow Warbler	Iduna	similis
Papyrus Yellow Warbler	Calamonastides	gracilirostris
LOCUSTELLIDAE		
Bamboo Warbler	Locustella	alfredi
Broad-tailed Warbler	Schoenicola	platyurus
Cinnamon Bracken Warbler	Bradypterus	cinnamomeus
Grauer's Swamp Warbler	Bradypterus	graueri
CISTICOLIDAE		
Wing-snapping Cisticola	Cisticola	ayresii
Siffling Cisticola	Cisticola	brachypterus
Singing Cisticola	Cisticola	cantans
Carruthers's Cisticola	Cisticola	carruthersi
Chubb's Cisticola	Cisticola	chubbi
Red-faced Cisticola	Cisticola	erythrops
Winding Cisticola	Cisticola	marginatus
Zitting Cisticola	Cisticola	juncidis
Croaking Cisticola	Cisticola	natalensis
Stout Cisticola	Cisticola	robustus
Trilling Cisticola	Cisticola	woosnami
Banded Prinia	Prinia	bairdii
Tawny-flanked Prinia	Prinia	subflava
White-chinned Prinia	Schistolais	leucopogon
Rwenzori Collared Apalis	Oreolais	ruwenzori
Buff-bellied Warbler	Phyllolais	pulchella
Lowland Masked Apalis	Apalis	binotata
Grey Apalis	Apalis	cinerea
Yellow-breasted Apalis	Apalis	flavida
Black-throated Apalis	Apalis	jacksoni
Mountain Masked Apalis	Apalis	personata
Chestnut-throated Apalis	Apalis	porphyrolaema
Buff-throated Apalis	Apalis	rufogularis
Grey-capped Warbler	Eminia	lepida
Grey-backed Camaroptera	Camaroptera	brevicaudata
Olive-green Camaroptera	Camaroptera	chloronota
Yellow-browed Camaroptera	Camaroptera	superciliaris
Black-faced Rufous Warbler	Bathmocercus	rufus
Rufous-crowned Eremomela	Eremomela	badiceps
Green-capped Eremomela	Eremomela	scotops
SYLVIIDAE		
Eurasian Blackcap	Sylvia	atricapilla
Garden Warbler	Sylvia	borin
Rwenzori Hill Babbler	Sylvia	atriceps
Barred Warbler	Curruca	nisoria
ZOSTEROPIDAE		
Northern Yellow White-eye	Zosterops	senegalensis
PELLORNEIDAE		
Brown Illadopsis	Illadopsis	fulvescens
Mountain Illadopsis	Illadopsis	pyrrhoptera
Pale-breasted Illadopsis	Illadopsis	rufipennis
LEIOTHRICHIDAE		
Capuchin Babbler	Turdoides	atripennis
Hartlau'bs Babbler	Turdoides	hartlaubi
Arrow-marked Babbler	Turdoides	jardineii
Black-lored Babbler	Turdoides	sharpei
MODULATRICIDAE		
Grey-chested Babbler	Kakamega	poliothorax
HYLIOTIDAE		
Southern Hyliota	Hyliota	australis
Yellow-bellied Hyliota	Hyliota	flavigaster
STURNIDAE		
Wattled Starling	Creatophora	cinerea
Purple Starling	Lamprotornis	purpureus
Rüppell's Starling	Lamprotornis	purpuroptera
Splendid Starling	Lamprotornis	splendidus
Violet-backed Starling	Cinnyricinclus	leucogaster
Chestnut-winged Starling	Onychognathus	fulgidus
Slender-billed Starling	Onychognathus	tenuirostris
Waller's Starling	Onychognathus	walleri
Narrow-tailed Starling	Poeoptera	lugubris
Stuhlmann's Starling	Poeoptera	stuhlmanni
Sharpe's Starling	Pholia	sharpii
BUPHAGIDAE		
Yellow-billed Oxpecker	Buphagus	africanus
Red-billed Oxpecker	Buphagus	erythrorynchus
TURDIDAE		
Fraser's Rufous Thrush	Stizorhina	fraseri
White-tailed Ant Thrush	Neocossyphus	poensis
Red-tailed Ant Thrush	Neocossyphus	rufus
Crossley's Ground Thrush	Geokichla	crossleyi
Grey Ground Thrush	Geokichla	princei
Abyssinian Ground Thrush	Geokichla	piaggiae
African Thrush	Turdus	pelios
Abyssinian Thrush	Turdus	abyssinicus
MUSCICAPIDAE		
Fire-crested Alethe	Alethe	castanea
Brown-backed Scrub Robin	Cercotrichas	hartlaubi
White-browed Scrub Robin	Cercotrichas	leucophrys
Forest Scrub Robin	Cercotrichas	leucosticta
Ashy Flycatcher	Fraseria	caerulescens
Fraser's Forest Flycatcher	Fraseria	ocreata
Grey-throated Flycatcher	Fraseria	griseigularis
Olivaceous Flycatcher	Fraseria	olivascens
Grey Tit-Flycatcher	Fraseria	plumbea
Yellow-eyed Black Flycatcher	Melaenornis	ardesiacus
Northern Black Flycatcher	Melaenornis	edolioides
White-eyed Slaty Flycatcher	Melaenornis	fisheri
Dusky-Blue Flycatcher	Bradornis	comitata
Sooty Flycatcher	Bradornis	fuliginosus
African Dusky Flycatcher	Muscicapa	adusta
Swamp Flycatcher	Muscicapa	aquatica
Cassin's Flycatcher	Muscicapa	cassini
Yellow-footed Flycatcher	Muscicapa	sethsmithi
Spotted Flycatcher	Muscicapa	striata
Little Grey Flycatcher	Muscicapa	epulata
White-starred Robin	Pogonocichla	stellata
Forest Robin	Stiphrornis	erythrothorax
White-bellied Robin Chat	Cossyphicula	roberti
Brown-chested Alethe	Chamaetylas	poliocephala
Red-throated Alethe	Chamaetylas	poliophrys
Blue-shouldered Robin Chat	Cossypha	cyanocampter
White-browed Robin Chat	Cossypha	heuglini
Red-capped Robin Chat	Cossypha	natalensis

Common Name	Genus	Species
Snowy-crowned Robin Chat	Cossypha	niveicapilla
Cape Robin Chat	Dessonornis	caffer
Archer's Ground Robin	Dessonornis	archeri
Equatorial Akalat	Sheppardia	aequatorialis
Lowland Akalat	Sheppardia	cyornithopsis
Collared Flycatcher	Ficedula	albicollis
Whinchat	Saxicola	rubetra
African Stonechat	Saxicola	torquatus
Mocking Cliff Chat	Thamnolaea	cinnamomeiventris
Sooty Chat	Myrmecocichla	nigra
Familiar Chat	Oenanthe	familiaris
Northern Wheatear	Oenanthe	oenanthe

NECTARINIIDAE

Common Name	Genus	Species
Grey-headed Sunbird	Deleornis	axillaris
Grey-chinned Sunbird	Anthreptes	tephrolaemus
Little Green Sunbird	Anthreptes	seimundi
Collared Sunbird	Hedydipna	collaris
Blue-headed Sunbird	Cyanomitra	alinae
Blue-throated Brown Sunbird	Cyanomitra	cyanolaema
Olive Sunbird	Cyanomitra	olivacea
Green-headed Sunbird	Cyanomitra	verticalis
Green-throated Sunbird	Chalcomitra	rubescens
Scarlet-chested Sunbird	Chalcomitra	senegalensis
Malachite Sunbird	Nectarinia	famosa
Scarlet-tufted Sunbird	Nectarinia	johnstoni
Bronzy Sunbird	Nectarinia	kilimensis
Purple-breasted Sunbird	Nectarinia	purpureiventris
Purple-banded Sunbird	Cinnyris	bifasciatus
Olive-bellied Sunbird	Cinnyris	chloropygius
Copper Sunbird	Cinnyris	cupreus
Red-chested Sunbird	Cinnyris	erythrocercus
Tiny Sunbird	Cinnyris	minulla
Marico Sunbird	Cinnyris	mariquensis
Northern Double-collared Sunbird	Cinnyris	reichenowi
Regal Sunbird	Cinnyris	regius
Rockefeller's Sunbird	Cinnyris	rockefelleri
Rwenzori Double-collared Sunbird	Cinnyris	stuhlmanni
Superb Sunbird	Cinnyris	superbus
Variable Sunbird	Cinnyris	venustus

PASSERIDAE

Common Name	Genus	Species
House Sparrow	Passer	domesticus
Northern Grey-headed Sparrow	Passer	griseus

PLOCEIDAE

Common Name	Genus	Species
Thick-billed Weaver	Amblyospiza	albifrons
Maxwell's Black Weaver	Ploceus	albinucha
Strange Weaver	Ploceus	alienus
Orange Weaver	Ploceus	aurantius
Baglafecht Weaver	Ploceus	baglafecht
Dark-backed Weaver	Ploceus	bicolor
Northern Brown-throated Weaver	Ploceus	castanops
Village Weaver	Ploceus	cucullatus
Brown-capped Weaver	Ploceus	insignis
Yellow-capped Weaver	Ploceus	dorsomaculatus
Yellow-legged weaver	Ploceus	flavipes
Lesser Masked Weaver	Ploceus	intermedius
Little Weaver	Ploceus	luteolus
Black-headed Weaver	Ploceus	melanocephalus
Black-billed Weaver	Ploceus	melanogaster
Vieillot's Black Weaver	Ploceus	nigerrimus
Black-necked Weaver	Ploceus	nigricollis
Spectacled Weaver	Ploceus	ocularis
Slender-billed Weaver	Ploceus	pelzelni
Compact Weaver	Ploceus	superciliosus
Yellow-mantled Weaver	Ploceus	tricolor
Holub's Golden Weaver	Ploceus	xanthops
Red-crowned Malimbe	Malimbus	coronatus
Red-bellied Malimbe	Malimbus	erythrogaster
Crested Malimbe	Malimbus	malimbicus
Blue-billed Malimbe	Malimbus	nitens
Red-headed Malimbe	Malimbus	rubricollis
Red-headed Quelea	Quelea	erythrops
Red-billed Quelea	Quelea	quelea
White-winged Widowbird	Euplectes	albonotatus
Red-collared Widowbird	Euplectes	ardens
Fan-tailed Widowbird	Euplectes	axillaris
Yellow Bishop	Euplectes	capensis
Black Bishop	Euplectes	gierowii
Black-winged Red Bishop	Euplectes	hordeaceus
Southern Red Bishop	Euplectes	orix

ESTRILDIDAE

Common Name	Genus	Species
Black-and-white Mannikin	Spermestes	bicolor
Bronze Mannikin	Spermestes	cucullata
Magpie Mannikin	Spermestes	fringilloides
White-collared Olive-back	Nesocharis	ansorgei
Yellow-bellied Waxbill	Coccopygia	quartinia
Green Twinspot	Mandingoa	nitidula
Dusky Crimson-wing	Cryptospiza	jacksoni
Red-faced Crimson-wing	Cryptospiza	reichenovii
Abyssinian Crimson-wing	Cryptospiza	salvadorii
Shelley's Crimson-wing	Cryptospiza	shelleyi
Chestnut-breasted Negrita	Nigrita	bicolor
Grey-headed Negrita	Nigrita	canicapillus
White-breasted Negrita	Nigrita	fusconotus
Pale-fronted Negrita	Nigrita	luteifrons
Common Waxbill	Estrilda	astrild
Black-headed Waxbill	Estrilda	atricapilla
Black-crowned Waxbill	Estrilda	nonnula
Kandt's Waxbill	Estrilda	kandti
Fawn-breasted Waxbill	Estrilda	paludicola
Crimson-rumped Waxbill	Estrilda	rhodopyga
Quailfinch	Ortygospiza	atricollis
Orange-breasted Waxbill	Amandava	subflava
Grant's Bluebill	Spermophaga	poliogenys
Red-headed Bluebill	Spermophaga	ruficapilla
Black-bellied Seed-cracker	Pyrenestes	ostrinus
Green-winged Pytilia	Pytilia	melba
African Firefinch	Lagonosticta	rubricata
Red-billed Firefinch	Lagonosticta	senegala

VIDUIDAE

Common Name	Genus	Species
Village Indigobird	Vidua	chalybeata
Pin-tailed Whydah	Vidua	macroura

MOTACILLIDAE

Common Name	Genus	Species
African Pied Wagtail	Motacilla	aguimp
Cape Wagtail	Motacilla	capensis
Mountain Wagtail	Motacilla	clara
Western Yellow Wagtail	Motacilla	flava
Yellow-throated Longclaw	Macronyx	croceus
Short-tailed Pipit	Anthus	brachyurus
Plain-backed Pipit	Anthus	leucophrys
African Pipit	Anthus	cinnamomeus
Long-billed Pipit	Anthus	similis
Tree Pipit	Anthus	trivialis

FRINGILLIDAE

Common Name	Genus	Species
Oriole Finch	Linurgus	olivaceus
Black-throated Canary	Crithagra	atrogularis
Thick-billed Seedeater	Crithagra	burtoni
Black-faced Canary	Crithagra	capistrata
African Citril	Crithagra	citrinelloides
Yellow-fronted Canary	Crithagra	mozambica
Streaky Seed-eater	Crithagra	striolata
Brimstone Canary	Crithagra	sulphurata
Yellow-crowned Canary	Serinus	flavivertex

EMBERIZIDAE

Common Name	Genus	Species
Golden-breasted Bunting	Emberiza	flaviventris
Cinnamon-breasted Rock Bunting	Emberiza	tahapisi

Appendix 6
Authors' biographies

BASTIEN ALARD

Having gained some initial professional experience with development aid NGOs, Bastien Alard moved to the DRC in 2015. His successive positions with Welthungerhilfe in Beni and Butembo allowed him to develop his expertise in rural development. In 2019, he joined Virunga National Park, where he heads the Agriculture Department and supervises the agricultural processing businesses (Virunga Chocolate, Virunga Enzymes, Sicovir, Virunga Origins).

NESTOR BAGURUBUMWE

Nestor Bagurubumwe, a retired Director of Virunga National Park, was born in Musezero in 1946. He began his career with the Syndicat National des Travailleurs Congolais (1964) and went on to work at the Bwisha chiefdom tax collection office (1965), as an archivist at the Rutshuru hospital and finally as a catechist, also in Rutshuru. In 1969, he started working at Virunga National Park as a patrol ranger at the Rwindi station. He moved on to the Chanzerwa and Ishasha patrol posts, before becoming a secretary-accountant at the Lulimbi station. After graduating from the Garoua Wildlife School (Cameroon) in 1985, he became a botany and soil science research technician and an ornithologist at the Lulimbi Research Centre, where he was appointed station manager.

MÉTHODE BAGURUBUMWE UHOZE

Méthode, son of Nestor Bagurubumwe, grew up in Virunga National Park, where he developed a passion for conservation. After earning a master's degree in Public Administration and Environmental Management (USA), he began his career at Kahuzi-Biega National Park. He went on to work for the World Wildlife Fund (WWF-East/DRC) from 2004 to 2016. In support of the PNVi, he became head of the project for sustainable participatory management of natural resources and protection of great ape habitats. He specialises in geomatics and conflict prevention/resolution relating to boundaries between local communities and protected areas. From 2016 to 2019, he was the geomatics and GIS coordinator at UN-Habitat/DRC. In 2020, he joined the PNVi as Director of External Relations and Community Engagement.

STANISLAS BAKINAHE

After graduating from the Technical Agricultural and Veterinary School in Butembo in 1961, Stanislas Bakinahe began his career at the ICCN as an assistant curator of Garamba National Park. From 1988 to 1993, he specialised in managing protected areas, obtaining a diploma from the École de Faune de Garoua (Cameroon). He worked in the Upemba, Maiko and Virunga parks and at the Okapis Wildlife Reserve before joining the ICCN General Directorate in Kinshasa. There, he successively held the positions of Inspector, Regional Coordinator for Province Orientale, Coordinator for the Provinces of South Kivu, North Kivu and Maniema, Provincial Director for North Kivu, and Administrative and Financial Director. He retired in 2010.

EPHREM BALOLE BWAMI LUBALA

Having earned a degree in Integrated Management of Tropical Landscapes and Territories from the University of Kinshasa, Ephrem Balole began his professional career in 2006 as Country Director of the Africa Conservation Fund. In 2008, he became Programme Manager for the Virunga Foundation. In 2014, he became the Director of Virunga Energies, managing the construction of power stations and networks and marketing electricity in North Kivu Province. After successfully defending his thesis on the socio-economic value of the PNVi (Ecole Régionale Postuniversitaire d'Aménagement et de Gestion intégrés des Forêts et Territoires tropicaux - ERAIFT, 2020) he is continuing his research on the contribution of renewable energies to the socio-economic development of protected areas.

LUKAMBO BANTU

Lukambo Bantu was born in Vitshumbi on the shores of Lake Edward. He has a degree in Nature Conservation. Since 2000, as Director of the non-profit organisation Innovation pour le Développement et la Protection de l'Environnement, he has been fighting on many fronts to protect the ecosystems of the DRC. His fight against trafficking of all kinds – abducted baby gorillas, ivory, etc. – has repeatedly resulted in him being taken prisoner by rebel groups. He has been awarded several tributes, including the IUCN Heritage Hero Award (2016).

GUILLAUME BOUDOIRE

Doctor Guillaume Boudoire is a lecturer in volcanology at the Magmas and Volcanoes Laboratory of the University of Clermont Auvergne (France). His keen interest in the operational aspects of monitoring active volcanoes has led him to focus his research on the architecture and dynamics of magma systems in the context of a continental rift and the role of volcanic gases. Since 2020, he has carried out several missions in Virunga National Park and lends his support to the monitoring activities of the Goma Volcanological Observatory.

PIERRE-YVES BURGI

Pierre-Yves Burgi is Assistant Director of the Information Systems Division at the University of Geneva (Switzerland). His expertise is in mathematical representations of physical processes to study volcanological phenomena. Since 2005, he has regularly visited the Nyiragongo and Nyamulagira volcanoes to study their dynamics, using computational approaches. His recent research, in collaboration with the Goma Volcanological Observatory and Franco-Italian teams, has resulted in the development of models to understand the mechanisms underlying the recent eruptions of these two volcanoes.

LARA COLLART

As a graduate in Economics (University of Maastricht, Netherlands) and Development Programme Evaluation (University of Antwerp, Belgium), Lara Collart has been working on a PhD in Development Economics since 2021 (BIO, Antwerp). As part of this, she is contributing to the research project on 'clean cooking' methods and deforestation in Virunga National Park.

JEAN-PIERRE d'HUART

Holder of a degree in Zoology and a doctoral degree in Science (PhD) from the Université Catholique de Louvain (Belgium), Jean-Pierre d'Huart began his career as a scientific warden and researcher at the Lulimbi station in Virunga National Park (1971–1975), supervising bird ringing activities and conducting the first ecological study of the giant forest hog. For 24 years, he held various management positions within TRAFFIC and WWF, including Head of Programmes in Central and East Africa, based in Nairobi (1992–1997), and Director of Programmes at WWF Belgium. Since 2004, he worked as an independent consultant, carrying out field missions in Africa, particularly in the Congo Basin, to support protected area management teams and design conservation projects.

EMMANUEL de MERODE

Emmanuel de Merode was born in Carthage (Tunisia) in 1970. He spent his childhood in Kenya, where he developed a passion for the savannahs and mountains of East Africa. He studied at Durham University (UK) and earned a doctoral degree in biological anthropology at University College London. He first went to the Congo in 1993 as a researcher in Garamba National Park. In 1999, he set up a lowland gorilla conservation programme in Gabon. In 2002, he returned to the DRC to launch the Zoological Society of London's activities in Virunga National Park. In 2003, he was appointed head of the EU development programmes coordination office in the eastern DRC, based in Goma. In 2008, the Congolese government asked him to take charge of Virunga National Park. A public–private partnership (PPP) between the Virunga Foundation and the Institute for Nature Conservation in Congo enabled him to launch the Virunga Alliance in 2013: a vast stabilisation and development programme based on the sustainable use of natural resources. His work is frequently mentioned in Congolese and international media.

GUY DEBONNET

Guy Debonnet, a graduate in agronomy from the University of Ghent (Belgium), worked for the German Society for International Cooperation (GIZ) in Kahuzi-Biega National Park from 1996 to 2001. In 1998, he co-initiated a joint programme for UNESCO, the ICCN and NGOs for safeguarding the five World Heritage Sites in the DRC. He has been the Head of the Natural Heritage Unit at the UNESCO World Heritage Centre since 2002. In this capacity, he supervises activities concerning natural sites included on UNESCO's World Heritage List, reporting to the World Heritage Committee.

FRANÇOIS-XAVIER de DONNEA

François-Xavier de Donnea, a doctor in Economics from Erasmus Universiteit (Rotterdam, Netherlands), held several university teaching posts before embarking on a political career. He has been a Member of Parliament, a Member of the European Parliament, Secretary of State for Development Cooperation, Minister of Defence, Mayor of Brussels, Minister-President of the Brussels-Capital Region, and Royal Mediator. From 2009 to 2018, he chaired the Sahel and West Africa Club, a network of countries working for economic development and security in the region. Between 2018 and 2019, he was appointed Facilitator of the Congo Basin Forest Partnership, which promotes the sustainable management of forest resources in Central Africa. In 2008, he created the Africa Conservation Fund (ACF) – later named Virunga Foundation – with Jan Bonde Nielsen and Emmanuel de Merode, and signed the first contract for the management of PNVi with the ICCN. He is currently a member of the Board of Directors of the Virunga Foundation, Chairman of the Virunga Belgium Fund, Chairman of the Board of Directors of Garamba National Park (in collaboration with African Parks) and a founding member of the Trust Fund for Protected Areas in the DRC ('Fonds Okapi').

SÉBASTIEN DESBUREAUX

Sébastien Desbureaux holds a doctoral degree in economics. His work uses statistical evaluation approaches to support the emergence of public policies conducive to the fight against extreme poverty and for the protection of living organisms. From 2019 to 2021, he supervised the Monitoring and Evaluation Department of the PNVi and he has since continued to set up experimental programmes with the Park. He currently holds a Junior Professorship at the Institut National de Recherche pour l'Agriculture, l'Alimentation et l'Environnement (INRAE, France) and is affiliated with the Centre d'Economie de l'Environnement in Montpellier (France).

JOSUÉ DUHA

Josué Duha holds a degree in economics and management from the Université Libre des Pays des Grands-Lacs (2015), where he specialised in industrial and development economics. In 2015, he was appointed assistant at the Institut Supérieur de Commerce Kiwanja. He joined Virunga Energies in 2016, first as a Public Relations Officer and then as a Sales Manager, before being appointed Assistant Managing Director. He is currently its Sales and Communications Director.

JACQUES DURIEUX (†)

Jacques Durieux, a vulcanologist specialising in eruptive dynamics and risk management, first became interested in Nyiragongo and the other Virunga volcanoes in 1970. After four years in Goma, he spent 25 years studying most of the world's active volcanoes and carried out several missions for the PNVi. Called in as an expert by the United Nations during the Nyiragongo eruption in January 2002, he remained in Goma as Director of the United Nations Volcano Risk Reduction Programme. He died in June 2009.

JÉRÔME GABRIEL

Having earned a degree in Management Engineering from Solvay Brussels Schools of Economics & Management (Belgium) and Politecnico di Milano (Italy), Jérôme Gabriel began his career in consultancy and strategy at McKinsey & Company before joining the PNVi as Head of Investments (2020–2021) and subsequently becoming the CEO of Virunga Energies (2021–2024).

AUDACE HAMULI

Having obtained a degree in Financial Management (DRC), Audace Hamuli worked as a consultant before joining Virunga Energies in 2017. In 2019, he became a financial analyst for the programme to support entrepreneurship by granting electricity loans, and subsequently its manager. In February 2024, he was appointed Director of Grameen Virunga SA, a micro-finance structure set up by the Virunga Foundation in partnership with the Grameen Trust.

FRÉDÉRIC HENRARD

Frédéric Henrard holds master's degrees in Political Science and Business Management (Belgium). For 10 years, he worked in the police sector, first with the Belgian Ministry of the Interior and Federal Police, then with the European police cooperation agency Europol. In 2009, he joined the Ministry of Foreign Affairs, to hold posts in Shanghai (China), Kabul (Afghanistan) and New York (at the United Nations). As he admired the work accomplished at Virunga National Park, he took leave in 2017 to go to Rumangabo, assisting the Director of PNVi as Head of Programmes and Operations. In 2021, he returned to the Ministry of Foreign Affairs, where he covers African political issues with the European Union.

VIANNEY HARAKANDI

Vianney Harakandi, a graduate in educational humanities, was a teacher before becoming a warden at Virunga National Park in 1989. He gained experience as a patrolman and guide before joining the PNVi tourism office in Goma. He holds a certificate from the College of African Wildlife Management (Mweka, Tanzania).

JOSÉ KALPERS

José Kalpers, a Doctor of Science, joined the PNVi in 1991 as the first regional coordinator of its International Gorilla Conservation Programme. In 1996, he developed a system for monitoring patrols and gorillas throughout the Virunga massif (Rwanda, Uganda, DRC). He also works as a consultant for several conservation organisations active in the DRC. In 2014, he moved to Australia to work with First Nations as the Director of a natural resource management programme.

MERDI KAMBALE BARAKA

Holder of a degree in Economics and Management (DRC) and a certification in Civic Leadership from Kenyatta University (Kenya), Merdi Baraka joined Virunga National Park in 2018 as a project supervisor for the Agriculture Support Programme. He is a specialist in value chains and contributes to project impact analysis.

JOSUÉ KAMBASU KATSUVA MUKURA

The son of a Lake Edward fisherman and a fisherman himself, Josué Mukura holds a master's degree in Environmental Management and Sustainable Development (DRC). He is the Secretary General of the Federation of Individual Fishermen's Committees of Lake Edward (FECOPEILE). He is also a lecturer at the Institut Supérieur de Pêche in Goma (DRC).

JACQUES KATUTU

Jacques Katutu has a degree in Environmental Science and Nature Conservation (DRC). He joined Virunga National Park in 2011. Initially a warden, he has been in charge of monitoring mountain gorillas since 2014. He took part in censuses in the Virunga massif in 2015–2016 and the Bwindi-Sarambwe forest (Uganda-DRC) in 2018. Between 2018 and 2021, he managed the habituation of two gorilla groups of around 60 individuals. An expert in the fight against environmental crime, he also monitors lowland gorillas as part of the reintroduction project at Mount Tshiaberimu. He is the focal point for the modelling of the impact of diseases on wild animals (Outbreak Network).

DEO KUJIRAKWINJA
Deo Kujirakwinja has a PhD in Environmental Sciences from Rhodes University, South Africa, and a master's degree in Conservation Biology from UCT, South Africa. He has worked in various protected areas in Africa since 2003. At Virunga National Park, he has supported the training of rangers and managers and cross-border collaboration. An employee of the Wildlife Conservation Society (WCS) since 2003, he is currently the Director of Kahuzi-Biega National Park (DRC) and an associate professor at the Institut Supérieur du Tourisme (ISTou, DRC).

ROBIN LAIME
Robin Laime grew up in Africa dreaming of one day working for Virunga National Park. After obtaining a master's degree in Sustainable Finance (The Netherlands), he joined the PNVi team in 2021. He is responsible for programming and developing work systems and procedures.

MARC LANGUY
Marc Languy holds a degree in Biology and a master's degree in Population Sciences, Development and Environment (UCL, Belgium). He was a lecturer at the University of Lyon I (France) before setting out to teach in Africa. He joined the WWF in 1992 as a project manager in Virunga National Park, then went to work for WWF in Gabon and BirdLife International in Cameroon. In 2002, he returned to WWF as the coordinator of a programme on the Albertine Rift. Between 2009 and 2013, he managed the ICCN reform support programme and became WWF Director for Central Africa. In 2019, he left this position to start coordinating cross-border conservation and development programmes in West Africa funded by the European Union.

ANNETTE LANJOUW
After successfully defending a thesis in Biology on the behaviour of bonobos (Universiteit Utrecht, Netherlands), starting in 1990, Annette Lanjouw led a chimpanzee conservation project in Tongo, in the southern sector of PNVi. She spent a year in the Ituri forest and another in Garamba National Park. From 1993 to 2005, she was Director of the International Gorilla Conservation Programme (AWF/FFI/WWF). She continued her conservation career by overseeing several great ape conservation projects through the Howard G. Buffett Foundation. Since 2007, she has been the Chief Executive of the Arcus Foundation (Cambridge, UK).

FRANCESCA LANATA
A forestry engineer with a master's degree in Parks and Landscaping (Italy) and a post-graduate diploma (DEA) in Urban Forestry (Belgium), Francesca Lanata coordinates projects in Africa for the Meise Botanical Garden (Belgium). Since 1990, she has taught and led several projects, notably in Chad, Gabon and Sao Tome. She has been working in the DRC as an expert since 2004, on the rehabilitation of the Kisantu Botanical Garden, the Kinshasa and Eala Botanical Gardens, the Bombo Lumene Hunting Reserve and the Yangambi Herbarium. At the PNVi specifically, she oversees the management of green spaces and reforestation projects.

PATRICK MACUMU HABAKARAMO
Patrick Macumu holds a PhD in environmental sciences and technologies on the ecological impact of active volcanoes (University of Campania, Italy). He is a Professor of Botanics, specialising in ecology and environmental pollution, at the University of Goma (UNIGOM). His main research activities focus on managing and protecting water resources, characterising and monitoring polluted sites, conserving and managing terrestrial biodiversity, and the chemical analysis of soils and edible plants.

SAMY MANKOTO MA MBAELELE
Samy Mankoto headed the ICCN from 1985 to 1995, focusing on international cooperation, sustainable tourism development and an innovative revenue-generation policy. He joined UNESCO from 1995 to 2012, and in 1999 contributed to the creation of the ERAIFT (Ecole Régionale Postuniversitaire d'Aménagement et de Gestion intégrés des Forêts et Territoires tropicaux). An honorary member of Belgium's Royal Academy of Overseas Sciences (ARSOM) and former IUCN regional advisor for Africa, he was President of the RAPAC (Réseau des Aires Protégées d'Afrique Centrale) from 2003 to 2013.

GEORGES MAVONGA TULUKA
Georges Mavonga is a senior researcher at the Goma Volcanological Observatory, specialising in assessing seismic hazards in sub-Saharan Africa. His work focuses on volcanic seismicity, emphasising the monitoring and modelling of the seismic precursors to the eruptions of the Nyiragongo and Nyamulagira volcanoes.

DIMITRI MOREELS
Dimitri Moreels holds several degrees in finance. His professional career began in the DRC, where he founded several companies in 2005, including Virunga Enzymes SARL, a leading exporter of papaya latex, and the Compagnie des Produits Agricoles du Kivu (COPAK SARL), a major exporter of cocoa and medicinal plants. Jointly with the Virunga Foundation and other partners, he founded Virunga Origins in 2021, which supports exports of processed agricultural products from the outskirts of Virunga National Park.

LÉONARD K. MUBALAMA
Holder of a master's degree in Conservation Biology (Canterbury, UK) and a thesis in Geography (Ghent, Belgium), Léonard K. Mubalama became a scientific curator at the PNVi from 1990 to 1994. A university professor and the Director of the Biodiversity Management and Climate Change Research Centre at ISDR-Bukavu (DRC), he is a member of several IUCN commissions and a corresponding member of the Royal Academy of Overseas Sciences (Belgium). He is currently a sub-regional expert for the CITES/MIKE-ETIS Technical Advisory Group for Central Africa.

OLIVIER MUNGUIKO MUNYAMAHORO
Olivier Munguiko is a researcher at the Goma Volcanological Observatory, where he studies volcanic seismology and geochemistry to understand the dynamics of the East African rift and the Virunga volcanoes. He is particularly involved in monitoring the Nyiragongo and Nyamulagira volcanoes. He is also a teacher at the Institut Supérieur pédagogique de Goma, the Institut Supérieur pédagogique de KANYATSI and the Institut Supérieur pédagogique de Maranatha (DRC).

RODRIGUE MUGARUKA KATEMBO
Rodrigue Mugaruka holds degrees in Science, Biology, Ecology and Animal Resource Management (DRC) and a post-graduate diploma in Biodiversity and Environmental Management (DRC). He joined the PNVi as a warden in 2003. After working in the Kahuzi-Biega National Park and the national parks of Katanga, he returned to the PNVi as Deputy Park Chief.

LUCIEN MUNYANTWARI
A member of the Bar at the Court of Appeal of North Kivu (DRC) since 2013, Lucien Munyantwari collaborated from 2016 to 2019 with the American Bar Association to provide access to justice and strengthen the rule of law in the DRC. In 2020, he joined Virunga National Park as a legal advisor before setting up an independent firm of lawyers specialising in environmental law in 2021, which provides legal representation for the PNVi.

NORBERT MUSHENZI LUSENGE
A graduate of the Ecole de Faune in Garoua (Cameroon), Norbert Mushenzi began his career at the PNVi in 1971 as a warden before working at other World Heritage Sites, notably at the Okapi Wildlife Reserve and at the Garamba and Kahuzi-Biega NP, where he helped habituate gorillas to the presence of humans. He was Director of Virunga National Park during the Congo wars before he retired in 2017.

GRACIEN MUYISA SIVANZA
Gracien Sivanza holds a degree in Environmental Management and Sustainable Development. He completed paramilitary training before joining Virunga National Park. He held several positions, within the canine unit in particular, while continuing his academic training, before being appointed Head of the new Lake Edward sector in 2021.

PATIENT NAMEGABE LIBALA
After his studies in Bukavu, Patient Libala fled to Rwanda in 2008 to escape the violence in the city, where he became a teacher. He was able to return to the DRC when he was employed as a warehouseman at Virunga National Park. His work in the tourism department was appreciated, which enabled him to move up the ranks. Today, he is a lodge manager and hospitality trainer.

ERASME NGENDE
Holder of a degree in Financial Management (DRC), Erasme Ngende began his career in the hospital sector. He worked for public institutions and a Dutch NGO while continuing his training in human resources management. He became Director of Human Resources at Virunga National Park in 2014.

MUSTAFA NSUBUGA
Mustafa Nsubuga is an expert in biodiversity conservation and management and has carried out assignments for the Uganda Wildlife Authority, the Wildlife Conservation Society and the Uganda Conservation Foundation. He is currently pursuing a master's degree in Natural Resources Management, while contributing to several research projects, focusing on lion conservation, human–wildlife conflict and ecological monitoring.

LAURA PARKER
Holder of a double degree (BA) in International Relations and History (USA), Laura Parker began her career in 2007 with the World Food Program in refugee camps in Chad and Sudan. She was transferred to Goma and joined the Howard G. Buffett Foundation in 2013. She has been working at the PNVi since 2018, as a manager of the key programmes for species recovery, habitat restoration and cross-border collaboration.

AUGUSTIN RWIMO
An avid birdwatcher, Augustin Rwimo became a ranger in 1984 at the Okapi Wildlife Reserve (DRC), where his knowledge of biodiversity gained him a position as a guide. While continuing his professional training, in 1997 he joined the PNVi where he took up various management positions in the field. He is currently attached to the Ecological Monitoring Department.

FILIPPO SARACCO
Holder of a master's degree and a PhD in Conservation of Genetic Resources and Seed Improvement (University of Turin, Italy), Filippo Saracco has been working for the European Union (EU) in the field of nature conservation in Africa since 1994. Since 2003, he designed and implemented several programmes in support to the DRC, including at Virunga National Park. He contributed to the creation of the Observatoire des forêts d'Afrique centrale and to EU biodiversity strategies for Africa, Asia and Latin America. The EU Green Deal's NaturAfrica initiative is notably inspired by the concepts tested at Virunga National Park.

DARIO TEDESCO
Dario Tedesco is a lecturer in Geochemistry and Volcanology at the University of Campania (Italy). His PhD focused on the geochemistry of volcanic fluids (Sorbonne University – Jussieu Paris 5, France). After several research stays in Japan and the USA, he focused on the volcanoes of Virunga National Park, sharing his expertise with the United Nations, the European Union and the World Bank. Starting in 1995, he has been collaborating with the Goma Volcanological Observatory on international projects that help build its researchers' capacity.

MIREILLE VANOVERSTRAETEN
An agricultural engineer with a PhD in agronomical science from the University of Liège-Gembloux, Mireille Vanoverstraeten worked as a scientific warden and researcher at the Lulimbi station (1978–1982) studying and evaluating the ecology of the Rwindi–Rutshuru plains. As a consultant to UNESCO's 'Man and the Biosphere' programme (MAB) within the Department of Earth and Environmental Sciences, she contributed to creating the Transboundary Biosphere Reserves on the African continent. She is a scientific collaborator at the University of Liège (Gembloux Agro-Bio Tech).

PATRICIA VAN SCHUYLENBERGH
Patricia Van Schuylenbergh holds a PhD in History, a specialised diploma in Development from UCL (Belgium) and a certification in Environmental Education (Université du Québec, Montréal). She is a senior researcher at the Royal Museum for Central Africa (AfricaMuseum, Tervuren, Belgium). Her main research and publications focus on the history of nature protection and conservation in Central Africa (DRC, Rwanda, Burundi) and natural resource management (wildlife, agriculture, fish farming). Her expertise also includes African national parks and the history of naturalist collections during and after the colonial period.

MICHEL VERLEYEN
A graduate in Civil Construction Engineering (ULg, Belgium) and Civil Engineering in Industrial Management (UCL, Belgium), Michel Verleyen began his career in Zaire in 1977, where he managed the construction of the Maréchal Bridge over the River Congo at Matadi for the Besix group, as well as several civil engineering works. In 1984, he became the Managing Director of the UNIBRA group and, in 1990, Chairman of Lonhro Zaire. In 2005, he oversaw the World Bank's urban rehabilitation programme in Goma. In 2008, he was appointed head of the European Union's infrastructure programmes in eastern Congo. In this capacity, between 2009 and 2024 he successively managed the construction of the Mutwanga I, Matebe, Mutwanga II, Luviro and Rwanguba hydroelectric power stations.

MARIJKE VERPOORTEN
Marijke Verpoorten holds a doctoral degree in Development Economics (KULeuven, 2006) and is an associate professor at the Institute for Development Policy at the University of Antwerp. Her research focuses on the socio-economic causes and consequences of armed conflict, as well as on natural resources and economic and institutional development in sub-Saharan Africa, with a particular focus on Rwanda, Benin and the DRC. She has been leading a research project in Virunga National Park since 2018, focusing on the impact of the electrification programme and the behaviour of armed groups.

JACQUES VERSCHUREN (†)
Holder of a degree in Zoology and a doctoral degree in Science (Belgium), Jacques Verschuren devoted his life to nature conservation and scientific research. As a biologist of the IPNCB and a Fellow of the Royal Belgian Institute of Natural Sciences, he worked in the Congolese parks between 1948 and 1990, particularly in Virunga National Park. He was Director General of the IZCN between 1969 and 1975. Outside the DRC, he continued his research and conservation activities in Paraguay, Indonesia, Rwanda, Burundi, Tanzania, Senegal, Mauritania, Liberia and Benin. He authored more than 250 scientific publications and popular articles.

JEAN DE DIEU WATHAUT
Jean de Dieu Wathaut is the son of an ICCN warden. He grew up in the PNVi and holds a degree in Development Management (DRC). In 2009, he joined the ICCN in Virunga National Park, where he specialised in geographic information systems, remote sensing and environmental monitoring, particularly for elephants and hippos. Since 2013, he has contributed to wildlife censuses and supervises the Park's ecological monitoring.

VIKTOR WEINAND
Viktor Weinand is a graduate of the Solvay Brussels School of Management (Belgium). He gained initial professional experience as a consultant with McKinsey before joining Virunga National Park in 2022. He manages its entrepreneurship support programme and its investments in partner companies.

JULIE WILLIAMS
Originally from Kenya, Julie Williams studied business management (Great Britain) and fashion (Great Britain) before moving into the tourism sector in Africa. She was a freelance guide and a lodge manager in Kenya, Tanzania and Botswana. In 2015, she joined Virunga National Park, where she heads the tourism department. She also leads the network of widows of deceased rangers established to provide support and an alternative income.

Appendix 7
Bibliography

This section presents the bibliography in two distinct parts. The first gathers the sources cited in the previous chapters, while the second provides a thematic list of the most important references regarding the PNVi and its history. Some references are cited in both sections.

1. References cited in the text

AGRECO-Union européenne, 2006. Revue institutionnelle et Programme de renforcement de l'ICCN et de l'IJZBC. Phase 1 : Bilan-Diagnostic ; Phase 2 : Plan de réforme et programme de renforcement de l'ICCN.

AGRECO-Union européenne, 2006. Revue institutionnelle et Programme de renforcement de l'ICCN et de l'IJZBC. Phase 1 : Bilan-Diagnostic ; Phase 2 : Plan de réforme et programme de renforcement de l'ICCN.

AGRECO-Union européenne, 2012. Projet d'Appui à la Réforme de l'ICCN. Projet FED/2207/018-886. Rapport final 2009-2012.

Akeley, C., 1923. *In Brightest Africa.* Doubleday, New York. 188–249.

Alliance Virunga, 2023. *Rapport annuel 2022 du Parc National des Virunga.* ICCN and Virunga Foundation. 35 pp.

Anderson, D. & Grove, R. (eds.), 1999. Conservation in Africa. *People, Policies and Practice.* Cambridge University Press.

Andersson, A. & Gibson, L. 2018. Missing teeth: Discordances in the trade of hippo ivory between Africa and Hong Kong. *African Journal of Ecology,* 56(2): 235-243.

Anon., 2002. A. von Beringe: On the Trail of the Man who discovered the Mountain Gorilla. *Gorilla Journal,* June 2002.

Aveling, C., 1990. *Comptage aérien total des buffles et éléphants au Parc National des Virunga, octobre 1990.* Unpublished report of the Kivu Programme (European Union), Virunga sub-programme. 6 pp.

Balole Bwami E., 2018. *Estimation de la valeur socio-économique du Parc National des Virunga.* Doctoral thesis, ERAFT/UNIKIN, 222 pp.

Balole Bwami, E., Mumbere, J.C., Matunguru, J., Kujirakwinja, D., Shamavu, P., Muhindo, E., Tchouamo, I.R., Michel, B., & Micha, J.C., 2018. Production et impacts de la pêche sur le Lac Edouard en République Démocratique du Congo. *Tropicultura* 36(3): 539-552.

Banque mondiale, 2021 : Densité de la population (personnes par kilomètre carré de superficie des terres) - Sub-Saharan Africa, Congo, Dem. Rep. | Data (banquemondiale.org) Referenced on 3/7/2024.

Bene, S., 2016. *Étude de la chaîne de valeur poisson, Parc Naturel des Virunga, République démocratique du Congo.* Advisory Service in Social Transfers (ASiST III). Report to the European Union.

Biodiversity Support Programme, 1999. *Study on the Development of Transboundary Natural Resource Management Areas in Southern Africa.* Biodiversity Support Programme, Washington DC.

Bishikwabo, K., 2000. *La situation du Parc National de Kahuzi-Biega au 20 mars 2000.* Unpublished Report.

Biswas, A.K. & Tortajada-Quiroz, H.C. 1996. Environmental Impacts on the Rwandan Refugees in Zaïre. *Ambio* 25: 403–408.

Biswas, A.K., Tortajada-Quiroz, H.C., Lutete, V., & Lemba, G., 1994. *Environmental impact of the Rwandese refugee presence in North and South Kivu (Zaïre).* United Nations Development Programme. 53 pp.

Blom, E., 2000. Conclusions and recommendations. In: Blom E., Bergmans, W. et al. (eds.), Nature in war. *Biodiversity conservation during conflicts* pp. 165–170. Netherlands Commission for International Nature Protection. Mededelingen, 37. Amsterdam.

Blondel, N., 1997. *L'impact des camps de réfugiés sur l'environnement local: étude de cas sur Goma (Nord-Kivu).* One-day seminar 'Satellite information for humanitarian aid', 28 May 1997. Contribution from I-Mage Consult. Unpublished report. 5 pp.

Borges, A.V., Lambert, T., Descy, J.P., Darchambeau, F., Deirmendjian, F., Roland, F., Bouillon, S., Morana, C., Soto, D., Snoeks, J., Van Steenberge, M., Decru, E., Vranken, N., Maetens, H., Diedericks, G., de Merode, E., Okello, W., Bwambale, M., Nankabirwa, A., Musinguzi, L., Nabafue, I., Stoyneva, M., 2021. *Human impacts on ecosystem health and resources of Lake Edward (Hipe).* Final Report. Brussels: Belgian Science Policy Office 2021 – 85 pp. (BRAIN-be - Belgian Research Action through Interdisciplinary Networks).

Bourlière, F. & Verschuren, J., 1960. *Introduction à l'écologie des ongulés du Parc National Albert.* Institut des Parcs Nationaux du Congo Belge. Exploration du Parc National Albert. Volumes 1 and 2. Brussels. 158 pp.

Brabant, H.R.H. the duke of, 1933. Speech delivered at the *African Society in* London, 16 November 1933: *Les Parcs Nationaux et la protection de la nature,* IPNCB, 1937, p. 17.

Bremer, F., 1996. *Réhabilitation du Parc National des Virunga.* Report on the ZOPP workshop of 7 to 9 February 1996 in Goma. GTZ/IZCN. Unpublished.

Burgi, P.-Y., Valade, S., Coppola, D., Boudoire, G., Mavonga, G., Rufino, F., & Tedesco, D., 2021. Unconventional filling dynamics of a pit crater. *Earth and Planetary Science Letters* 576 art. n° 117230.

Cambridge Econometrics, 2020. *Impact économique du Parc National des Virunga 2020-2030.* Report to the Virunga Foundation. Cambridge. 36 pp.

Cammaert, L. & Jadin, Y. 2017. De l'archéologie dans le PNVi au Bâton d'Ishango. In: P. Van Schuylenbergh and H. De Koeijer (eds.), Virunga, Archives et Collections d'un Parc national d'exception. Tervuren, Royal Museum for Central Africa, 107-115.

Christensen, M. & Arsanjani, J.J., 2020. Stimulating implementation of sustainable development goals and conservation action: predicting future land use/cover change in Virunga National Park, Congo. *Sustainability* 2020, 12: 1570.

Cooper, J. & Cooper, M., 1996. Mountain Gorillas, a 1995 update. *African Primates* 2: 30–31.

Cornet d'Elzius, C., 1996. *Ecologie, structure et évolution des Populations des Grands Mammifères du Secteur Central du Parc National des Virunga (Parc National Albert) Zaïre (Congo Belge).* Fondation pour Favoriser les Recherches Scientifiques en Afrique, Belgium. 231 pp.

Crevecoeur, I., Skinner, M.M., Bailey, S.E., Gunz, P., Bortoluzzi, S., et al., 2014. *First Early Hominid from Central Africa (Ishango, Democratic Republic of Congo).* PLoS ONE 9(1): e84652. doi:10.1371/journal.pone.0084652.

Decaro, A. & Debeve, C., 2017. Parc des Virunga : entre préservation de la nature et développement des populations. *Justice & Paix.* 11 October 2017.

de Jong, Y. & Butynski, T., 2023. *Pocket Identification Guide of the Primates of East Africa (Second Edition).* Re: wild, Tropical Pocket Guide Series. R.A. Mittermeier & A. B. Rylands (eds.).

Delvingt, W., 1978. *Ecologie de l'hippopotame au Parc National des Virunga.* Doctoral thesis, Gembloux Agro-Bio Tech (Liège), 2 volumes. 333 pp.

Delvingt, W., 1994. Étude préparatoire du programme spécial de réhabilitation pour les pays voisins du Rwanda (PSSR), volet environnement. Report of a mission to Zaïre. Gembloux Agro-Bio Tech (Liège), Forestry. 28 pp.

Delvingt, W., 1996. L'intervention de l'Union Européenne dans le Parc National des Virunga. *African Primates* 2: 28–30.

Delvingt, W., Lejoly, J. & Mankoto, M., 1990. *Guide du Parc National des Virunga.* Commission des Communautés Européennes. 192 pp.

de Saint Moulin, L., 1987. Essai d'histoire de la population du Zaire. In : Zaire-Afrique. Kinshasa Gombe, Vol. 27(217): 389-407.

Desbureaux, S., 2021. Subjective modeling choices and the robustness of impact evaluations in conservation science. *Conservation Biology,* 35(5): 1615-1626.

d'Huart, J.P., 1971. *Révision et nouvelles recherches sur la biologie du phacochère* (Phacochoerus aethiopicus Pallas). Mémoire de Licence en Sciences Zoologiques. UC. 187 pp.

d'Huart, J.P., 1978. *Ecologie de l'hylochère* (Hylochoerus meinertzhageni Thomas) *au Parc National des Virunga.* Exploration du Parc National des Virunga, 2ème série, Fasc.25. Fondation pour Favoriser les Recherches Scientifiques en Afrique. Brussels. 156 pp.

d'Huart, J.P., 1987. *Parc National des Virunga (Kivu, Zaïre): état des lieux et recommandations pour un projet d'appui de la Commission des Communautés Européennes.* Mission report to the EC. 89 pp.

d'Huart, J.P., 2003. *Statut de conservation et proposition de réhabilitation des Parcs Nationaux de la Garamba et des Virunga (RDC).* Report on an identification mission and proposition for an intervention to prepare a GEF/World Bank support project. 59 pp.

d'Huart, J.P. & Brugière, D., 2013. *Rapport d'évaluation à mi-parcours de la mise en œuvre du Plan stratégique GVTC 2006-2016.* Greater Virunga Transboundary Collaboration. June 2013. BRLi/GVTC. 28 pp.

Gill, F., Donsker, D. & Rasmussen, P. (eds.), 2024. *IOC World Bird List* (v14.1). doi: 10.14344/IOC.ML.14.1. http://www.worldbirdnames.org/

Gray, M., Fawcett, K., Basabose, A., Cranfield, M., Vigilant, L., Roy, J., Uwingeli, P., Mburanumwe, I., Kagoda, E. & Robbins, M., 2013. *Virunga Massif Mountain Gorilla Census 2010.* Summary Report.

Groom, A.F.G., 1973. Squeezing out the mountain gorillas. *Oryx,* 2: 207-215.

Harcourt, A.H., & Groom, A.F.G. 1972. Gorilla census. *Oryx,* 11: 355-363.

Harcourt, A.H., Kineman, J., Campbell, G., Yamagiwa, J., Redmond, I., Aveling, C., & Condiotti, M., 1983. Conservation and the Virunga gorilla population. *African Journal of Ecology,* 21: 139–142.

Harroy, J.P., 1949. *Afrique, terre qui meurt.* Marcel Hayez, Éditeur-Imprimeur, Brussels. 557 pp.

Harroy, J.P., 1985. Soixantième anniversaire d'un parc national zaïrois. *Bull. Séances. Acad. Roy. Sci. Outre-Mer*, 31(4): 507-516.

Henquin, B. & Blondel, N., 1996. Étude par télédétection sur l'évolution récente de la couverture boisée du Parc National des Virunga. Project Report PSRR/PNVi, UE-ADG-UNHR-IZCN. 80 pp.

Henquin, B. & Blondel, N., 1997. Étude par télédétection sur l'évolution récente de la couverture boisée du Parc National des Virunga, deuxième partie (période 1995-1996). Project Report PSRR/PNVi, UE-ADG-UNHCR-IZCN. 63 pp.

Hickey, J.R., Granjon, A.C., Vigilant, L., Eckardt, W., Gilardi, K.V., Cranfield, M., Musana, A., Masozera, A.B., Babaasa, D., Ruzigandekwe, F., Leendertz, F.H., & Robbins, M.M., 2019. *Virunga 2015–2016 surveys: monitoring mountain gorillas, other select mammals, and illegal activities.* GVTC, IGCP & partners' Report. Kigali, Rwanda.

Hoier, R., 1952. *Mammifères du Parc National Albert.* Collections Lebègue et Nationale n° 105. Brussels. 111 pp.

Hubert, E.J., 1947. *La faune des grands mammifères de la plaine Rwindi-Rutshuru (Lac Édouard). Son évolution depuis sa protection totale.* Institut des Parcs Nationaux du Congo Belge. Brussels. 84 pp.

ICCN, 1999. Séminaire sur les Sites du Patrimoine Mondial en danger en République Démocratique du Congo. Naivasha, 12–16 April 1999. Final Report. 37 pp.

ICCN, 2006. *Liste du personnel de l'ICCN.* Kinshasa.

ICCN & Virunga Foundation, 2015. Contrat de Gestion du Parc National des Virunga. 14 pp.

INCN/IZCN, 1973–1977. *Léopard* magazines 1 - 5.

IPNCB, 1935. *Rapport du Conseil Colonial sur le projet de décret organisant l'IPNCB.* Bulletin Officiel 1935, p. 64.

IPNCB, 1937. *Les Parcs Nationaux et la Protection de la Nature.* Institut des Parcs Nationaux du Congo Belge. 88 pp.

IPNCB, 1942. *Premier rapport quinquennal, (1935–1939).* Institut des Parcs Nationaux du Congo Belge. 75 pp.

IPNCB, 1956, 1960. *Rapports annuels 1956 et 1960.* Institut des Parcs Nationaux du Congo Belge.

IUCN, 1994. *Guidelines for protected area management categories.* IUCN and WCMC. Gland, Switzerland and Cambridge, UK.

IZCN, 1975. Annual Report 1975. 80 pp.

Kalpers, J., 1996. *Suivi systématique de deux sites du patrimoine mondial: PN des Virunga et PN de Kahuzi-Biega. Mission du 22 avril au 9 mai 1996.* Mission Report to the Office of the World Heritage Committee. Unesco, Paris. 30 pp.

Kalpers, J., 1998. *Projet de réhabilitation des capacités de gestion de l'ICCN au Parc National des Virunga, secteur sud.* Activity report 2nd semester of 1997 from IGCP to UNHCR and WWF-NL.

Kalpers, J. & Lanjouw, A., 1997. Potential for the creation of a peace park in the Virunga volcano region. *Parks*, 7: 25-35.

Kalpers, J. & Lanjouw, A., 1998. *Projet de réhabilitation des capacités de gestion de l'ICCN au Parc National des Virunga, secteur sud. Financement UNHCR, premier semestre 1997.* Activity report from the International Gorilla Conservation Programme. Nairobi.

Kalpers, J., Williamson, E., Robbins, M., McNeilage, A., Nzamurambaho, A., Lola, N. & Mugiri, G., 2003. Gorillas in the crossfire: Population dynamics of the Virunga mountain gorillas over the past three decades. *Oryx*, 37(3): 326-337.

Kambere Mulwahali, J.C., Balole, E., Shamavu, P., Muhindo, E., Kambale, E., Biloko, F., Mukura, J., van Damme, P., Lain, T., Matunguru, J., Kalemeko, C., Biloko M., & Kitambala, B., 2015. *Le lac Édouard en RDC: leçons pour la gestion de la pêche.* Unpublished UICN-NL report.

Kasonia, F. & Mushenzi, N., 2006. L'histoire de la COPE-VI: l'utilisation et la gestion du lac Edouard. pp 165-169. In: Languy, M. & de Merode, E. (eds): *Virunga: survie du premier Parc d'Afrique.* Lannoo, Tielt.

Kujirakwinja, D., Plumptre, A., Moyer, D., & Mushenzi, N., 2006. *Parc National des Virunga. Recensement aérien des grands mammifères 2006.* Unpublished report to the ICCN, Kinshasa.

Kujirakwinja, D. & Balole, E., 2013. *Recensement des Hippopotames au Parc National des Virunga 2013.* Unpublished ICCN-WCS report.

Kujirakwinja, D., Shamavu, P., Wathaut, J.D., Plumptre, A., de Merode, E. & Muhindo, E., 2016. Conservation of the common hippopotamus in Virunga National Park, eastern Democratic Republic of Congo. *Suiform Soundings.* 15(1): 5-10.

Kümpel, N.F., Quinn, A., Queslin, E., Grange, S., Mallon, D., & Mapilanga, J.J., 2015. *Okapi* (Okapia johnstoni): Stratégie et Revue du statut de conservation. Gland, Switzerland: IUCN and the Congolese Institute for Nature Conservation (ICCN), 62 pp.

Lamprey, R., 2024. *Aerial survey of wildlife in Virunga National Park and Queen Elizabeth Protected Area. June 2023.* Report to UWA and ICCN.

Languy, M., 1994. *Recensement des hippopotames dans le Parc National des Virunga, 14-17 juillet 1994.* Unpublished report. WWF International, Gland, Switzerland. 15 pp.

Languy, M., 1995. *Problèmes environnementaux liés à la présence des réfugiés rwandais. Identification des interventions réalisées. Coordination entre les organismes et propositions d'interventions complémentaires.* Mission report to the UNDP. 29 pp.

Languy, M., 2005. *Compilation et analyse des textes légaux délimitant le Parc National des Virunga. Programme de renforcement des capacités de gestion de l'ICCN et appui à la réhabilitation d'aires protégées en RDC.* Technical sheet no1. WWF-EARPO, Nairobi. 20 pp.

Languy, M. & de Merode, E. (eds.), 2006. *Virunga : survie du premier Parc d'Afrique.* Lannoo, Tielt, Belgium. 352 pp.

Languy, M., Hugel, B. & Buliard, Y., 2011. *Le processus de démarcation participative des limites du Parc National des Virunga.* Programme to strengthen the management capabilities of the ICCN-CINC and support the rehabilitation of protected areas in the DRC. Technical sheet n°5. WWF-ESARPO, Nairobi, 30 pp.

Lebrun, J., 1947. *La végétation de la plaine alluviale au sud du Lac Edouard.* Exploration du Parc National Albert. Institut des Parcs Nationaux du Congo Belge. 800 pp.

Leusch, M., 1995. HCR Goma–Unité Environnement. Interim Report 15 February - 11 August 1995. UNHCR, in collaboration with partners of the Environmental Information Office (European Union, GTZ Goma, PNUD Goma). 105 pp.

Lippens, L. & Wille, H. 1976. *Les Oiseaux du Zaïre.* Lannoo, Tielt, Belgium. 512 pp.

Lunanga, E., Maombi, E., Stoop, N. & Verpoorten, M., 2022. *Powering development, stabilization and conservation? The impact of electricity rollout by Virunga Alliance in Eastern DR Congo.* Ongoing IOB research project, University of Antwerp.

Mackie, C., 1989. *Recensement des Hippopotames au Parc National des Virunga. Leur impact sur la végétation et sur les sols.* Unpublished report to the Zairian Institute for the Conservation of Nature, Kinshasa. 78 pp.

McPherson L., 1991. Étude institutionnelle de l'Institut Zaïrois pour la Conservation de la Nature. Partie 1 : organisation, gestion, ressources humaines. *Banque Mondiale.* (Abstract). 20 pp.

Mertens, H., 1983. Recensements aériens des principaux ongulés du Parc National des Virunga, Zaïre. *Revue d'Ecologie Terre et Vie*, 38: 51–64.

Minissale, S., Casalini, M., Cucciniello, C., Balagizi, C., Tedesco, D., Boudoire, G., Morra, V., & Melluso, L., 2019. The petrology and geochemistry of Nyiragongo lavas of 2002, 2016, 1977 and 2017 AD, and the trace element partitioning between melilitite glass and melilite, nepheline, leucite, clinopyroxene, apatite, olivine and Fe-Ti oxides: a unique scenario. *Lithos* 332/333: 296-311.

Mondol, S., Moltke, I., Hart, J., Keigwin, M., Brown, L., Stephens, M., & Wasser, S. K., 2015. New evidence for hybrid zones of forest and savanna elephants in Central and West Africa. *Molecular Ecology*, 24(24): 6134-6147.

Morisho, N., Lubula, M.E., Sematumba, O., Barengeke, A., & Senzira, P., 2022. *Financement des groupes armés à l'est de la RD Congo, fondement d'une économie criminelle. Le cas de la Province du Nord-Kivu.* Technical report. Pole Institute. 61 pp.

Musana, A., Masozera, A.B., Babaasa, D., Ruzigandekwe, F., Leendertz, F.H. & Robbins, M.M., 2019. *Virunga 2015–2016 surveys: monitoring mountain gorillas, other select mammals, and illegal activities.* Report GVTC, IGCP & partners. Kigali, Rwanda.

Mushenzi, N., 1996. *Rapport de mission: état actuel du Parc National des Virunga dans les Secteurs Centre et Sud. Infrastructures, administration et surveillance.* Direction Régionale des Parcs Nationaux, Région du Nord-Kivu. Goma, DRC.

Muzinga Lola, N., 2001. *Les conflits ethniques et les problèmes d'identité dans la République Démocratique du Congo, cas des Banyamulenge.* Mémoire, Université de Sherbrooke, Montréal. 174 pp.

Ndaywel è Nziem, I., 1998. *Histoire du Congo. De l'héritage ancien à l'âge contemporain.* Duculot, Paris, 955 pp.

Nzabandora, N., 2003. *Histoire de conserver : évolution des relations socio-économiques et ethno écologiques entre les parcs nationaux du Kivu et les populations avoisinantes (RD Congo).* Doctoral thesis in history, Université Libre de Bruxelles, 600 pp.

Petit P., 2006. *Les pêches dans la partie congolaise du lac Edouard: Analyse de la situation actuelle.* Report Vredeseilanden (VECO), 54 pp.

Petrželková, K.J., Uwamahoro, C., Pafčo, B., Červená, B., Samaš, P., Mudakikwa, A., & Modrý, D., 2021. Heterogeneity in patterns of helminth infections across populations of mountain gorillas (Gorilla beringei beringei). *Scientific Reports*, 11(1): 10869.

Pironio, E. & Mayaux, P. (eds.), 2016. *Larger than elephants: input for an EU strategic approach for African Wildlife Conservation.* DG for International Cooperation and Development. European Commission. Brussels, 500 pp.

Plumptre, A., Davenport, T., Behangana, M., Kityo, R., Eilu, G., Ssegawa, P., Ewango, C., Meirte, D., Kahindo, C., Herremans, M., Kerbis, J., Pilgrim, J., Wilson, M., Languy, M., & Moyer, D., 2007. The Biodiversity of the Albertine Rift. *Biological Conservation* 134. 178-194. 10.1016/j.biocon.2006.08.021.

Plumptre, A., Kujirakwinja, D., Moyer, D., Driciru, M., & Rwetsiba, A., 2010. *Greater Virunga Landscape: large mammal surveys 2010.* Report to ICCN-UWA-WCS.

Refisch, J. & Jenson, J., 2016. Transboundary collaboration in Greater Virunga Landscape: From gorilla conservation to conflict-sensitive transboundary landscape management. in: *Governance, Natural Resources, and Post-Conflict Peacebuilding.* Carl Bruch, Carroll Muffett, Sandra S. Nichols (eds.). 825-841. Earthscan, Routledge.

Robbins, M.M., Gray, M., Fawcett, K.A., Nutter, F.B., Uwingeli, P., Mburanumwe, I., & Robbins, A.M., 2011. Extreme conservation leads to recovery of the Virunga mountain gorillas. *PloS one* 6(6), e19788.

Rutagarama, E., 1999. *Initiatives d'implication des populations dans des micro-projets de gestion du Parc National des Volcans. Rapport préliminaire d'exécution des projets.* Unpublished report to PICG, Rwanda. 9 pp.

Schaller, G., 1963. *The mountain gorilla: Ecology and Behavior.* Ph.D. Thesis. University of Chicago Press, Chicago.

Schoelynck J., Subalusky, A.L., Struyf, E., Dutton, C.L., Unzue-Belmonte, D., Van de Vijver, B., Post, D.M., Rosi, E.J., Meire, P. & Frings, P., 2019. Hippos (*Hippopotamus amphibius*): The animal silicon pump. *Science Advances*, 5(5): eaav0395.

Sclater, P.L., 1901. (sans titre). *Proc. Zool. Soc. Lond.* 1901 (1): 50.

Shamavu, P., Wathaut, J., Standaert, S., Mashagiro, D., Katutu, J., Kakiri, M., Kazerezi, M., Musafiri, A., & de Merode, E. 2018. *Parc National des Virunga: Comptage aérien des grands mammifères – Août 2018.* ICCN – WCS Report.

Stoop, N. & Verpoorten, M., 2024. *Jobs and Violence: Evidence from a policy experiment in DR Congo*. IOB Policy brief, University of Antwerp, June 2024.

Stuhlmann, F., 1894. *Mit Emin Pascha in Herz von Afrika. Ein Reisebericht mit Beiträge von Dr Emin Pasha, in seinem Auftrage geschildert,* Berlin, Dietrich Reimer, 1894. 205-305.

Tedesco, D., Tassi, F., Vaselli, O., Poreda, R.J., Darrah, T., Cuoco, E., & Yalire, M.M. 2010. Gas isotopic signatures (He, C, and Ar) in the Lake Kivu region (western branch of the East African rift system): Geodynamic and volcanological implications. *Journal of Geophysical Research: Solid Earth* 115 (1), art. n° B01205.

Thorsell, J.W. (ed.), 1991. *Parks on the Borderline: Experience in Transfrontier Conservation.* IUCN Gland, Switzerland. 98 pp.

Tombola, J.P. & Sanders, C., 1994. *Résultats de l'enquête sur l'impact des réfugiés rwandais sur le Parc National des Virunga (secteur sud).* Unpublished report to the UNHCR, technical department.

Treves, A., Plumptre, A., Hunter, L., & Ziwa, J., 2009. Identifying a potential lion *Panthera leo* stronghold in Queen Elizabeth National Park, Uganda and Parc National des Virunga, Democratic Republic of Congo. *Oryx*, 43: 658.

UNESCO, 1995. Convention concerning the Protection of the World Cultural and Natural Heritage. World Heritage Committee. 19th session, Berlin, 4-9 December 1995.

UNESCO, 1999. *Biodiversity conservation in regions of armed conflict: protecting World Heritage in the Democratic Republic of the Congo (DRC). Project Review Form.* Unesco World Heritage Centre, Paris.

UNESCO, 2000. *Rapport synthétique de la mission intermédiaire de l'UNESCO sur les sites du patrimoine mondial en péril en République démocratique du Congo.* 24th session of the Office of the World Heritage Committee.

Upham, N., Burgin, C., Widness, J., Liphart, S., Parker, C., Becker, M., Rochon, I., Huckaby, D., 2022. *Mammal Diversity Database*. Version 1,9. https://zenodo.org/doi/10.5281/zenodo.4139722 Referenced on 3/7/2024

Vakily, J.M., 1989. *Les pêches dans la partie zaïroise du Lac Idi Amin: analyse de la situation actuelle et potentiel de développement.* Report to DAFECN and the EC. Kinshasa. 18 pp.

Van Schuylenbergh, P., 2006. *De l'appropriation à la conservation de la faune sauvage. Pratiques d'une colonisation : le cas du Congo belge, 1885-1960*. Doctoral thesis in history. UC Louvain, 327 pp.

Van Schuylenbergh, P., 2015. Virunga, star des médias. Les tribulations du plus ancien parc naturel d'Afrique, in: *Le Temps des médias*, 25(2): 85-103.

Van Schuylenbergh, P., 2016. Contribution à l'histoire du lac Edouard : enjeux socio-économiques et environnementaux autour des ressources halieutiques (ca 1920-1960), in: P. Mantuba-Ngoma et M. Zana Etambala (eds.), *La société congolaise face à la modernité (ca.1700-2010). Mélanges eurafricains offerts à Jean-Luc Vellut*, Cahiers africains, 89. MRAC/ L'Harmattan, Tervuren/Paris. pp 127-163.

Van Schuylenbergh, P. & de Koeijer, H. (eds.), 2017. *Virunga. Archives et collections d'un parc national d'exception.* Royal Museum for Central Africa, Tervuren (MRAC and IRSNB Collections Series). 189 pp.

Van Schuylenbergh, P. 2019a. Entre chasse, science et diplomatie. Le "Parc national Albert" et la question de l'internationalisme. In: Vanderlinden, J. and Vanthemsche, G. (ed.), *The Belgian Congo between the Two World Wars*. International Conference, Brussels, 17-18 March 2016, Royal Academy for Overseas Sciences, Brussels, pp 211-240.

Van Schuylenbergh, P., 2019b. *Faune sauvage et colonisation. Une histoire de destruction et de protection de la nature congolaise (1885-1960)*. Collection Outre-Mers, vol. 8. Peter Lang, Bruxelles-Bern-Berlin-Istanbul-New York-Oxford-Warsawa-Wien, 376 pp.

Vedder, A. & Aveling, C., 1986. *Census of the Virunga population of Gorilla gorilla beringei.* Unpublished report, September 1986.

Veetil, B. K. & Kamp, U., 2019. Global disappearance of tropical mountain glaciers: observations, causes, and challenges. *Geosciences*, 9(5): 196.

Verschuren, J., 1965. Un facteur de mortalité mal connu, l'asphyxie par gaz toxiques naturels au Parc National Albert, Congo. *La Terre et la Vie* 3: 215-237.

Verschuren, J., 1972. *Contribution à l'écologie des Primates, Pholidota, Carnivora, Tubulidentata et Hyracoidea (Mammifères).* Exploration du Parc National des Virunga, Mission F. Bourlière et J. Verschuren, 3:1-61.

Verschuren, J., 1986. *Observation des habitats et de la faune après soixante ans de conservation.* Exploration du Parc National des Virunga (Zaïre), Fondation pour Favoriser les Recherches Scientifiques en Afrique, Belgium. Fascicule 26. 44 pp.

Verschuren, J., 1993. *Les Habitats et la Grande Faune: Evolution et Situation Récente.* Exploration du Parc National des Virunga (Zaïre). Fascicule 29. 133 pp.

Verschuren, J., 2001. *Ma Vie, Sauver la Nature.* Editions de la Dyle. Ghent. 529 pp.

Vikanza, K., 2018. *La protection du Parc national des Virunga en région de Butembo (R. D. Congo) : développement durable ou développement des populations?* Mondes en développement 181(1): 57-70.

von Götzen, G., 1899. Durch Afrika von Ost nach West. Resultaten und Begebenheiten einer Reise von der Deutsch-Ostafrikanischen Küste bis zur Kongomündung in den Jahren 1893/94, Berlin, Dietrich Reimer, pp 201-246.

Wanyama, F., Balole, E., Elkan, P., Mendiguetti, S., Ayebare, S., Kisame, F., Shamavu, P., Kato, R., Okiring, D., Loware, S., Wathaut, J., Tumonakiese, B., Mashagiro, D., Barendse, T., & Plumptre, A. 2014. *Aerial surveys of the Greater Virunga Landscape.* Technical Report WCS-ICCN-UWA.

Wathaut, A., 1996. État des lieux du PNVi-sud, une année et demi après l'*installation des réfugiés rwandais dans et en bordure du parc.* Zaïrian Institute for Nature Conservation. Virunga National Park. Rumangabo station, RDC.

Wathaut, J.D. et al. 2017, 2018, 2019, 2020, 2021, 2022. Bi-annual monitoring of the Hippopotamuses. ICCN-Virunga Foundation Reports.

Weber, W., 1989. *Conservation and Development on the Zaïre-Nile Divide. An analysis of value conflicts and convergence in the management of afro-montane forests.* PhD Thesis, University of Wisconsin, Madison, 329 pp.

Weber, W. & Vedder, A., 1983. Population Dynamics of the Virunga Gorillas: 1959–1978. *Biological Conservation,* 26: 341-366.

Werikhe S., Mushenzi Lusenge, N. & Bizimana, J., 1997. *The impact of war on protected areas in Central Africa. Case study of Virunga Volcanoes Region*. International Conference on Transboundary Protected areas as a vehicle for international co-operation, Cape Town, South Africa, 16-18 September 1997. 8 pp.

Werikhe S., Mushenzi Lusenge, N., & Bizimana J., 1998. L'impact de la guerre sur les aires protégées dans la région des Grands Lacs. Le cas de la région des volcans Virunga. *Cahiers d'Ethologie,* 18: 175-186.

William (Prince) of Sweden, 1923. *Among Pygmies and Gorillas. With the Swedish zoological expedition to central Africa, 1921,* Gyldendal. Copenhagen-Berlin-Christiania, 148-149.

Wilson, D.E. & Reeder D.M. (eds.), 2005. *Mammal Species of the World. A taxonomic and geographic reference.* 3rd edition, Vols. 1 and 2. The Johns Hopkins University Press, Baltimore, USA. 2141 pp.

2. A selection of important references specific to the Albert National Park/ Virunga National Park

A. General references

Akeley, C., 1923. *In Brightest Africa*. New York, Doubleday. 188-249.

Anon., 1934. *Parc National Albert, Congo Belge*. Commission du Parc National Albert. 61 pp.

Anon., 1964. *Victor Van Straelen : Tel qu'il demeure*. Renson International Marketing. Brussels. 126 pp.

Auguste, C., 1934. La protection de la nature au Congo belge et le rôle du Roi des belges. Historique du Parc National Albert. *Revue de botanique appliquée et d'agriculture coloniale*, 153: 317-322.

Balole Bwami E., 2018. *Estimation de la valeur socio-économique du Parc National des Virunga*. Doctoral thesis, ERAFT/ UNIKIN, 222 pp.

Cambridge Econometrics, 2020. *Impact économique du Parc National de Virunga 2020-2030*. Report to the Virunga Foundation. Cambridge, 36 pp.

Curry-Lindahl, K., 1956. *Ecological studies on Mammals, Birds, Reptiles and Amphibians in the Eastern Belgian Congo. Part I*. Ann. Musée Roy. Congo Belge, Tervuren, Sciences Zoologiques, vol 42. 75 pp.

Curry-Lindahl, K., 1960. *Ecological studies on Mammals, Birds, Reptiles and Amphibians in the Eastern Belgian Congo. Part II*. Ann. Musée Roy. Congo Belge, Tervuren, Sciences Zoologiques, vol 87. 170 pp.

de Heinzelin de Braucourt, J., 1955. *Le fossé tectonique sous le parallèle d'Ishango*. Exploration du Parc National Albert, Mission J. de Heinzelin de Braucourt, fasc.1. Institut des Parcs Nationaux du Congo Belge. 150 pp.

de Heinzelin de Braucourt, J., 1957. *Les fouilles d'Ishango*. Exploration du Parc National Albert, Mission J. de Heinzelin de Braucourt, fasc.2. Institut des Parcs Nationaux du Congo Belge. 128 pp.

Delvingt, W. & d'Huart, J.P., 1972. Conservation et recherche scientifique au Parc National des Virunga : la Station de Lulimbi, Zaïre. *Biological Conservation,* 4(5): 397.

Delvingt, W., 1994. Étude préparatoire du programme spécial de réhabilitation pour les pays voisins du Rwanda (PSSR), volet environnement. Rapport d'*une mission effectuée au Zaïre, 24/11-05/12/94*. Faculté des Sciences Agronomiques de Gembloux, Sylviculture, 28 pp.

Delvingt, W., Lejoly, J. & Mankoto, M., 1990. *Guide du Parc National des Virunga*. Commission des Communautés Européennes. 192 pp.

Derscheid, J.M., 1927. *La protection scientifique de la nature*. Self-published, 77 pp.

De Saeger, H., 1955. Le Parc National Albert : la Plaine. *Parcs Nationaux* 10(4): 3-12.

De Saeger, H., 1957. Les Parcs nationaux du Congo belge : Le Tourisme. *Parcs Nationaux* 12(4): 3-16.

de Witte, G.F., 1937. *Exploration du Parc National Albert. Introduction.* Mission G.F. de Witte, (1933–1935), fasc.1. Institut des Parcs Nationaux du Congo Belge. 39 pp.

d'Huart, J.P., 2003. *Renforcement des capacités de gestion et réhabilitation des aires protégées en République Démocratique du Congo*. Report on an identification mission and funding proposition submitted to the European Commission.

d'Huart, J.P., 2018 : *Plan d'aménagement et de gestion du Parc National des Virunga 2018-2022*. Draft submitted to the Virunga Foundation/ICCN. 101 pp.

d'Huart, J.P. & Verschuren, J., 2014. National background to Conservation in Congo: Early History. pp 100-

114. in: Hillman Smith, K., Kalpers, J., Arranz, L., & Ortega, N. (eds.) 2014: *Garamba: Conservation in Peace and War.* Published by the authors. 448 pp.

Frechkop, S., 1941. *Animaux protégés au Congo Belge.* Institut des Parcs Nationaux du Congo Belge. 469 pp.

Harroy, J.P., 1941. Les parcs nationaux du Congo Belge en 1939 et 1940. *Bull. Agric. Congo Belge,* 32(3): 454-495.

Harroy, J.P., 1987. Soixantième anniversaire d'un parc national zaïrois. *Bull. Séances. Acad. Roy. Sci. Outre-Mer,* 31(4): 507-516.

Harroy, J.P., 1993. *Contribution à l'histoire jusque 1934 de la création de l'Institut des Parcs nationaux du Congo belge.* in : Thoveron, G. et Legros, M., Mélanges Pierre Salmon, t. II: pp. 427-442. Histoire et ethnologie africaines, ULB. Brussels.

Hoier, R., 1950. *A travers plaines et volcans au Parc National Albert.* Institut des Parcs Nationaux du Congo Belge. Brussels. 173 pp.

INCN/IZCN, 1973–1977. *Léopard* magazine, n° 1-5.

IPNCB, 1935. *Rapport du Conseil Colonial sur le projet de décret organisant l'IPNCB.* Bulletin Officiel, 1935, p. 64.

IPNCB, 1935. *Décret Constitutif.* Institut des Parcs Nationaux du Congo Belge. 27 pp.

IPNCB, 1937. *Les Parcs Nationaux et la Protection de la Nature.* Institut des Parcs Nationaux du Congo Belge. 88 pp.

IPNCB, 1942. *Premier rapport quinquennal, (1935–1939).* Institut des Parcs Nationaux du Congo Belge. 75 pp.

IPNCB, 1944. *Recueil à l'usage des membres du personnel d'Afrique et spécialement des conservateurs de l'IPNCB. Edition provisoire.* Institut des Parcs Nationaux du Congo Belge. 122 pp.

IPNCB, 1946. *Parc National Albert. Liste des Localités.* Institut des Parcs Nationaux du Congo Belge. 19 pp.

Kabala, M., 1976. *Aspects de la conservation de la Nature au Zaïre.* Institut zaïrois pour la Conservation de la Nature, Editions Lokole, Kinshasa. 312 pp.

Languy, M., 1994. *Parc National des Virunga, Zaïre. Stratégie de la conservation à long terme des écosystèmes et ébauche d'un plan directeur du parc national.* WWF/IZCN report to the World Bank. 50 pp.

Languy, M., 2005. *Compilation et analyse des textes légaux délimitant le Parc National des Virunga. Programme de renforcement des capacités de gestion de l'ICCN et appui à la réhabilitation d'aires protégées en RDC.* Technical sheet no 1. 20 pp.

Languy, M. & de Merode, E. (eds.), 2006. *Virunga : survie du premier Parc d'Afrique.* Lannoo, Tielt, Belgium. 352 pp.

Languy, M., Hugel, B. & Buliard, Y., 2011: *Le processus de démarcation participative des limites du Parc National des Virunga.* Programme de renforcement des capacités de gestion de l'ICCN et appui à la réhabilitation d'aires protégées en RDC. Technical sheet n°5. WWF-ESARPO, Nairobi, 30 pp.

Lippens, L., 1937. *Parmi les bêtes de la brousse. Instantanés.* Ed. Raymond Dupriez. Brussels. 129 pp.

Mankoto ma Mbaelele, S., 1978. *Problématique de la mise en valeur globale et intégrée du Parc National des Virunga, Zaïre.* Master's thesis, Université Laval (Canada). 303 pp.

Mankoto ma Mbaelele, S., 1989. *Problèmes d'écologie au Parc National des Virunga. Exploration du PNVi.* Fondation pour favoriser les recherches scientifiques en Afrique, 2ème série, fascicule. 28. 63 pp.

McPherson L., 1991. *Étude institutionnelle de l'Institut Zaïrois pour la Conservation de la Nature. Partie 1 : organisation, gestion, ressources humaines.* Report to the World Bank (abstract). 20 pp.

Plumptre, A. (ed.), 2012. *The Ecological Impact of Long-term Changes in Africa's Rift Valley.* Environmental science, engineering and technology series. Nova Science Publishers, 308 pp.

Plumptre, A., Davenport, T., Behangana, M., Kityo, R., Eilu, G., Ssegawa, P., Ewango, C., Meirte, D., Kahindo, C., Herremans, M., Kerbis, J., Pilgrim, J., Wilson, M., Languy, M., & Moyer, D., 2007. The Biodiversity of the Albertine Rift. *Biological Conservation* 134. 178-194. 10.1016/j.biocon.2006.08.021.

Plumptre, A., Kayitare, A., Rainer, H., Gray, M., Munanura, I., Barakabuye, N., Asuma, S., Sivha, M., & Namara, A., 2004. *The socio-economic status of people living near protected areas in the central Albertine rift.* Albertine Rift Technical Reports n°4. 127 pp.

Prigogine, A., 1987. Quelques commentaires à l'occasion du soixantième anniversaire du Parc National des Virunga. *Bull. Séances Acad. Roy. Sci. Outre-Mer,* 31(4): 551–554.

Shalaby, H., Bangui, C., d'Huart, J.P., & Bal, J., 2012. *Evaluation Environnementale Stratégique de l'exploration/exploitation pétrolière dans le nord du Rift Albertin. Phase 1 : Etude de cadrage.* Demande n° 2011/268166. Bureau CCM/SAFEGE. 79 pp. + annual report submitted to the UE/DRC.

Van Schuylenbergh, P., 2015. Virunga, star des médias. Les tribulations du plus ancien parc naturel d'Afrique. In: *Le Temps des médias,* 25(2): 85-103.

Van Schuylenbergh, P. & de Koeijer, H. (eds.), 2017. *Virunga. Archives et collections d'un parc national d'exception.* Royal Museum for Central Africa, Tervuren (Series MRAC and IRSNB Collections). 189 pp.

Van Straelen, V. 1943. Le concept de la réserve naturelle intégrale au Congo Belge. *Bull. Inst. Colon. Belge* 14(2) : 398-417.

Verschuren, J., 1988. *Problèmes scientifiques et techniques au Parc National des Virunga (Zaïre).* Mission report to the Belgian General Administration for Development Cooperation and the Zairian Institute for Nature Conservation. 132 pp.

Virunga Foundation, 2008: *Virunga Alliance: Stability through Sustainable Development in Eastern Congo.* Presentation folder.

B. Mammals

Aveling, C., 1990. *Comptage aérien total des buffles et éléphants au Parc National des Virunga, octobre 1990.* Unpublished report. Kivu programme, Virunga sub-programme. 6 pp.

Aveling, C. & Harcourt, A.H., 1984. A census of the Virunga gorillas. *Oryx,* 18: 8–13.

Bashonga, G., 2006. *A propos de la présence des Okapis et autres mammifères sur la rive gauche de la moyenne Semliki, Secteur Nord, Parc National des Virunga.* WWF mission report. 19 pp.

Bourlière, F. & Verschuren, J., 1960. *Introduction à l'écologie des ongulés du Parc National Albert.* Institut des Parcs Nationaux du Congo Belge. Exploration du Parc National Albert. Fasc.1 and 2. Brussels. 158 pp.

Cornet d'Elzius, C., 1996. Écologie, structure et évolution des populations des grands mammifères du secteur central du Parc National des Virunga (Parc National Albert) Zaïre (Congo Belge). Fondation pour Favoriser les Recherches Scientifiques en Afrique, Belgium. 231 pp.

Curry-Lindahl, K., 1961. *Contribution à l'étude des Vertébrés Terrestres en Afrique tropicale.* Institut des Parcs Nationaux du Congo et du Ruanda-Urundi, fasc.1. 331 pp.

Delvingt, W., 1978. *Ecologie de l'hippopotame au Parc National des Virunga.* Doctoral thesis, Fac. Sc. Agr. Gembloux, 2 vols. 333 pp.

de Witte, G.F., 1938. *Mammifères.* Exploration du Parc National Albert. Institut des Parcs Nationaux du Congo Belge, Brussels.

d'Huart, J.P., 1978. *Ecologie de l'hylochère* (Hylochoerus meinertzhageni *Thomas) au Parc National des Virunga.* Exploration Parc National des Virunga, 2ème série, fasc. 25. Fondation pour Favoriser les Recherches Scientifiques en Afrique. Brussels. 156 pp.

Frechkop, S., 1938. *Mammifères.* Exploration du Parc National Albert. Mission G.F. de Witte (1933–1935), fascicule 10. Institut des Parcs Nationaux du Congo Belge. Brussels. 103 pp.

Frechkop, S., 1943. *Mammifères.* Exploration du Parc National Albert. Mission S. Frechkop (1938), fasc. 1. Institut des Parcs Nationaux du Congo Belge. Brussels. 186 pp.

Frechkop, S., 1950. Parmi les mammifères de l'est du Congo Belge. *La Terre et la Vie,* 1: 1–15.

Gray, M., McNeilage, A., Fawcett, K., Robbins, M.M., Ssebide, B., Mbula, D. & Uwingeli, P., 2005. *Virunga Volcano Range Mountain Gorilla Census 2003.* Unpublished report to UWA/ ICCN/ ORTPN.

Harcourt, A.H., Kineman, J., Campbell, G., Yamagiwa, J., Redmond, I., Aveling, C., & Condiotti, M., 1983. Conservation and the Virunga gorilla population. *African Journal of Ecology,* 21: 139–142.

Hediger, H., 1951. *Observations sur la psychologie animale dans les parcs nationaux du Congo belge.* Exploration des Parcs Nationaux du Congo, 1: 84 pp.

Hickey, J.R., Granjon, A.C., Vigilant, L., Eckardt, W., Gilardi, K.V., Cranfield, M., Musana, A., Masozera, A.B., Babaasa, D., Ruzigandekwe, F., Leendertz, F.H., & Robbins, M.M., 2019. *Virunga 2015–2016 surveys: monitoring mountain gorillas, other select mammals, and illegal activities.* GVTC, IGCP & partners, Kigali, Rwanda.

Hillman Smith, A.K., de Merode, E., Smith, F., Amube, N., Mushenzi, N., & Mboma, G., 2003. *Parc National des Virunga–Nord: comptages aériens de mars 2003.* Report to the ICCN. 38 pp.

Hoier, R., 1952. *Mammifères du Parc National Albert. Collections Lebègue et Nationale no 105.* Brussels. 111 pp.

Hubert, E.J., 1947. *La faune des grands mammifères de la plaine Rwindi-Rutshuru (Lac Édouard). Son évolution depuis sa protection totale.* Institut des Parcs Nationaux du Congo Belge. Brussels. 84 pp.

Kalpers, J., Williamson, E., Robbins, M., McNeilage, A., Nzamurambaho, A., Lola, N., & Mugiri, G., 2003. Gorillas in the crossfire: Population dynamics of the Virunga mountain gorillas over the past three decades. *Oryx* 37(3): 326-337.

Kujirakwinja, D., Shamavu, P., Wathaut, J.D., Plumptre, A., de Merode, E., & Muhindo, E., 2016. Conservation of the common hippopotamus in Virunga National Park, eastern Democratic Republic of Congo. *Suiform Soundings* 15(1): 5-10.

Kümpel, N.F., Quinn, A., Queslin, E., Grange, S., Mallon, D., & Mapilanga, J.J., 2015. *Okapi* (Okapia johnstoni)*: Stratégie et Revue du statut de conservation.* Gland, Switzerland: UICN and ICCN, 62 pp.

Lamprey, R., 2024. *Aerial survey of wildlife in Virunga National Park and Queen Elizabeth Protected Area. June 2023.* Report to UWA and ICCN.

Languy, M., 1994. *Recensement des hippopotames dans le Parc National des Virunga, 14–17 juillet 1994.* Unpublished report to WWF International, Gland, Switzerland. 15 pp.

Mackie, C., 1989. *Recensement des Hippopotames au Parc National des Virunga. Leur impact sur la végétation et sur les sols.* Unpublished report to the Zairian Institute for Nature Conservation, Kinshasa. 78 pp.

Mertens, H., 1983. Recensements aériens des principaux ongulés du Parc National des Virunga, Zaïre. *Revue d'Ecologie (Terre et Vie)* 38: 51–64.

Mertens, H., 1984. Détermination de l'âge chez le topi (*Damaliscus korrigum* Ogilby) au Parc National des Virunga (Zaïre). *Mammalia* 48(3): 425–435.

Mertens, H., 1985. Structures de population et tables de survie des buffles, topis et cobs de Buffon au Parc National des Virunga, Zaïre. *Revue d'Écologie. (Terre Vie)* 40: 33–51.

Misonne, X., 1963. *Les rongeurs du Ruwenzori et des régions voisines.* Exploration du Parc National Albert. Institut des Parcs Nationaux du Congo et du Rwanda. 2ème série, fasc. 14. 164 pp.

Mubalama, L., 2000. Population and Distribution of Elephants (*Loxodonta africana africana*) in the Central Sector of the Virunga National Park, Eastern DRC. *Pachyderm* 28: 44–55.

Mushenzi, N., de Merode, E., Smith, F., Hillman-Smith, K., Banza, P., Ndey, A., Bro-Jorgensen, J., Gray, M., Mboma, G., & Watkin, J., 2003. *Aerial Sample Count of Virunga National Park, Democratic Republic of Congo.* Unpublished report. USFWS & ICCN.

Owiunji, I., Nkuutu, D., Kujirakwinja, D., Liengola I., Plumptre, A., Nsanzurwimo, A., Fawcett, K., Gray, M., & McNeilage, A., 2005. *The Biodiversity of the Virunga Volcanoes.* Unpublished report. WCS, DFGF-I, ICCN, ORTPN, UWA & IGCP.

Rahm, A., 1960. Les muridés des environs du lac Kivu et régions voisines (Afrique Centrale) et leur écologie. *Rev. Suisse Zool.,* 74(9): 439–519.

Rahm, A., 1972. Note sur la répartition, l'écologie et le régime alimentaire des Sciuridés au Kivu (Zaïre). *Rev. Suisse Zool.,* 85(3-4): 321–339.

Robbins, C. & van der Straeten, E., 1982. A new specimen of *Malacomys verschureni* (Rodentia, Muridae) from Zaïre, Central Africa. *Rev. Zool. Bot. Afr.* 96: 216-220.

Schouteden, H., 1947. De zoogdieren van Belgisch-Congo en van Ruanda-Urundi. *Ann. Museum van Belgisch Congo, Tervuren, Zoologie,* 2(3). 576 pp.

Vedder, A. & Aveling, C., 1986. *Census of the Virunga population of Gorilla gorilla beringei.* Unpublished report, September 1986.

Verheyen, R., 1954. *Monographie éthologique de l'hippopotame.* Institut des Parcs Nationaux du Congo Belge. 91 pp.

Verschuren, J., 1967. *Introduction à l'écologie et à la biologie des Cheiroptères.* Parc National Albert, Institut des Parcs Nationaux du Congo, fasc. 2. 65 pp.

Verschuren, J., 1972. *Contribution à l'écologie des Primates, Pholidota, Carnivora, Tubulidentata et Hyracoidea (Mammifères).* Exploration du Parc National des Virunga, Fondation pour Favoriser les Recherches Scientifiques en Afrique, fasc. 3. 61 pp.

Verschuren, J., 1986. *Relations entre la faune, principalement les vertébrés supérieurs, et les eaux thermales.* Exploration du Parc National des Virunga, Fondation pour Favoriser les Recherches Scientifiques en Afrique. 2ème série, fasc. 27. 21 pp.

Verschuren, J., 1987. L'action des éléphants et des hippopotames sur l'habitat, au Parc National des Virunga, Zaïre. Évolution chronologique de leurs populations. *Bull. Inst. Roy. Sc. Nat. Belg., Biologie,* 57: 5–16.

Verschuren, J., 1987. Liste commentée des mammifères des Parcs Nationaux du Zaïre, du Rwanda et du Burundi. *Bull. Inst. Roy. Sci. Nat. Belg., Biologie,* 57 : 17–39.

Verschuren, J., 1993. *Les habitats et la grande faune: évolution et situation récente.* Exploration du Parc National des Virunga, Fondation pour favoriser les recherches scientifiques en afrique, 2ème série, fasc. 29. 133 pp.

Verschuren, J., Van der Straeten, E., & Verheyen, W., 1983. *Rongeurs.* Exploration Parc National des Virunga. Fondation pour favoriser les recherches scientifiques en Afrique, 2ème série, fasc. 4. 121 pp.

Verschuren, J., 2008. *Insectivora.* Exploration Parc National des Virunga et régions proches. (Manuscrit non publié) Fondation pour favoriser les recherches scientifiques en Afrique, Bruxelles. 48 pp.

Wanyama, F., Balole, E., Elkan, P., Mendiguetti, S., Ayebare, S., Kisame, F., Shamavu, P., Kato, R., Okiring, D., Loware, S., Wathaut, J., Tumonakiese, B., Mashagiro, D., Barendse, T., & Plumptre, A., 2014. *Aerial surveys of the Greater Virunga Landscape.* Technical Report WCS-ICCN-UWA.

Weber, A.W. & Vedder, A., 1983. Population Dynamics of the Virunga Gorillas: 1959–1978. *Biological Conservation,* 26: 341–366.

C. Birds

Bataille, J. Bourguignon, L. Pagezy, H. & Trotignon, J., 1972. Dénombrement des Sauvagines et d'aigles pêcheurs (*Cuncuma vocifer*) sur le lac Edouard (R.D. Congo). *L'oiseau et la R.F.O.,* 42: 183–192.

Chapin, J.P., 1932. The birds of the Belgian Congo. *Bull. Amer. Mus. Nat. Hist.,* 65. 756 pp.

Chapin, J.P., 1938. The birds of the Belgian Congo. *Bull. Amer. Mus. Nat. Hist.,* 75. 632 pp.

Chapin, J.P., 1954. The birds of the Belgian Congo. *Bull. Amer. Mus. Nat. Hist.,* 75B. 846 pp.

d'Huart, J.P., 1977. Station de baguage de Lulimbi (Parc National des Virunga, Zaïre): rapport d'activités 1971-1975. *Le Gerfaut* 67: 161–168.

Demey, R., Herroelen, P. & Pedersen, T., 2000. Additions and annotations to the avifauna of Congo-Kinshasa (ex Zaïre). *Bull. Br. Ornithol.,* 120: 154–172.

Lippens, L., 1938. Les oiseaux aquatiques du Kivu. *Le Gerfaut,* 28. Fasc. spécial. 103 pp.

Lippens, L. & Wille, H., 1976. *Les Oiseaux du Zaïre.* Lannoo, Tielt, Belgium. 512 pp.

Mertens, H., 1986. Contribution à l'ornithologie du Parc National des Virunga. *Le Gerfaut* 76: 213–219.

Prigogine, A., 1953. Contribution à l'étude de la faune ornithologique de la région à l'ouest du lac Edouard. *Ann. Mus. Congo Tervuren, Zoologie,* 24. 117 pp.

Schouteden, H., 1938. *Oiseaux.* Exploration du Parc National Albert. Institut des Parcs Nationaux du Congo Belge, Brussels. 107 pp.

Schouteden, H., 1954. *Faune du Congo belge et du Ruanda-Urundi. iii. Oiseaux non passereaux.* Annales du Musée Royal du Congo belge. Série in-8°, Sciences zoologiques, vol.29. 434 pp.

Schouteden, H., 1957. *Faune du Congo belge et du Ruanda-Urundi. iv. Oiseaux passereaux (1).* Annales du Musée Royal du Congo belge. Série in-8°, Sciences zoologiques, vol. 57. 314 pp.

Schouteden, H., 1960. *Faune du Congo belge et du Ruanda-Urundi. v. Oiseaux passereaux (2).* Annales du Musée Royal du Congo belge. Série in-8°, Sciences zoologiques, vol. 89. 328 pp.

Schouteden, H., 1968. *La faune ornithologique du Kivu. i. Non passereaux.* Musée Royal d'Afrique Centrale. Documents zoologiques, no 12. 168 pp.

Schouteden, H., 1969. *La faune ornithologique du Kivu. ii. Passereaux.* Musée Royal d'Afrique Centrale. Documents zoologiques, no 15. 188 pp.

Verheyen, R., 1947. *Oiseaux.* Exploration du Parc National Albert. Institut des Parcs Nationaux du Congo Belge, Brussels. 87 pp.

Verschuren, J., 1966. *Contribution à l'Ornithologie.* Exploration du Parc National Albert, Mission F. Bourlière - J. Verschuren (1957-1961), fasc.2. 3-24.

Verschuren, J. 1978. Observations ornithologiques dans les parcs nationaux du Zaïre. *Le Gerfaut* 68 : 3-24.

D. Reptiles, amphibians, fish

de Witte, G.F., 1941. *Batraciens et reptiles.* Exploration du Parc National Albert, Mission G.F. de Witte (1933-1935), 1. Institut des Parcs Nationaux du Congo Belge, Brussels. 39 pp.

de Witte, G.F., 1965. *Les caméléons de l'Afrique Centrale.* Annales du Musée Royal de l'Afrique centrale, sciences zoologiques, no 142. 200 pp.

Laurent, R, 1972. *Amphibiens.* Exploration du Parc National Albert. Institut des Parcs Nationaux du Congo belge, Brussels. 125 pp.

Damas, H., 1937. *Recherches hydrobiologiques dans les lacs Kivu, Edouard et Ndagala. Mission H. Damas (1935-1936).* Exploration du Parc National Albert. Institut des Parcs nationaux du Congo belge. 128 pp.

Poll, M., 1939. *Poissons.* Exploration du Parc National Albert, Mission G.F. de Witte (1933-1935), fasc. 33. Institut des Parcs Nationaux du Congo Belge, Brussels. 81 pp.

Poll, M., 1939. *Poissons.* Exploration du Parc National Albert, Mission H. Damas (1935-1936), fasc. 6. Institut des Parcs Nationaux du Congo Belge, Brussels. 73 pp.

Roux-Estève, R., de Witte, G.F., & De Saeger, H., 1975. *Serpents.* Fondation pour Favoriser les Recherches Scientifiques en Afrique, Belgique. 2ème série, fasc. 24. 121 pp.

Snoeks, J., 2000. *How well known is the ichtyodiversity of the large East African Lakes.* In: Rossiter, A. & Kawanabe, H. (eds). Ancient lakes: Biodiversity, ecology and evolution. Advances in Ecological Research, 31. Academic Press. 17–38.

Verschuren, J., Mankoto ma Mbaelele, S., & Luhunu K., 1989. L'apparition des crocodiles au Lac ex-Edouard, Parc National des Virunga, Zaïre. *Revue d'Ecologie (Terre Vie),* 44: 387–397.

E. Vegetation

Chifundera, K.Z., Nyakabwa, M., Bashonga, M.G., Masumbuka, N.C., & Kyungu, J.C., 2003. *The Mount Tshiabirimu in the Albertine Rift: biodiversity, habitat and conservation issues.* Unpublished report to the Dian Fossey Gorilla Fund Europe.

Cornet d'Elzius, C., 1964. Évolution de la végétation dans la plaine au sud du Lac Edouard. Institut des Parcs Nationaux du Congo et du Rwanda. 23 pp.

Languy, M. & Banza P., 2006. *Utilisation des photos périodiques au PNVi dans le cadre du suivi du parc. Programme de renforcement des capacités de gestion de l'ICCN et appui à la réhabilitation d'aires protégées en RDC.* Technical sheet no 2. WWF International.

Lebrun, J., 1942. *La végétation du Nyiragongo. Aspects de végétation des Parcs nationaux du Congo belge.* Série I. Parc National Albert, vol I, fasc. 3-4-5. Institut des Parcs Nationaux du Congo Belge. 121 pp.

Lebrun, J., 1947. *La végétation de la plaine alluviale au sud du Lac Edouard.* Exploration du Parc National Albert. Institut des Parcs Nationaux du Congo Belge. 800 pp.

Lebrun, J., 1960. Études sur la flore et la végétation des champs de lave au Nord du lac Kivu (Congo Belge). Exploration Parc National Albert. Mission J. Lebrun (1937-1938). Institut des Parcs Nationaux du Congo Belge. 352 pp.

Pierlot, R., 1966. Structure et composition des forêts denses d'Afrique Centrale, spécialement celles du Kivu. Académie royale des Sciences d'Outre-Mer. 367 pp.

Plumptre, A., 1991. *Plant-herbivore dynamics in the Birungas.* Ph.D. thesis. University of Bristol, United Kingdom.

Robyns, W., 1937. *Aspects de végétation des Parcs Nationaux du Congo Belge.* Série 1, Parc National Albert. Institut des Parcs Nationaux du Congo Belge. Vol 1, fasc. 1 et 2. 42 pp.

Robyns, W., 1947. *Flore des Spermatophytes du Parc National Albert. 2. Sympétales.* Institut des Parcs Nationaux du Congo Belge. 626 pp.

Robyns, W., 1948. *Flore des Spermatophytes du Parc National Albert. 1. Gymnospermes et Choripétales.* Institut des Parcs Nationaux du Congo Belge. 745 pp.

Robyns, W., 1948. *Les territoires biogéographiques du Parc National Albert.* Institut des Parcs Nationaux du Congo Belge. 51 pp.

Robyns, W., 1955. *Flore des Spermatophytes du Parc National Albert. 3. Monocotylées.* Institut des Parcs Nationaux du Congo Belge. 571 pp.

Van Gysel, J. & Vanoverstraeten, M., 1982. *Inventaire des potentialités pédo-botaniques pour l'élaboration du plan d'aménagement d'un parc africain.* Report on the International Symposium on tropical livestock production for the benefit of mankind. Institute of Tropical Medicine, Antwerp, Belgium. 417–422.

Vanoverstraeten, M., 1989. *Apport de la morphopédologie à l'étude de la dynamique des écosystèmes. Application à l'aménagement du Parc National des Virunga.* Doctoral thesis. Fac. Sc. Agr. Gembloux, Belgium. 280 pp.

Vanoverstraeten, M., Van Gysel, J., Mathieu, L. & Bock, L., 1984. Étude intégrée au Parc National des Virunga (PNVi Centre – Zaïre Oriental). Les milieux morphopédologiques, support des écosystèmes. *Bull. Rech. Agron. Gembloux,* 19(3/4): 189–225.

Vanoverstraeten, M., 1991. L'organisation du réseau hydrographique, conséquences sur la morphogenèse et sur la pédogenèse au Parc national des Virunga. *Bulletin de la Société géographique de Liège*, 27 : 109-123.

Verschuren, J., 1986. *Observation des habitats et de la faune après soixante ans de conservation.* Fondation pour Favoriser les Recherches Scientifiques en Afrique, Belgique. 2ème série, fasc. 26. 44 pp.

F. Virunga volcanoes and Ruwenzori

de Grunne, X., Hauman, L., Burgeon, L., & Michot, P., 1937. *Vers les glaciers de l'Equateur. Le Ruwenzori, Mission scientifique belge 1932.* Ed. R. Dupriez, Brussels. 300 pp.

de Heinzelin de Braucourt, J.,1935. *Les stades de récession du glacier Stanley occidental (Ruwenzori, Congo Belge).* Exploration du Parc National Albert, série 2(1). Institut des Parcs Nationaux du Congo Belge. 25 pp.

de Heinzelin de Braucourt, J. & Mollaret, H., 1956. *Biotopes de haute altitude : Ruwenzori I.* Exploration du Parc National Albert. Institut des Parcs Nationaux du Congo Belge, Brussels. 2ème série, fasc. 3. 31 pp.

De Mulder, M., 1985. The Karisimbi Volcano (Virunga). *Ann. Mus. Roy. Afr. Centr.- Série in-8° - Sc. Géologiques* n°90, 101 pp.

De Saeger, H., 1958. Le Ruwenzori. *Parcs Nationaux. Ardenne et Gaume*, 13(4): 1-12.

Mollaret, H., 1961. *Biotopes de haute altitude : Ruwenzori II et Virunga. Etudes diverses.* Exploration du Parc National Albert. Institut des Parcs Nationaux du Congo et du Ruanda-Urundi, Brussels. 2ème série, fasc. 11. 101 pp.

Sahama, T.G. & Meyer, A., 1958. *Study of the volcano Nyiragongo.* Mission d'études vulcanologiques. Institut des Parcs Nationaux du Congo Belge. Fasc. 2. 85 pp.

Verhaeghe, M., 1958. *Le volcan Mugogo.* Exploration du Parc National Albert. Mission d'Études vulcanologiques, fasc. 3. Institut des Parcs Nationaux du Congo Belge. 29 pp.

Verhoogen, J., 1948. *Les éruptions 1938-1940 du volcan Nyamuragira.* Institut des Parcs Nationaux du Congo Belge. 186 pp.

Verschuren, J., 1965. Un facteur de mortalité mal connu, l'asphyxie par gaz toxiques naturels au Parc National Albert, Congo. *La Terre et la Vie* 3: 215-237.

G. Lake Edward

Balole Bwami, E, Mumbere, J.C., Matunguru, J, Kujirakwinja., D., Shamavu, P., Muhindo, E., Tchouamo, I.R., Michel, B., & Micha, J.C., 2018. Production et impacts de la pêche sur le Lac Edouard en République Démocratique du Congo. *Tropicultura* 36(3): 539-552.

Bene, S., 2016. Étude de la chaîne de valeur poisson, Parc Naturel des Virunga, République démocratique du Congo. Advisory Service in Social Transfers (ASiST III). Report to the European Union.

Kambere Mulwahali, J.C., Balole, E., Shamavu, P., Muhindo, E., Kambale, E., Biloko, F., Mukura , J., van Damme, P., Lain, T., Matunguru, J., Kalemeko, C., Biloko, M., & Kitambala, B., 2015. *Le lac Édouard en RDC: leçons pour la gestion de la pêche.* UICN-NL Report.

Petit P., 2006. *Les pêches dans la partie congolaise du lac Edouard: Analyse de la situation actuelle.* Report Vredeseilanden (VECO), 54 pp.

Vakily, J.M., 1989. *Les pêches dans la partie zaïroise du Lac Idi Amin: analyse de la situation actuelle et potentiel de développement.* Report to DAFECN and CEE. 18 pp.

Van Schuylenbergh, P., 2016. *Contribution à l'histoire du lac Edouard : enjeux socio-économiques et environnementaux autour des ressources halieutiques (ca 1920-1960)* in: P. Mantuba-Ngoma et M. Zana Etambala (dir.), La société congolaise face à la modernité (ca.1700-2010. Mélanges eurafricains offerts à Jean-Luc Vellut, Cahiers africains, 89. MRAC/ L'Harmattan, Tervuren/Paris. pp 127-163.

H. Crises

Biswas, A.K. & Tortajada-Quiroz, H.C., 1996. Environmental Impacts on the Rwandan Refugees in Zaïre. *Ambio* 25: 403-408.

Biswas, A.K., Tortajada-Quiroz, H.C., Lutete, V., & Lemba, G., 1994. *Environmental impact of the Rwandese refugee presence in north and south Kivu (Zaïre).* United Nations Development Programme. 53 pp.

Blom, E., 2000. Conclusions and recommendations. in: Blom E., Bergmans W. et al. (eds.), Nature in war. *Biodiversity conservation during conflicts* pp. 165-170. Netherlands Commission for International Nature Protection. Mededelingen, 37. Amsterdam.

Blondel, N., 1995. *Un an de présence des camps de réfugiés en périphérie du secteur sud du Parc National des Virunga: bilan des dégâts.* Unpublished report to FED/PSRR-PNVi. 20 pp.

Blondel, N., 1997. *L'impact des camps de réfugiés sur l'environnement local: étude de cas sur Goma (Nord-Kivu).* Study day «l'information satellitaire au service de l'aide humanitaire», 28 mai 1997. Contribution from bureau I-Mage Consult. Unpublished report. 5 pp.

d'Huart, J.P. & Hart, T., 2000. *Conservation de la biodiversité dans les zones de conflits armés: protection des sites du Patrimoine Mondial en République Démocratique du Congo.* Report of the interim diplomatic mission to prepare for the UNESCO/UNFIP/RDC Project. Centre du Patrimoine Mondial de l'UNESCO. 60 pp.

Kalpers, J., 2005. *Biodiversité et urgence en Afrique sub-saharienne: la conservation des aires protégées en situation de conflit armé.* Doctoral thesis. Université de Liège. Faculté des Sciences. 234 pp.

Languy, M., 1995. *Problèmes environnementaux liés à la présence des réfugiés rwandais. Identification des interventions réalisées. Coordination entre les organismes et propositions d'interventions complémentaires.* Mission report to the UNDP. 29 pp.

Mugangu, S., 2001. *Conservation et utilisation durables de la diversité biologique en temps de troubles armés. Cas du Parc National des Virunga.* Report to the IUCN – Central African Programme, Yaoundé. 107 pp

Shambaugh, J., Oglethorpe, J., & Ham, R., 2001. *The Trampled Grass: mitigating the impacts of armed conflict on the environment.* Biodiversity Support Program, Washington DC.

Steklis, H.D., Gerald, C.N., & Madry, S., 1997. The mountain gorilla – conserving an endangered primate in conditions of extreme political instability. *Primate Conservation* 17: 145–151.

Tombola, J.P. & Sanders, C., 1994. *Résultats de l'enquête sur l'impact des réfugiés rwandais sur le Parc National des Virunga (secteur sud).* Unpublished report to the UNHCR, Technical department.

UNESCO, 2000. *Rapport synthétique de la mission intermédiaire de l'UNESCO sur les sites du patrimoine mondial en péril en République démocratique du Congo.* 24th session of the Bureau of the World Heritage Committee.

Werikhe S., Mushenzi Lusenge, N., & Bizimana, J., 1998. L'impact de la guerre sur les aires protégées dans la région des Grands Lacs. Le cas de la région des volcans Virunga. *Cahiers d'Ethologie* 18: 175–186.

I. Cross-border aspects

Biodiversity Support Programme, 1999. Study on the Development of Transboundary Natural Resource Management Areas in Southern Africa, *Biodiversity Support Programme*, Washington DC.

d'Huart, J.P., Kramkimel, J.D., & de Merode, E. 2008: *Proposition de financement pour un projet d'appui de l'Union européenne à la collaboration transfrontalière entre les aires protégées contiguës de RDC, Ouganda et Rwanda.* AGRECO/ Groupe SOGES Report to the EU. 38 pp.

Kalpers, J. & Lanjouw, A., 1997. Potential for the creation of a peace park in the Virunga volcano region. *Parks* 7: 25-35.

Lanjouw, A., Kayitare, A., Rainer, H., Rutagarama, E., Sivha, M., Asuma, S., & Kalpers, J., 2001. *Transboundary Natural Resource Management: A Case Study by International Gorilla Conservation Programme in the Virunga-Bwindi Region.* Biodiversity Support Program. 60 pp.

Plumptre, A., Kujirakwinja, D., Treves, A., Owiunji, I., & Rainer, H., 2007. Transboundary conservation in the Greater Virunga Landscape: its importance for landscape species. *Biological Conservation* 134(2): 279-287.

Refisch, J. & Jenson, J., 2016. *Transboundary collaboration in Greater Virunga Landscape: From gorilla conservation to conflict-sensitive transboundary landscape management.* In: Governance, Natural Resources, and Post-Conflict Peacebuilding. Carl Bruch, Carroll Muffett, Sandra S. Nichols (eds.). 825-841. Earthscan, Routledge.

Weber, W., 1989. *Conservation and Development on the Zaïre-Nile Divide. An analysis of value conflicts and convergence in the management of afro-montane forests.* PhD Thesis, University of Wisconsin, Madison. 327 pp.

Acknowledgements

The present book is the fruit of the collaboration of 54 authors of 9 different nationalities, under the direction of a 6-person editorial board, including the three editors.

This project was achievable only with the support of the PNVi's financial partners. The European Union, a long-standing supporter of the Park, has made a major contribution to its realisation. In addition to this key institutional partner, we must also thank the sponsors of the 2006 edition, on which the current book is based.

Our thanks also go to the Institut Congolais pour la Conservation de la Nature, which encouraged the project from the outset. We are particularly indebted to its Director General, Yves Milan Ngangay, and all the managers who supported the PNVi's projects and research in the past century. The current team at the ICCN headquarters in Kinshasa is part of this long tradition.

It would be impossible to mention each PNVi employee who has contributed to the various chapters in one way or another. First and foremost, we thank those who collected the extensive field data. The institutional memory of the retired managers has fed the writing of several historical sections. Nestor Bagurubumwe, Stanislas Bakinahe, Deo Kajuga, Samy Mankoto, Norbert Mushenzi and Alexandre Wathaut proved invaluable in that respect. Thanks also to Jérôme Lombart who, like a talented conductor, made possible what appeared impossible.

Several among the many authors and co-authors played a part that went beyond mere writing: Patricia Van Schuylenbergh, Méthode Bagurubumwe, Ephrem Balole, Guy Debonnet, Sébastien Desbureaux, Jérôme Gabriel, Marc Languy and Annette Lanjouw. We thank them warmly for their enthusiastic contributions. Our gratitude also goes to those who clarified various content issues: Conrad Aveling, Tom Butynski, Thierry Claeys Boúúaert, Yvonne de Jong, José Kalpers, Hadelin Mertens, Pierre-Denis Plisnier, Pierre-Yves Renkin and René Van Acker.

Numerous maps and illustrations illustrate the various chapters. We are grateful to the people who authorised their reproduction: at the Royal Museum for Central Africa (Africa Museum, Tervuren), Bart Ouvry, Patricia Van Schuylenbergh, Isabelle Gérard and Anne Welschen; at the Royal Belgian Institute of Natural Sciences, Michel Van Camp, Luc Janssens de Bisthoven, Han De Koeijer and Thomas Wouters; at the Botanical Garden of Meise, Steven Dessein and Francesca Lanata. Jean de Dieu Wathaut and Zachary Maritim are to be credited with creating the new maps – a complex, highly accurate piece of work.

The many photographers mentioned in the photo credits list have graciously ceded the right to reproduce their superb images. Special thanks go to Brent Stirton, Bruce Davidson, Melihat Veysal and Marc Languy. Hanna Cooper, Rita Ngoyi and Katya Vinywasiki helped us find contemporary photographs.

We are immensely indebted to Aurore D'Haeyer, who coordinated the editing of the book. She read, re-read and again re-read the successive proofs to guarantee the quality of writing and layout. Jacqueline d'Huart also contributed to this work, as did Nick Borrow, who checked the English translations provided by Lannoo. Philippa Terreblanche provided useful design advice.

Finally, our gratitude goes to the staff at Lannoo – Maarten Van Steenbergen, Carolijn Domensino, Ann Brokken, Nele Reyniers, Stef Lantsoght, Anne Baudouin, Heather Sills, Cécile Wastiaux – who rose to this ambitious challenge and met the many demands of the authors.

In conclusion, the three editors would like to thank their family and friends, who saw them engrossed in screen work in front of their computers for almost a year, all too regularly abandoning their nearest and dearest and their other occupations.

This book is dedicated with the greatest respect to the memory of the staff members who lost their lives protecting Virunga National Park.

Photo credits[1]

Adam Kiefer: 10.28, 10.29 (ur, dl, dr), 11.2
American Museum of Natural History: 2.3
Boone & Crockett Club: 7.2
LuAnne Cadd: page 17, 3.21, 5.10, 8.1, 8.3, 8.14, 9.7, 17.13 (r), 17.14 (l), 18.1
Tristan Chopard: 10.16 (ul, ur)
Bruce Davidson/Naturepl.com: page 12, 1.7, 1.8, 1.10, 1.12, 1.14 (l), 1.15, 1.35, 5.1, 5.3, 10.1
Yolaine de Donnéa: 6.8, 6.15
Yolente Delaunoy/WWF: 13.10
Jean-Pierre d'Huart: 3.8, 4.4, 4.5, 4.6, 4.9, 4.10, 4.11, 4.13, 4.14, 4.16
Jacques Durieux: 8.10
Jean Fontaine/Plisnier: 2.11
Dian Fossey/National Geographic Magazine: 7.5
Pierre Gallez/pgkivu: 17.9
Goldman Environmental Prize: 7.11
Sven Erik Harklåu: 1.25, 1.52 (u), 9.1
Martin Harvey/WWF: 0.2, 5.7
Chris Horsley: page 8, 0.1
Royal Belgian Institute of Natural Sciences (IPNCB): 2.1, 2.2, 2.4, 2.5, 2.7, 2.9, 2.10, 2.12, 2.13, 2.14, 2.16, 2.17, 3.25, 3.3, 3.4 (all), 3.5, 3.6, 3.7, 3.9, 3.11, 3.12, 3.13, 3.14, 3.15, 3.16, 3.17, 3.18, 3.20, 3.22, 3.23, 3.24, 4.1, 4.2, 4.3, 4.7, 4.8, 4.18, 4.19, 7.3, 7.4, 7.8, 9.25, 10.30, 11.4, 11.5 (all), 12.1, 17.6, 17.15 (l)
Joseph King: page 1, 1.24, 1.26, 9.5, 9.12
Déo Kujirakwinja/WCS: 16.5
Denys Kutsevalov: Front cover
Stéphane Laime: 1.30, 1.34
Marc Languy: 1.16, 1.18, 1.19, 1.21, 1.22, 1.44, 1.54, 4.20, 13.5, 16.2 (d)
Samy Mankoto: 7.15
Musée Royal de l'Afrique Centrale/Africa Museum: 2.6 (HP.1956.15.4070, coll. MRAC, 1926), 2.8 (HP.2001.20.23-22, fonds J-P. Harroy), 2.15 (HP. 2001.20.21-93, fonds J-P. Harroy), 3.2 (EP.0.0.1204, coll. MRAC), 3.19 (HP.2011.62.22-233, coll. MRAC), 8.4 (HP.1956.15.7197, coll. MRAC; photo H. Tazieff/Inforcongo 1948, © MRAC), 11.7 (EP.0.0.11830, coll. MRAC; photo Léopold III, 1957 © Fonds Léopold III pour l'Exploration et la Conservation de la Nature), 16.2 (u) (HP.2010.8.397, coll. MRAC, photo Service cinématographique militaire 1955), 17.7 (Coll. MRAC Tervuren)
Robert Muir/SZF: 5.8, 15.12
Augustin Ndimu/WWF: 1.17
Bobby Neptune: 9.27 (d), 17.26
Mustafa Nsubuga: 10.23 (l)

Parc National des Virunga[2]: page 10, p. 59, p. 171, 1.14 (r), 1.20, 1.27, 1.33, 1.39, 1.45, 1.48, 1.49, 1.50, 1.51 (ul, cl, d), 1.52 (c+d), 5.2, 5.4, 5.5, 5.6, 5.11, 5.12, 6.1, 6.2, 6.3, 6.9, 6.10, 6.12, 6.13 (all), 6.14 (u+d), 6.16 (r), 6.17 (u+d), 6.18 (u+d), 6.19, 6.20, 7.10 (u+c), 7.12, 7.13, 7.14, 8.13 (l+r), 9.1, 9.2, 9.3, 9.4, 9.9, 9.10, 9.11, 9.23, 9.27 (u), 9.29, 10.2, 10.3, 10.6, 10.7, 10.10, 10.13, 10.14, 10.15 (u), 10.19 (dl), 10.20, 10.23 (r), 10.24, 10.25, 10.29 (ul), 10.31, 11.3, 11.12 (all), 11.13, 11.19, 11.20, 11.21, 11.22, 11.24, 11.25, 11.26, 11.27, 11.28 (all), 11.30, 11.31 (all), 12.3, 12.4, 12.5, 12.6, 12.7, 12.8, 12.9 (dl, ur), 12.10 (all), 12.12, 12.13 (all), 12.14, 12.15, 12.16, 12.17, 12.18, 12.19, 12.20, 12.21, 12.23, 13.2, 13.3, 13.7 (all), 13.8 (all), 13.9 (all), 14.2, 14.3, 14.4, 14.5 (l), 14.8, 15.1, 15.2 (all), 15.4, 15.5, 15.7, 15.8, 15.9 (all), 15.10, 15.13, 15.16, 15.17, 15.18, 15.19, 15.20, 15.21, 15.22, 16.3, 16.6, 16.8, 16.9, 16.10, 16.11, 16.12 (all), 16.13 (all), 16.15, 16.17, 16.19, 17.1, 17.3, 17.4 (all), 17.5, 17.8, 17.12 (all), 17.13 (l), 17.14 (r), 17.15 (r), 17.16 (all), 17.17 (d), 17.18, 17.19 (u), 17.20, 17.21 (all), 17.22, 17.23, 17.24, 17.25, 17.27, 17.28 (all), 17.29, 17.32, 17.33, 17.34, 17.35 (all), 17.36, 17.39, 17.40, 17.41, 17.42, 17.43, 17.44, 17.45, 17.46 (all), 17.48, 17.49, 17.51, 17.54, 17.55, 17.56, 17.57, 17.58 (all), 17.59, 17.60, 17.61, 17.62, 17.63, 17.64, 17.65, 17.66 (all), 17.67 (all), 17.68, 17.69, 17.70, 17.71, 17.72, 17.73, 17.74, 17.75, 17.76, 17.77, 17.78, 17.79, 17.80, 17.81 (all), 17.82, 17.83, 18.2
Nick Philipson: 10.15 (d)
PlanetImage/Landsat: 8.5
Andrew Plumptre/WCS: 13.6
Rafael Reyna: 10.27
Roelof Schutte: 10.16 (dr)
Brent Stirton: page 2-3, p. 4-5, p. 7, p. 139, p. 235, p. 319, p. 324-325, Back cover, 1.23, 1.51 (d), 6.4, 6.5, 6.6 (all), 6.7, 6.11, 6.16 (l), 8.7, 9.8, 9.26, 9.28, 10.8, 10.17, 10.18, 11.1, 11.9, 11.10, 11.17, 11.18, 11.23, 11.26, 12.9 (ul, dr), 13.4, 14.1, 14.5 (r), 14.6, 14.7, 15.11, 15.14, 15.15, 16.1, 17.2, 17.10, 17.17 (u), 17.19 (d), 17.52, 18.1
Paul Taggart: 7.1
Dario Tedesco: 8.6, 8.8, 8.9, 8.11, 8.12
Michel Verleyen: 12.11, 17.30, 17.31, 17.38
Jacques Verschuren: 1.9, 3.1, 3.10, 3.18, 4.15, 4.17, 7.6, 8.16, 9.6
Melihat Veysal: 1.32, 1.36, 1.37, 1.38, 1.40, 1.41, 1.42, 1.43, 10.16 (dl)
Jean-Pierre von der Beck : 4.12, 11.8
Orlando von Einsiedel/Netflix: 7.9
WWF: 1.46, 5.9, 7.7

The publisher has made every effort to respect the rights relating to illustrations following legal requirements. Despite this research, certain rights holders may remain unknown. They are invited to contact the publisher.

---

[1] The letters associated with certain photos mean: u = up, c = centre, d = down, l = left, r = right.
[2] Photos taken by PNVi staff, in particular: Méthode Bagurubumwe, Ephrem Balole, Merci-Dieu Kambale Baraka, Sekibibi Bonge, Anthony Caere, Sébastien Desbureaux, Josué Duha, Jérôme Gabriel, Audace Hamuli, Gael Hassani, Jean de la Croix Kambere, Eric Kytakya, Robin Laime, Francesca Lanata, Jérôme Lombart, Jose Luque Luque, Lucien Munyantwari, Sarah Kangendo Musavuli, Norbert Mushenzi, Laura Parker, Gracien Sivanza, Jean de Dieu Wathaut, Julie Williams. Katya Vinywasiki, the Park's photographer, is the author of a large number of photos.